SHAKESPEARE SURVEY

ADVISORY BOARD

SHAKESPEARE SURVEY

AN ANNUAL SURVEY OF

SHAKESPEARE STUDIES AND PRODUCTION

48

EDITED BY

STANLEY WELLS

CAMBRIDGE
UNIVERSITY PRESS

Published by the Press Syndicate of the University of Cambridge
The Pitt Building, Trumpington Street, Cambridge CB2 IRP
40 West 20th Street, New York, NY 10011–4211, USA
10 Stamford Road, Oakleigh, Melbourne 3166, Australia

© Cambridge University Press 1995

First published 1995

Printed in Great Britain at the University Press, Cambridge

A cataloguing in publication record for this book is available from the British Library

ISBN 0 521 55030 0 hardback

Shakespeare Survey was first published in 1948. Its first
eighteen volumes were edited by Allardyce Nicoll. Kenneth
Muir edited volumes 19 to 33.

EDITOR'S NOTE

Volume 49 of *Shakespeare Survey*, which will be at press by the time this volume appears, will have as its overall theme '*Romeo and Juliet* and its Afterlife'. Volume 50, on 'Shakespeare and Language', will include papers from the 1996 International Shakespeare Conference; the theme of Volume 51 will be 'Shakespeare in the Eighteenth Century'.

Submissions should be addressed to the Editor at The Shakespeare Institute, Church Street, Stratford-upon-Avon, Warwickshire CV37 6HP, to arrive at the latest by 1 September 1996 for Volume 50 and 1 September 1997 for Volume 51. Pressures on space are heavy; priority is given to articles related to the theme of a particular volume. Please either enclose postage (overseas, in International Reply coupons) or send a copy you do not wish to be returned. All articles submitted are read by the Editor and at least one member of the Editorial Board, whose indispensable assistance the Editor gratefully acknowledges.

Unless otherwise indicated, Shakespeare quotations and references are keyed to the modern-spelling Complete Oxford Shakespeare (1986).

Review copies of books should be addressed to the Editor, as above. In attempting to survey the ever-increasing bulk of Shakespeare publications our reviewers inevitably have to exercise some selection. We are pleased to receive offprints of articles which help to draw our reviewers' attention to relevant material.

S. W. W.

CONTRIBUTORS

JONATHAN BATE, *University of Liverpool*
JOHN RUSSELL BROWN, *University of Michigan*
MARK THORNTON BURNETT, *The Queen's University of Belfast*
INGA-STINA EWBANK, *University of Leeds*
MAIK HAMBURGER, *Deutsches Theater, Berlin*
PETER HOLLAND, *Trinity Hall, Cambridge*
PIERRE ISELIN, *University of Nanterre*
NICO KIASASHVILI, *Shakespeare Society of the Republic of Georgia*
LAURENCE LERNER, *Vanderbilt University*
DAVID LINDLEY, *University of Leeds*
JEAN-MARIE MAGUIN, *University of Montpellier*
STEVEN MARX, *California Polytechnic State University*
MARK MATHESON, *University of Utah*
TOM MATHESON, *The Shakespeare Institute, University of Birmingham*
TOM MCALINDON, *University of Hull*
MICHAEL NEILL, *University of Auckland*
NIKY RATHBONE, *Birmingham Shakespeare Library*
JAMES SHAPIRO, *Columbia University*
ZDĒNĚK STŘÍBRNÝ, *Charles University, Prague*
YASUNARI TAKAHASHI, *Showa Women's University*
H. R. WOUDHUYSEN, *University College, London*

CONTENTS

ILLUSTRATIONS

LIST OF ILLUSTRATIONS

SHAKESPEARE TRANSLATION AS CULTURAL EXCHANGE

INGA-STINA EWBANK

In August 1994 the *Guardian*'s drama critic concluded his review of Peter Zadek's production of *Antony and Cleopatra* at the Edinburgh Festival by claiming that its value to him lay in its not being in English: 'Shakespeare in a foreign tongue', he wrote, 'becomes an analogue to the original that gives the director new freedom', and 'it will be hard', after this, 'to go back to traditional productions'.[1] While it could be argued that Michael Billington, in journalistic haste, is confusing the strength of a 'startling, radical, Brechtian' production with the alienation effect of a foreign language, this was not so with Clement Scott, the formidable *Daily Telegraph* reviewer, when nearly a hundred years ago he praised Sarah Bernhardt in his book on *Some Notable Hamlets of the Present Time* (1900). Amazingly he manages to go into raptures over Madame Bernhardt's performance without once commenting on her gender; but he is explicit about the language of this Hamlet: 'With the French version of the immortal text I was charmed. It conveyed Shakespeare's idea in a nutshell' (p. 51). Both then and now, it seems, drama reviewers can be Sentimental Travellers: 'They order this matter better in France' . . . or in Germany . . . or Japan.

But I wonder, when it comes to thinking about the implications of Billington's and Scott's proclaimed positions, if academic critics are such travellers? And, how seriously do we think about those implications? I wonder, that is, whether to the immensely fertile body of current Shakespeare studies, the study of translations might not be a stepchild – 'an interesting and harmless occupation for researchers abroad', as the editors of the recently published and excellently thought-provoking collection of essays on *European Shakespeares* put it, lamenting the lack of reciprocity between their discipline and English and American Shakespeare studies.[2] Seminars on translation are now an inalienable part of Shakespeare Conferences and World Congresses, but how many native speakers of English attend them?

From a sense, then, that the title of my paper is not as much of a truism as it seems, my aim is to probe the notion of *exchange*. The *Oxford English Dictionary* defines this word (*sb* 1.1.a) as 'The action, or an act, of reciprocal giving and receiving' and quotes, as part of the definition, the proverb 'Exchange is no robbery.' Whatever our theoretical position in regard to Shakespearian texts – their stability, their meaningfulness, or otherwise – do we not tend to feel that any translation of those texts into another language involves an element of 'robbery'? Or, to put it less adversarially, that, if exchange is a matter of give and take, from the point of view of English it is all give and no take?

---

[1] Michael Billington, 'Sexual Itch in the Sand', The *Guardian*, 18 August 1994, tabloid section, pp. 6–7.

[2] Dirk Delabastita and Lieven D'hulst, eds., *European Shakespeares: Translating Shakespeare in the Romantic Age* (Amsterdam and Philadelphia, 1993), p. 19.

And yet it is difficult to avoid an adversarial note, in so far as current critical practices are far more comfortable talking about cultural colonialism than cultural exchange; and if we believe with George Steiner that 'the translator invades, extracts, and brings home',[3] then translating Shakespeare becomes, from the point of view of English, a somewhat embarrassing kind of inverse colonialism. Language, we know only too well, is intimately connected with national, or racial, or gender identity; and history is only too full of examples of linguistic colonialism where the Calibans of this world learn to curse[4] – or where, as in Brian Friel's play *Translations*, the English re-map an Irish county, re-name its hills and streams and villages, and re-place the Gaelic language, 'a syntax opulent with tomorrows', with an English as sterile as the only phrase that the Irish girl Maire knows (the kind of phrase familiar to many of us who learned English as a foreign language): 'in Norfolk we besport ourselves around the maypoll [*sic*]'.[5] We – and our students – now have the critical equipment to deal with aspects of translation where English means power and hegemony: translations where the movement 'out of honesty into English' can be read rather more seriously and politically than Pistol reads Falstaff's translation of Mistress Ford's body language. But we are less well equipped to deal with situations where the translation is, as it were, out of English into honesty. Not so long ago I attended a performance of *The Merchant of Venice* in Hong Kong, which is of course for yet a short while one of the few remaining British colonies, and theoretically bilingual. The text was in Cantonese, which meant that there were virtually no expatriates in the audience. The director, Daniel S. P. Yang, tells me that the same production had been performed in English in the United States, with the mixed emotional impact that this problematic comedy tends to elicit. In the Kowloon outdoor theatre where I saw it, with a Chinese cast and audience, the play was received as a glorious comedy. In a society

honestly and unashamedly materialistic there is nothing suspect about the commercial values which prevail in Venice and invade Belmont, nothing to problematize the ending. And above all, Shylock, the speculator who misjudged the rate of exchange, was to this audience the uncontested clown of the piece. He was a creation for a culture which does not know anti-semitism. What had I seen: a kind of cultural collusion to turn Shakespeare into something he isn't? Not long thereafter, I saw *The Tempest* in Oslo in *nynorsk* – the second Norwegian language, constructed as 'accents yet unknown' out of dialects – and again was struck by the untroubled comedy of the performance: it bespoke a culture which does not need to have a postcolonial conscience. Whales, possibly, may elicit guilt, but not Caliban. So, was what I had seen and heard a kind of pollution of Shakespeare?

It may be obvious by now that, pondering such questions, I have found the paradigm for this paper in the exchange between Holofernes and Dull (*Love's Labour's Lost* 4.2.35–49) where Holofernes translates Dull's riddle about 'what was a month old at Cain's birth, that's not five weeks old as yet' and insists that 'Th'allusion holds in the exchange', whereupon Dull demonstrates his 'capacity' for dullness by his 'mistakings': turning 'allusion' first into 'collusion' and then into 'pollution'.

Holofernes may think that his allusion to '*Dictynna* ... Phoebe ... *luna*' holds in the exchange for 'the moon'; but, for all the existence now of translations into untold languages, I doubt if many would agree that Shakespeare *holds* in the exchange, if with 'hold' we infer identity. This may be the point to confront the old irritant (which, however old, may still, as a

---

[3] George Steiner, *After Babel. Aspects of Language and Translation* (London, 1975), p. 298.

[4] *The Tempest* 1.2.365–7. Cf. Stephen J. Greenblatt, *Learning to Curse. Essays in Early Modern Culture* (London, 1990).

[5] Brian Friel, *Translations* (London, 1981), p. 42 and p. 51.

resentment at appropriation, be one of the elements in the kind of embarrassment I referred to above): the claims that certain translations are superior to the Shakespearian original. With his customary lack of tact, Strindberg, who read Shakespeare both in English and in translation, claimed this, for at least parts of the monumental Swedish mid-nineteenth-century translation by Karl August Hagberg.[6] Several European nations have such 'classic' Shakespeare translations with a literary status of their own – notably of course Germany, with the great translation by August Wilhelm Schlegel and Ludwig Tieck. (Strictly, Schlegel translated sixteen of Shakespeare's plays between 1797 and 1801 and added *Richard III* in 1810, whereupon some of his work was revised and the translation of the corpus completed, 1825–33, by Graf Boudessin and Tieck's daughter Dorothea, with a certain amount of guidance from Tieck himself.) In 1855 George Eliot wrote an essay in the *Leader* on 'Translations and Translators', prompted by her own struggles with Strauss, Feuerbach and Spinoza, but moving almost immediately on to Shakespeare translations and naturally to Schlegel. An entry in her journal earlier that year – which incidentally goes to suggest that Victorian culture was rather more genuinely pluralistic than our own – tells how she and George Henry Lewes spent evenings reading and comparing scenes of *Hamlet* in Schlegel and in Shakespeare. In her article she admits that 'sometimes the German is as good as the English – the same music played on another but as good an instrument', but also dismisses what she calls 'the illusion, encouraged by some silly English people, that Shakespeare according to Schlegel is better than Shakespeare himself – not simply to a German as being easier for him to understand, but absolutely better as poetry'.[7] But later in the century Georg Brandes, the Danish critic who had a way of speaking for all of Europe, and whose three-volume study of *William Shakespeare* (1895–6) was to be translated into English and widely read, could still

write of the Schlegel-Tieck translation as a re-birth of Shakespeare, man and text. 'It is', he writes, 'as if – at the side of Goethe and Schiller – in the middle of the eighteenth century Shakespeare too had been born in Germany. He was born in 1564 in England; he was re-born in 1767 in his German translator. In 1597 *Romeo and Juliet* was published in London; in 1797 this tragedy was published in Berlin as a newly-born work.'[8]

With George Eliot, we can easily reject the myth of re-birth; but in doing so we would do well to remember her informed appreciation of 'another but as good an instrument'. Perhaps we have to be open to a notion of transmigration. When Friedrich Gundolf (himself a Shakespeare translator) writes, in *Shakespeare und der deutsche Geist* (1911), that what was 'absolutely new, indeed world-historical' about Schlegel's translation was 'die Wiedergeburt Shakespeares als eines deutschen Sprachganzen' ('the re-birth of Shakespeare as a German language phenomenon'),[9] then this is not so much German chauvinism as a historical fact – one to which we could add the re-appearance of Shakespeare as a French language phenomenon. For Shakespeare was discovered in continental Europe through translations into these two – culturally dominant – languages, and well into the nineteenth century was often translated indirectly. Early Russian translations, for

---

6 In, e.g., his essay on *A Midsummer Night's Dream* in the fourth of his *Öppna brev till Intima Teatern*, in *Samlade Skrifter*, ed. John Landqvist, vol. 50 (Stockholm, 1921), pp. 231–3. English translation by Walter Johnson, *Open Letters to the Intimate Theatre* (Seattle, n.d.), pp. 231–3. Hagberg's translation was published 1847–51.

7 George Eliot's essay in *The Leader*, 7, 20 October 1855, 1014–15, is reprinted in Thomas Pinney, ed., *Essays of George Eliot* (London, 1963), pp. 207–11; see p. 210. For journal entry, see Pinney, p. 55, n. 7.

8 Georg Brandes, *Hovedstrømninger i det nittende Aarhundreds Litteratur*, 6 vols. (Copenhagen 1872–90), vol. 6 (new edn, Copenhagen, 1966), pp. 56–7.

9 Friedrich Gundolf, *Shakespeare und der deutsche Geist* (Berlin, 1911), p. 355.

example, were based on French neo-classical versions, including those of Jean-François Ducis who, though he knew no English, was the author of acting versions which brought Shakespeare to the Parisian stage as well as (indirectly) to other parts of Europe. In Poland the earliest translations were from the German; in Scandinavia Schlegel-Tieck underlay both the Danish and the Swedish classic mid-nineteenth-century translation, even though their authors worked from English texts as well.[10] Not only that, but 'Shakespeare' had also come to mean critical commentaries and discussions, largely German. Hence, in the Swedish Shakespeare of Hagberg one may now and then find a line that corresponds less to Shakespeare's line than to Schlegel's comment on that line; and one may find the whole approach to the language of a play coloured by Tieck's reading. Tieck's commentary on *Troilus and Cressida* describes it as a 'tragische Parodie'; Hagberg explains in his Introduction and notes that he has pushed the tone towards a 'huge joke on Homer'.[11]

History, of course, colludes in the exchange in another fashion, too, in that the discovery of Shakespeare was – in Germany, in Scandinavia, and in much of the rest of Europe, if more hesitantly in France – a stimulus to national literature. Translators looked before and after, sometimes with as articulate a sense of mission as Hagberg's in his note at the end of the twelfth and last volume of Shakespeare's *Dramatiska Arbeten*: 'If Shakespeare, made part of Swedish language and literature, can contribute to raising and strengthening the general Swedish public's sense of what is old and beautiful, and can also encourage the development of a dramatic art in our country, then the translator has his reward for labours – which have been very great indeed.' Discovering Shakespeare gave an impetus, both dramatic and political, towards the creation of a national and often a popular drama – a subject beautifully dealt with by Philip Edwards in his book *Threshold of a Nation*.[12] Here I need only return

to a reminder that it may be appropriate to think of the world as full of transmigrated, rather than appropriated, Shakespeares and in that context to heed Feste's warning to 'fear to kill a woodcock, lest thou dispossess the soul of thy grandam' (*Twelfth Night* 4.2.59–60).

That the 'allusion' becomes 'pollution' may seem to be inherent in the act of inter-lingual translation as such. Of Samuel Beckett, who wrote in two languages and translated his own work from French to English or vice versa, we are told that, attending a rehearsal of *Endgame* in London and hearing his own translation of Clov's punning remark about the telescope, he exclaimed: 'It's a rotten line. Bad translation . . . The more I go on the more I think things are untranslatable.'[13] Any translator worth his/her salt takes the supremacy of the original text for granted and so dissatisfaction is deeply rooted in the activity itself. Even August Wilhelm Schlegel spoke of his work as 'a thankless task, in which one is continuously tormented by the sense of ineluctable imperfections'.[14] So, second-hand, second-rate – and also thankless,

---

[10] See the essays by, respectively, Yuri D. Levin, Brigitte Schulze and Kristian Smidt in Delabastita and D'hulst, *European Shakespeares*; and also Paul V. Rubow, *Shakespeare paa dansk* (Copenhagen, 1932), p. 42 (on Edvard Lembcke, whose translation of Shakespeare's works into Danish appeared in 18 volumes, 1861–73, working with the English text on the left, and Schlegel-Tieck on the right, of his desk).

[11] See Nils Molin, *Karl August Hagberg som Översättare* (Lund, 1929) (published as the second half of a volume also containing Walter Raleigh, *William Shakespeare*, translated by Ruben Nöjd), p. 318.

[12] Philip Edwards, *Threshold of a Nation. A Study in English and Irish Drama* (Cambridge, 1979). See also the wide-ranging essays in José Lambert and André Lefevere, eds., *La traduction dans le développement des littératures* (Bern, 1993).

[13] 'Ça alors, pour une longue-vue c'est une longue-vue': 'That's what I call a magnifier'. See Harry Cockerham, 'Bilingual Playwright', in Katharine Worth, ed., *Beckett the Shape Changer* (London, 1975), p. 144.

[14] Letter to Goethe, 15 March 1811, quoted in Margaret E. Atkinson, *August Wilhelm Schlegel as a Translator of Shakespeare* (Oxford, 1958), p. 4.

in so far as one's best praise is not to be noticed, to be 'transparent' (a favourite accolade for translations, before it became a buzz-word in another sense, but not the best colour for the spur of fame).

As a result, the study of translations, and in particular of Shakespeare translations, has traditionally served mainly to demonstrate the outstanding qualities of the original and the failings of one or more translators. It is therefore worth pointing out, as Werner Habicht has done,[15] that at the level of 'allusion' – of language as semantics, and of poetry as creating meaning through a variety of devices – the translator is bound to function as a 'New Critic', however heretical such an approach may seem at present. Probably in that sense no one, not even an editor, knows the workings of the language in a play so well as a translator who has had to confront every word in a peculiarly intense way and in its relation to every other sign in the verbal texture of the play. The editor and the critic can comment on, and safely admire, Shakespeare's stylistic qualities; the translator alone has, painfully, the acute experience which Victor Hugo sums up as 'Shakespeare échappe'. How, Hugo asks, do you translate 'unsex', or 'buttock of the night', or 'green girl', or the phrase where – as in Virgil's 'sunt lacrymae rerum' – 'l'indictible est dit': 'We have kissed away / Kingdoms and provinces'?[16] But this is never a one-to-one process: 'collusion' immediately slips in, for (moving from the stylistic to the linguistic level) the confrontation is also intensely with the peculiar qualities, the whole more or less closed language system, of each of the two languages involved – the source and the target. Schlegel, again, lamented his inability to do justice to Shakespeare's puns, for, he said, the German language 'always wants to work, never to play'.[17] A number of scholars – Kristian Smidt in Norway, the late Professors Toshiko and Toshikazu Oyama in Japan, to mention only a few – have written fascinating explorations of the problems encountered at this level (such as, how do you translate 'To be

or not to be' into Japanese when there is no verb for simply 'to be'?). Many of these have appeared in *Shakespeare Translation*, the journal started by the two Oyamas and continued now under the significantly wider title of *Shakespeare Worldwide*. These are objective studies, throwing much light not only on Shakespeare but also on general linguistic issues. But for those with a subjective interest (involved in 'collusion'?) the gap between languages can also become a battle ground for the defence of one's vernacular. Thus Victor Hugo, in the Preface to his son François-Victor Hugo's translation into French prose of the complete works of Shakespeare (and the Apocrypha), makes much of English being to French like the night to the day, the moon to the sun. Out of 'cloudy' English, his son has made a 'clear' translation: 'fidèle' and 'définitive'.[18]

Seen in its full context, however, Hugo's statement is not only, or even mainly, about the French language as such: it is about poetics, in that implicitly it defines this prose translation of Shakespeare against earlier French translations in rhymed alexandrines. Even more implicitly, it also enters, via Shakespeare, the larger battle where French Classicism was fighting it out with German Romanticism on the cultural and political map of Europe – a battle in which England was very much on the side-lines. In questions of translation, poetics readily slides into politics. Thus Willa Muir, writing soon after World War II on translating from the German (albeit Kafka and other twentieth-century novelists rather than Shakespeare), sees

---

[15] In Delabastita and D'hulst, *European Shakespeares*, p. 51.

[16] Victor Hugo, 'Préface pour la nouvelle traduction de Shakespeare par François-Victor Hugo' (1864), in *Oeuvres complètes*, ed. Jean Massin, vol. 12/1 (Paris, 1969), pp. 329–30.

[17] *August Wilhelm Schlegel: Sämtliche Werke*, ed. E. Böcking, vol. 4 (Leipzig, 1846), p. 128. Quoted and translated by Atkinson, *Schlegel as Translator*, p. 24.

[18] Victor Hugo, 'Préface', p. 330. François-Victor Hugo's translation, *Oeuvres complètes de Shakespeare*, appeared in 18 vols. (Paris, 1859–66).

the German sentence as 'less ruthless than the Latin sentence, but also less realistic. The Romans preferred concrete statements to abstract ones, while the Germans roll compound words into sausages of abstraction, and then roll these sausages into bigger ones . . . So the right image for the German sentence . . . is that of a great gut, a bowel, which deposits at the end of it, a sediment of verbs.' And she goes on to ask: 'Is not this like the Reich desired by Hitler, who planned to make mincemeat of Europe?'[19] Whether it is or not, her analysis may explain why a speech like that of Claudius which opens *Hamlet* 1.2 goes apparently so much more happily into German than into French. The speech depends on Claudius' rhetoric laying a smoke-screen over the embarrassing features of his 'o'er-hasty marriage' to Gertrude. So Shakespeare gives him three and a half lines between the introduction of the object, subject and auxiliary verb –

> Therefore our sometime sister, now our queen,
> Th'imperial jointress of this warlike state,
> Have we –

and the arrival – by which time his listeners are befuddled by a series of images of oxymoronic events – at the predicate proper: 'Taken to wife'. Schlegel out-Claudiuses Claudius. After an imposing introduction –

> Wir haben also unsre weiland Schwester,
> Jetzt unsre Königin, die hohe Witwe
> Und Erbin dieses kriegerischen Staats –

he rolls oxymorons into compounds like 'Leichenjubel' and 'Hochzeitklage' ('mirth in funeral' and 'dirge in marriage') and then rolls these into a four-line 'sausage' which finally deposits the verb: 'Zur Eh' genommen'.[20] André Gide, on the other hand, continuing the post-Hugo French tradition of translating Shakespeare into prose (while also convinced that his translation of *Hamlet* was 'hautement supérieure à toutes les précédentes'),[21] first disposes of all the oxymorons and then has Claudius explain with suicidal clarity: 'Nous avons pris pour femme notre soeur d'hier qui est aujourd'hui notre reine.' It is perhaps not surprising that Claude Mauriac congratulated Gide on making the play of *Hamlet* 'moins mystérieuse, plus claire'.[22]

Translation is never a purely philological activity but a collusive re-creation in which cultural differences cling to grammar and syntax and history mediates the effect even of single words. I cannot refrain here from underlining this point with a personal anecdote: a true story of how a word can encapsulate the political and spiritual history of Europe in this century. Swedish schools used for a very long time the same standard German grammar, which was updated with new editions as needed. In my home we had three editions; the one my father had used was dated 1904 and, in the section on irregular verbs, the verb 'schaffen' ('create') was illustrated with the sentence 'Gott hat die Welt geschaffen': 'God has created the world'. By 1938, in the edition used by my older brothers and sisters, that sentence had become: 'Der Führer hat Ordnung geschaffen': 'the Führer has created order'. And in the 1943 edition, which I used, it read: 'Der Künstler hat ein Meisterwerk geschaffen': 'the artist has created a masterpiece'.[23]

---

19 Edwin Muir and Willa Muir, 'Translating from the German', in Reuben A. Brower, ed., *On Translation* (Cambridge, Mass. 1959), cited from Galaxy Press edn (New York, 1966), pp. 95–6. The passage quoted is by Willa Muir.

20 *Shakespeare's dramatische Werke nach der Übersetzung von August Wilhelm Schlegel und Ludwig Tieck*, ed. H. Ulrici, vol. 6 (Berlin, 1877), p. 24.

21 André Gide, *Journal 1939–1949*, p. 130. Cited from Jean Claude, *André Gide et le théâtre*, 2 vols. (Paris, 1992), 1.204. Gide's *Hamlet* translation is in vol. 7 of *Théâtre complet d'André Gide* (Paris, 1947–9).

22 Mauriac, letter to Gide on 28 November 1946, cited from Claude, *André Gide et le théâtre*, I.213. Gide worked with Jean-Louis Barrault who staged this *Hamlet* at the Marigny theatre in the autumn of 1946.

23 Hjalmar Hjort, *Tysk Grammatik* (3rd edn, Uppsala, 1904); edited by Sven Lide (15th edn, Uppsala, 1938, and revised 1945).

If this seems a long way from the subject of Shakespeare translation, it is by way of a reminder that, before a translator even begins consciously to appropriate Shakespeare, the language he is translating into has done a great deal of appropriating for him. Thereafter, as Shakespeare texts are mediated through the particular poetics and politics of a culture, translations move on a sliding scale towards adaptations. The theatrical aesthetics and traditions of a culture are of course also involved: in, for example, French versions that make Shakespeare aspire to be Racine, or in Schröder's German adaptations. But the divide between translations for the stage and for reading, respectively, is not a simple binary one: as Werner Habicht has pointed out, German acting versions in the nineteenth century were often based on the Schlegel-Tieck translation, although this was in itself famous for its beauty as a reading text rather than for its expressiveness in the theatre.[24]

Translation, then, is only one form of rewriting, and needs to be thought about and studied as such. In cutting, suppressing, restructuring and adding, theatre directors and (we must admit) academic critics are, each in his or her way and for his or her particular purpose, translators/re-writers of Shakespeare. I wish to illustrate this point by a brief and selective excursus through some versions of *Coriolanus* – a play that has served many functions at many times in many languages.

In English culture, *Coriolanus* has been a kind of litmus paper. In 1682 Nahum Tate's *The Ingratitude of a Commonwealth, or, The Fall of Coriolanus*, staged at the Theatre Royal, was an intervention in the Exclusion Crisis, its Dedicatory Epistle spelling out the moral: 'to recommend Submission and Adherence to establisht Lawful Power'. In Charlotte Brontë's novel *Shirley* (1849) a reading of *Coriolanus* provides an analogue to the local Luddite riots and enables the heroine to address the rather more cautious moral to the hero: 'you must not be proud to your workpeople; . . . and you must

not be of an inflexible nature, uttering a request as austerely as if it were a command'.[25] And a tract by William Miller, CIE, DD, LLD, *Shakespeare's 'Coriolanus' and Present-Day Indian Politics*, published by the Christian Literature Society in London and Madras (1906), translates the play into a lesson to teach civil servants in India the meaning of national unity, that is not to listen to those who cry 'India for the Indians':

The men who in many varied ways are bringing the thought of the West to bear upon the East are as indispensable for India's future as the patrician order, small although it was, compared with the overwhelmingly superior number of the people, was indispensable to Rome.   (p. 76)

Less politically, *Coriolanus* has served to translate actors into stars: J. P. Kemble, Edmund Kean (for whom it rather failed), Laurence Olivier, Ian McKellen, and others. W. C. Macready was to play Coriolanus in several productions, but the first, in 1819, was for him a kind of apotheosis. The testimony to his performance that he most esteemed, he tells in his reminiscences, was 'the graceful sonnet' published in the *Literary Gazette* by Barry Cornwall and entitled 'Mr Macready in *Coriolanus*':

'This is the noblest Roman of them all;'
And he shall wear his victor's crown, and stand
Distinct amidst the genius of the land,
And lift his head aloft while others fall.

. . .

And therefore fit to breathe the lines of him
Who, gayly, once, beside the Avon river
Shaped the great verse that lives, and shall live
     for ever.
But he now revels in eternal day
Peerless among the earth-born cherubim.[26]

---

[24] In *European Shakespeares*, p. 50.
[25] *Shirley*, ed. Herbert Rosengarten and Margaret Smith (Oxford, 1979), p. 105.
[26] See Frederick Pollock, ed., *Macready's Reminiscences* (new edn, 1876), p. 153.

Character, actor and author collapse into each other, as the clichés blur the antecedents of pronouns; and Macready is – like Bottom – translated. But the text itself has of course also been translated within English culture. James Thomson's *Coriolanus*, staged at Covent Garden in 1749, was a new play, based on Shakespeare's plot but re-written to ennoble the hero and at the same time conform to Augustan poetics. It ends with a speech by one of the deputies of the Volscian state who, standing over the dead body of Coriolanus, both eulogizes him and defines his fatal flaw:

> This Man was once the Glory of his Age,
> Disinterested, Just, with every Virtue
> Of Civil Life adorn'd, in Arms unequall'd.
> His only Blot was This, that, much provok'd,
> He rais'd his Vengeful Arm against his Country.

The fate of Coriolanus thus affirms poetic justice and points a moral:

> And lo! the Righteous Gods have now chastis'd
>   him,
> Even by the Hands of Those for whom he
>   fought.
> Whatever Private Views and Passions plead,
> No Cause can justify so black a Deed:
> . . .
> Then be this Truth the Star by which we Steer:
> Above ourselves our Country should be dear.
>   (5.4.24–39)[27]

This may be a translation out of English into English but, compared to the dialectical uncertainty of Shakespeare's ending, the heroic couplets at the end dictate and delimit both the meaning and the method of delivery as much as does the French prose of Pierre Le Tourneur (who, Victor Hugo claimed, did not translate Shakespeare but 'parodied' him).[28]

Closer to our own time, the most famous translation of *Coriolanus* is undoubtedly Bertolt Brecht's, usually discussed as a theatrical adaptation and in socio-political terms. But it was also Brecht's own translation, from an eclectic medley of source texts: he used two editions in English as well as a modern edition of Dorothea

Tieck's translation, and the prompt book from Erich Engel's 1936 staging of the play at the Deutsches Theater as well as Livy and Plutarch for additional historical material.[29] The German text that he arrived at was to be a challenge to what he saw as German Shakespeare: a tradition of 'lumpy, monumental' drama, 'beloved of middle-class Philistines' because it celebrated the heroic struggle of a single individual.[30] His leading idea, which he discusses in journals and notes, was that the play must not become the tragedy of an 'unersätzlich' – 'indispensable' or 'irreplaceable' – individual. Hence, after playing Coriolanus down and the Roman people up, throughout the text, he added a final scene in which the Roman Senate learns of Coriolanus' death but, after a brief silence, carries on with its agenda. This includes a request from the Marcius family to be allowed to wear mourning; and the play ends on the one ruthless word, 'Abgeschlagen' ('Rejected') and the stage direction '*The Senate continues its normal business.*'[31]

I have found a striking contrast to Brecht's *Coriolanus* in another German translation which is also a case of ideologically motivated re-writing: Johannes Falk's *Coriolan. Frei nach Shakespeare*, published in 1812 as a kind of hypertext with a summary of criticism, sources, and so on, a prefatory piece on Shakespeare's genius (which knows neither death, nor space, nor time) and a 'Nachschrift' on the art of translation. Falk, a minor writer and major

---

27 *The Plays of James Thomson, 1700–1748*, ed. John C. Greene, 2 vols. (New York, 1987), 2.553–4.

28 Victor Hugo, 'Préface', p. 329, on Pierre Le Tourneur's *Shakespeare. Traduit de l'anglois*, 20 vols. (Paris, 1776–83).

29 See the notes on Brecht's work on *Coriolanus* in Bertolt Brecht, *Stücke*, ed. Werner Hecht et al., vol. 9 (Frankfurt am Main, 1992), pp. 344–5.

30 See Brecht's comments on his 1924 production of Marlowe's *Edward II*, cited from John Rouse, *Brecht and the West German Theatre: The Practice and Politics of Interpretation* (Ann Arbor and London, 1989), p. 16.

31 *Stücke*, 9.81.

philanthropist, had moved to Weimar in 1797 and was a frequent guest of Goethe's.[32] Though his play was never put on at the theatre over which Goethe presided, its spirit is that of the classical Weimar theatre – a civic institution intent on moulding its audience into a harmonious society through experiences of beauty and truth. Falk's Preface, referring to Weimar as 'a new Rome', suggests a nationalistic agenda, all the more relevant in a city invaded by the French after the battle of Jena in 1806; and the text presents Coriolanus as the noblest Roman of them all, dying on a prayer for the city's protection ('Beschützet euer Rom, ihr ew'gen Götter', p. 290). This hero is as 'unersätzlich' as Brecht's is 'ersätzlich'. Falk, too, has a non-Shakespearian final scene in which two senators discuss at length the state of affairs in Rome; but here the subject is the creation of a memorial to 'the one and only great man', and they decide on building a temple to 'the womanly Fortuna' on the *Via Latina* to mark the spot where Coriolanus was persuaded not to attack Rome. Virgilia will be its first priestess. At this point a procession of Roman matrons enters, led by Volumnia who carries an urn containing the ashes of Coriolanus and who concludes the play with an extended 'Klagerede', lamenting her own broken heart and inviting the seven hills and the Tiber to weep with her:

Er ist für uns, er ist für euch gestorben!
Ich trage Rom in diesem Aschenkrug!
  (pp. 297–8)
(He has died for us, he has died for you!
I carry Rome in this urn of ashes!)

So this Coriolanus *is* Rome, and Volumnia's exclamations are a far cry from Sicinius' question 'What is the city but the people?' (3.1.199)

Obviously the *exchange* between these various versions of a Shakespeare play is in the mind of the beholder, as they establish a dialogue, across the ages and through the different languages, speaking about a translated and transmigrating Shakespeare. They remind us, too, that it is through theatrical performance that a veritable exchange can take place. If Brecht had developed some of his ideas of the theatre from his work on Elizabethan drama, so they were in turn fed back into English theatre. The Berliner Ensemble did not bring a Shakespeare play on their first visit to London in August 1956: they did not stage *Coriolanus* until 1964, and then in a re-adapted version as far from Brecht's text, according to one German reviewer, as Brecht's was from Shakespeare's.[33] But in opening up English theatre to influences from 'abroad', the visit was in its way as historical, and as much the cause of a re-birth, as was the publication of the Schlegel translation in Germany. Perhaps what is crucial in a genuine cultural exchange is that both sides see themselves from the outside: 'What shall they know of England / That England only know?'[34] The point is poignantly made by Brecht's last message to the Berliner Ensemble, pinned to the notice board in the Theater am Schiffbauerdamm on 5 August 1956. (Brecht died on 14 August, and the Ensemble's London season opened on 27 August.) 'For our London season', Brecht wrote,

we need to bear two things in mind. First: we shall be offering most of the audience a pure pantomime, a kind of silent film on the stage, for they know no German. . . . Second: there is in England a long-

---

[32] Falk's *Coriolan*, written in 1810, is cited from the edition published in Amsterdam and Leipzig, 1812. For details of his literary production (which probably included a posthumously published and anonymous memoir of Goethe), see Fritz Fink, *Johannes Daniel Falk*, Heft 4 of *Persöhnlichkeiten des klassischen Weimar* (Weimar, 1934). Falk's daughter's reminiscences of her father concentrate on his philanthropy; she quotes him as being grateful that God used him, not as 'Schreibpapier' ('writing paper') but as 'Charpie' to dress 'the open wounds of the age': Rosalie Falk, *Johannes Falk. Erinnerungsblätter* (Weimar, 1868), p. 142.

[33] R. W. Leonhardt, 'Können wir den Shakespeare ändern?', *Die Zeit*, 2 October 1964, quoted in Rouse, *Brecht and the West German Theatre*, p. 100.

[34] Kipling, 'The English Flag', is also quoted, via Harry Levin, by the editors of *European Shakespeare*, p. 21.

standing fear that German art (literature, painting, music) must be terribly heavy, slow, laborious, pedestrian.

So our playing needs to be quick, light, strong.[35]

As scholars, critics, and teachers we have opportunities to further cultural exchange as real as, if less spectacular than, those which are given to theatre people and others working in the performing arts. We also have the advantage of being able to see the whole process of exchange historically. So, if August 1956 was a moment of tangible exchange, the history of Shakespeare translations, on and off stage, offers networks of less tangible ones; and in conclusion I wish to explore just one such.

The *loci* for this are Dresden, London and Bergen in June–July 1852. In Bergen the Norwegian Theatre – really the first national theatre of Norway – had recently been established and had appointed as its 'stage instructor' a young student, Henrik Ibsen, himself recently delivered from the cultural backwater of a small coastal town where he had been an apothecary's apprentice. His main claim to fame was a blank verse tragedy, *Catiline*, never performed, written in subversive sympathy with the 1848 revolutions in Europe and as a distant Shakespearian transmigration, out of *Julius Caesar* (in Danish translation, for he had no English) and such *Sturm und Drang* drama as Schiller's *The Robbers*. In the summer of 1852 the management of the Norwegian Theatre sent Ibsen out to learn from theatre practices abroad; and, after a stay in Copenhagen, where he saw his first Shakespeare on stage, he arrived in Dresden on 9 June. He left no record of what he saw at the Court Theatre there, only a complaint that ticket prices were so high. Possibly he had, like Dull, no 'capacity': no language for what he must have seen.

By 1852 the Dresden Court Theatre, though less famous than some of its counterparts in other German states and cities, had a flourishing Shakespeare tradition.[36] Ludwig Tieck had

been its *Dramaturg* between 1824 and 1842; and Ibsen would have seen his famous pseudo-Elizabethan staging of *A Midsummer Night's Dream*, for which Mendelssohn had written the music.[37] He would also have seen two Shakespeare tragedies, *Hamlet* and *Richard III*, both long in the repertoire as vehicles for the Court Theatre's star actor, Emil Devrient.[38] But instead of Devrient, famous as a dreamy, idealist Hamlet, a 'Mondscheinprinz', Ibsen would have seen Bogumil Dawison who, as a Polish Jew who had decided to become a German actor and was now shocking Dresden audiences with his demonic energy, was himself virtually a personification of cultural exchange.[39] During these same weeks Emil Devrient was in London, leading a troupe of German players in a guest season at St James's Theatre where they opened – in the presence of the Queen and Prince Albert, who were to return for four more performances – with Goethe's *Egmont* and went on to present a range of plays, including *Hamlet* in Schlegel's translation.[40]

As a cultural exchange, this visit – unlike the

[35] Cited from *Brecht on Theatre*, translation and notes by John Willett (London, 1964), p. 283.

[36] See Robert Prölss, *Geschichte des Hoftheaters zu Dresden* (Dresden, 1878) and Egon Frohberg, *Die Entwicklung des Schauspiels am Dresdner Hoftheater zur Zeit Eduard Devrients* (Munich, 1926).

[37] See Robert Prölss, 'Shakespeare-Aufführungen in Dresden vom 20. Oct. 1816 bis Ende 1860', *Jahrbuch der deutschen Shakespeare-Gesellschaft*, 15 (1880): pp. 173–210.

[38] On the theatrical Devrient family, see Julius Bab, *Die Devrients* (Berlin, 1932); Friedrich Kummer, *Dresden und seine Theaterwelt* (Dresden, 1938); and Heinrich Hubert Houben, *Emil Devrient* (Frankfurt, 1903).

[39] See the diary of Emil Devrient's brother for a first-hand reaction to Dawison's acting: *Eduard Devrient: Aus seinen Tagebüchern: Berlin-Dresden 1836–1852*, ed. Rolf Kabel (Weimar, 1964), pp. 594–8. Also, Peter Kollek, *Bogumil Dawison: Die Schaubühne 70* (Kastellaun, 1978).

[40] See Henry Morley, *The Journal of a London Playgoer* (London, 1866), pp. 40ff., and Barry Duncan, *The St James's Theatre* (London, 1964), p. 90.

Berliner Ensemble's, some hundred years later – seems to have been more momentarily inspirational than lastingly developmental for English theatre, although Emil Devrient arrived back in Dresden 'full of England' and believing that he had 'created a space for ever, there, for German art'.[41] In 1900 Clement Scott still remembered Devrient as an actor 'supposed to be the greatest Hamlet who ever lived', but preferred Sarah Bernhardt.[42] As a seasoned playgoer, Henry Morley in 1852 was very conscious that he was experiencing *Hamlet* through a foreign language: 'The "Hamlet" of A. W. Schlegel is a wonderful translation', he writes, 'but the terse philosophy of Shakespeare is not to be fully translated'. He measured the performance against Victorian expectations of how the title role should be acted and missed the 'points of stage business familiar to the English . . . which the Germans have not been able to discover for themselves'; and, seen through a film of unfamiliarity, the production struck him – ironically, in view of Emil Devrient's notoriety in Dresden as an egotistical virtuoso player – as an example of ensemble playing.[43]

Ibsen meanwhile returned to Norway, apparently unable to translate any of his Dresden experiences into work for the Bergen stage, although they must have left a Shakespearian stratum somewhere in his consciousness. Eventually, as he found his own form of dramatic expression, he was explicitly to reject Shakespeare as a model – that is the 'lumpy, monumental drama' that Brecht also rejected.[44] But he went on reading Shakespeare, in Danish and German translation, and undoubtedly there is transmigrated Shakespeare in the works for which Ibsen is best known around the world – including a version of *Coriolanus* in *An Enemy of the People* (1882). Like Shakespeare's 'enemy to the people', Ibsen's Dr Stockmann is a passionately arrogant fighter for what he, and only he, sees as the truth; and in the mass meeting in act 4 – a crowd scene unique in Ibsen's 'contemporary' plays – he confronts his fellow citizens with an energy of vituperation and an élitism of attitude which could well have been passed down from Shakespeare's 'too absolute' hero.[45] Above all, Ibsen sets up a dialectic around his protagonist so that, as with Coriolanus, we have to view him from more than one viewpoint: he is objectively justified in his action over the polluted bath-water, but he is also subjectively occupied with his own heroism. 'Alone I did it' is his theme in the ironically constructed closing scene where his words say one thing and the stage image another:

DR STOCKMANN . . . Now I am one of the strongest men in the whole world . . . I've made a great discovery.
MRS STOCKMANN Not again!
DR STOCKMANN . . . (*gathers his family around him and says confidently*) The fact is, you see, that the strongest man in the world is he who stands most alone.
MRS STOCKMANN (*smiles and shakes her head*) Oh, Thomas – !
PETRA (*trusting, takes his hands*) Father![46]

Arthur Miller made his adaptation of *An Enemy of the People*, which opened at the Broadhurst Theatre, New York, in December 1950, without knowing Norwegian, working indirectly (as so many Shakespeare 'translators' have done), from a literal translation. In the then current political situation his *Enemy* had a subversive aim: to celebrate the courage to speak up for the truth against oppression. But, as he explains in his autobiography, he had to

41 *Eduard Devrient: Aus seinen Tagebüchern*, p. 598.
42 Scott, *Some Notable Hamlets*, pp. 43–4.
43 Morley, *The Journal of a London Playgoer*, pp. 40–9.
44 See I-S. Ewbank, 'Shakespeare, Ibsen, and Rome', in Tetsuo Kishi, Roger Pringle and Stanley Wells, eds., *Shakespeare and Cultural Traditions* (Newark, London and Toronto, 1994), pp. 229–42.
45 I am grateful to Thomas VanLaan for drawing my attention to *Coriolanus* as a 'source' of Ibsen's play.
46 Literally translated from the text in Henrik Ibsen, *Samlede Verker*, ed. Didrik Arup Seip, 3 vols. (Oslo, 1960), vol. 2, p. 628.

write out of the text what he saw as 'the play's implied social Darwinism' and to cut dangerous proto-fascist suggestions in Stockmann's speeches.[47] The result is a play that has lost the irony of the original; and instead of the dialectic of Ibsen's final scene, Miller's ends on a stance of unquestioned heroic defiance. Unlike Ibsen's Stockmann, Miller's identifies himself with his family and supporters – 'We [not an Ibsen pronoun] are the strongest people in the world' – and then, in a scene which is for all the world like a would-be Ibsenite *High Noon*, walks alone into danger:

The crowd is heard angrily calling outside. Another rock comes through a window.
DR STOCKMANN – and the strong must learn to be lonely!
 The crowd noise gets louder. He walks upstage toward the windows as a wind rises and the curtains start to billow out toward him.
    The Curtain Falls.

In its celebration of an 'unersätzlich' hero, Miller's *An Enemy of the People* relates to Ibsen's much as Falk's *Coriolanus* does to Brecht's. When it was performed at the Young Vic in London in October 1988, *The Daily Telegraph* hailed it with a 'Miller does Ibsen proud.'[48] To

some of us, this is no less outrageous than praising a Shakespeare translation for being better than the original. It is easier to come to terms with the complete cultural re-writing of *An Enemy of the People* in Satyajit Ray's Indian film (1989), because for all its Ibsenite allusion it stands alone as a beautiful piece of didacticism, with an almost utopian upbeat ending where Dr Gupta, who has discovered bacteria in the holy water of a Hindu temple, and his young supporters face a brave new world. But here we are dealing with translation both into another medium and into a non-European cultural context – both of which are outside my ken.

No one would say that Miller's play, let alone Ray's film, does *Shakespeare* proud. And yet, through layers of cultural exchange, through allusion and collusion and pollution, there is a Shakespearian grandam inside these woodcocks. Truly, the study of Shakespeare translation, like the study of human relationships, ends nowhere.

---

[47] Arthur Miller, *Timebends* (1987), quoted from the Postscript in the Nick Hern paperback edition of *An Enemy of the People* (London, 1989), from which the text of the play is also quoted.
[48] Quoted on the back cover of Miller's play.

SHAKESPEARE, THEATRE PRODUCTION, AND CULTURAL POLITICS

JOHN RUSSELL BROWN

Shakespeare's plays, with their inherently flexible structure and openness of style, positively invite distinctive re-interpretations in performance. They can be cut and amplified, bent this way or that in translation, and, in staging, transported lock, stock, and barrel into the here-and-now or almost any other time and place. Even at their most intense and sustained moments – perhaps especially then – the dialogue can support a wide variety of characterizations: Shylock, Hamlet, Falstaff, Prince Hal, Prospero have all served many purposes, taking shape and spirit from the actors and directors who have laid hands on the very same printed words. Arguments can be readjusted at will, so that a Shakespeare play becomes a director's opportunity to say whatever he or she wishes under cover of serving its author and taking advantage of his reputation. In a politically conscious world, Shakespeare's plays can speak politically, in an anxious world psychologically, in a religious world religiously; in a closed world of theatre-making they can become gentle or hectic fantasies of minimal moral or political interest. In most theatres, a director's conceptual choices are reinforced by a quartet of designers, for set, costumes, light, and sound, whose overwhelming effects thrill an audience and render it submissive to each new interpretation.

Any production can be read as an indication of the culture that supports its theatre, but that message is not always clear. What is far more readily perceived is a distinctive reading, concept, or message created by the production's director, which uses the text in ways which challenge accepted notions of the play's meanings. Representations of something as complex as a culture would be work of a quite different order. There is little chance of exercising considered or inspired judgement on such matters in a theatre production which has been worked on for a year or two in circumstances not entirely under anyone's control, not even the director's who must work within the bounds of the finance, administration, and market of the theatre company. No one has opportunity for free and unrestricted investigation. Besides, in most English-speaking theatres a director seldom has more than four or five weeks to work full-time with the actors, some of whom he or she will be meeting for the first time. Directorial reinterpretations are likely to be enlightening in much the same way as a reputable newspaper article about the state of Europe or the way we live now. A journalist is no Homer, a director no Shakespeare; and neither is a Margaret Mead, Clifford Geertz, or James Clifford attempting to interpret an entire culture. Most directors are like journalists looking for a quick fix, a way of making a striking, accessible, and saleable commodity, fit to last for only a comparatively short time, after which another production must be made ready for immediate consumption. Most directors are so busy 'making their names', turning out material to catch the eye, and keeping their company afloat, that they stand little chance of probing the deeper issues of politics and still less the slow-moving and hidden wellsprings of a culture. Taking them seriously beyond what is due to purveyors of fashionable opinion and flashes of idiosyncratic insight is to underestimate the potential of theatre and the ingrained and complex nature of culture. Re-interpretations created by actors of experience and originality repay rather fuller attention, because a Shakespeare play requires the leading actors to put their whole lives and experience on the line – if the director has not sent them chasing after more easily recognized objectives.

However, Shakespeare's plays make such wide and deep demands on all those who stage them that any production achieves rather more than its director intends. By looking away from what is glossy-new in each re-interpretation, we may still say that theatre is a mirror of its age in which both the form and pressure of the time are revealed. Performance will always overflow the measure of a director's mind in one way or another. Each play we see in the theatre is the product of a whole company working more or less together and Shakespeare's scripts are so written that they are especially sensitive to this corporate effort. The power-structure of a theatre company and the relationships implicit in its culture are represented in the product of varied people working, of necessity, in close contact with each other and using whatever they bring from life into this new and demanding endeavour. In the process, to adapt the words of Shakespeare's Henry the Fifth, they will inevitably 'show the mettle of their pasture;'[1] the cultural politics of a theatre will be implicit in its productions and will communicate to an audience, whether a director likes it or not. Arguably this hidden content of a performance communicates the better because an audience is not in general aware of what is happening.

Most experienced directors know this very well. Productions by Sir Peter Hall depend as much on what he is given by the company as on his own ideas and initiative. He has explained that:

In the early stages of rehearsal, the shape and pace of a scene must not be imposed. The actors should be free to create while their director helps to release their imaginations; and if that means going very fast or very slow, or taking enormous pauses, it must happen; everything must be allowed. But once the truth of the scene is found, the director becomes the editor.[2]

Or, again:

The director is the leader of a group who are on a journey to discover the play; neither he nor the group members know necessarily where that journey will lead them.[3]

In effect, members of a company discover themselves in the play, and the political and cultural realities of what they have brought with them are displayed for all to see. Peter Brook made much the same point in more radical terms, referring to the entire process of production and performance. At the end of a long series of rehearsals he confided to an attentive note-taker:

We are a small group of human beings. If our way of living and working is infused with a certain quality, this quality will be perceived by the audience, who will leave the theatre subliminally coloured by the working experience we have lived together. Perhaps that is the small contribution we can make, the only thing we have to convey to other human beings.[4]

By putting on show a 'working experience lived together' theatre will express the 'form and pressure' of the times – its cultural politics – no matter what a director might want to achieve or a censor to say.

Companies producing Shakespeare today work in a variety of organizations and therefore represent different modes of contemporary culture. But a few dominant forms are everywhere

---

[1] Cf. *Henry V* 3.1.27.
[2] *Making an Exhibition of Myself* (London, 1993), pp. 99–100.
[3] Ibid., p. 83.
[4] *Peter Brook: A Theatrical Casebook*, compiled by David Williams (London and New York, 1988), pp. 348–9.

present, expressing cultural politics repetitively and confidently, as if there were no hope of change or regeneration. Taking the phrase from Fredric Jameson and looking at the most admired Shakespeare productions of the last few years, Dennis Kennedy has identified signs of 'late monopoly capitalism' in the way that successful theatre works at this time.[5] Like Coca-Cola and McDonalds' hamburgers, this mode of production 'works by transcending national borders and creating attractive images of its material products designed to make their consumption inevitable'. He can point to productions by Brook, Mnouchkine, Bergman, Strehler, Sturua, Ninagawa which thrive on this political-cultural situation and are made available for purchase around the world. These well-financed productions share another cultural mark with many that are less famous, less skilled and polished, and less travelled: they are all the products of an accepted dictatorship, a supposedly benevolent exercise of power by a 'final voice', a daily submission to an experienced 'editor' who is relatively distant from the work because never on stage and personally involved with enacting the play. The authority of this over-riding dictator/director/editor is often said to be inevitable because the complicated technical resources which are brought nowadays to the staging of Shakespeare require a single person to be in sole command.

If theatre is to be efficient, it is said, there is no choice in this matter. As with any successful business in the world market-place, its production-process must be thoroughly organized and carefully controlled, and only one central authority should be responsible for this and, ultimately, for everything else. Do work-councils have much effective influence over *product*? Can individuals compete with a computer-assisted intelligence? For maximum effectiveness and world-wide availability must there not be some sacrifice of individual freedoms and initiatives? These questions are pertinent across the whole spectrum of society and usually only one set of answers is given. In the theatre, the same logic holds: urged on by theatre's administrators, the directors of productions go their forceful ways, carefully and sometimes almost apologetically; and their productions bear traces of compulsion, as if bound to achieve strength through unity and happiness through organized labour.

Pursuit of obvious success and development of compelling brand-images are among the most pervasive elements of our culture and politics, and the ways we stage Shakespeare's plays have been made to fit these necessities of the global market-place. Theatre remains the mirror of the age: directors seduce audiences into uncritical acceptance by superb organization – as high in quality as that of the most ruthless business – consistent quality, and stunning visual presentation. The interests of local audiences, the individual talents and imaginations of actors, and a sense of exploration and adventure all tend to lose out.

Cultural and political realities can be identified most easily in productions of Shakespeare when two versions of the same play are available for comparison, such as *Richard III* staged by the Royal National Theatre of Great Britain in 1990–1 and by the Odeon Theatre of Bucharest in 1993–4. In the English version the director's intelligence organized activities on stage as if he had inherited an old-fashioned taste for military parade: grand and formal effects were carried out with precision, but without allowing much scope for the independent and idiosyncratic creativity of participants. Certainly the scheme of Richard Eyre's production was grand, offering not only Shakespeare's play but also twin pictures of dictatorship in Nazi Germany and the resurgence of the extreme right wing of politics in post-war Europe, and in England more especially. The production was making much the same comment on contemporary

---

[5] 'Shakespeare and the Global Spectator', *Shakespeare Jahrbuch* (forthcoming, 1995).

politics as Brecht's *Resistible Rise of Arturo Ui* of 1957 but, in London in 1990, Shakespeare's text was kept intact while being fingered incessantly by the director. The actors appeared to order in formal white-tie evening dress, black-shirt uniforms, or serviceable everyday clothes with armbands displaying the cross of St George or the image of a boar; they employed banners and slogans, public-address systems, board-room rituals; they posed for a group photo, managed to act alongside a toy train, and then provided a red-carpet welcome at a railway station together with a review of attendant troops. These superimposed visuals were used to plug a political message into the words of the text and keep the actors in line. Richard himself was defined by what he looked like and his manner of speaking. At first a Sandhurst-trained officer bearing the psychological and physical wounds of war and an élitist education, he then became, one after the other, a right-wing demagogue and a melodramatic actor in medieval costume performing before a huge painting showing himself naked and in triumph, astride a rearing white horse. In Richard's dream before the final battle of Bosworth, the ghosts of those he had slaughtered took on fantastic life, regardless of the stiff formality of their speeches: Clarence tried to force wine down Richard's throat, Anne danced with Richmond, the two young princes played games, and Buckingham brought on a crown of thorns; Queen Margaret, restored to youth and dressed in white, roamed the stage in gloating triumph. Here the director had pushed his actors beyond the limits of Brecht's play, seeking to add images of infantile competitiveness and hackneyed horror as signifiers of Richard's terminal state and, possibly, of his motivation throughout the action. None of this could have been achieved without tight discipline on stage and in the design-rooms, workshops, and control booths. Even the intense and compelling Richard of Ian McKellen had its effects nailed down and sometimes upstaged by what had been busily provided around him: having wooed Elizabeth to allow

him to marry her daughter, Richard's comment on her departure, 'Relenting fool, and shallow, changing woman' (4.4.362), registered less as sardonic humour than as an occasion for his attendant henchmen to break out into a guffaw, reminding the audience of 'male barrack-room mockery of all women'.[6]

What this interpretation said about the play and about cultural politics was very obvious and self-limited, one more appropriation of this text to join others put on stage in the present century. But viewed as a political and cultural product, expressing the nature of the theatre that made it, its very thorough workmanship and consistency have wider interest. The most obvious challenges of Shakespeare's text had been ducked: its great variety of independent engagement for actors and the complex dynamic of its central role – egocentric, anti-establishment, mercurial, buffoonish, coldly cruel, and highly intelligent. Actors, designers, and the whole company had been subdued and energized by the dictates of a skilled director with a political point to make. A brilliant and well-executed production could then play in privileged repertory and on a heavily subsidized foreign tour. The play had become the means to a productive end; the text, both respected and patronized, played its sometimes passive part in producing a distinctive product for exploitation within the world of subsidies, prestige publicity, and assured excellence of workmanship. For those members of its audiences who resented being nudged repeatedly towards the director's view of twentieth-century history, many more would have been pleased to find an easily understood 'treatment' of a masterpiece. Often slow and sometimes shrill, nicely judged and yet completely achieved, so carefully consistent in every effect that it seemed afraid of attempting anything

---

[6] Peter Holland, 'Shakespeare Performances in England, 1990–1991', *Shakespeare Survey 44* (1992), p. 187; many of the details from this production recorded in this paper are corroborated by this careful and perceptive review.

uncertain, the production was praised for stage-business rather than acting, interpretation rather than either passion or intellectual exploration. Critics were kept so busy noting the period and political details that they had little space to consider whether the production was entertaining in any interesting sense.

The 'working experience lived together' by the National Theatre company as sensed in this production could scarcely be further from that of theatres in Shakespeare's day. Then a theatre was run by a group of actors who benefited directly from success and bore the cost of failure. Actors dominated what was shown on stage as they performed before a lively and diverse public, sitting or standing in the same light as themselves. We have no idea how the text was 'interpreted', but we do know that *Richard III* was a great popular success for its author and theatre. The actor playing the hero also grew in fame in the process of a large number of single performances spread out over many years. There was no director/dictator, no designer, few technicians, and almost no budget for scenic effects: in contrast with this way of working, and by most other standards as well, the political and cultural reality of the National Theatre production must be judged over-wrought, repressive, and defeatist.

The production of *Richard III* by the Odeon Theatre playing in its own Majestic Hall in the centre of Bucharest won prizes for leading actor and director. It was also exploited in the overseas marketplace and was a triumph of 'benevolent' dictatorship. But there was both more slavery for members of the cast and more freedom for the star than at the National Theatre. Twelve of the actors were uniformly dressed and drilled as a support-team for Richard, his attentive listeners, playmates, and agents of destruction; they were as little individualized as a chorus in classical ballet, and worked as hard. But Marcel Iures as Richard had been encouraged to act in extrovert, smiling, impulsive, and playful manner, with a great show of energy and charm. He gave the role a hyped-up dynamism which made it hard to believe every effect calculated and hard to make consistent sense of his commitment to the play's action beyond the achievement of a self-satisfied and increasingly manic childishness. The other named roles achieved little individuality: tough, aggressive males in long, heavily padded robes, uniform in style and stiff with appliqué decoration; strong-voiced and demonstrative females, in vibrant colours. They all had been given essentially the same orders, so that they played along with Richard in the idiom of the production, throwing their bodies around and sharing energetic embraces, salutes, kneeling, kissing of hands and faces. On-stage laughter seemed to come whenever bidden, as victims were strangled or as Richard ordered 'Off with his head!' Buckingham shared an apple with Richard who insisted on having the bigger half, and then gave Buckingham a bite out of his. In such a setting Richard's freedom had obvious limitations, as if he had been allowed free scope in a selected and limited environment, a freedom not of the world, but confined within a theatrical fantasy where 'anything goes'. Besides cutting and altering its text, the director made one striking addition to the play, providing Richard with an attendant who was half-wolf, half-fool, who howled and chattered with laughter, and breathed deeply in shared commitment. With a calculated *coup de théâtre*, this attendant lost his mask at the end of the play and revealed the face of a Medusa; this creature then cradled Richard and, as he died, kissed him.

Here again was a single-minded interpretation, but applied almost exclusively to showing the central character in a non-specific theatrical environment. The triumph of the production was its elevation of a simple political story into an infectiously riotous, but circumscribed, celebration of performance. With the exception of the leading actor, the company acted on orders and subdued individuality to corporate discipline. Little money had been spent on set or stage-effects, but great attention was paid to music, choreography, and the martial arts which together gave the director an unstoppable power to seduce the audience; he might have been staging a mega-musical. In cultural and political terms, this Shakespeare production revealed a company committed to long-term success, every bit as much as the National Theatre in London, but less cunning and careful, and less self-consciously solemn and restrained. Most noticeably, the Odeon Theatre was more content to create a work that had no precise reference outside the theatre, as if the real world, past or present, was better avoided. A comparison with the cultural politics of Shakespeare's theatre serves to accentuate the well-drilled life of all but one of the actors, the isolated theatricality of the operation, and the picturesque engagement in violence and martial arts.

Control of the production-process is not always so effective in other theatres. Regional companies in the United States, for example, give very limited powers to the 'visiting' director for their annual Shakespeare production. First priority goes to the on-going needs of a large number of patrons buying their seats by the season; the company is geared to a supply-economy, not to meeting exceptional challenges or creating new audiences. Choice of cast is governed by the availability of local talent and the high cost of bringing in additional actors. Rehearsal period is likely to be three or four weeks, with not all the actors available all the time. A significant proportion of the company may have spent most of the previous few years acting in television serials, films, or new plays representing modern speech and living; some members may have been doing other work than acting for much of the time. Knowledge of each other and a shared attitude to Shakespeare's text are likely to be found only at Festival Theatres specializing in Shakespeare, and there the actors are sometimes without other significant theatre experience. The political and cultural consequences of these arrangements can be clearly seen, not least in the boldest strokes of directional invention. Productions are therefore given as much song and dance as possible, while decoration and display, broad comedy and up-to-the-minute caricature, are all devised to grab attention. A Shakespeare production in such a theatre will usually show signs of unease or uncertainty alongside corporate submission, relieved by some individual exertion or even defiance. These qualities are not essentially Shakespearian, but an index of the politics and culture of this time and place. They have a pervasive and inescapable effect on performance and consequently on the reactions of an audience.

Not all theatres go along with the dictates of the market place, whether global or local. As better-off, better organized theatres become the market leaders and eliminate long-standing opposition, alternative modes of operation are attempted with ever-greater frequency. The super-theatres are so powerful that they have learnt to live in uneasy peace at a distance from one another, but the dispossession their policies bring about among the under-privileged leads to outbreaks of civil war among theatres, and sometimes these disturbances penetrate into what had previously been considered safe areas. In fact theatre reflects contemporary politics as described by Hans Magnus Ensensberger:

Few dispute that the world market, now that it is no longer a vision of the future but a global reality, produces fewer winners and more losers as each year passes . . . The losers, far from regrouping under a common banner, are hard at work on their own self-destruction, and capital is retreating from the battlefields wherever possible . . .

[In] New York as well as in Zaire, in the industrial cities as well as in the poorest countries, more and more people are being permanently excluded from the economic system.[7]

The excluded and disadvantaged in theatre find opportunity to produce Shakespeare outside

---

[7] *Civil War* (1993; tr. Piers Spence, 1994), pp. 34–6.

the control of the major companies. They set up business on their own, aggressively and self-importantly. Freedom and independence beckon, even if this means scrapping a working-wage and other hard-won rights, and doing without new and powerful technical equipment, an effective propaganda machine, and an assured audience – all the fruits of successful trading. These uprisings cause little permanent damage to the large companies which remain virtually unscathed, but the emergence of small-scale, independent Shakespeare producers is a part of present-day cultural politics which should not be ignored. Some of the work is inefficient, rushed, ill-advised, or even crippled, but there it is and making its own commotion. With little thought or little access to capital investment, small, independent theatres thrive on the challenge of Shakespeare's plays, working with excitement and unpredictability.

Some small companies do not look very much as if they could wage a 'civil war', because they do not parade their weaponry. They look more like units of a cottage industry which serves a small clientèle living in remote areas and having a peculiar taste for individually crafted performances. But in their small world, these theatres are starkly and boldly opposed to the processes which create expensive and durable productions with recognizable brand images. Even in their most painstaking work belligerence usually shines through. These people believe passionately that they are taking part in a necessary struggle and perform as if the plays and their own initiatives provided all the necessary armaments.

A two-fold division of Shakespeare productions into the mass-market and the pirate and small scale drastically simplifies a complex situation. For example, the Bucharest and London *Richard III*s differed significantly in the relationship developed between the show on stage and its audience. The Opera Theatre's Richard was able to make contact and invite connivance or wonder. A reviewer from the London *Times* noted both the company discipline and the free-booting hero:

His soldiers worship him – and this production can afford to give him a bodyguard of 12 devoted swordsmen who step, turn and threaten in unison. [Marcell] Iures [as Richard] tosses a smile at the audience after putting them through their paces.

(13 May 1994)

In contrast, Ian McKellen's Richard was on stage for the audience to see for itself and figure out its meaning. Up there, in the carefully created world of the play, the actor made no concessions to the silent spectators below and above him. Nevertheless such contrasts of style do not affect the common purpose of such exercises; both these financially viable companies were providers of a show that had been developed to run for a long time and impress their audiences in ways decided by a director. The small-scale, upstart, and pirate companies are basically different in operation, seeing themselves as sharers with their audiences, or as representatives or leaders of them, or as provocateurs and instigators for them.

Despite stylistic variations, the two-fold distinction holds good in most aspects of production. Market leaders are possessors and purveyors, providing their public with what they think will sell. (No subsidy is big enough to allow a theatre company to escape the financial restrictions and responsibilities of commercial enterprise.) They manipulate the market through the media and their own self-promoting propaganda, and their skills in this work grow ever more impressive. Necessarily they try to become highly distinctive on the surface while their products become more and more similar in substance: they operate in the same market place and use very much the same exploitive means. On the other side of the divide, variations are essential to existence and each company will flaunt its difference from the rest of theatre. One uses all male actors, another all female; one casts actors from a single ethnic background, another insists on a mix of racial traditions. Here all the performers are dancer-actors, or singer-actors, or mimes, or clowns. Another company insists on using only contemporary costumes and fashionable manners and intonations. When money will stretch so far, a company may employ only actors who are also musicians, so that productions can be accompanied at all times by music, creating mood and sustaining forward movement and unity. Another company will maximize doubling, so that *Macbeth* is produced with three actors, *King Lear* with five; and in a contrary way, two Ophelias or three Hamlets may be on stage at the same time. Another theatre will use only the minimum of company rehearsals, trying to 'free' their actors from prescribed movements and interpretations, and from a director's all-seeing control. Others use film clips to provide a contemporary context or parallel for the play's action. Some will always perform in small, intimate spaces where there is little division between stage and auditorium. Or performances may be for special audiences, the old, the very young, or people living in particular places or social conditions. All are united in trying to break through the limitations of monopoly commercial practice, craving their own kinds of success as if struggling to draw the very breath of life.

Sometimes, briefly, the dividing wall is breached. A benevolent dictatorship may set up a small company-within-the-company to ape the freer spirits outside its bounds; this much smaller unit will mount workshop, studio, 'educational', 'outreach', or 'mobile' productions on very tight budgets. But every enterprise of this sort remains subordinate to the dictates of its masters. Directors and actors do not stay here for long, the best being promoted into 'mainstage' productions where they will earn and spend more money, and learn the necessities of the market place. The other way around, small independent companies can be corrupted by success, restricting their own freedom by mounting productions which are able

to tour for long periods or take up residence in a large theatre run by commercial producers seeking the profits and stability of established suppliers. Cheek by Jowl is a British company which took its name from the defiance flung at his rival by the callow Demetrius in *A Midsummer Night's Dream* (3.2.338) and, back in 1981, it started life in this vein:

there's no-one who leads, no-one who follows in a Cheek by Jowl production. All participants go together in a world of the imagination. There's a spirit in Cheek by Jowl which is intimate but raucous, private yet public, cerebral but celebratory ... Theirs is the regeneration game, the fruition of impulses from a collective creative imagination.

So runs the Introduction to a publication celebrating the company's first ten years of life.[8] But almost from the start, in its choice of a succession of productions of Shakespeare, European classics in new translations, and adaptations of well-known novels, the company was trading on the reputation of household names; it was also balancing its books and boosting its image by holding on to productions for long tours around the world. By 1994 a production of *Measure for Measure*, after months of constant touring, settled for a further month into the Lyric Theatre, Hammersmith, close to the West End of London. While this show had started as workshops in the summer of 1993, by July of the following year the actors seemed to be enacting routines and their performance took some quarter of an hour longer than at first. The word was that the company's all-male version of *As You Like It*, which had played for many months in 1991, was to be revived with a West End management as a Christmas show; for this to work, the intimate, raucous, and impulsive band of actors must become ordered enough for their product to be repeated and exploited for greatly increased consumption.

---

8 Simon Reade, *Cheek by Jowl: Ten Years of Celebration* (1991), p. 11.

Other companies, especially in Britain, which started small, free, and valiant, have advanced right up to the gates of established citadels and then failed to continue. Some lacked the finance or skill to enter that market place; others found that the energies and purposes with which they had started life could not sustain work in the larger scale. When the rebellious freely commit themselves to a strong leader, they may manage to straddle the divide long enough to give large-scale performances which are adventurous and glowing with independent life. The English Shakespeare Company, led by director Michael Bogdanov and actor Michael Pennington, managed this at least once when they finished a nationwide tour at the Old Vic in London in 1987, and presented *Richard II, Henry IV, Parts I and II,* and *Henry V* in a single day. The productions had all been played in repertoire for some months and bore the marks of directorial decisions in every scene, but the occasion provided a quite exceptional boost with which predictability was cast away. When Falstaff (John Woodvine) entered on a handcart and astride a barrel his disquisition on Honour was timed, effortlessly, to the unscripted responses of a crowded audience which had been watching the story unfold for well over seven hours. This was not a display of secure excellence or smart efficiency, though the standard of work was comparable with that of many market leaders. Nor was it a carnival entertainment as historians usually describe one, because all had been carefully prepared and all performers knew their script, their places, and their art. Rather it was a triumph of free thought and feeling within a prescribed production, a pleasure shared between actors and audience. The effect was only partly anarchic, because it was lodged securely in the whole unfolding and prearranged drama, and in the audience's sense of that achievement; but, quite unexcep-

tionally, the experience was intense, joyous, palpable, and unprecedented.

A sufficient number of moments like this keep recurring to remind us that Shakespeare's plays in performance need not be clearly packaged and processed by directors working for the market leaders and need not be distorted by the exaggerations and aggressions of insurrection and anarchy. But the politics and culture of our age are so strongly ingrained that productions which are alive in confident interplay with the text, and between individual performers and their audiences, remain highly exceptional. We get the Shakespeare we deserve and in theatre it would take more than a few zealots to reverse current trends. Perhaps a programme of reform could succeed, but it would have to start with the organisms that create theatre, not with new ideas for staging or with yet more re-interpretations: as Falstaff said of mere 'reasons', both of those are 'as plentiful as blackberries' and on their own will not improve matters at all (*1 Henry IV*, 2.4.243). Reform would have to engage all those elements of corporate theatrical life which Shakespeare supposed would be in force for the staging of his plays and it would have to draw upon an 'experience of working and living together' in the present time.

It may seem impossible to alter the cultural politics of our time, but theatre can be an agent for the practical testing of ideas which society as a whole will not admit. This has been proved in very recent years by the theatres of Eastern Europe and is being proved again by theatres in Africa, South America, and India. Change may be more possible in theatres than elsewhere, because theatre is being forced to redefine itself over against film, TV, videos, and pop music: competition with these more exploitable and profitable forms of entertainment is already raising questions which strike to the root of many present-day habits and conformities.

'AMPHITHEATERS IN THE BODY': PLAYING WITH HANDS ON THE SHAKESPEARIAN STAGE

MICHAEL NEILL

In more than one respect, man's hands have been his destiny.   Elias Canetti, *Crowds and Power*

The hand is a peculiar thing.   Heidegger

'Hath not a Jew hands?'[1] What exactly does Shylock mean when he makes the hand a defining mark of humanity? The gesture called for by his rhetorical demand is likely to make us feel that something more than the mere possession of opposable thumbs is involved; but we might be hard pressed to say precisely what. I should like to begin answering the question in a somewhat oblique way by invoking a powerful piece of ritual from Frank McGuinness's drama, *Observe the Sons of Ulster Marching Towards the Somme*, a play whose action displays an almost fetishistic fascination with the human hand – gesturing, reaching, clasping, crafting, drumming, striking, 'seeing', and bleeding. At the climax of the second act, the protagonist, Kenneth Pyper, signs his reluctant allegiance to the atavism of Protestant tribal history by slashing his left hand: 'Red hand,' goes the chant, 'Red sky. Ulster.'[2] In the London production the significance of this gesture was underlined by the backdrop against which the entire action was performed – a huge Ulster flag with the blood-red hand at its centre.[3] Despite the fact that the Red Hand was originally a native Irish device, the clan badge of the Northern O'Neill, and although (as the Irish Labour Movement's 'Red Hand of Liberty') it served as a Republican emblem in 1916, it has by now become almost exclusively associated in

most minds with the intransigent politics of Orange Unionism. Simplified to a political traffic sign, an Ulster *no passaran*, what it says is 'No Surrender!' McGuinness's ritual, however, complicates this message by re-activating the emblem's origins in the Milesian foundation myth, where the soil of Ireland was successfully claimed by one of two brothers who severed his own hand and hurled it ashore before his rival could touch land. What results is an odd kind of alienation-effect that bathes all the hands of the play in an unfamiliar light, investing them with a density of semiotic suggestiveness that the modern hand has lost. In this way, as I shall try to show, McGuinness's hands belong (like so much else in Northern Ireland) to an archaic, seventeenth-century world.

The political effectiveness of the foundation myth embodied in the Red Hand clearly depends on its ability to concentrate the symbolism of possession and sacrifice into a single extraordinary gesture. Yet at some level its darkly suggestive power refuses to be contained by the allegory; and it resonates, in ways that help to explain why Freud should have considered severed hands amongst the most potent

---

[1] *Merchant of Venice* 3.1.59; all citations from Shakespeare are to G. Blakemore Evans (ed.), *The Riverside Shakespeare* (Boston: Houghton Mifflin, 1974).

[2] Frank McGuinness, *Observe the Sons of Ulster Marching Towards the Somme* (London: Faber, 1986), p. 37.

[3] The ambivalence of Pyper's gesture is underscored by the fact that it is his left hand that he mutilates, whilst the heraldic device displays a bloody right hand.

signs of the uncanny,[4] with other episodes of mutilation whose surface meanings are very different – the terrifying story of an American slave about to be sold away from her family who cut off her hand and flung it in her master's face; or (to choose a literary example that may seem closer to our business here) the grotesque episode in Shakespeare's *Titus Andronicus* where the protagonist lops off his hand and sends it to the Emperor by way of ransom for his sons. For the Irish hero the hand is the instrument of seizure and appropriation; for the slave woman it is the tool of labour, the determinant of her market-value; for Titus it is the shield-hand, the sign of his role as Rome's defender ('Tell him it was a hand that warded him / From thousand dangers', 3.1.194–5); yet in each case the amputated member seems charged with an overplus of obscure significance that threatens to rupture the semiotic boundaries of the gesture, rendering it as impossibly full (or empty) of meaning as a scream. For Freud, predictably enough, the feeling of uncanniness aroused by such images 'springs from [their] proximity to the castration complex';[5] and the mutilated hands that uncannily linked the two 1993 prize-winners at the Cannes Film Festival – Jane Campion's *The Piano* and Chen Kaige's *Farewell My Concubine* – reflect the explanatory force of his conjecture. Yet the vagueness of Freud's 'proximity' seems to hint that he was less than fully satisfied with his own explanation; and the three very differently inflected mutilations I have cited are perhaps enough to indicate that the persistence of the hand as a suggestive motif in human culture has less to do with any single universal significance than with its extraordinary symbolic adaptability.

Of course the mysterious stencilled handprints in Neolithic rock paintings are a recognizable reminder that the hand has an ancient metonymic pedigree as a mark of human presence. As the instrument of making and acting it is a widely recognizable symbol of power – like the 'hand of God' in which scripture imagines the absolute authority of Jehovah, or the hand

of Fatima which in North African Muslim belief serves as a potent talisman for warding off the Evil Eye. The meaning of hands seems also to have been shaped by the peculiar relation to the bicameral brain,[6] which has made them a crucial element in the deep structure out of which human beings shape their understanding of the world – the dualistic oppositions of right and left that are so densely inscribed in the language and practices of every culture.[7]

---

[4] Sigmund Freud 'The Uncanny' in S. Freud, *Art and Literature*, trans. James Strachey et al.; ed. Albert Dickinson, the Pelican Freud Library, 14 (Harmondsworth: Penguin, 1985), p. 366: 'Dismembered limbs, a severed head, a hand cut off at the wrist, as in a fairy tale of Hauff's ["The Story of the Severed Hand"], feet which dance by themselves . . . all these have something peculiarly uncanny about them' (p. 366).

[5] Ibid. However his placing of the discussion in the general context of animism, magic, sorcery, and madness as uncanny phenomena (pp. 365–6) suggests other parameters. Earlier he relates feelings of the uncanny to the 'intellectual uncertainty as to whether an object is alive or not' (p. 354). Elias Canetti, *Crowds and Power*, trans. Carol Stewart (Harmondsworth: Penguin, 1973), suggests that the symbolic power of the hand has much to do with its 'faculty of independent life' (p. 256).

[6] Robert Hertz, *Death and the Right Hand*, trans. Rodney & Claudia Needham (Aberdeen: Cohen & West, 1960), notes the difficulty of resolving whether 'We are right handed because we are left brained' or vice versa (p. 90).

[7] See Hertz, (pp. 89–106): 'To the right hand go honours, flattering designations, prerogatives: it acts, orders, and *takes*. The left hand, on the contrary, is despised and reduced to the role of a humble auxiliary: by itself it can do nothing; it helps, it supports, it *holds*. The right hand is the symbol and model of all aristocracy, the left hand of all common people . . . The former is used to express ideas of physical strength and 'dexterity', of intellectual 'rectitude' and good judgement, of 'uprightness' and moral integrity, of good fortune and beauty, or juridical norm; while the word 'left' evokes most of the ['sinister'] opposites of these . . . the right is the 'side of life' (and of strength) while the left is the 'side of death' (and of weakness) . . . (as in the iconography of the Last Judgement) the right represents what is high, the upper world, the sky; while the left is connected with the underworld and the earth . . . The right is the *inside*, the finite, assured well-being, and peace; the left is the *outside*, the infinite, hostile, and the perpetual menace of evil . . . The right hand stands for *me*, the left for *not-me*, *others* . . . The left hand is the hand of perjury, treachery, & fraud'.

1   Vesalius demonstrating the anatomy of the hand. Frontispiece to Andreas Vesalius, *De Humani Corporis Fabrica* (1543)

But as the chequered history of the Red Hand reminds us, such universals are invariably overlaid with a superstructure of historically and locally specific meanings – meanings that are inseparable from those of the culturally assembled body to which the hand belongs. For bodies, as recent work in cultural history has made us aware, are artefacts of culture as much as nature: infants come naked into the world, but they are swaddled in meanings almost as quickly as they are swathed in clothes; and those meanings are constitutive of the 'body' recognized by culture. We have gradually begun to understand how profoundly unlike, in its (only too legible) physiological operations, its thresholds of shame, its peculiar kind of interiority, was the early modern body to our own.[8] Variously allegorized as a complex heraldic device, a castle, a landscape, a model of the state, a *mappamundi*, or a microcosm of God's creation, this was a body that invited decipherment, blazoning, mapping, and discovery. Through its humoural relation to the material world on the one hand, and its sympathetic relation to the astrological universe on the other, it was seen as indelibly marked with the signs of its own nature and with the signatures of its fate; while in social terms it was understood as a carefully fashioned semiotic structure organized according to elaborate rules of gender and rank, whose meanings became thicker the higher its position in the societal pyramid. The minutely ordered codes of the 'vestimentary system' ensured that the very clothes which covered it did not so much adorn as complete this body, enclosing it in a membrane of metaphor that was felt to constitute an inalienable part of the 'person'.

The hand had a peculiar role in the hierarchy of this construction that is not easily recaptured. Something of its symbolic prominence is indicated by the way in which early modern anatomists from Vesalius and Giulio Casserio to Rembrandt's Dr Tulp often chose to have themselves represented while engaged in the dissection of the hand.[9] More was involved

here than a mere self-referential play upon the idea of anatomy as a manual art; for the hand, in the words of Vesalius' disciple, Columbus, was *organum organorum*, 'the organ of organs', and had been cited by such diverse authorities as Aristotle and Galen as the most characteristically human part of the whole body.[10] To anatomize such an organ was to demonstrate anatomy's claim to fulfil the ancient philosophical goal of self-knowledge (*nosce teipsum*):[11] to know the hand was to know the self.

The hand was also privileged by this culture as an expressive instrument. In contemporary Anglo-Saxon culture, the hand is most characteristically experienced, perhaps, as a site of embarrassment, something we don't quite know what to do with: it may still have access

---

[8] Important contributions to the process of reimagining this body include: Norbert Elias, *The History of Manners* (1939), vol. 1 of *The Civilizing Process*, trans. Edmund Jephcott (New York: Pantheon, 1978); Thomas Laqueur, *Making Sex: Body and Gender from the Greeks to Freud* (Cambridge, Mass.: Harvard University Press, 1990); Gail Kern Paster, *The Body Embarrassed: Drama and the Disciplines of Shame in Early Modern England* (Ithaca: Cornell University Press, 1993); Peter Stallybrass, 'Patriarchal Territories: The Body Enclosed', in *Othello: Critical Essays*, ed. Susan Snyder (New York: Garland, 1988), pp. 251–74; and Stallybrass, 'Reading the Body: *The Revenger's Tragedy* and the Jacobean Theater of Consumption', *Renaissance Drama*, ns, 18 (1987): 121–48; Nancy Vickers, '"The Blazon of Sweet Beauty's Best:" Shakespeare's *Lucrece*', in Patricia Parker and Geoffrey Hartman (eds.), *Shakespeare and the Question of Theory* (New York & Methuen: Methuen, 1985), pp. 95–115.

[9] For an exceptionally thorough analysis of Rembrandt's anatomy scene, see William S. Heckscher, *Rembrandt's Anatomy of Dr Nicholaas Tulp* (New York: New York University Press, 1958).

[10] See Heckscher, p. 73; and Jonathan Goldberg, *Writing Matter: From the Hands of the English Renaissance* (Stanford, Cal: Stanford University Press, 1990), pp. 84–6.

[11] See e.g. Helkiah Crooke, *Mikrocosmographia. A Description of the Body of Man* (London, 1618). Chap. v '*How profitable and behoouefull Anatomy is to the knowledge of Mans selfe*'; and Caspar Barlaeus cited in Heckscher, p. 14.

to a diminished range of symbolic gestures, but they are generally deployed in an unconscious and incoherent way; and its full expressive power is glimpsed only in very specialized contexts – in certain forms of dance, for example, or in the dazzling manual choreography of the deaf. For Shakespeare and his contemporaries, by contrast, it was not only a primary site of meaning, but the conduit of extraordinary energies. Thus, for example – as the delicate gestural ballet of *Romeo and Juliet* 1.5 seems designed to remind us[12] – the simple ritual of handfasting was still considered sufficient to establish the mystical bond of marriage between man and wife without intervention by the church – a bond traditionally emblematized in the clasped hands of *fede*, or wedding rings.[13] In certain highly charged circumstances, moreover, the hand (infused, as it were, with the spiritual current that passes between the hands of God and Adam on the Sistine ceiling) might become a surrogate for the divine hand itself. This was the source of the power which in early modern belief informed not merely the sanctified hands of priests and kings,[14] but those of ordinary parents in the daily rites of family blessing. Such details are enough to remind us that, like the rest of the human body, the hand is not what it was; and that it must once have occupied a quite different place in the psychic topography of the human body.

SIGNATURES OF THE HAND

If the early modern body was a densely textualized site, no part of it was more prominently inscribed than the hand. When the Soothsayer of *Antony and Cleopatra* offers to read from 'nature's infinite book of secrecy' (1.2.10) it is to the scripture of the palm that he turns. According to seventeenth-century chiromantic theory there was a '*Secret Concordance, and Harmony*' between the stars and the human hand, whose lines were reckoned to be produced 'from the *Imagination* [of the soule] of the Greater *Worlde* . . . in the Generation of *Man*'. This power,

'otherwise called *Predistination, Science, Fate*', performed 'its Authority & Office by the *Stars*' which engraved the '*Signatures*' of fate on the infant's palm.[15] Such signatures, according to Sir Thomas Browne, were made by '[t]he Finger of God [which] hath left an Inscription upon all His works' – one that, if we learn how to read it, contains the Adamic name in which is expressed the true nature of every creature. In human beings, the inscription is jointly composed of 'Characters in our Faces' and of 'certain mystical figures in our Hands, which I dare not call meer dashes, strokes *a la vollee*, or at random, because delineated by a Pencil that never works in vain; and hereof I take more particular notice, because I carry that in mine own hand which I could never read of nor discover in another.'[16]

The potent signatures of identity and destiny borne by the hand help to account for the occult power ascribed to it in rituals of witchcraft – such as those which the Duchess of Malfi fearfully associates with the amputated hand sent by her brother,[17] or those which the witches perform with 'pilot's thumb' and

---

[12] 'Good pilgrim you do wrong your hand too much . . . For saints have hands that pilgrims' hands do touch, / And palm to palm is holy palmers' kiss' (1.5.97–100).

[13] Ernest Schanzer, 'Marriage-Contracts', *Shakespeare Survey 13* (1960), pp. 81–9. On the *fede*, see Dale J. Randall, 'The Rank and Earthy Background of Certain Physical Symbols in *The Duchess of Malfi*', *Ren.D. n.s.* XVIII (1987): 171–203 (esp. 172–9).

[14] The blasphemous effrontery of Marlowe's *Tamburlaine* is thus perfectly expressed in the power of the 'hand' which he claims to 'turn fortune's wheel about' (*1 Tamburlaine*, 1.2.175). Citations from Marlowe are to J. B. Steane (ed.), *The Complete Plays* (Harmondsworth: Penguin, 1969).

[15] Johan Rothmann, *Cheiromantia: or, The Art of Divining by The Lines and Signatures Engraven in the Hand of Man, By the Hand of Nature . . . Wherein you have the Secret Concordance, and Harmony betwixt It, and Astrology*, trans. George Wharton (London: 1642), pp. 175–6.

[16] Sir Thomas Browne, *Religio Medici* in *Religio Medici and Other Writings* (London: Dent, 1965), pp. 68–9.

[17] On the wider symbolism of the *Malfi* hand, see Randall 'Physical Symbols in *The Duchess of Malfi*', section 1,

'Finger of birth-strangled babe' in *Macbeth* (1.3.27; 4.1.30); but they also seem to contribute to the talismanic authority invested in the written signature and the writer's 'hand'. The very act of writing indeed may seem to involve an uncanny mimesis; for if scripture routinely represents 'the hand of God' as the instrument of divine power, it also expresses destiny as a kind of script – like the fatal handwriting of Belshazzar's Feast (Daniel 5: 5, 24–8). According to the chiromancer Johann Rothmann, the hand was chosen to bear its potent signs of difference precisely as a result of qualities which gave it a kind of natural sympathy with the inscribing hand of destiny – its powers not merely of 'action' but of signification:

if you desire to know wherefore these *Signatures* are found in the *Hand*, and perhaps not in any other *Part* of the *Body*: you must conceive, that our *Hands* are the most *Noble Members* in perfecting of al manner of *Actions*; they are the executors of our *Primary Conceptions* . . . therefore our *Fate* for the most part, and Our *Power* are very much reposed in our *Hands*.[18]

On a more mundane level the hand was invested with the social authority of handwriting, whose enhanced prestige, reflected in the pedagogic practice of Tudor grammar schools, has been amply documented by Jonathan Goldberg.[19] The hand here had a double role: it was both that which made possible full participation in the new print culture, and that which served as a symbolic guarantor of individual difference, privacy, and possession against the mechanical usurpations of print.[20] The quasi-magical authority of handwriting was most evident in the power invested in the signature as a sign of individual presence and consent. The symbolic equivalence between the appending of a signature and the giving of a hand is neatly registered in Middleton and Rowley's *The Changeling*, where Alsemero's 'confirmation by the hand royal' punningly equates the act of signing with the ritual of handfasting (1.1.80–1).[21] But the written 'hand' was also more generally under-

stood as a mark of authenticity. Thus one could speak metaphorically of the presence of a writer's 'hand' in a printed work, meaning that it bore the authentic marks of his peculiar genius. The 1623 Folio of Shakespeare's plays is famously prefaced by Droeshout's portrait engraving, a 'Figure' whose illuminated head is designed, as Ben Jonson's accompanying verses suggest, to advertise the contents as the distinctive product of the poet's 'wit'. In their address 'To the great Variety of Readers', however, the actor-editors, Heminge and Condell, place as much emphasis upon the creative function of the poet's *hand*: they offer the plays as the work of one 'Who, as he was a happie imitator of Nature, was a most gentle expresser of it. His mind and hand went together: And what he thought, he vttered with that easinesse, that wee haue scarse receiued from him a blot in his papers.' Just as Hamlet's 'character' is punningly made vivid in his 'hand' (*Hamlet* 4.7.51–2), or as Edgar's allegedly unfilial 'character' is exposed in the vicious 'hand' of the conspiratorial letter flourished by Edmund (*Lear* 1.2.56–68),[22] so it is as if the poet is most

---

'The Dead Man's Hand', pp. 172–9. Randall describes the hand as 'a horrid, mixed hand-in-hand image that is part sadistic trick part erotic gesture, part *memento mori*, part perversion of the traditional *fede*, and part reminder of the Duchess's own marriage scene' (pp. 178–9). Middleton and Rowley rework this episode in *The Changeling*, where an amputated finger and a mutilated hand become the visible signs both of Beatrice's violated bond with Piracquo and of the new bond which his murder has established with de Flores (3.4.37–8, 88; 4.1.0.9–10).

18 Rothmann, p. 183.

19 See above, n. 9.

20 On the manuscript hand as a sign of privacy, inwardness, and the secrets of the heart see Bruce R. Smith, *Homosexual Desire in Shakespeare's England* (Chicago: University of Chicago Press, 1991), pp. 235–45.

21 Citations from *The Changeling* are to the New Mermaid edition by Joost Daalder (London: A. & C. Black, 1990).

22 Cf. also *Twelfth Night* 2.5 and 3.4 where Malvolio's excited identification of Olivia's 'sweet Roman hand' becomes tantamount to possession of her 'sweet heart': 'this is my lady's hand . . . 'Tis my lady' (2.5.86–93; 3.4.28–31).

present to his colleagues' imagination through the manuscript signatures of his genius – the unblotted 'papers' they received from him in the playhouse, the 'True Originall[s]' from which the Folio itself has supposedly been produced.

Thus the very existence of the Folio becomes a powerful testimony to the growing power and prestige of the writer's hand; and it is a sense of the unbroken chain linking the printed text, the manuscript, the writing hand, and the author's individual genius that shapes the controlling conceit of Hugh Holland's encomiastic sonnet 'Vpon the Lines and Life of the Famous Scenicke Poet, Master William Shakespeare'. Summoning the audience to wring their own generous hands in mourning (as they once brought them together in applause), Holland finds in the dead playwright's printed verses a testimony to the immortality of his 'hand': 'For though his line of life went soone about, / The life of his lines shall neuer out.' Holland was no doubt remembering that in the Sonnets Shakespeare had registered his own sense of the peculiar metonymic authority of the writer's hand: in 65 the 'swift foot' of Time is challenged by the 'strong hand' whose presence is miraculously preserved in the black ink of the text (lines 10–14);[23] while in 49, the poet's hand is playfully 'uprear[ed]' against himself (line 11) as if it were a kind of malign double – rather as Benedick and Beatrice discover in their written professions of love 'our own hands against our hearts' (*Much Ado* 5.4.91–2).[24]

Such conceits, in which the hand develops an uncanny life of its own – as though it were a kind of second, or alternative self, mediating between the writer and his book, and capable of standing for either (or both) – are by no means exceptional. The feminist pamphleteer 'Constantia Munda', for example, dedicates a tract to her mother, reaffirming the filial 'bond' with an extraordinary metonymic flourish – 'I here present you with my writing hand'[25] – in which the printed text stands in for the manuscript, which in turn stands for the hand now

vicariously offered as a pledge and token of her essential self. But perhaps the most elaborate examples of such play occur in a text exclusively devoted to the expressive power of the human hand, John Bulwer's two-part treatise on 'manual rhetoric', *Chirologia/Chironomia*.[26] For Bulwer's encomiasts the author's hand is consubstantial with the text, in which 'each line's a line of life';[27] whilst Bulwer himself, playfully maintaining that his '*Fancie*' is ruled by his '*Hand's Genius*', attributes the book's very authorship to the invention of 'my Soul's inspired *Hand*', making it a work of 'autography' in which 'the *Hand* . . . hath . . . proved its own Biographer'.[28] In writing itself the hand writes the self.

THE SIGNIFYING HAND

But if the hand writes the self, it also speaks it; and this, for Bulwer, is its greatest glory. It is, he notes, an ancient 'symbole of action',[29] but it specially excels in rhetorical *actio* – the repertory of bodily signals with which orators and actors amplified and intensified their verbal

---

23 In line 10 a quibble associates the 'foot' of time with the metrical feet whose mastery by the poet's writing hand will enable him to keep time – the hand's struggle to hold back the foot of Time being imaged in the extra stressing of this heavily spondaic line. This complex of word-play also includes line 4's 'action', which because of its legal-oratorical context must involve gestural *actio* as well as 'action' in the sense of 'case'.

24 Benedick's conceit wrily undoes the familiar hand-on-heart gesture that expresses the ideal integration of inner and outer selves.

25 Constantia Munda, *The Worming of a Mad Dog*, in Katherine User Henderson and Barbara F. McManus (eds.), *Half Humankind: Contexts and Texts of Controversy about Women in England, 1550–1640* (Chicago: University of Chicago Press, 1985).

26 John Bulwer, *Chirologia: or the Natural Language of the Hand and Chironomia: or, The Art of Manual Rhetoric* (London, 1644).

27 *Chirologia*, p. 82.

28 Ibid., p. 82, *Chironomia*, p. 146.

29 Bulwer, *Chirologia*, p. 95; Bulwer attributes the symbol to the Stoics.

performances – through which it is able to 'translate a thought into discoursing signes . . . while the articulated Fingers supply the office of a voyce'.[30] For Bulwer gesture is not a mere ornament of speech, but a vehicle of communication in its own right, a 'language' with its own rules. Thus he can describe the hand as 'the *Spokesman* of the body', and second only to the tongue, whose '*Substitute* and *Vicegerent*' it is. He calls it 'the Tongue of *hearty goodwill*', 'the Engineere of invention, and wits true *Palladium* . . . couzen german to the Fancie', and the 'relative' of the heart.[31] Often, indeed, this 'famous *companion of Reason*' begins to sound superior to the tongue, which it is able 'to over-match . . . in speaking labours, and the significant varietie of important motions'.[32] In the Dedication to *Chirologia* the hand's expressive capacity is conveyed by a remarkable theatrical conceit: Bulwer imagines the body as a piece of biological architecture, whose most arresting features are 'Two Amphitheaters', (hence the title of this article) upon whose stages are displayed 'the voluntary motions of the Minde'; these structures, are identified as 'the *Hand* and the *Head*';[33] and of the two it turns out to be the hand which, by virtue of its expressive immediacy, is capable of the greatest eloquence. 'An *active Wit*', as one of his encomiasts puts it, 'employs a *speaking Hand*', because the hand is privileged to express the motions of the mind with a directness denied to any other organ.[34]

Like the head, of course, the hand stands in need of education through *The Art of Manuall Rhetorique* outlined in *Chironomia*; but (also like the head) it is endowed with natural gifts that are among the defining characteristics of humankind: 'in regard of the Rhetoricall properties of the *Hand*,' writes Bulwer, '*Man may well be called Chirosophus, id est Manu sapiens*, Hand-wise';[35] and such, he insists, is its 'force and estimation among all Nations', that anyone who fails to master its techniques of '*benevolent insinuation*' will seem 'to be disarmed of all humanity'.[36]

Far from representing the eccentric enthusiasm of a self-styled 'chirosopher', such views (as Bulwer was at pains to remind his reader) were grounded in the authority of a number of classical philosophers – notably Aristotle, who argued (*De Anima*, II, ix, 421a) that humans were 'far more intelligent than [other animals]' precisely because they had 'a far more accurate sense of touch', and Anaxagoras, who maintained that man was 'the wisest of all creatures, because he had *Hands*'.[37] This perception of a deep causal link between human intelligence and the unique capacities of the human hand anticipates the conclusions of those modern anthropologists who argue that it was in the hand, rather than its symbolic double the head, that the crucial developments occurred which separated human beings from other primates. Indeed, if Elias Canetti is right, it is to the activities of the hand that we must look for the origins of language itself.[38]

Renaissance theorists of communication like Bulwer, similarly convinced that 'The *Hand*

---

[30] John Bulwer, '*Dactylogia, or Dialects of the Fingers*' in *Chirologia: or the Natural Language of the Hand and Chironomia: or, The Art of Manual Rhetoric* (London, 1644), p. 157.

[31] Ibid., pp. 2, 86, 110, 111.

[32] *Chironomia*, p. 2; *Chirologia*, p. 8.

[33] Ibid., p. 6.

[34] Thomas Diconson in *Chirologia*, A2v.

[35] *Chironomia*, p. 2.

[36] *Chirologia*, p. 114.

[37] *Chironomia*, p. 1. Without any apparent sense of contradiction Bulwer also cites Galen's opinion 'that because Man was the wisest of all creatures, therefore he had *Hands* given him' (p. 1).

[38] '[A]s a man watched his hands at work, the changing shapes they fashioned must gradually have impressed themselves on his mind. Without this we should probably never have learnt to form symbols for things, nor, therefore to speak', *Crowds and Power*, p. 254. The peculiar (and supposedly proper) articulacy of the right hand, stressed by rhetoricians from classical times onwards, may indeed be related to the fact it is controlled by the same hemisphere of the brain that contains 'the centre for articulate speech' (Hertz, *Death and the Right Hand*, p. 90).

and meaning ever are ally'de',[39] further justified their claims by appealing to scripture. Bulwer claimed that gesture

hath since been sanctified and made a holy language by the expression of our Saviors *Hands*; whose gestures have given a sacred allowance to naturall significations of ours. And God speaks to us by the signes of his *Hand* (as *Bernard* observes) when he works wonders which are the proper signs of his *Hand* . . . And as God speaks to us with his *Hand*, by a supernaturall way: so we naturally speake to Him, as well as unto men, by the *appeale* of our *Hands* in *admiration, attestation*, and *prayer*.[40]

Moreover, as 'the onely speech that is natural to Man',[41] gesture seemed to preserve the universal transparency of prelapsarian speech. Identifying in it the traces of an Adamic eloquence that had 'had the happinesse to escape the curse at the confusion of Babel', Bulwer acclaimed it as 'the *Tongue and generall language of Humane Nature*, which, without teaching, men in all regions of the habitable world doe at the first sight most easily understand'.[42]

Such views were widespread amongst early modern theorists of language. Thus Montaigne, for example, could describe gesture as constituting 'a language common and publike to all . . . [which] must be . . . deemed the proper and peculier speech of humane nature;'[43] whilst the Italian apostle of manual rhetoric Giovanni Bonifacio devoted his *L'arte de'cenni* (1616) to the task of restoring the 'universal language' which humankind had foolishly abandoned 'in favour of so many different artificial ways of speaking, that one region cannot understand or agree with another'.[44] The anxiety which such texts display about the problems of cultural exchange is a useful reminder that, whilst their notions of gestural universality were solidly grounded in manuals of classical rhetoric,[45] they had a direct application, as Dilwyn Knox has observed, to the 'exploring, converting and plundering [of] the New World and elsewhere'.[46]

From one point of view, indeed, a work such as Bulwer's *Chirologia* deserves to be placed

---

[39] William Diconson, commendatory verses on *Chirologia*, A1v. This alliance is one of the things that Claudius has in mind when he insists that the 'hand is . . . instrumental to the mouth' (*Hamlet*, 1.2.48).

[40] *Chirologia*, p. 7.

[41] Ibid., p. 2.

[42] Ibid., pp. 7, 2.

[43] John Florio (trans.), *Montaigne's Essays*, ed. L. C. Harmer, 3 vols. (London: Dent, 1965), II, xii, 'An Apology of *Raymond Sebond*', pp. 144–5. The passage is worth quoting in greater detail: arguing that human beings might 'argue and tell histories by signes', Montaigne emphasizes the infinitely expressive capacity of the hand: 'Doe we not sue and entreat, promise and performe, call men unto us and discharge them, bid them farwell and be gone, threaten, pray, beseech, deny, refuse, demand, admire, number, confesse, repent, feare, bee ashamed, doubt, instruct, command, incite, encourage, sweare, witnesse, accuse, condemne, absolve, injurie, despise, defie, despight, flatter, applaud, blesse, humble, mocke, reconcile, recommend, exalt, shew gladnesse, rejoyce, complaine, waile, sorrow, discomfort, dispaire, cry out, forbid, declare silence and astonishment . . . [w]ith so great variation, and amplifying, as if they would contend with the tongue' (p. 144).

[44] Giovanni Bonifacio, *L'arte de'cenni* (Vicenza, 1616), pp. 11–12; cited in Dilwyn Knox, 'Ideas on gesture and universal languages c. 1550–1650', in John Henry and Sarah Hutton (eds.), *New Perspectives on Renaissance Thought* (London: Duckworth, 1989), pp. 101–36 (p. 129).

[45] In passages cited in successive editions of Omer Talon's *Rhetorica* (Paris, 1552; Frankfurt, 1581) Cicero (*De oratore*, III, lix, 223) had observed that 'a certain power is bestowed by nature on everything pertaining to gesture. For this reason it has a great effect even on the uneducated, the common people and indeed savages'; and Quintilian (*Inst. orat.* XI, iii, 87) had gone so far as to suggest that 'gesture . . . seems a language common to mankind'. (quoted from Knox, 'Ideas on gesture', pp. 121–2). But no classical rhetorician had theorized this conjecture as Bulwer was to do.

[46] Knox, pp. 130–3. Knox has described a significant shift from the precepts of the medieval world in which 'gesture var[ied] from one profession or vocation to another', forming a 'Babel of vernaculars' which could be learned only through 'observation and practice', to the late sixteenth-century belief that gesture is 'amenable to theory' because it belongs (despite local variations) to a universal human language; in response to this shift, rhetorical manuals from the middle of the sixteenth century begin to discuss delivery and gesture in much greater detail (pp. 102–4).

alongside Hakluyt's *Voyages* and Purchas's *Pilgrims*, as a primary text of English imperialism. For Bulwer, along with his encomiasts, makes it abundantly clear that the burgeoning interest in the science of universal languages was a direct product of early voyaging enterprise, and of the desire for trade that was the principal driving force of English expansionism.[47] Already, Bulwer assured his readers, the language of hands had enabled English merchants to open 'commerce with those salvage nations . . . of the West . . . driving a rich and silent Trade, by signes, whereby many a dumb bargaine without the crafty Brocage of the tongue is advantageously made'.[48] Properly mastered, according to one of his encomiasts, this 'grand, / And expresse Pantotype of speech', would 'redeem [humankind] . . . from *Babels* doome' by establishing a 'universall Idiome' in which 'All Tribes shall now each other understand / Which (though not of one lip) are of one Hand'; in the ensuing golden age of communication commerce would flourish even with those 'rationall Brutes' of Africa, 'the dumb *Ginnie Drills*'.[49] As though in fulfilment of Bulwer's dream, the frontispiece of Cave Beck's *The Universall Caracter* (1657) features an Englishman in converse with a turbanned Hindu, an African, and a Brazilian Indian who raises his hand in a gesture of silent eloquence.

THE ACTOR'S HAND

Shakespeare appears to mock such touching faith in the capacity of gesture to transcend the culture-bound limits of ordinary speech in *The Comedy of Errors*, where the luckless Dromio of Ephesus is baffled by the forceful manual rhetoric of the Syracusan stranger whom he takes for his own master: 'He told his mind upon my ear. / Beshrew his hand, I scarce could understand it . . . he strook so plainly, I could too well feel his blows, and withal so doubtfully, that I scarce could understand them' (2.1.48–54); and in *The Tempest*, it is typically the sentimental Gonzalo who celebrates the

2   The transparent eloquence of the hand. Frontispiece to Cave Beck, *The Universall Caracter* (1657)

perfect transparency of the 'excellent dumb discourse' employed by the monstrous 'people of the island' (3.3.30, 39). It is, of course, part of Shakespeare's irony that the creatures of Ariel's antimasque should be not true 'islanders' at all but 'actors', spirit-performers in a 'living drollery', reminding us that the theatre had its

---

[47] Bulwer's interest in New World culture is amply illustrated in his treatise on bodily adornment *Anthrometamorphosis; Man Transform'd* (1653).

[48] *Chirologia*, pp. 3–4.

[49] See the verses of *Chirologia* by Thomas Diconson and Jo. Harmanus, pp. A2v–A4. On the belief of early explorers in the universal accessibility of gesture, see Tzvetan Todorov, *The Conquest of America: The Question of the Other* (New York: Harper and Row, 1984), p. 30; Stephen Greenblatt, 'Learning to Curse' in *Learning to Curse: Essays in Early Modern Culture* (New York: Routledge, 1990), pp. 16–39; and Eric Cheyfitz *The Portius of Imperialiom* (New York: Oxford University Press, 1991), p. 109.

3 The orators Demosthenes and Cicero taking instruction from the actors Andronicus and Roscius. Frontispiece to John Bulwer, *Chironomia* (1644)

own particular reasons for nourishing an interest in the communicative efficacy of bodily 'action'; indeed the very term 'acting' referred originally only to the player's art of gesture, and did not acquire its expanded meaning until the early seventeenth century.[50]

The frontispiece that Bulwer commissioned for *Chironomia* acknowledges the role of theatre as an ancient nursery of manual rhetoric – even if the author is anxious to distinguish between the more restrained style of gesture proper to the orator and that which 'is scenicall, and belongs more to the theater, then the forum'.[51]

In the engraving the stage-players Andronicus and Roscius are shown tutoring the orators Demosthenes and Cicero;[52] Andronicus holds up a mirror to his pupil, inscribed with the word *actio*; and Bulwer explains that his task was to reform 'the defect that was before in [Demosthenes'] Orations for want of Action.'[53] It is *actio*, more than anything, that endows rhetoric with the active power of eloquence.

B. L. Joseph long ago recognized the relevance of Bulwer's treatises for an understanding of sixteenth and seventeenth-century theatrical convention. The chirosopher's elaborate codification of oratorical practice identifies appropriate 'actions' for practically every imaginable affective context – and some of these, as Joseph was able to demonstrate, have an obvious application to particular theatrical moments in Shakespeare. For example, Bulwer's account of *Gestus LVIII Injurias remitto* ('TO PRESSE HARD AND WRING ANOTHERS HAND . . . a naturall *insinuation of love, duty, remembrance, supplication, peace, and of forgivenessse* of all injuries') actually cites the same passage in Plutarch from which Shakespeare derived the famous stage direction for Coriolanus' reconciliation with his mother, '*holds her by the hand, silent*' (*Cor.* 5.3.182). Yet it is also clear, as Andrew Gurr has shown, that by the end of the sixteenth century, gestural pedantry of the kind favoured by Bulwer was regarded in theatrical circles as somewhat old-fashioned.[54] More important than the details of Bulwer's system, I would argue, is what it implies about the extraordinary *visibility* of hands in Elizabethan

---

50 See Andrew Gurr, *The Shakespearean Stage, 1574–1642*, 2nd edn (Cambridge: Cambridge University Press, 1980), p. 97.

51 *Chironomia*, pp. 103–4. Bulwer instances 'The trembling *Hand*' and 'strik[ing] the Breast with the *Hand*' as 'Scenicall' affectations.

52 Bulwer explains the significance of these figures on p. 17.

53 *Chironomia*, p. 17.

54 See Gurr, *The Shakespearean Stage*, pp. 99–100.

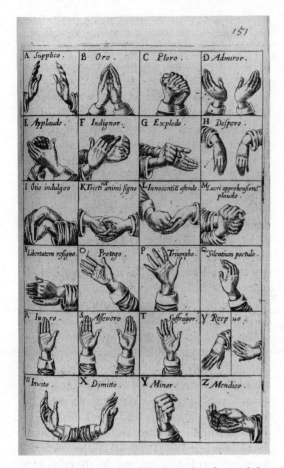 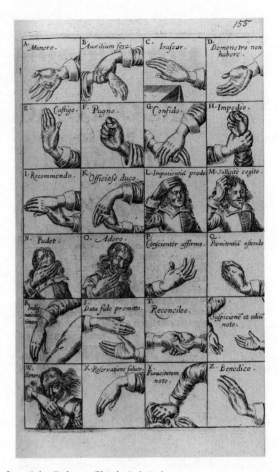

4a and b Examples of manual rhetoric from John Bulwer, *Chirologia* (1644)

society generally, and on Shakespeare's stage in particular.

An emphasis on the power of *actio* is understandable in a theatre whose rhetorical inheritance and playing conditions combined to give particular prominence to the actor's body in all its corporeal fulness of presence; but it also reflected the practical necessities of an industry that was engaged in its own form of mercantile expansionism. In the first half of the seventeenth century English touring companies found a significant market for their talents in continental Europe, where (as the pantomimic arts of *Hamlet*'s 'Tragedians of the City' arguably remind us), cultivation of the language of

gesture became especially important.[55] Indeed when Fynes Moryson witnessed the performance of a rather down-at-heel English company at Frankfurt in 1592, he observed that, despite the actors' want of decent scripts and 'any good apparel [or] ornament of the stage . . . the

---

[55] One may see this reflected in the concern for gestural precision apparent in Hamlet's advice to the players. If the 'Tragedians of the City' are in some sense to be identified as a touring London company (as their unlucky experiences with boy-players and the 'late innovation' half suggest) it is easy to see why they might wish to preface their performance with a dumb show that exactly summarizes the subsequent action – a use of mime otherwise unparalleled in English theatre.

Germans, not understanding a word they said
... flocked wonderfully *to see their gesture and action*.[56] It was, evidently, their hands that spoke.

SPEAKING HANDS

'Speak hands for me!' When, in *Julius Caesar* (3.1.76), Casca thrusts his envious dagger into Caesar's body, he might seem, at first sight, to be simply renouncing language in favour of action: 'where words prevail not', as Kyd's Lorenzo has it, 'violence prevails' (*Spanish Tragedy* 2.1.108).[57] Certainly Casca's *actio* puts into practice his earlier insistence that 'every bondman in his own hand bears / The power to cancel his captivity' (1.3.101–2) – at the same time consciously reversing Brutus' kiss of feigned submission to the power of Caesar's hand (3.1.52). But his apostrophe is energized by a viciously witty play upon the idea of the hand as 'the *Spokesman* of the body'[58] in Bulwer's phrase: this will be speech that kills, killing that speaks – a gesture that collapses the distinctions between speech, *actio* and action, just as it cancels out the distance between the literal and the metaphorical.

As Shakespeare stages the assassination scene, however, the unmediated directness of utterance to which Casca lays claim will be complicated and confused by an obsessive focus upon hands – gesticulating, clasping, and smeared with blood.

[BRUTUS] Stoop, Romans, stoop
And let us *bathe our hands in Caesar's blood*
Up to the elbows,[59] and besmear our swords
. . .
And waving our red weapons o'er our heads,
Let's all cry, 'Peace, freedom, and liberty!'

[ANTONY] I do beseech ye, if you bear me hard,
Now whilst *your purpled hands do reek and smoke*,
Fulfil your pleasure . . .

[BRUTUS] Though now we must appear bloody and cruel,
As by our *hands* and this our present act

You see we do, yet see you but our *hands*,
And this the bleeding business they have done.
Our hearts you see not; they are pitiful . . .
    (3.1.103–9, 157–9, 165–9 [emphases added])

The symbolic fulcrum of the scene is Brutus' hand-washing ritual, with its uncanny fulfilment of Calphurnia's dream, in which 'many lusty Romans . . . did bathe their hands' in the blood fountaining from Caesar's statue (2.2.78–9); and it is significant that both details appear to have been entirely of Shakespeare's

---

[56] Fynes Moryson, *Itinerary*, cited from G. Blakemore Evans (ed.), *Elizabethan and Jacobean Drama* (London: A. & C. Black, 1989), p. 50, emphasis added. A complete account of the place of hands in the theatre would need to consider the important role played by the audience's hands: for at the end of a performance convention allowed the actors to reach out and claim the gestural acknowledgement of a special bond:

> Give me your hands, if we be friends,
> And Robin shall restore amends. (*Dream* 5.1.437–8)

> Ours be your patience then, and yours our parts;
> Your gentle hands lend us, and take our hearts
>   (*All's Well* Epil. 5–6)

> But release me from my bands
> With the help of your good hands.
>   (*Tempest*, Epil. 9–10)

Through such characteristically English variations on the ancient Latin *plaudite*, it is possible to glimpse how in this theatre even applause had a subtly different meaning from the mechanical expression of pleasure with which we are familiar; for it was expressly located as the crowning gesture in a carefully orchestrated rhetorical sequence – one that completed a graceful circle of mutual 'benefits', in a metaphorical 'giving' and 'joining' of hands.

[57] Citations from *The Spanish Tragedy* are to Andrew S. Cairncross's Regents Renaissance Drama edition (London: Edward Arnold, 1967). The gestural significance of this scene is briefly glanced at from the perspective of stage history by Robert Hapgood in 'Speak Hands for Me: Gesture as Language in *Julius Caesar*', *Drama Survey*, 5 (1966): 162–70.

[58] *Chirologia*, p. 2.

[59] This detail seems to register the fact that Roman 'manus' (hand) included the forearm.

invention.[60] The hand-washing is a gestus whose power to shock depends partly on its travesty of one of the most familiar of all manual signs – one that plays a key role in the action of at least two other Shakespeare plays, *Richard II* and *Macbeth*,[61] – the Pilate-like gesture called by Bulwer '*Innocentiam ostendo*', and used, he says

by those who would *professe their innocency* and declare *they have no Hand in that foule business, not so much as by their manuall assent* ... A gesture very significant, for the *Hands* naturally imply, as it were in Hieroglyphique, mens acts and operations; and that cleansing motion denotes the *cleannesse of their actions*. As this expression is heightened by the addition of water, 'tis made by the AEgyptians the Hieroglyphique of innocency.[62]

Ironically designed as a symbolic 'profession of innocency' – demonstrating Brutus' claim that the murder is the work of priestly 'sacrificers [and] not butchers', 2.1.166 – the ritual becomes a 'hieroglyphique' of guilt, whose meaning is brought home to the audience by Antony's ambiguous counter-ritual of hand-clasping. As a vicious replay of the rite of bonding to which Brutus invited the conspirators in 2.1: 'Give me your hands all over, one by one' (line 112), Antony's gestures shockingly invert the elaborate symbolism of truce-making, faith-pledging, reconciliation and 'forgivenesse of all injuries' discovered by Bulwer in the act of shaking and pressing another's hand:[63]

[ANTONY] Let each man render me his bloody
    hand
First, Marcus Brutus, will I shake with you;
Next, Caius Cassius, do I take your hand;
Now, Decius Brutus, yours; now yours,
    Metellus;
Yours Cinna, and my valiant Casca, yours;
Though last, not least in love, yours, good
    Trebonius.   (3.1.184–9)

Antony's falsification of 'manual faith' coincides with the transfer of blood from the conspirators' hands to his own. The hand that in this way vicariously imbrues itself in the victim's

blood is, the action compels us to notice, the same hand that two scenes later licenses a new round of murder ('look, with a spot I damn him', 4.1.6). A modern audience will respond immediately to the theatrical cruelty of this moment through the tactile immediacy of those hands, sticky with blood, but may have difficulty re-imagining the original force of the

---

[60] Conceivably both were suggested by the brief passage in Plutarch that records the wounding and bloodying of Brutus' hand in the mêlée around Caesar's body. The conspirators' gesture of waving their bloodied hands also seems to resonate uncannily with Casca's description of the slave who 'Held up his left hand, which did flame and burn ... and yet ... remain'd unscorch'd' (1.3.16–18). The singling out of the ill-omened left hand is a Shakespearian addition to Plutarch's anecdote. Interestingly, John Bulwer also seems to have been sensitive to the suggestive resonances of hands in Plutarch: discussing the significance of handclasping, he is reminded of a serendipitous quibble in Sir Thomas North's version of the *Life of Brutus*, where Caius Ligarius, taking the hero *by the right hand* enquires if he has 'any great enterprise in *Hand*', *Chirologia*, p. 95 (italics original).

[61] See also *Richard III* 1.4.172, where the Second Murderer laments: 'How fain, like Pilate, would I wash my hands'; 4.1.67, where Anne recalls Richard's wooing 'When scarce the blood was well wash'd from his hands'; and *Hamlet* 3.3.43–4 where, in an even more obvious anticipation of *Macbeth*, Claudius broods over his 'cursed hand ... thicker than itself with brother's blood'.

[62] *Chirologia*, Gestus XI, p. 40.

[63] The context makes it plain that Antony's handshakings combine aspects of three closely allied gestures described by Bulwer:

Gestus LVI Data fide promitto: 'TO STRIKE ANOTHERS PALM ... the habit and expression of those who *plight their troth, give pledge of faith and fidelity, promise, offer truce, confirme a league ... warrant* and *assure.*'

Gestus LVII Reconcilio: 'TO SHAKE THE GIVEN HAND ... an expression usual in *friendship, peacefull love, benevolence ... reconciliation,* and *well-wishing ...* An expression usuall between those who *desire to incorporate, commixe, or grow into one, and make a perfect joynt*'

Gestus LVIII Injurias remitto: 'TO PRESSE HARD AND WRING ANOTHERS HAND ... a naturall *insinuation of love, duty, remembrance, supplication, peace,* and of *forgivenesse* of all injuries.' (*Chirologia*, pp. 93, 109, 116)

handclasping itself or in recognizing its important symmetry with the gesture that closes the scene, when Antony reaches out to Octavius' servant: 'Lend me your hand' (3.1.297). While the celebrated Arafat-Rabin handshake of 1993 is evidence that in particularly charged circumstances such gestures can regain something of their old emblematic power, it remains true (as one historian of gesture has recently argued) that the meanings of the early modern handshake were richer and more intense than those which are preserved in the commonplace courtesy of today.[64] The reason for this, not surprisingly, lay not so much in the gesture as in the instrument; for the hand, as Bulwer explained, possessed occult properties that made it not merely a passive vehicle, but an active agent in such affective transactions. 'There is,' he writes, 'some Pythagoricall mystery in this authenticke guise of the *Hand* in *warrantizing faithfull dealings*', a mystery which 'flowes from a secret and religious reverence to that comprehensive number *Ten* . . . since meeting in their formall close they seem to greet one another in that number';[65] and he further observes that 'Physitians the subtile and diligent observers of nature, thinke that there is in the *Hand* a certaine secret and hidden vertue, and a convenient force or philtre to procure *affection*,' so that the holding of hands does not merely represent, but actually *produces* the '*kniting together of hearts*'.[66] There is, moreover, an inherent 'sympathy between the will and the *Hand*: for, the will affectionately inclined and moved to stretch forth her selfe, the *Hand*, that is moved by the same spirit, willing to goe out and set a glosse upon the inward motion, casts it selfe into a forme extending to a semblance of the inward appetite'. Thus, Bulwer argues,

nature . . . seems to have ordained the *Hand* to be the generall instrument of the minde. Therefore when the minde would disclose the virtue, strength, and forcible operation of her *favour* and *good-will*, out of the abundance of her *love he puts forth the hand*, and in that as it were the *heart* it self, with *affectionate love*; and receives them againe by a natural bill of ex-

change in the *Hand of another; which is verily a signe of mutuall agreement*, and of a *perfect conjunction*; for which cause *Pindarus a Poet* of an aspiring wit, placed the heart and *Hand* as relatives under one and the same parallel.[67]

What Bulwer describes is a 'conjunction' that is as much literal as it is symbolic; and it is just such a 'conjunction' that visibly binds the 'inward souls' of the French and English Kings in Act 3, Scene 1 of *King John*:[68]

> This royal hand and mine are newly knit,
> And the conjunction of our inward souls
> Married in league, coupled, and link'd together
> With all religious strength of holy vows.
>
> . . .
>
> And shall these hands, so lately purg'd of blood,
> So newly join'd in love, so strong in both,

---

[64] Herman Roodenburg, 'The "hand of friendship": shaking hands and other gestures in the Dutch Republic,' in Jan Bremner and Herman Roodenburg (eds.), *A Cultural History of Gesture* (Ithaca, NY: Cornell University Press, 1992), pp. 152–89. Perhaps the most graphic illustration of the symbolic power invested in the early modern handclasp is in the parodic stage business of *King John* 3.1.226–321 where the frenetic making and breaking of royal treaties is expressed in the successive grasping and dropping of hands.

[65] *Chirologia*, p. 101.

[66] *Chirologia*, pp. 116–17. For the heart as symbolic double of the hand see e.g. *RII* 5.1.82 'Hand from hand my love, and heart from heart' or Bassanio's 'forfeit of my hands, my head, my heart' (*Merchant* 4.1.212). In Webster's *The Duchess of Malfi* Ferdinand's sinister practical joke, in which he gives his sister a dead man's hand (supposedly cut from her husband's body) to kiss in lieu of his own, depends upon the same conceit: 'here's a hand . . . bury the print of it in your heart, / I will leave this ring with you, for a love token; / And the hand, as sure as the ring: and do not doubt / But you shall have the heart too' (4.1.43–9); cited from the New Mermaid edition, ed. Elizabeth M. Brennan (London: A. C. Black, 1983).

[67] *Chirologia*, pp. 110–11.

[68] The New Cambridge edition plausibly adds a direction that Philip and John should enter 'hand in hand' at I. 74; presumably the newly married Dauphin and Blanche should use the same gesture; see L. R. Beaurline (ed.), *King John* (Cambridge: Cambridge University Press, 1990).

Unyoke this seizure and this kind regreet?
Play fast and loose with faith? so jest with heaven?
Make such unconstant children of ourselves,
As now again to snatch our palm from palm,
Unswear faith sworn . . .   (3.1.226–45)

The theatrical power of Philip's repudiation ('England, I will fall from thee', line 320), can thus be fully realized only through the implied direction to drop John's hand[69] – a gesture that does not merely *stand for*, but vividly *embodies* their spiritual rupture.

It is, more than anything, this intense intimacy with mind, will, and heart that makes the hand (as it is again for Brutus in *Julius Caesar* 2.1.58) into a metonymic extension of the self, so that it is with no sense of exaggeration or paradox that Bulwer can assert that anyone who 'forfeits the Recognizance of his *Hand* . . . by falsifying his manuall faith proves a kind of renegado to himselfe.'[70] No wonder, then, that Othello should scan Desdemona's 'liberal hand' with such ferocious intensity for the signs of her 'liberal [libertine] heart' (*Othello* 3.4.36–47); and no wonder either, perhaps, that the token of her supposed betrayal should be a *hand-kerchief* promiscuously passed from hand to hand, a handkerchief fittingly 'dyed in mummy . . . Conserved of maidens' hearts' (3.4.74–5).

THE SEVERED HAND

Julius Caesar's simultaneous association of hands with blood and rhetoric suggests that just behind the action of the murder scene lie recollections of one of the most notorious atrocities that followed in the wake of Caesar's assassination – the killing and mutilation of Cicero, whose philippics against Julius Caesar had incurred the enmity of Mark Antony. Antony had the orator's body dismembered, commanding that 'his head and his hands should straight be set up over the pulpit for orations, in the place called Rostra'.[71] This display not only drew sarcastic attention to the dead man's hands as (silenced) instruments of eloquence, but also (according to Plutarch's *Life of Antony*) gave special prominence to the right hand 'with the which he had written the invective orations (called *Phillippides*) against Caesar'.[72] The meaning of this vindictive display was abundantly clear to the populace who in this 'fearefull and horrible sight . . . thought they saw not Cicero's face, but an image of Antonius' life and disposicion'.[73] According to Bulwer

the malice of *Antonie* forced teares and lamentations into the eyes of the Romans, when they saw *Cicero's* Right Hand, instrument of his divine Eloquence, with which he penn'd and pronounced the Phillipiques, nail'd fast unto his head, and set upon the . . . Pulpit of Common Pleas in the *Forum*.[74]

If *Julius Caesar* displaces the sanguinary symbolism of Antony's revenge on to the blood-stained hands of the conspirators, it is relished and elaborated in the barbaric spectacles of Shakespeare's first Roman tragedy, *Titus Andronicus* (1589). The play's notorious parade of mangled limbs bodies forth the dismemberment of the body politic itself; and partly because the injured Titus *is* himself the hand that wards the royal head from danger (just as Coriolanus is imagined 'the arm our soldier', 1.1.116), severed hands are especially conspicuous here. Even the play's title seems designed

---

[69] Beaurline once again supplies the necessary direction at 3.1.320.

[70] *Chirologia*, p. 101. Compare also Hubert's insistence upon the correspondence between his 'maiden . . . innocent hand' and the purity of his 'thought' and 'mind' (*King John* 4.2.251–9).

[71] Plutarch, 'The Life of Marcus Tullius Cicero', trans. Sir Thomas North, cited from Geoffrey Bullough (ed.), *Narrative and Dramatic Sources of Shakespeare*, 5 vols. (London: Routledge and Kegan Paul, 1964), 5, p. 140.

[72] 'The Life of Marcus Antonius', in Bullough, 5, p. 269.

[73] 'Life of . . . Cicero', p. 140.

[74] *Chironomia*, p. 17. Like Shakespeare, Bulwer was probably familiar with Sir Thomas North's translation of Plutarch's 'Life of Marcus Tullius Cicero'; for North's version of this episode, see Geoffrey Bullough (ed.), *Narrative and Dramatic Sources of Shakespeare*, 5 vols. (London: Routledge and Kegan Paul, 1964), 5, p. 140.

to alert the audience to the metonymic importance of such images; for while 'Andronicus',
like the other characters of Shakespeare's tragedy, is entirely fictional, his name recalls those
of three historical characters: the Byzantine
Emperor Andronicus Commenus (1183–5)
whose right hand was cut off by the mob who
butchered him;[75] the Andronicus of 2 Maccab-
bees 4.34, who entrapped his enemy by the
fraudulent offer of his hand;[76] and (most per-
tinently of all) the Greek actor whose figure
adorns the title-page of Bulwer's *Chironomia* as
an embodiment of the communicative power
of theatrical *actio* – and that in a context that
directly associated him with the fatally eloquent
hand of Cicero.[77] In Shakespeare, as in Plutarch,
the severed hand is identified as an emblem of
silenced eloquence – a sign, like Lavinia's
severed tongue, of speech cut off at the very
root.

But whilst educated playgoers would have
been reminded of the Roman orator's fate by
the spectacle of mutilated tongues, heads, and
hands that expresses the tragedy's preoccupation with the breakdown of language and the
disintegration of the body politic that follows
from it, more hands than Cicero's are being
remembered here. Titus' willing surrender of
his own hand also seems calculated to recall one
of the most celebrated demonstrations of
Roman *virtus* – the sacrifice of his right hand by
the captured warrior Gaius Mucius Scaevola–an
episode spectacularly dramatized in Heywood's
The Rape of Lucrece (1607).[78] Heywood's Scevola
thrusts his 'base hand' into the fire to punish it
for his own failure to assassinate the Etruscan
King Lars Porsena (lines 2739–45).[79] Just as
Scevola's mutilation of his right hand expresses
his contempt for Rome's royal enemy, so Titus
sacrifices his left as a defiant offering to his own
tyrannic emperor, Saturninus. If *Titus Andronicus* played off such recollections, it was able to
do so partly because these classical anecdotes in
turn resonated so powerfully with much more
recent events. Mutilated hands figure prominently in several Protestant martyrologies –

[75] See J. C. Maxwell's Introduction to his Arden edition
(London: Methuen, 1953), p. xxx. For an extensive
discussion of the significance of hands and manual
dismemberment in *Titus*, see Katherine A. Rowe,
'Dismembering and Forgetting in *Titus Andronicus*',
Shakespeare Quarterly, 45 (1994): 279–303. Rowe's essay
has affinities with my own, and I regret that it did
not appear in time for me to make full use of its
arguments.

[76] This Andronicus is actually cited in *Chirologia*
(pp. 99–100) as a rare instance of manual hypocrisy:
'Thus *Andronicus* comming to *Onias* who had fled to the
sanctuary at *Daphne*, hard by Antiochia, counselled
him craftily, GIVING HIM HIS RIGHT HAND / with
an oath, by that faire shew of peace perswaded him
to come out: whom incontinently without any regard
of righteousnesse, he slew according to *Menelaus*
instigation' (pp. 99–100). This episode is grotesquely
reworked in Act 3, Scene 1 of Shakespeare's play, where
Titus instructs Aaron to 'give his majesty my
[amputated] hand' as a prelude to his treacherous
revenge.

[77] On the proverbial eloquence of Cicero's hand, see
Goldsmith's commendatory verses on Cicero's hand in
Bulwer, and cf. Bartolome de Las Casas, *Historia de Las
Indias* [1527–], ed. Augustin Millares Carlo, 3 vols.
(Mexico, 1951), II, p. 27: 'To give substance (*encarnecer*)
to the greatness of the Indies one would need all the
eloquence of Demosthenes and the hand of Cicero',
cited in Pagden, *American Encounters*, p. 61. The mutilation of Cicero seems also to be remembered in
Marlowe's *Massacre at Paris*, when Anjou triumphs over
the murdered Admiral: 'Cut off his head and hands, /
And send them for a present to the Pope' (Scene 6,
43–4).

[78] See Maxwell, p. xxx. Gaius Mucius Scaevola's name
appears to be echoed in that of Andronicus' son, Mutius.
The episode was well enough known to be cited in
Foxe's *Book of Martyrs*. Foxe describes the burning of
Rose Allin's hand by the papist, Edmund Tyrell (1557)
and of a blind harper's hand by the Marian Bishop
Bonner (8, pp. 385–6), comparing both episodes to the
voluntary mutilation of Scaevola, and adding 'But thus
to burn the hands of poor men and women which never
meant any harm unto them . . . we find no example of
such barbarous tyranny, neither in Titus Livius, nor in
any other story amongst the heathen' (p. 386).

[79] Scaevola's hand resonates with the '*Ioviall* hand' which
Brutus makes a synecdoche for Jupiter, and the 'purple
hands of death and ruine' that stand for the Tarquins
(lines 2616–20). Citations from Heywood's *The Rape of
Lucrece* are to the edition by Alan Holaday (Urbana:
University of Illinois Press, 1950).

most famously in Foxe's account of Cranmer's burning (1556), where the Archbishop punishes the hand that has written his recantation, thrusting it into the flames in a gesture that rewrites Gaius Mucius' heroism in the language of Christian bodily discipline: 'And if thy hand offend thee, cut it off' (Mark 9: 43).[80] Just ten years before the staging of *Titus*, moreover, England had been scandalized by the punishments inflicted upon the Protestant polemicist John Stubbs and his publisher William Page for a pamphlet attacking Elizabeth's prospective marriage to the Duke of Alençon. Stubbs and Page were prosecuted under a statute of Mary's that prescribed amputation of the right hand for 'the authors and sowers of seditious writings'; and when Titus offered his ambivalent proof of allegiance to the emperor many in the audience might have recalled Stubbs's stubborn display of loyalty to Elizabeth: 'notwithstanding the bitter pain and doleful loss of my hand immediately before chopped off, I was able, by God's mercy, to say with heart and tongue, before I left the block, these words, "God save the Queen!"'[81]

Characteristic of all these narratives, as of Shakespeare's play, is the apparently disproportionate sense of outrage and revulsion that attaches to mutilation of the hands. In both his accounts of Cicero's death Plutarch emphasizes the special 'cruelty' of Antony's proceeding, and his indignation is further highlighted by North's marginalia. Yet compared with the treatment of Philologus, forced to broil and eat 'litle morsells' of his own flesh – a punishment whose 'goodness' Plutarch commends by way of contrast – the 'wicked' treatment of Cicero's corpse seems relatively mild. By the same token, many worse torments were inflicted upon the long-suffering bodies of Elizabeth's subjects than those experienced by Stubbs and Page, yet their case seems to have been regarded as especially shocking – and it is probably significant that the Marian statute under which they were condemned, though fully consistent with a language of punishment that habitually

marked the criminal body with the signs of its crime,[82] was very rarely invoked. According to the Spanish Ambassador, the penalty appalled even Alençon himself, who averred that 'he was very sorry they had cut off the hands of the men concerned with the book, and he would indeed be glad if could remedy it, even at the cost of two fingers of his own hand . . .'[83]

Such reactions make sense, it seems to me, only in terms of the extraordinary symbolic value invested in the hand – a value which the circumstances of early modern culture had, if anything, enhanced. It was no accident the bodies of early modern suicides should have been symbolically punished for their self-cancelling crime by the amputation of their right hand.[84] When Thomas Beard wanted to demonstrate the exemplary meaning of Marlowe's inadvertent suicide (to take a notorious example), he gloatingly stressed the way in which, through a murderous frenzy of self-division, 'the very hand that had writ those blasphemies' became the chosen instrument of divine vengeance against the poet's equally blasphemous head. Nor was such symbolism only a tool of oppression, since the victims were often as anxious as their tormentors to exploit the symbolic potential of their hands: just as the captured Roman warrior disdainfully sacrificed his defeated sword-hand, so the Henrician cleric

---

80 John Foxe, *The Acts and Monuments*, ed. Josiah Pratt, 8 vols. (London: Religious Tract Society, n.d.), vol. 8, pp. 86–90.

81 John Stubbs, letter to Sir Christopher Hatton, cited from Lloyd E. Berry, *John Stubbs's* Gaping Gulf *with Letters and Other Relevant Documents* (Charlottesville, Va: University of Virginia Press for the Folger Shakespeare Library, 1968), p. 111.

82 See Michel Foucault's now classic account of the language of public mutilation in *Discipline and Punish* (New York: Vintage, 1977).

83 Letter of Mendoza to Philip, 13 January 1580 (*Calendar of State Papers Spanish, 1580–86*, pp. 1–2) cited in Berry, pp. xxxviii–ix.

84 Michel Ragon, *The Space of Death*, tr. Alan Sheridan (University of Virginia Press, Charlottesville, Va, 1991), p. 85.

resolved to punish his writing-hand for signing things 'contrary to my heart';[85] and the pamphleteer, as if remembering Cranmer's example, declared upon the scaffold, 'I will not have a guiltless heart and an infamous hand', before offering his arm to the executioner's axe; while his publisher held up a bleeding stump as the signature of his violated loyalty to the queen: 'I have left there a true Englishman's hand.'[86]

The force of such gestures depends on the way in which, as we have already seen, the hand is figured as the locus of a kind of second self[87] – one that can be distanced, and if necessary separated, from the true self. Thus it can be made to suffer as a scapegoat, drawing punishment away from those symbolic loci of identity with which it is so often paired – the head and the heart. Stubbs is at pains to admit that his writing has 'offend[ed] the laws' but 'without an evil meaning' (p. xxxv): thus his hand can be 'infamous' and deserving of punishment, even as his heart remains 'guiltless'; and just as Gaius Mucius' actions rehabilitated the normally 'sinister' left hand (to the point where he was henceforth proud to be known by the ill-omened name of Scaevola – 'left-handed'), so John Stubbs is at pains to demonstrate the continuing loyalty of his left hand: 'Stubbs, having his right hand cut off, put off his hat with his left, and said with a loud voice, "God save the queen"' (p. xxxvi) – thus re-establishing, as he later insisted, an essential consonance of inner and outer self, of heart and tongue. Using the same codes to rather different effect, Shakespeare's Titus offers his sinister hand to the emperor as a (deliberately ambivalent) sign of loyalty and integrity – while his right hand is used to deal out symbolic discipline to his refractory heart:

> This poor right hand of mine
> Is left to tyrannize upon my breast,
> Who, when my heart, all mad with misery,
> Beats in this hollow prison of my flesh,
> Then thus I thump it down.   (3.2.7–11)

This readiness of victims to turn the symbolic power of the hand against their oppressors helps to illustrate how the very things that made the hand such a potent token in the language of punishment, also made it a dangerous and volatile instrument. For what finally seems to have rendered the treatment of a Stubbs or a Cicero so objectionable was less any simple excess of cruelty, or even the vicious symmetry between offence and retribution, than a sense that violence inflicted upon the hand broke an important taboo, making its exemplary implication in the process of punishment somehow unbearable. What is at issue, I want to suggest, is a threat to the body's power to mean – a threat, that is, to its very humanity. *Titus Andronicus* can help us to see how.

In *Titus* the visual prominence accorded to hands is more than matched by a compulsive rhetorical elaboration that drives the deranged Titus to his infamous quibble 'O, handle not the theme to talk of hands' (3.2.29). This rebuke has a brutally comic redundancy that serves only to emphasize the 'theme' it pretends to suppress, drawing attention to the way the play can't stop handling hands. The troping of hands begins in the opening scene, where the hand of paternal blessing to which Lavinia appeals ('O, bless me here with thy victorious hand', 1.1.163) is transformed to the bloody hand of murder ('Lord Titus here . . . With his own hand did slay his youngest son', 1.1.415–18). Then from the reaching and clasping hands which seal the fates of Martius and Quintus in the pit

---

85 Foxe, 8, p. 88. Cranmer's hand is on conspicuous display throughout this part of the narrative: on his way to the fire Cranmer self-consciously shakes the hands of sympathetic bystanders, but is rebuffed by a priest named Ely who 'drew back his hand, and refused, saying it was not lawful to salute heretics, and specially such a one as falsely returned unto the opinions that he had foresworn . . . and chid those sergeants and citizens which had given him their hands' (p. 89).

86 Cited from Berry, pp. xxxv, xxxviii.

87 The idea of the hand as a second self is what underpins Stephano's favourite oath 'by this hand' (*Tempest* 3.1.69; 4.1.227).

(2.3.327–45) and the fatal handwriting that supposedly confirms their guilt, through the successive amputations of Lavinia's (2.4) and Titus' hands (3.1.191), and on to the final clasping of Marcus' and Lucius' hands (5.3.132–9) which signifies the knitting up of Rome's 'broken limbs ... into one body' (5.3.72), both action and language compulsively highlight the physical presence, the vulnerability and violence, as well as the expressive power of hands.

Most striking of all is the weird procession contrived by Titus at the end of 3.1, in which the handless Lavinia is required to carry her father's severed hand in her own tongueless mouth. If this, by once again forcing together the two mutilated organs of expression, seems to mimic Antony's vindictive emblem, the connection is appropriate because of *Titus Andronicus*'s persistent association of hands with writing and speech. Titus sees his hands first as the instruments of martial action ('For hands to do Rome service is but vain,' 3.1.80), to the point where his heroic identity becomes embodied in his severed hand ('give his majesty my hand. / Tell him it was a hand that warded him / From thousand dangers, bid him bury it', 3.1.193–5) – just as Lavinia's feminine identity was invested in the 'lily hands' described by Marcus, that 'could have better sew'd than Philomel' and 'Tremble[d] like aspen leaves upon a lute' (2.4.43–5).[88] But once severed from the body their hands cease to bear the print of gender, and are almost exclusively imagined as the instruments of rhetorical *actio*, tools of signification. Lavinia's hands are amputated not only to prevent her from writing ('See how with signs and tokens she can scrowl,' 2.4.5), but to deny her the eloquence of gesture. Deprived of hands as well as tongue, she becomes in a double sense a 'Speechless complainant' – forced to the painful foot-and-mouth calligraphy of 4.1. Her very 'signs' are 'martyr'd', her very 'action' rendered 'dumb' (3.2.36–40). If language, as Aristotle had maintained, defines the human *polis*, then the Rome

for which Lavinia stands is close to becoming an absolute wilderness, shorn, by the 'barbarous, beastly' trimming (5.1.97) of Goth and Moor, even of the universal language to which the most barbarous peoples had access.

Titus symbolically participates in his daughter's dumbness when he consents to the amputation of his own left hand:

> Thy niece and I, poor creatures, want our hands,
> And cannot passionate our tenfold grief
> With folded arms. (3.2.5–7)

> No, not a word, how can I grace my talk,
> Wanting a hand to give it action.[89] (5.2.17–18)

Thereafter he must painstakingly attempt to reassemble his disintegrated world, 'perfecting' himself in a 'dumb action' that wants even the assistance of hands. Finally, as if returning to the very origins of language, Titus finds a way to make his remaining hand speak for him, as he repeats the founding act of the Roman hero Virginius by slaying 'his daughter with his own right hand' (5.3.37).[90] Like the political order from which it is ultimately inseparable, speech, the play suggests, begins in the violence of the hand that kills, just as it ends in the violence of the mouth that eats.[91]

---

88 Similarly in *Antony and Cleopatra* the gendered oppositions of the play can be traced through an elaborate pattern of contrasts between the erotic power associated with the 'flower-soft hands' of Cleopatra's court ('a hand that kings / Have lipp'd, and trembled kissing', 2.5.29–30), and the violent hand of power associated with the Roman world ('that self hand / Which writ his honour in the acts it did', 5.1.21–2) – the masculinized hand to which Cleopatra finally trusts herself (4.16.51).
89 I prefer the F reading here to Q's 'give['t] that accord', printed in Riverside.
90 For the Virginia story as a Roman foundation myth, see Patricia Kleindienst Joplin, 'Ritual Work on Human Flesh: Livy's Lucretia and the Rape of the Body Politic', *Helios*, 17 (1990): 51–70.
91 The two are collapsed together in the monstrous pageant of 3.1, where Lavinia's mouth appears to devour her father's severed hand as if grotesquely literalizing Lear's paradigm of filial ingratitude: 'Is it not as this mouth should tear this hand / For lifting food to it' (3.4.15–16).

At the same time, it is as if any assault upon the hand, as a crucial, even originary site of meaning, can be interpreted as an assault on meaning itself. Thus 'the stern, ungentle hands' that have stripped Lavinia's trunk 'Of her two branches', have (in Marcus' quibbling conceit) cut the 'mean' from her – not merely the means of expression, but the ability to 'mean' at all (2.4.16–18, 40), leaving her father to reinvent language, as it were, from scratch:

> That shalt not sigh, nor hold thy stumps to heaven,
> Nor wink, nor nod, nor kneel, nor make a sign,
> But I, of these, will wrest an alphabet,
> And by still practice, learn to know thy
> meaning.   (3.2.42–5)

These verbal and gestural quibbles on 'mean' and 'meaning' themselves belong to an elaborate scheme of word-play associated with hands – a scheme which is often regarded simply as a function of the play's conceited Ovidian rhetoric or of its archaic 'moral heraldry'[92] – but which serves to advertise the polysemous identity of hands. It is as if, over and above their much-emphasized connection with writing, gesture, and the language of signs, hands are invested with a semantic surplus that overflows in sequences of spontaneous word-play:

> Speak, Lavinia, what accursed *hand*
> Hath made thee *handless* in thy father's sight?
> . . .
> 'Tis well, Lavinia, that thou hast no *hands*,
> For *hands* to do Rome service is but vain.
>   (3.1.66–7, 79–80)

> Lend me thy *hand*, and I will give thee mine . . .
> Good Aaron, give his majesty my *hand* . . .
>   (3.1.187, 193)

> What violent *hands* can she lay on her life?
> Ah, wherefore dost thou urge the name of *hands*
>   . . .
> O, *handle* not the theme, to talk of *hands*
> Lest we remember still that we have none.
> Fie, fie, how frantically I square my talk,
> As if we should forget we had no *hands*,
> If Marcus did not name the word of *hands*!
>   (3.2.25–33)

> As sure a card as ever won the set . . .
> I play'd the cheater for thy father's *hand*
>   (5.1.100, 111)

> [TITUS] O sweet Revenge, now do I come to thee,
> And if one arm's embracement will content thee,
> I will embrace thee in it by and by.

> [TAMORA] This closing with him fits his lunacy
>   . . .
> I'll find some cunning practice *out of hand*,
> To scatter and disperse the giddy Goths,
> Or at the least make them his enemies.
>   (5.2.67–79)

Nor are such bouts of manual quibbling peculiar, as is often supposed, to the black humour of a play in which severed hands are self-consciously 'cut off and made a merry jest' (5.2.174) – on the contrary they can be matched in a number of contemporary texts where the semiotic importance of the hand is foregrounded. Porsena, overcome by the heroism of the 'handlesse' Scaevola, protests 'And were we not so much *ingagde* to *Tarquin*, / We would not *lift a hand* against that nation that breeds / Such noble spirits' (lines 2746–8; emphasis added). Even Stubbs on the scaffold cannot resist punning: 'The hand ready on the block to be stricken off, he said often to the people, "Pray for me, now my calamity is at hand",'[93] whilst his appeals from prison are studded with references to the Queen's 'merciful hands' and to the plight of one who 'hath no longer his own hand to declare his own grievous plight' or to demonstrate the loyalty of his 'unfeigned heart'.[94]

---

92 See A. C. Hamilton, '*Titus Andronicus*: The Form of Shakespearean Tragedy', *Shakespeare Quarterly*, 14 (1963): 201–13; M. C. Bradbrook, *Shakespeare and Elizabethan Poetry* (Harmondsworth: Penguin, 1964), pp. 96–101.

93 Folger Ms. v.b.142, f. 54v, quoted in Berry, pp. xxxv–vi.

94 See Berry, pp. 108, 111. The persecuted Rose Allin, recalling Tyrell's burning of her hand, quibblingly remarked that she might have struck him in the face with the pot in her left hand, 'for no man held my hand to stay me therefrom' (Foxe, p. 386).

5a and b   Spaniards amputating the hands of Amerindians. Engravings by J. T. and

Stubbs's word-play asserts an essential connection not merely between the hand that writes, the hand that gestures, and the hand that pledges, but also between these hands and the hands of power (shadowed in the violent hands of the executioner) to which his missing hand makes its pathetic appeal.

The prefatory material that introduces Bulwer's treatises on 'manual rhetoric', is full of such play on the practical and symbolic functions of the hand. Bulwer dedicates *Chirologia* to Edward Goldsmith, with the reflection that 'However this *Chirosophie* or first Fruits of my *Hand* be accepted abroad, having put forth my

Right Hand in signe of amity to you, and for performance of promise: there remains nothing (most noble *Chirophilus*) but that you take it between Yours in token of warranty and protection'; and the text is prefaced with a clutch of commendatory verses praising 'the Very Pure and Beloved Hand of John Bulwer' in elaborately quibbling language – most notably those by 'F.W.':

> I feele my Hand, deep struck in friendships
>   veine,
> With rich invention flowing out amaine.
> And where such force the *Pens* inagagement
>   draws,

J. L. de Bry, from Bartolome de Las Casas, *Narratio Regionum Indicarum* (1614)

There an unskilful *Hand* may give applause.
Were I *Bellona's* Darling, I would fight:
But at that Spirits rate that Thou dar'st write;
Mercurial valour in Thy conquering Pen
Equals the Hand of War in ord'ring men.
I find Thee (Friend) well armed to repell
Th'affronts of any scoffing Ismael;
Whose carping Hand 'gainst every man is bent,
And each mans Hand 'gainst his Hands crosse intent.
Thou may'st such blowes without a Gauntlet ward
. . .
But if a Viper through the glove invade
Thy harmlesse *Hand*; shak't off, and to thy aide
Raise thy own new Militia, thy Hands,
Natures best squadron, and Arts Trained Bands.[95]

95 A5. Cf. also pp. A1–A1v; A2; A3v; A4: 'We may know
Alcides by his foot, and a lion by his claw; / I rejoice that
you can be known by your hand'; 'I joy (deare friend) to
see thy *Palme* display / A new *Chirosophie*, which hidden
lay / In Natures Hieroglyphique grasp'd'; 'We all desi-
rous are to limb Thee forth: / But blushing, must
confesse, none can command / A pencil worthy Thee,
but Thy own *Hand*'; 'See here appeares a *Hand*, one
limbe alone, / Borne to the World, a perfect *sunalon*
[companion] / And marke how well 'tis muscled, how it
speakes / Fresh from the Presses wombe . . . By *Chiro-
mancies* leave I must divine: / He need not feare bold
Atropos her knife, / For in his *Hand* each line's a line of
life.'

In the case of *Titus*, however, the word-play is given particular significance by its association with spectacles of barbaric violence and dismemberment, culminating in an extraordinary cannibal fantasy – a conjunction which makes sense once it is recognized that *Titus* plays out, in a displaced form, one of the recurrent nightmares of early modern culture – the encounter with the barbaric threat of unmeaning on the beaches of the New World. It is no accident, I think, that among the most powerful images of atrocity that accompany the 'Black Legend' of Spanish imperialist desecration, are the de Bry engravings in which the 'civilized' conquerors hack the hands from their 'savage' victims, stripping them of the very instruments of 'natural language' in which the universal kinship of humankind was embodied; symbolically amputating them from the body of meaning itself (Figs. 5a and b).

THE BLOODY HAND

The severed hand effectively disappears from Shakespeare after *Titus*,[96] but the bloodstained hand remains as a recurrent symbol – not merely of guilt, but of the necessary intimacy of violence and power – from *Richard III* to *Macbeth*. *Richard II*, for example, systematically opposes the sacred dialect of Richard's hands to the machiavellian idiom of Bolingbroke's. The sacramental gesturing that marks Richard's return to England shows how the imagined power of his 'royal hands' is expressed in their ability to confer blessing on the earth, to 'salute' and 'do . . . favours' to a soil that is allegedly rendered 'gentle' by his touch (3.2.6–11). Bolingbroke's hand, by contrast, is defined as 'royal' simply by its acts of 'possession' (4.1.110). Bolingbroke's is identified with the naked force of 'the hand of death' (3.1.30), Richard's with the invisible puissance of 'the hand of god' (3.3.77), from which its sanctity is vicariously derived ('For well we know no hand of blood and bone / Can gripe the sacred handle of our sceptre, / Unless he do profane,

steal, or usurp', lines 79–81). In the deposition scene the context between the rival ideas of monarchy for which their hands stand, is perfectly expressed in the gestural emblem that Richard devises: 'here cousin, seize the crown . . . On this side my hand, and on that side thine . . .' (4.1.181–3); just as the self-undoing paradoxes of Richard's surrender are expressed in the gestures in which he gives up the trappings of royalty: 'Now mark me how I will undo myself: / I give this heavy weight from off my head, / And this unwieldy sceptre from my hand . . . With mine own hands I give away my crown, / With mine own tongue deny my sacred state' (lines 203–9).

Cleansed by the blandly self-exculpatory gestures with which he washes away all guilt for the execution of Richard's favourites (3.1.5–6), Bolingbroke's is the coldly efficient hand of policy; yet it remains tainted, even in the imagination of the trimmer York, by its association with 'the rude misgoverned hands' that throw 'dust and rubbish' on Richard's 'sacred head' (5.2.5–6, 30); and it is even more damningly marked by its identification with the 'fierce hand' of Exton, whose murderous blows 'stain'd the King's own land' in an impious reversal of Richard's sanctifying favours (5.5.109–10). It is not only Richard who identifies his oppressors with Pilate ('Though some of you, with Pilate, wash your hands . . . yet . . . Water cannot wash away your sin', 4.1.239–42), but Bolingbroke himself who is haunted by the image of his own guilt, as he stares aghast at Exton's 'fatal hand': 'I'll make a voyage to the Holy Land, / To wash this blood off from my guilty hand' (5.6.35, 49–50).

The same opposition between the blood-stained 'unlineal hand' (*Macbeth* 3.1.62) of *de*

---

[96] But see Warwick's defiant asseveration in *3 Henry VI*: rather than submit to York, he maintains, 'I had rather chop this hand off at a blow / And with the other fling it at thy face' (5.1.50–1); and Bassanio's hyperbolic 'Why I were best to cut my left hand off, / And swear I lost the ring defending it' (*Merchant* 5.1.178).

facto power and the sanctified hand of divinely ordained monarchy underlies the action of the tragedy in which Shakespeare's language of hands is at once most eloquent and most brutally limited. The central symbol of *Macbeth* is, of course, the hand that cannot be cleansed:

What hands are here? . . .
Will all great Neptune's ocean wash this blood
Clean from my hand? No, this my hand will rather
The multitudinous seas incarnadine,
Making the green one red.   (2.2.56–60)

Here's the smell of the blood still. All the perfumes of Arabia will not sweeten this little hand.
(5.1.50–1)

And such is the imaginative force of the horror with which Shakespeare invests this symbol of pollution that the play's first recorded viewer, the physician and magus Simon Forman, was convinced that he had actually *seen* the Macbeths vainly scouring the blood from their hands 'by which means they became . . . much amazed and affronted'. The overwhelming power of the image is not, however, simply a local effect of the poetry that creates the killers' inflamed imaginations, but grows out of the play's obsessive preoccupation with sanctified and unsanctified hands. The very infection which devours the body politic of Scotland is spread by Macbeth's 'hand accurs'd' (3.6.49), whilst the miraculous power of 'Gracious England' to cure 'the evil' is attributed to the special 'sanctity' which 'heaven [hath] given his hand' (4.3.144). Indeed Lennox's prayer for English aid to redeem Scotland from its sufferings expressly equates the war against Macbeth with the gesture of 'blessing' by which 'the King's Evil' was supposedly cured.

Yet if the idea of sacred monarchy is treated less equivocally in this play than in *Richard II*, that is perhaps only because its mystical aura, though posthumously attached to the 'sainted' Duncan (4.3.109), is primarily invested in the shadowy offstage figure of the (significantly unnamed) Edward the Confessor. The blessed hand of ideal kingship is given an emblematic presence as the instrument of life-giving fertility and wisdom in Act 4's apparitions of '*A Child crowned, with a tree in its hand*' and '*the last king with a glass in his hand*'; but otherwise the only hands which are granted a significant physical presence in the play are the blood-soaked hands of the Macbeths and the withered claws of the witches. Moreover it is impossible to ignore how the healing touch of England's hand is achieved only through an action that (as critics have often observed) uncannily replicates Macbeth's first action in the play, the decapitation of Macdonwald: '*Enter Macduff with Macbeth's head*'. Banquo conceived of a world where each one stood 'In the great hand of God' (2.3.130); but when the 'hands uplifted in [Malcolm's] right' (4.3.42) merely seem to repeat the murderous gestures of Macbeth's 'heavy hand' (3.1.89), then the 'even-handed justice' that haunted the protagonist's imagination (1.7.10) becomes difficult to distinguish from the blind handy-dandy logic of revenge; and the spectacle of Macduff with the 'dead butcher['s]' head in his hand can seem to exhibit the same cruel and absurd reflexiveness as Lady Macbeth's taking of her own life 'by self and violent hands' (5.9.35–6).

No longer the instruments of bonding, but violent cancellers of humane bonds (3.2.48–9), hands in this play become so exclusively the violent 'symbole of action' that even such familiar gestures of affection and fellowship as the handclasp are admitted only by way of grotesque irony, as in the description of Macbeth's encounter with Macdonwald –

Which nev'r *shook hands*, nor bad farewell to him,
Till he unseam'd him from the nave to th' chops,
And fix'd his head upon our battlements.
(1.2.21–3)

– or in the sinister dance of the Weird Sisters with its travesty of the Three Graces' circle of giving, receiving and returning:

The weird sisters, *hand in hand* . . .
Thus do go, about, about;
Thrice to thine, and thrice to mine,
And thrice again to make up nine.   (1.3.32–6)

When the Sisters make their first appearance, their gestures seem to Banquo to speak the same universal language that offered travellers access to the world of the Other: 'You seem to understand me, / By each at once her choppy finger laying / Upon her skinny lips' (1.3.43–5). This might be the *gestus* which Bulwer calls *Inventione laboro*, indicating that they are momentarily at a loss for words to answer his questions; it is more likely, however, to be the familiar *Silentium indico*, a gesture which, in the wider context of the play, might be read as a refusal of meaning – a forbidding of interpretation, in Banquo's terms. For the witches, with all the sinister gobbledygook of their doggerel incantations, and the self-cancelling doubleness of their prophetic utterances ('Lost and won', 'Fair is foul, foul is fair', 'lesser and . . . greater' 'Not so happy, yet much happier') inhabit the very world of meaningless 'sound and fury' into which they lure Macbeth – a world of desperate contingency whose only watchword is 'I'll do, and I'll do, and I'll do' (1.3.10). In such a world the only thing to be done is 'a deed without a name' (4.1.49). Bloody hands are the sign of that doing – the symbol of a kind of action which, because it turns out to be related only to itself, must in the end turn on itself.

'Strange things I have in head, that will to hand, / Which must be acted ere they may be scann'd' (3.4.138–9): the 'strange things' of which Macbeth speaks at the end of the banquet scene are precisely deeds which cannot be named, because to name them would be to 'scan' them, exposing them to the intolerable 'speculation' that has manifested itself in the 'glare' of Banquo's ghost. The contradiction in Macbeth's figure – it speaks deeds that in Lady Macbeth's phrase 'must not be thought' (2.2.30) – is entirely characteristic of their willed self-division: 'To know my deed, 'twere best not know myself' (2.2.70). Although the hand

nominally translates into action the ideas of the head (3.4.138) or the impulses of the heart ('The very firstlings of my heart shall be / The firstlings of my hand,' 4.1.147–8), the murderous compulsiveness of doing is such that thought can seem the unlucky consequence of action rather than its necessary precursor. In terms of the play's dominant figurative scheme, it is once again as if the hand had a life of its own separate from the head, as if acting were detached from seeing, the hand severed from the eye: 'This deed I'll do before this purpose cool. / But no more sights!' (4.1.154–5).

Not only should the eye guide the hand, it is also bound to it by the language of gesture, which, as the play's patron, James I, had once remarked, 'speaketh to the eye';[97] without the eye, guiding and interpreting, the hand cannot 'make sense', it is capable of signifying nothing. But *Macbeth* presents a world in which eye and hand, seeing and doing, are set in unnatural opposition to one another:

Let not light see my black and deep desires;
The eye wink at the hand; yet let that be
Which the eye fears, when it is done, to see.
                                        (1.4.51–3)

In Macbeth's vision of the dagger with its handle temptingly 'toward my hand', eye and

---

[97] The remark is cited by Bacon in *The Advancement of Learning*: 'your Majesty saith most aptly and elegantly, *As the tongue speaketh to the ear, so the gesture speaketh to the eye*' – quoted from the edition by G. W. Kitchin (London: Dent, 1915), p. 107; later in the *Advancement* Bacon discusses the use of gesture 'in the commerce of barbarous people, that understand one another's meaning' (p. 137). The first Bacon passage is cited in Bulwer's Dedication to *Chirologia*, A5v. Cf. also Bulwer's Dedication to *Philocophus; or, The Deafe and Dumbe Mans Friend* (London, 1648), where he promises to teach the deaf to *'heare with your eye'* in 'a happy *metamsychosis* or *transmigration* of your senses' A6–A6v; and Thomas Diconson's verses on the same treatise which declare that through it 'The Deafe and Dumb get Hearing Eies, which breake / Their Barre of Silence, and thence learn to speake / Words may be seene or heard: W'are at our choyce / For to give Eare, or Eie unto a Voyce', A8.

hand seem briefly to collude, until that vision discloses itself as one of impotence ('I have thee not, and yet I see thee still', 2.1.35) and guilt ('And on thy blade and dudgeon gouts of blood', line 46). The more Macbeth is tormented by the 'filthy witness' of his 'hangman's hands' (2.2.25, 44), the more violently his hands seem to turn against his eyes, in an impossible rage for self-cancellation:

What hands are here? Ha! they pluck out mine eyes?
(2.2.56)

As the eye functions only in the daylight world from which Macbeth recoils, so his imagination consigns the hand to the occult world of 'night's black agents', where it operates less as the blindman's substitute for sight than as a literal 'instrument of darkness'. So intense, indeed, does this identification become that night itself comes to be figured as a 'bloody and invisible hand' blindfolding 'the tender eye of pitiful day' (3.2.47–8).[98]

Because that 'tender eye' inevitably recalls the fearful and compassionate 'eye of childhood' whose 'sorry sight' Lady Macbeth sought to suppress in 2.2, and Macbeth's own terrified glimpse of 'pity, like a naked new-born babe . . . blow[ing] the horrid deed in every eye' (1.7.21–4), it inevitably becomes proleptic of the actual infanticide in 4.2, identifying it as a kind of self-murder. And there is a sense, of course, in which all of those 'secret murders sticking on his hands' belong to a chain of self-destructive doing in which Macbeth repeatedly attempts to destroy his own double (Macdonwald, Cawdor, Duncan, Banquo, Macduff – a line stretching potentially to the crack of doom). All that the tyrant does however is to 'murder sleep' – as it were to tear the very eyelids from his eyes, so that nothing can occlude their fascinated stare. And even as he is about to hurl himself into the dark, the repressed returns (how else?) in the sleep-walking figure of the represser, her uncannily open eyes fixed in horror upon the very hands that she once offered to cleanse with 'a little water' – 'What, will these hands ne'er be clean?' (5.1.43). The sleepwalking scene ends with a gesture that recalls Macbeth's vain grasping at the air-drawn dagger, as Lady Macbeth reaches out for her husband's hand, to find inscribed upon its phantasmagoric palm the implacable signature of their fate: 'Come, come, come, give me your hand. What's done cannot be undone' (lines 67–8) – the lines of a narrative 'signifying nothing'.

THE BARE HAND

The 'nothing' of *Macbeth* is an effect of cancelled human bonds, imagined as writings torn by the 'bloody and invisible hand' of power (3.2.48) – bonds for which, ironically enough, the human hand itself should properly stand. The last play I want to look at, *King Lear*, is also haunted by the self-annihilating violence of the 'bloody hand' – a phrase that echoes through the play (3.2.53; 3.4.92; 4.6.160), and is brought to hallucinatory life in the 'robbers' hands' that tear out Gloucester's eyes (3.7.40). *Lear* begins with a scene that initiates a progressive unstitching of the social fabric through the king's formal undoing of the bond that ties him to his daughter. The repudiation of Cordelia is expressed in a powerfully gestural language that formally reverses the rite of parental blessing ('So be my grave my peace, as here I give / Her father's heart from her', 1.1.125–6) – the very rite which Cordelia vainly tries to re-invoke in the restoration scene: 'O, look upon me, sir, / And hold your hand in benediction o'er me' (4.7.57–8). In the last of many reversals which characterize this Prodigal Father fable, Lear responds by kneeling in the posture of the suppliant child – a gesture which by the final

---

[98] In the complex word-play of this passage 'that great bond / Which keeps me *pale*' refers not simply to the bond of moral law which has kept Macbeth fenced in, but to the bond of common humanity which has not only made him tender-hearted but kept him in the world of light.

scene has come to express for him the essence of their new relationship ('When thou dost ask me blessing I'll kneel down / And ask of thee forgiveness', 5.3.10–11). But Cordelia's hand is extended only to raise him to his feet ('sir, you must not kneel', 4.7.58); neither's hand is now invested with magical power.[99] For one of the things that this play has witnessed, in its remorseless stripping away of all those meanings in which the Renaissance body was clothed, is something like the discovery of a modern hand – the desanctified hand that Gloucester must not kiss because it 'smells of mortality' (4.6.133); a hand that is no longer a magic vehicle of eloquence of power, but offers itself as an inarticulate token of mere animal presence, an instrument of bare sensation:

> I know not what to say.
> I will not swear these are my hands. Let's see,
> I feel this pin-prick.   (4.7.53–5)

This is the unadorned 'friendly hand' that Edgar repeatedly offers to his blind father (4.6.25, 223, 230, 284; 5.2.5, 7); the hand that is foregrounded in the extraordinarily moving Quarto stage direction that begins 5.2 'Enter the powers of France over the stage, Cordelia with her father in her hand'. It is a hand that has learned to 'see . . . feelingly' (4.6.149) perhaps – 'Be your tears wet? Yes, faith' (4.7.70) – but one whose only eloquence is touching. This hand has forgotten how to speak. It is a hand that lays claim to what the novelist J. M. Coetzee calls 'the innocence of hands';[100] a hand that, like the 'scrubbed and sour humble hands' of Dylan Thomas's Ann Jones, seems to mean no more (or less) that what it does: 'Pray you undo this button' (5.3.310). It is (to return to the text with which I began this essay), the hand which Frank McGuinness's play sets up against the over-inscribed dead hand of mythic history: 'When I touched your hand, I smelt bread of it. I smelt life.'[101]

---

[99] Cf. also Gloucester's apparent inability to respond to Edgar's request for blessing (5.3.196–200).

[100] J. M. Coetzee, *The Master of Petersburg* (London: Secker & Warburg, 1994), p. 10: 'The innocence of hands, ever renewed. A memory comes back to him: the touch of a hand, intimate in the dark. But whose hand? Hands emerging like animals, without shame, without memory, into the flight of day.'

[101] *Observe the Sons of Ulster*, p. 54.

'SHAKESPUR AND THE JEWBILL'

JAMES SHAPIRO

Two hundred and twenty-five years ago David Garrick's Stratford Jubilee helped establish Shakespeare as a national poet and as a permanent cultural fixture, one who, in Jane Austen's familiar phrase, would soon enough become part of an Englishman's constitution.[1] Garrick's subsequent play – called *The Jubilee* and written for those unable to attend the celebrations in Stratford – further secured this reputation, while positioning Shakespeare against those at the periphery of English culture. *The Jubilee* includes a bumbling unnamed 'Irishman' who travels from Dublin to witness the festivities only to sleep through them and return, as he says, to 'go home and be nowhere'. The play also contains a comic exchange between Stratford locals, who, when they hear celebratory fireworks, fear that ''Tis certainly a plot of the Jews and Papishes', a confusion no doubt exacerbated by the fact that to them, the word 'ju–bil–ee' sounded a lot like 'Jew Bill'. Sukey, a young woman of Stratford, explains to her friend Nancy (who wonders 'who is this Shakespur, that they make such a rout about 'en?') that had 'you lived at Birmingham or Coventry, or any other polite cities, as I have done, you would have known better than to talk so of Shakespur and the Jewbill'.[2] By framing the Jubilee events with the skewed perspective of these outsiders, incapable of grasping the difference between a local hero and a Jewish threat, Garrick offers up a Shakespeare who cannot possibly belong to Stratford, let alone to the boorish Irish, but is

the rightful property of a cultivated London society that can properly know his worth. This essay is about that Jew Bill, formally known as the Jewish Naturalization Act of 1753, and the ways in which Shakespeare, Englishness, and Jewishness crossed paths at this historical moment, and in so doing helped illuminate and redefine each other.

The facts of this alien legislation and the ensuing controversy have been well documented.[3] In January 1753, after some debate within the Jewish community in England, a Jewish banker named Joseph Salvador decided to petition the government to relax restrictions on

---

[1] As Jonathan Bate neatly puts it, 'Shakespeare was constituted in England in the eighteenth and early nineteenth century', and 'cultural life during that period was by constitution Shakespearean', *Shakespearean Constitutions: Politics, Theatre, Criticism, 1730–1830* (Oxford: Clarendon Press, 1989), p. 1. See too Michael Dobson, *The Making of the National Poet: Shakespeare, Adaptation and Authorship, 1660–1769* (Oxford: Clarendon Press, 1992).

[2] See David Garrick, *The Jubilee* (1769) in *The Plays of David Garrick*, ed. Harry W. Pedicord and Frederick L. Bergmann (Carbondale: Southern Illinois University Press, 1980), vol. 2, pp. 125, 104, 122.

[3] See Thomas W. Perry, *Public Opinion, Propaganda, and Politics in Eighteenth-Century England: A Study of the Jew Bill of 1753* (Cambridge: Harvard University Press, 1962); Todd Endelman, *The Jews of Georgian England, 1714–1830: Tradition and Change in a Liberal Society* (Philadelphia: Jewish Publication Society of America, 1979), esp. pp. 50–117; and David S. Katz, *The Jews in the History of England 1485–1850* (Oxford: Clarendon Press, 1994), pp. 240–53.

Jewish naturalization. With the support of the ruling Whig party a bill to this effect was introduced on 3 April into the House of Lords, where it was rapidly approved and soon passed through Commons as well. Then, unexpectedly, opposition gradually mounted, and then erupted; by autumn, the clamour for repeal reached a deafening roar. Before 15 November, when the Whigs led the way in repealing the bill that they themselves had first advocated, more than sixty pamphlets, endless newspaper columns, various satiric illustrations, sermons, and an assortment of related books had been printed, pro and con, on the Jew Bill. Almost as rapidly, the Jew Bill and the issues circulating around it virtually disappeared from print and public scrutiny.

The flavour of the debate is nicely conveyed in a column by a contemporary polemicist, Arthur Murphy, who writes that:

The English have naturally interwoven in their Constitution a peculiar Kind of national Self-Love, and the least Attempt to dispense a Favour to Foreigners alarms their Fears, and awakens that Jealousy which is natural to their very Frame. It is to this we owe the general Discontent, which has broke out among all Ranks of People upon the late Occasion ... As it is apparent from what has been observed already, that the Christian Religion has no longer a Footing in this Country, it may not be improper to repeal the sacramental Test, and to substitute in its Room the Act of Circumcision.[4]

A month after the Jew Bill was overturned Murphy wrote on a related topic that 'with us islanders Shakespeare is a kind of established religion in poetry'.[5]

At first glance, the Jew Bill seems harmless enough: a slight alteration or two in the requirements for becoming a naturalized British subject. Considerably more proved to be at stake, however, than updating alien laws that had remained unchanged since the reign of James I.[6] The controversy not only touched upon what legal rights foreigners living in England should be accorded, but also called into question what is 'naturally woven' into what

Murphy calls the English 'constitution', for the act of redefining the place of Jews in English society raised some troubling questions about the essential nature of English culture and identity.

While there is little disagreement about *what* happened in the summer and fall of 1753, there is considerable difference of opinion over *why* this controversy occurred. Two main explanations have been offered.[7] The first, that the episode reveals yet another chapter in the history of traditional English antisemitism: the legislation thus provided an opportunity for Jew-baiting that was not to be missed. This position is lent support by the fact that until recently mainstream British historians have tended to ignore the episode completely, overlooking in the process evidence such as the report in the *London Evening Post* from November 1753 that on the previous 'Saturday Night amidst the Rejoicings for the celebrating his Majesty's Birth-Day in the Borough of Southwark, the Populace dress'd up the Effigy of a Jew, and burnt him in a large bonfire'.[8] There is certainly enough evidence in the Jew Bill controversy of the crudest sort of prejudice. Charges of Jewish ritual murder resurfaced at this time and the public was reminded of the Jews' 'insatiable thirst for the blood of Christians, especially of Christian children, which they often steal and solemnly crucify'.[9] The English Enlightenment was built on the solid foundations of sixteenth- and seventeenth-

---

[4] *The Gray's-Inn Journal*, 2 vols. (London, 1756), vol. 1, pp. 222, 224 (16 June 1753).

[5] As cited in Dobson, *The Making of the National Poet*, p. 7, from *Gray's Inn Journal*, 15 December 1753.

[6] See J. M. Ross, 'Naturalisation of Jews in England', *Transactions of the Jewish Historical Society of England*, 24 (1975): 59–72.

[7] See Robert Liberles, 'The Jews and Their Bill: Jewish Motivations in the Controversy of 1753', *Jewish History*, 2 (1987): 29–36.

[8] *London Evening Post* (13–15 November 1753), p. 4.

[9] Anon., *The Rejection and Restoration of the Jews, According to Scripture, Declar'd* (London, 1753), pp. 34–5.

century conceptions of Jewish criminality and racial and national difference, foundations with a very long half-life.

Mainstream historians, sceptical (and at times dismissive) of this antisemitic explanation, have countered that what was actually at stake in this conflict was a political struggle in an election year between entrenched Whigs and the aggressive out-of-power Tories who seized on this convenient issue to wrest more Parliamentary seats.[10] As Thomas Perry puts it in his book on the Jew Bill, 'the clamor was meant to prepare the ground not for a pogrom, but for a general election', and its 'real targets were the Court Whig politicians, not the Jews'.[11]

Problems with each of these interpretations persist, however: why fight so heatedly over the place of Jews in England if this was merely partisan political struggle? On the other hand, if this was an unleashing of antisemitic sentiment, why was there almost no physical violence directed against English Jews? To these binary and partial positions, both of which contain arguments of considerable merit, I offer a third and supplementary one that tries to be sensitive to the nuances of eighteenth-century English politics yet at the same time not too hasty in reconstruing the substance of the polemical literature as something other than what the polemicists actually wrote. I'd like to suggest that the buried threat occasioned by the naturalization of Jews had to do with the surprising vulnerability of English social and religious identity at this time: if even a Jew could be English, what could one point to that defined essential Englishness? The anonymous author of the satiric tract The Exclusion of the English, written five years before the Jew Bill debate, may well be the first English writer to ask, in print, that most nagging of questions: 'If You consider rightly, it will be very hard to answer the question What is an Englishman?'[12] And a poem that appeared in the popular Gentleman's Magazine – 'The Jew naturalized, or the English alienated' – makes much the same point in 1753: 'Such actions as these most apparently shews, / That if the Jews are made English, the English are Jews.'[13]

Racial thinking about the Jews was hardly limited to the margins of English political discourse. In fact, it even informed the Parliamentary debate during the effort to repeal the Jew Bill. When the Duke of Newcastle, who had initially supported the Bill but recognized the political necessity of its repeal, nonetheless insisted that he 'knew that every Jew born here was, by the common law, a natural born subject', his opponent, the Duke of Bedford, would have none of it: 'whatever opinion the noble Duke may have of our common law, with respect to Jews born in this kingdom . . . no Jew born here can be deemed a natural born subject whilst he continues to be a Jew'. The Jews must 'always continue a people separate and distinct from the people that naturalize them'.[14] Bedford presses this racist line of thought by maintaining that Jewishness was an essence even more ineradicable than the blackness of colonial slaves:

I shall suppose, that for strengthening our sugar colonies, and for peopling them with subjects instead of slaves, a scheme were proposed for naturalizing all the blacks born in any of them without any other condition whatsoever: I will say that our adopting such a scheme would be ridiculous, because their progeny would continue to be a distinct people; but if the conditions were added that no blacks should be naturalized unless they declared themselves Christians, and that no such black man should be naturalized unless he married a white woman, nor any black woman unless she married a white man, the ridicule

---

[10] See G. A. Cranfield, 'The London Evening-Post and the Jew Bill of 1753', Historical Journal, 8 (1965), 16–30.

[11] Perry, Public Opinion, p. 194. See too, Nicholas Rogers, Whigs and Cities: Popular Politics in the Age of Walpole and Pitt (Oxford: Clarendon, 1989), pp. 89–93.

[12] Anon., The Exclusion of the English; an Invitation to Foreigners (London, 1748), p. 10.

[13] Gentleman's Magazine, July 1753, p. 346.

[14] For the 'Debate for the Repeal of the Jewish Naturalization Act, November 1753', see The Parliamentary History of England, vol. 15, 1753–65 (London: Hansard, 1813), p. 92.

of the scheme would be very much softened, because their progeny would in time unite and coalesce with the rest of the people: it might a little alter the complexion of the people of these islands; but they would all be the same people and would look upon themselves in no other light than as subjects of Great Britain. This must shew the imprudence, and even the ridiculousness, of our adopting the doctrine, that all Jews born here are to be deemed natural-born subjects, for their latest posterity whilst they continue Jews, will continue to be, and will consider themselves as a people quite distinct and separate from the ancient people of this island.[15]

The Jew Bill controversy clearly needs to be situated within the broader context of a century of English debate over alien immigration and naturalization as well as within emerging notions of racial difference.[16] The kind of incoherent racial ideas found in Bedford's speech had their roots in late sixteenth- and early seventeenth-century English thought. This is where Shakespeare's play enters the picture, because its exploration of Jews as nation, race, and aliens resonated with – and indeed for many writers at this time, helped identify – inchoate but powerfully felt anxieties circulating in this 1753 controversy. Historians have scratched their heads and wondered in footnotes why so many of the polemicists writing about the Jew Bill simply ignored the political and economic implications of the legislation and discussed instead the threat of Jews circumcizing Englishmen, taking Christian servants, and racially contaminating the English nation. I'd like to argue here that Shakespeare's play, with its knife-wielding Jew, its conversion and intermarriage, its Christian servant, and its disturbing exploration of the Jews as members of an international nation and as political aliens (we might recall here that it is Shylock's violation of a law against aliens that enables Portia to trip him up) became a powerful weapon in the arsenal of those opposed to the naturalization of Jews in England.

The history of *The Merchant of Venice* in the early eighteenth century – including the success of Granville's revision, *The Jew of Venice*, and Macklin's impressive revival – is well known,[17] though one feature of its stage history in these years that has been largely overlooked is *when* Londoners might have expected to see the play performed. Since Macklin's production had been staged at the opening of Drury Lane on 15 September 1747 an informal tradition emerged that the play would be performed near the start of each autumn season at Drury Lane (along with *The Beggar's Opera*). Thus, after a fairly late appearance in 1748 (3 November), it was the fourth play performed in 1749 (9 September), the opening play in 1750 (8 September), and the second play in both 1751 (9 September) and 1752 (19 September). In the months leading up to the Jew Bill debate the play remained in repertory, appearing on 4 January 1753 at Covent Garden, a week later at Drury Lane, once again at Covent Garden on 26 January, and on Shakespeare's birthday in April at Covent Garden, before the controversy developed in earnest in May.[18]

When the autumn season came around once more in early September 1753 the patrons of Drury Lane must have been looking forward to the return of *The Merchant of Venice* with unusual interest. The controversy over the Jew Bill was reaching the boiling point; another two months would pass before Parliament would meet and discuss its repeal. A column in

---

[15] *The Parliamentary History of England*, vol. 15, p. 106.

[16] See, in this regard, John Toland, *Reasons for Naturalizing the Jews in Great Britain, on the Same Foot with All Other Nations. Containing also, a Defence of the Jews against All Vulgar Prejudices in All Countries* (London, 1714). Toland's work was immediately challenged by the anonymous *A Confutation of the Reasons for Naturalizing the Jews* (London, 1715).

[17] See Toby Lelyveld, *Shylock on the Stage* (London: Routledge and Kegan Paul, 1961); and James C. Bulman, *The Merchant of Venice* (Manchester: Manchester University Press, 1991).

[18] For the record of performances, see George Winchester Stone, Jr, ed. *The London Stage 1660–1800*, part 4: 1747–76 (Carbondale, Illinois: Southern Illinois University Press, 1962).

the politically neutral *Cambridge Journal* on 25 August, two weeks before the theatres re-opened in London, reported that 'We are credibly informed, that some of the most eminent among the Children of Israel, have made Interest with the Patentee of Covent Garden Playhouse, not to engage Mr Macklin for the ensuing Season, to prevent his playing the Character of Shylock in the *Merchant of Venice*, which it is apprehended will certainly be called for by the Public'.[19] Though perhaps tongue-in-cheek about the Jews' attempts to silence Macklin, the *Cambridge Journal* was correct in reckoning that Shakespeare's play would most assuredly be called for. Yet on opening night, 8 September, the management of Drury Lane refused to stage *The Merchant of Venice*, offering instead *The Beggar's Opera*. The disappointment was palpable enough to elicit protest. We learn from the manuscript diary of the theatre's manager, Richard Cross, that the public clamour for the play was ignored:

Ye Naturalizing Bill having made some Noise against the Jews, some people call'd out for ye *Merch[an]t of Venice*, & a Letter was thrown upon ye Stage desiring that play instead of the Opera, but we took no Notice of it, some little hissing but it dy'd away.[20]

Cross draws the obvious connection between the 'noise' over the 'Naturalization Bill' and the 'hissing' in the theatre, but the call for Shylock was not heeded. There would be no performances of *The Merchant* at either Drury Lane or Covent Garden that autumn. Not until 6 April, months after the bill had been repealed and interest in the controversy had died down, was the play staged again in London. Some form of censorship, or self-censorship, was clearly at work.

A hint as to the source of this censorship can be found in an unusual manuscript note included in the Gabrielle Enthoven Theatre Collection in the Victoria and Albert Museum, placed in the Drury Lane file:

Last Sunday – 8th July. 1753. An Order came from the Lord Chamberlains Office to the Managers of both Theaters, forbidding them under the severst Penalty, to exhibit a certain scandalous Piece, highly injurious to our present happy Establishment, entitled the Merchant of Venice.[21]

Since 26 May marked the end of the 1753 theatre season, and the theatres remained closed until September, why would the Lord Chamberlain send such a note in July? And send it on a Sunday? As L. W. Conolly notes, it turns out that the facetious entry was actually copied from a newspaper column entitled 'News for One Hundred Years hence in the *Hebrew Journal*', which had first appeared in the *Craftsman*. This 'News' column offers a glimpse at life in a future England ruled by Jews, and includes a now Jewish Lord Chamberlain's warning not to stage Shakespeare's 'scandalous Piece, highly injurious to our present happy establishment, entitled, *The Merchant of Venice*'.[22] Clearly, in such a Judaized England, no place could be found for Shakespeare's anti-Jewish play. Capitalizing on how accurate this forecast for a hundred years in the future soon proved, the issue of the *London Evening Post* immediately following the reopening of the theatres in September made much of the suppression of Shakespeare's play: 'It is shrewdly suspected that one Part of the *Hebrew Journal* for One Hundred Years hence, will be fu'filled this Winter, by the Neutrality of both our Theatres, in not obliging the Town with the *Merchant of Venice*.'[23] Of particular interest here is the inference on the part of this pro-Tory newspaper that it was the 'neutrality' and self-

---

[19] *Cambridge Journal*, 25 August 1753, 1.

[20] As cited in Stone, *The London Stage*, part 4, vol. 1, p. 377.

[21] See L. W. Conolly's fine detective work in '*The Merchant of Venice* and the Jew Bill of 1753', *Shakespeare Quarterly*, 25 (1974): 125.

[22] As quoted from *The London Magazine, Or Gentleman's Monthly Intelligencer*, July 1753, p. 302, which reprinted the column from the *Craftsman*, 14 July 1753; no copies of the *Craftsman* survive.

[23] *London Evening Post*, 11 September 1753, p. 1.

censorship of the theatres, rather than bias towards the Jews or the Whigs that had initially supported the Jew Bill, which accounted for the suppression of *The Merchant* at this time. Apparently London's theatres were simply trying to stay out of the political crossfire.

Quite a few of the pamphlets and books published in 1753 illustrate how *The Merchant of Venice* served the ends of those opposed to Jewish naturalization. 'J. E., Gent[leman]', the author of *Some Considerations on the Naturalization of the Jews*, in the midst of a long diatribe against Jewish naturalization, turns to the matter of the Jews' 'exorbitant avarice'. The subject immediately put him 'in mind of a passage in the *Merchant of Venice*', and he begins by citing Shylock's hatred of Antonio: 'I hate him for he is a Christian.' He then proceeds to quote at length from *The Merchant of Venice*, including the lines from the trial scene where Shylock gloats over having been awarded a pound of Antonio's flesh. Shakespeare's play provides for him indisputable evidence of the danger to the English threatened by the Jews. After three uninterrupted pages of quotation from Shakespeare's play, he confidently asks his readers: 'And now, Englishman and country-man, judge ye, what advantage it can be to you to have these Jews naturalized! What can you get by them? They are all griping usurpers. And what can they get out of you, but your very Blood and Vitals? It can never be your temporal interest to see such persons made Englishmen.'[24]

Additional evidence of how Shakespeare's play was invoked in opposition to the Bill also appears in the anonymous *The Repository*, a collection which includes several allusions to Shylock. Thus, we find 'The Prophecies of Shylock', a passage in biblical prose addressed to the Jews about the English, which reads in part: 'Therefore, thus saith the Lord, I will destroy them in mine Anger, . . . give you their Land for a Possession', and 'establish you as their Rulers'.[25] Another allusion to Shakespeare's protagonist comes near the end of the

pamphlet, in a poetic dialogue between 'Shylock and Zimri'. Shylock's last verses like-wise turn on Jewish revenge against the Christians:

> How sweet are the Thoughts of that glorious
>   Scene,
> When none but a Jew over Jewry shall reign!
> No Ruler, nor King, over Jews shall have Place,
> But who is descended from David's great Race.
> From around all the Globe each Nation shall
>   meet
> And the Gentiles shall lick up the Dust of his
>   Feet.[26]

A similar invocation of Shylock appears during the election campaign in an attack on one of the supporters of the Jew Bill, Sir William Calvert. A note in *Gray's Inn Journal* describes an imaginary cabal of Jewish stock-jobbers and other 'Children of Israel' who support the candidate 'on account of his attachment to our cause in the last Parliament'. Predictably, one of the signers is 'Josephus Shylock'.[27] Shylock also appeared in contemporary political cartoons: one of those in circulation at this time – 'Shylock's Race from the Chequer Inn to Paris' – depicts the Jew Sampson 'Gideon's involve-ment in the 1753 lottery', and shows Shylock riding on a pig's back with the devil.[28] And according to John Smith's *Poetical Description* of

---

24 J. E., *Some Considerations on the Naturalization of the Jews*, pp. 17–21.

25 Anon., *The Repository: For the Use of the Christian Electors of Great-Britain; In Opposition to All Jews, Turks, and Infidels*, number 2 (London, 1753), p. 33.

26 *The Repository*, number 2, p. 51.

27 As cited in Perry, *Public Opinion*, p. 166, from *Gray's Inn Journal*, 27 April 1754.

28 For a reproduction of this cartoon see Isaiah Shachar, 'The Emergence of the Modern Pictorial Stereotype of "the Jews" in England', in *Studies in the Cultural Life of the Jews in England*. Folklore Research Center Studies 5, eds. Dov Noy and Issachar Ben-Ami (Jerusalem: Magnes Press, Hebrew University, 1975), p. 346. See too, Israel Salomons, 'Satirical and Political Prints on the Jews' Naturalization Bill, 1753', *Transactions of the Jewish Historical Society of England*, 7 (1912): 205–33.

Hogarth's xenophobic series of *Election* prints executed at this time, an impatient 'Shylock' – that 'Money-loving Soul' – appears in the service of a corrupt Tory candidate whose subsequent victory precipitates in the final print of the series a vision of a future Judaized England.[29]

Shylock also emerged as a ringleader in fantasies of Jewish attempts to take over England. In a column entitled 'The Thirty-fourth Chapter of Gen[esis]' that first appeared in the *London Evening Post*, Shylock is introduced along with real figures in the controversy, such as the Pelhams and Salvador, supplanting Jacob's sons in a parodic version of the rape of Dinah:

And it came to pass, in the Year Seventeen hundred sixty-three, that the Daughters of the Britons, which their Wives bear unto them, went into the Synagogues of the Jews, to see the Daughters of the Israelites.

And when the Sons of Gid—, of Shylock, of Men—, Fran—, and Salv—, saw them, they took them, and defiled them . . .

And Gid— and Shylock came to the Gate of the Change, and communed with the Men of their own Nation . . .

And unto Gid— and Shylock hearken'd all the Jews that went unto the Change; and they told the Pelh—tes, who ordered every male to be circumcised . . .

And it came to pass on the Third Day, whilst their Private Parts were sore, that the Jews took their Swords, and slew every Male of the Britons.[30]

Here, the biblical and Shakespearian narratives are conflated, with Shylock taking the role of father of the rapists, and then (since the story is reversed with the Jews as both violators and revengers), as one who first arranged for the Britons to be circumcised, then slain.

Recalling Shylock's threat to cut a pound of flesh from the part of Antonio that pleaseth him best, the anonymous author of the satiric tract, *Seasonable Remarks on the Act Lately Pass'd in Favour of the Jews*, offers Shakespeare's play as 'proof' that the Jews 'have not forgot their old

practices of circumcising, crucifying, etc.', reminding his readers of 'an instance on record with regard to a Jew at Venice', that 'seems to show that nothing less than our flesh as well as our money will satisfy their unchristian appetites'.[31] Again and again in the literature of 1753, the Jewish threat was imagined in terms of circumcision and emasculation.[32]

The pamphlets and newspaper column also register a shift in Shylock from stage character to one who steps out of the theatre into the daily lives of English men and women and whose influence extended out of the City into the countryside. In The *London Evening Post*, for example, an account appears of 'a Gentleman', who, 'travelling on the Uxbridge Road overtook a Farmer, who look'd very disconsolate; . . . he ask'd him the Matter; when the Farmer replied, Lord, Sir, I have had no Sleep for these three Nights, the Thoughts of the Jews ever running us distracting me; For we hear, in the Country, that the Jews will Circumcise all their Tenants; and my Landlord having ruined himself by Cards and Dice, is about selling my Farm, and several others in the Neighborhood, and we hear to a Jew. For last Week two strange-looking Men (one they called Shylock) came to look at mine.'[33] Further evidence that these examples offer not simply a Shylock abstracted and separate from *The Merchant of Venice*, but one very much

---

[29] John Smith, *A Poetical Description of Mr Hogarth's Election Prints* (London, 1759), p. 9. For a discussion of Hogarth's prints in relation to the Jew Bill, see Ronald Paulson, *Hogarth* (Cambridge: Lutterworth Press, 1993), vol. 3, pp. 166–73.

[30] *London Evening Post*, 18–20 October 1753.

[31] Anon., *Seasonable Remarks on the Act Lately Pass'd in Favour of the Jews*, pp. 27–8.

[32] See Roy S. Wolper, 'Circumcision as Polemic in the Jew Bill of 1753: The Cutter Cut?', *Eighteenth Century Life*, 7 (1982): 28–36. And see, for example, Anon., *The Christian's New Warning Piece: Or, a Full and True Acount of the Circumcision of Sir E. T. Bart.* (London, 1753).

[33] *London Evening Post*, 11–14 August, 1753.

based on the character of Shakespeare's play is apparent from allusions in the pamphlet literature to Lancelot Gobbo, Shylock's servant. One example appears in *Gray's Inn Journal*; following 'More News for One Hundred Years hence, in the Hebrew-Journal' there is an advertisement, dated August 1853 and signed by Lancelot Gobbo, addressed 'To the Gentlemen, Rabbi and Freeholders of the County of Sussex; Gobbo beg[s] the Favour of your Votes and Interest.'[34] The attack is clearly aimed at Prime Minister Henry Pelham, and the joke is straightforward enough: like Gobbo, Pelham is merely a servant – and a lowly one at that – of Jewish masters. Yet another reference to Shylock, this time as a 'Christian Imposter', immediately follows in the advertisement below the allusion to Gobbo: 'By Desire, At the Theater-Royal in Drury-Lane, on Sunday next, will be presented a COMEDY, called, I believe ... The Christian Impostor. The Part of Dr Tillotson to be performed by Rubens Shylock.'[35] Shylock's name continued to be invoked long after the furore over the Jew Bill had passed. By 1765 he had become not simply a character but an author, responsible for the second and third books of *The Jew Apologist*. Three years later a defeated Shylock would take up his pen again in defence of Jewish naturalization, this time offering *The Rabbi's Lamentation upon the Repeal of the Jew Act*.

It appears that in 1753 even the English theatres were not immune from expressions of anti-Jewish sentiment. In recounting the 'only instance of actual public unpleasantness towards Jews' that he found 'in any contemporary source' – a definition narrow enough to exclude attacks against itinerant Jewish peddlers, one of whom was slain – Thomas Perry quotes from the following account in the *London Evening Post*: 'After the second musick, some Jewish ladies and gentlemen were noticed in one of the balconies, when the cry immediately began, *No Jews, out with them, circumcise them*, &c. &c. and was followed with showers of apples, &c. with

great rudeness, till the company were obliged to leave their seats; but upon remonstrance from a gentleman that sat next to them, to some others in the pit, a loud clap ensued, the company were reinstated, and met with no other molestation.'[36] Why members of the audience would call for the circumcision of Jewish men – or for that matter of Jewish women – is not entirely clear. The incident perhaps cast further light on why London's theatre managers were loathe to stage *The Merchant of Venice* or any other plays about Jews at this time.

The popular pressure to see Shylock on-stage and the possibilities of capitalizing on popular interest in the Jew Bill, while resisted in London, did not extend to provincial touring, where self-censorship and a desire to please Whig patrons were not as strong. While standard stage histories of *The Merchant of Venice* and of English provincial touring companies offer no extant records of performances of the play outside London in 1753, I was fortunate to stumble upon an account of just such a touring production, probably staged in late spring or summer of that year, perhaps in the north of England, or perhaps in Edinburgh. The sole evidence of this production survives in John Cunningham's *Poems* (1766). Cunningham was an actor and poet who also penned occasional prologues.[37] Included in his collected verse is one such occasional piece, composed by Cunningham at the age of twenty-four: 'A Prologue, Spoke by Mrs G——, in an itinerant Company, on reviving the MERCHANT of VENICE, at the

---

34 *Gray's Inn Journal*, 6 October 1753, p. 12.
35 *Gray's Inn Journal*, 6 October 1753, p. 12.
36 As cited in Perry, *Public Opinion*, pp. 75–6.
37 According to the *Dictionary of National Biography*, Cunningham, after 'travelling about a great deal as a strolling actor ... eventually appeared at Edinburgh, where he became a great favourite with the manager, Mr Digges, and the leading lady, Mrs George Anne Bellamy, and wrote many occasional prologues for them'.

Time of the Bill passing for naturalizing the Jews.'

We have no other record of the performance or performances. There is little doubt that 'Mrs G—' is Mrs George Anne Bellamy, a leading actress of the 1750s and a friend of Cunningham's. We know from the entries recorded in *The London Stage* that she was in London from February 1753 until at least 7 May, where she played the leading roles in *Lady Jane Gray*, *The rothers*, *Venice Preserved*, *Othello*, *The Orphan* and *Macbeth*, all at Drury Lane. She only resumed playing in London, this time for Rich's company at Covent Garden, some time in September or October 1753. In sum, one of the stars of the London theatre apparently went on tour some time between late May and September, at the height of the uproar over the Jew Bill. Presumably, she played the part of Portia, and as befitted the leading performer, recited the twenty-line Prologue that Cunningham wrote for the occasion:

'Twixt the sons of the stage, without pensions
    or places,
And the vagabond Jews, are some similar cases;
Since time out of mind, or they're wrong'd
    much by slander,
Both lawless, alike, have been sentenc'd to
    wander;
Then faith 'tis full time we appeal to the nation,
To be join'd in this bill for na-tu-ra-li-za-ti-on;
Lord, that word's so uncouth! – 'tis so irksome
    to speak it!
But 'tis Hebrew, I believe, and that taste, as I
    take it.
Well – now to the point – I'm sent here with
    commission,
To present this fair circle our humble petition:
But conscious what hopes we should have of
    succeeding,
Without (as they phrase it) sufficiently bleeding;
And convinc'd we've no funds, nor old gold we
    can rake up,
Like our good brothers – Abraham, Isaac, and
    Jacob;
We must frankly confess we have nought to
    present ye,

But Shakespear's old sterling – play let it
    content ye.
Old Shylock, the Jew, whom we mean to
    restore ye,
Was naturaliz'd oft by your fathers before ye;
Then take him to-night to your kindest
    compassion,
For to countenance Jews is the pink of the
    fashion.[3]

This is an unusually rich document, one that powerfully connects the latent anxieties circulating through Shakespeare's play with the cultural dread produced by the Jew Bill. The Prologue also partakes of the self-contradiction characteristic of many of the polemical pamphlets, not least of all in the itinerant actors' simultaneous denigration of and identification with Jews in the opening lines. The legal status first assigned to wandering players in the late-sixteenth century – vagabonds – is here applied, as elsewhere in the pamphlet literature of 1753, to the wandering Jews as well. In the witty tone that pervades the entire Prologue, Mrs Bellamy protests that the similarity with the Jews stops there: the actors hope to win audience approval without having to be circumcised, that is, '(as they phrase it) sufficiently bleeding'.

In the most telling lines of the Prologue, Mrs Bellamy recites how 'Old Shylock, the Jew, whom we mean to restore ye, Was naturaliz'd oft by your fathers before ye.' A remarkable conflation of naturalization and conversion takes place here: for in Shakespeare's original, Shylock is not naturalized, after all, but threatened with conversion to Christianity. Shakespeare's play is reimagined here as one that depicts a legal and political transformation rather than a religious one, a change not all that surprising in an eighteenth-century England in which national and racial affiliations were gradually superseding theological ones. We are nonetheless left with the paradox that despite the fact that he has been 'naturaliz'd oft',

---

[3] John Cunningham, *Poems, Chiefly Pastoral* (London, 1766), pp. 165–6.

Shylock's Jewishness prevents him from being fully English (even as baptism could not fully wash away his essential Jewishness). Cunningham's Prologue, no less than the Duke of Bedford's comparison of Jews and Blacks, calls into question current theories of nationalism that ignore just how racialized nationalism was in eighteenth-century England, a fact that may explain why cultural historians continue to pass over this popular controversy in silence, a silence that extends to the work of recent scholars intent on identifying Shakespeare's place in the formation of British identity.[39]

This story does not end in 1753, for Shakespeare continues to be invoked by those who need to protect Englishness from the potentially contaminating influence of Jewishness. The taboo over dealing with this subject was recently broken by Elliott Baker in his book *Bardolatry*, where in a chapter entitled 'Was Shakespeare Jewish?' Baker describes an international conspiracy in which Jewish scholars have taken over the Shakespeare business and now dare to trespass on the very 'banks of the Avon'. 'Greenblatt and Levi', he laments, was 'once a good masthead for a clothing store.' He even seizes on Peter Levi's self-identification as 'British as opposed to English' as confirmation that this Jewish scholar's 'devotion to Shakespeare' is 'that of an outsider seeking identification with the core of Englishness'.[40] Baker's message is clear: this latest Jewish invasion must be exposed and resisted. It should come as no surprise that precisely the kind of arguments which first circulated in the Jew Bill debate – the inscrutability of the scheming Jews, anxiety over a Jewish presence on hallowed English ground, the idea that Jews could control English religion (this is 'bardolatry' after all), and the identification of Shakespeare with Englishness itself – form the basis of Baker's polemic. Although the irony may be lost on Baker, his book serves to confirm that the Jew Bill, along with Garrick's Jubilee, was instrumental in the creation of a Shakespeare who from that time on would be bound up with fantasies of social exclusion and cultural longing.

[39] I'm thinking in particular of Linda Colley's influential work, which invites us to look abroad to France to discover Britain's Other rather than to the dark racial and religious currents circulating around marginal groups like England's Jews (*Britons: Forging the Nation 1707–1837* (New Haven and London: Yale University Press, 1992). For an important exception, see Frank Felsenstein, *Anti-Semitic Stereotypes: A Paradigm of Otherness in English Popular Culture, 1660–1830* (Baltimore: The Johns Hopkins University Press, 1995), published as this article was going to press. See too, my forthcoming *Shakespeare and the Jews* (New York: Columbia University Press, 1996). For a critique of class-based theories of nationalism that occlude race, see David Theo Goldberg, *Racist Culture: Philosophy and the Politics of Meaning* (Oxford: Blackwell, 1993), esp. pp. 78–80.
[40] Baker, *Bardolatry* (London: Holofernes, 1992), pp. 30–3.

WILHELM S AND SHYLOCK

LAURENCE LERNER

Who is the mysterious dramatist who has shot to world-wide fame in our century because of his political relevance? His plays were performed before the incipiently fascist public in France and the actually fascist public in Germany during the 1930s, and he was acclaimed for his vigorous portrayal of the dangers of mob rule and the need for strong leadership, as well as for his awareness of the ineradicable enmity between Christian generosity and the Jewish fixation on money. At some point during the war he appears to have moved to England, since he wrote a film script for Laurence Olivier depicting the courage and resourcefulness of the English when fighting on the continent, and was much praised for his patriotism. After the war, his series of plays on English history showed the desirability of hereditary monarchy and the dangers of civil war; but after the student uprisings of 1968 he appears to have treated revolution much more sympathetically. His taste for a deliberately antiquated style and archaic diction lends (paradoxically) a sharpness to his critique of contemporary politics; his passion for anonymity and seclusion has kept biographers guessing, and has fascinated the public; and his obvious wanderlust has enabled him to exert an influence in every major country in the world.

There is some uncertainty even about his name: it has come to us in various spellings, and there are even theories that this was not his name at all, but that of an actor whom the dramatist used to disguise his true identity.

Since in this essay I intend to discuss the anti-Semitic play he wrote when in Nazi Germany, I shall use the German form of his given name, and avoid all orthographical controversy by abbreviating his surname: I shall call him Wilhelm S. Although we cannot be sure that he was actually German, there is no doubt about the great success he enjoyed there. He was congratulated for his awareness of Nordic profundity, and for the Nordic traits in the characterization of Hamlet: the tendency to muse about life and its meaning, and the melancholy with which he responds to the death of his father and the marriage of his mother. One critic saw these Nordic traits as interacting with other, more Latinate ('westisch') traits in Hamlet, and attributed the mixture to a corresponding interaction in the dramatist himself. Since biographical information about S is so hard to come by, this claim can hardly be tested.[1]

For a valuable bibliography of discussions of S in Germany in the 1930s, see Ruth Freifrau von Ledebuhr, 'Der deutsche Geist und S: Anmerkungen zur S-Rezeption 1933–45' in *Wissenschaft und Nazionalsozialismus* (Herausgeber: R. Geissler and W. Popp, 1988). I have also used Werner Habicht, 'S and Theatre Politics in the Third Reich', in *The Play out of Context*, ed. Scolnicov and Holland (1989); and *S im dritten Reich* by Georg Zähringer (Magisterarbeit: Universität München, 1988).

[1] Alex Niederstenbruch, 'Einige Gedanken zur rassischen Betrachtung von S's Hamlet', *Zeitschrift für neusprachlichen Unterricht* 41 (1942): 31–3. This and all other German passages are translated by me.

But the play which particularly led Nazi Germany to congratulate S for his understanding of racial psychology was *The Merchant of Venice*, in which he rewrote the old folk-tale of the Jew who lent three thousand ducats to a Christian merchant in return for a 'merry bond' by which, if the money was not repaid in time, he would be entitled to a pound of the debtor's flesh. The grotesque power of this anti-Semitic story obviously appealed to the German audience because of its brilliant portrayal of the racial characteristics of the Eastern Jew, and the contrast with the nobility of the Christian merchant, 'the royal merchant who loved money not for its own sake but in order to help his friends, who in order to put it in the service of life is willing to renounce everything. He keeps his word and is ready to carry it out to the bitter end.'[2]

That the play contains one apparently philo-semitic speech, the well-known self-defence 'Hath not a Jew eyes . . .', need not worry us: the Nordic reader, who shares S's insights into racial psychology, will not err in reading the play, but will realize that this torrent of words is judged and refuted by Antonio, who expresses the poet's own opinion in his speech in the trial scene asserting that reasoning with the Jew is as futile as trying to alter nature:

> You may as well do anything most hard
> As seek to soften that – than which what's
>   harder? –
> His Jewish heart.   (4.1.77–9)

We know today, in the light of racial biology, that Shylock is mistaken in his claim that a Jew is human like the rest of us (or them), since 'der Jude eben rassenbiologisch ein anderer, artfremder Mensch für uns ist': that is, he is 'biologically distinct' and so alienated from us – a point made by the Duke when he speaks of 'the difference of our spirit'.[3]

There is an ideological as well as a racial dimension to the contrast between Shylock and the Christians, which can be interestingly formulated as that between justice and the rule of law:

Rationalism and technical formalism are constitutive elements of every modern system of law. S's parody is not quite directed at these, but should be seen rather as an attack on that ideology of the rule (or the reliability) of law which submits so fully to these technical elements in law that it allows the just decision to yield without struggle to the calculable one. It justifies itself by claiming that it is more important to put an end to struggle than to put a just end to it; that the existence of a legal system is more important than its justice; and that the rule of law has as its prime duty the bringing about of peace. According to this concept (which, I add in parenthesis, is very like the rules by which the police work in our society) peace depends on security and is independent of justice. One only needs to attend to the meaning of these words in terms of foreign politics and national rights to realise what view of law is here in question: it is that of western positivism, the politics of the status-quo, or bourgeois security . . . in the legal consciousness of the Old Testament and of Jewry the element of security is of special importance. In the figure of Shylock this connexion is vividly expressed.[4]

This seems a very perceptive reading of *The Merchant of Venice*: precisely this contrast is dealt with in the exchange between Bassanio and 'Balthazar', in which Bassanio begs:

> Wrest once the law to your authority.
> To do a great right, do a little wrong,
> And curb this cruel devil of his will. (4.1.212–14)

– and Portia, as Balthazar, replies:

> It must not be. There is no power in Venice
> Can alter a decree establishèd:
> 'Twill be recorded for a precedent,
> And many an error by the same example
> Will rush into the state. It cannot be.   (4.1.215–19)

---

[2] Dr Karl Pempelfort, 'Er besteht auf seinem Schein', *Königsberger Tageblatt*, 31 March 1935; reprinted in Joseph Wulf, *Theater und Film im dritten Reich* (1964) p. 257.

[3] Gregor Schwartz-Bostunitsch, 'Shylock und wir', *Der Weltkampf*, 17 (1940): 17.

[4] Wilhelm Grewe, 'Shylock, oder die Parodie der Rechtssicherheit', *Deutsche Volkstum*, 18 (1936): 77–9.

– asserting in other words that the most important thing in law is its reliability, that the rule of law must not be overturned in the interests of justice ('a great right') because – the classic objection of the legalist – it would set a precedent. Shylock too asserted the same contrast:

> The pound of flesh which I demand of him
> Is dearly bought. 'Tis mine, and I will have it.
> If you deny me, fie upon your law:
> There is no force in the decree of Venice.
>
> (4.1.98–101)

That is to say, it is not the task of the court to pass judgement on the law, but to enforce it. And Shylock sees too that this conception of law is the basis of property: that is why he draws the parallel with slavery. His sarcastic suggestion about the 'purchased slaves' – 'Let them be free, marry them to your heirs' – could be paraphrased (if we remove the sarcasm) as 'let justice override legality', and he correctly indicates that this is out of the question by giving the conventional reply: 'The slaves are ours.' Is it not therefore correct to describe Shylock's view of law as positivist, as based on bourgeois security and the status quo?

Even the love story of S's play can be given a racial interpretation. The annual lecture for 1937 to the German Association for the study of Wilhelm S (yes, he was sufficiently celebrated to have his own Association) was delivered by a Eugenicist, 'someone who has inquired what conception of love and marriage will be suitable or necessary to improve the stock of a people, someone who has further inquired what kind of girls and women the young men of a people ought to incline to in order to beget a more effective, more handsome and nobler posterity'. The lecturer concluded that Portia was just the ticket: she shows the needed 'mixture of reserve, strong feeling and clarity of mind, along with a talent for the masterful assurance that belongs to an inherently aristocratic being. We cannot doubt that she will develop into a truly Germanic mistress of the house (Hausherrin germanischer Prägung).'[5]

It is hard to believe, after all this, that *The Merchant of Venice* has also been performed in Israel (though we must add that it has not always been popular there). Did the Israelis not realize what they were doing, when they put on this anti-Semitic play before their own people? Or were they so committed to a non-political aestheticism that they allowed the dramatic genius of S to override his ideology?

Particularly interesting is the production in 1936, when Israel was still Palestine, because after it took place the theatre organized a public debate, in which author, theatre and director were put on trial, accused of producing 'a play in which [they] involved an anti-Jewish theme without being informed enough to treat the subject'.[6]

I can find no evidence that Wilhelm S, world traveller though he has since become, came to Palestine for this 'trial', so he was no doubt represented by proxy. Play and production were attacked both for what they said and for what they did not say: for attributing to Shylock a spirit of revenge wholly alien to the Jews, 'in whom an ancient spiritual culture is coupled with the long experience of humiliation and suffering', and for not admitting that the responsibility for turning Jews into usurers rested with Christian society, 'because you never let us survive in any other way: you have turned us into usurers and profiteers'. I shall return shortly to this objection.

But first I wish to perform a thought-experiment. Let us imagine that so little is known about S not because he has kept himself hidden but because he lived a long time ago; that he did not write *The Merchant of Venice* as an act of homage to Nazi ideology, but that it was written in a quite different time and place,

---

[5] Hans F. K. Günther, 'S's Mädchen und Frauen' (Vortrag vor der deutschen S-Gesellschaft), *S-Jahrbuch*, 75 (1937): 85, 104.

[6] Ya'akov Fikhman, quoted in Avraham Oz, 'Transformations of Authenticity', *S-Jahrbuch* (1983): 169.

and was appropriated by the Nazis. What difference would this make? Obviously it would introduce a historical factor. It would enable us to ask whether the Nazi interpreters were distorting the play to fit their own ideology, or whether the distant age in which S wrote (say three or four centuries ago) shared their anti-Semitic assumption.

And instead of being impressed with the enterprise shown by S in writing in so many countries and so many different political situations, we shall now say that it was the various countries and societies that were enterprising, helping themselves to his plays and interpreting them as they wished or felt compelled to. We shall then find ourselves asking whether interpreting an old play is fundamentally different from writing a new one. To some the difference will seem obvious; but to some schools of criticism now flourishing (represented, say, by Stanley Fish or Terence Hawkes) there will be no significant difference: for if the meaning of a text is constituted entirely by an interpretive community, if we can attribute no qualities to the text itself but only to the way it is read, then there can be no appeal to an author living in the past, outside of the community of readers. This view is now so influential that it is worth pausing to discuss it, since it is central to my thought experiment.

I choose Terence Hawkes as the representative of this position, which he sets forth with great vigour in *That Shakespeherian Rag* and *Meaning by Shakespeare*. The two books maintain that 'great' works of art have 'no claim to existence "in themselves"', and that we should study the ways in which they have been 'worked upon . . . as part of the struggle for cultural meaning'.[7] As an example of how he applies his claim that 'meaning is made rather than found' we can look at his discussion of Nedar, a character who is mentioned but does not appear in *A Midsummer Night's Dream* (Helena is Nedar's daughter). The witty changes that Hawkes rings on Nedar's name culminate in the claim that she should be regarded as a woman, Helena's mother rather than her father, 'not because Nedar necessarily *is* female, but because, in twentieth-century terms, the suggestion that she could be unseats a number of presuppositions investing the play, and demonstrates an indeterminacy, an undecidability, that is a feature of all texts'.[8]

Now since we do not know whether Nedar is male or female (the phrase 'old Nedar's daughter' allows, as Hawkes rightly points out, either meaning) the play can be said to license the claim that she is female, and the fact that previous commentators have seen 'her' as male certainly confirms the view that we have here 'a struggle for cultural meaning'. But that kind of indeterminacy cannot possibly be seen as 'a feature of all texts'. The existence of some indeterminate elements does not show that all elements are indeterminate, it rather reminds us how determinate others are. To claim that 'in twentieth-century terms' Shylock should be turned into a woman would raise very different issues – and much more resistance.

The twentieth-century issue I am here concerned with, however, is not gender but prejudice. Wilhelm S offers us an anti-Semitic *Merchant of Venice*, and we, reacting like good liberals, are upset by it. My 'thought experiment' was a way of asking how important is the difference between writing an anti-Semitic play, and offering an anti-Semitic interpretation of a play written in 1597. According to the theory that meaning is made rather than found, there can be no difference; and in that case, treating *The Merchant of Venice* as if it was written by Wilhelm S in Nazi Germany is not the (ingenious or tiresome) gimmick which my readers have no doubt assumed it to be, but indistinguishable from the normal study of Shakespeare.

It will now be clear that I believe they *are*

---

[7] Terence Hawkes, *That Shakespeherian Rag: Essays on a Critical Process* (London 1986), p. 123.
[8] Hawkes, *Meaning by Shakespeare* (London and New York 1992), p. 39.

distinguishable, and appealing to history is the obvious way to distinguish them. But, as we are all aware nowadays, to appeal to the thought system of sixteenth-century England as a guide to correct understanding of S's plays soon raises problems. The appeal to history can alter our reading of a text only if some kind of direct access to the past is possible; if it produces the same kind of arguments as already rage about the plays, we may find ourselves reasoning in a circle.

And if we do appeal to history we shall soon find that German critics in the 1930s anticipated us, and were prepared to defend *their* reading on historical grounds:

The Merchant of Venice is not the tragedy of Shylock, as was believed by the sentimental sympathy of the 19th Century, which, closely related to semitic ways of thinking, thought that higher justice sided with the Jew, downtrodden and spat upon, and wanted to reopen the trial to Shylock and decide it in favour of the enemy of the Christians. The play begins with Antonio's puzzling and unhealthy melancholy, and ends in complete serenity. The concluding scene in Belmont follows consistently from the preceding struggles and decisions, as the Empire is the consequence of the return of the Jews to the Church. The so-called Jewish tragedy is an enchanting comedy of incomparable political power and beauty, transfigured by theology. The prominent use of music should be explained by the fact that great music is to be seen as part of a great political system. The final scene is not to be understood as lyrical in the way bourgeois moonlight romanticism is lyrical, but in its connexion with heavenly matters and eternal glory, with peace as the final goal of all politics in accordance with essential human nature, with the libera securitas et secura tranquillitas, the union of nature and grace symbolised by the wedding of Portia and Bassanio, the transfiguration of the body and the harmony of blessed spirits.[9]

Clemens Lang here is (almost) impeccably historical. He abuses the sentimental sympathy of the nineteenth century in a way that has been a commonplace since Irving Babbitt and T. S. Eliot, adding, however, one detail that sticks out like a sore thumb: the assertion that this

sentimentality is closely related to a Jewish way of thinking ('semitische Geisteart'). If, as his hostile critics have sometimes suggested, Eliot would have liked to say that too, at least he never did; but it is not difficult to guess where Lang got the idea. The view that *The Merchant of Venice* is the tragedy of Shylock was put forward by Heine in *Shakespeares Mädchen und Frauen* in a memorable and eloquent paragraph:

When I saw this play produced in Drury Lane, there was a beautiful pale British woman standing behind me in the box, who wept copiously at the end of the fourth act, and cried out several times 'The poor man is wronged!' [The exclamation is in English in the original]. She had a face of the noblest Grecian profile, and her eyes were large and black. I have never been able to forget them, those large black eyes which wept over Shylock!

And when I think about those tears, I have to count *The Merchant of Venice* among the tragedies, although the framework of the play is decorated with the liveliest masques, images of satyrs and cupids, and although the poet actually wanted to give us a comedy . . .[10]

Even though Heine, in an elegant touch, is careful to attribute the exclamation to a pale and beautiful young woman 'vom edelsten griechischen Schnitt', the conclusion that the play is the tragedy of Shylock belongs to Heine himself, and to Clemens Lang, writing in the 1930s, it is an example of the 'semitische Geistesart'. Of course Lang has generalized wildly in attributing not just this interpretation of *The Merchant of Venice* but the whole of the 'sentimentalisches Mitleid des neunzehnten Jahrhunderts' to the Jewish way of thinking; and each of the passages I have quoted from the Nazi critics contains a similar touch of wanton anti-Semitic generalization that can be removed

---

[9] Clemens Lang, 'S's Kaufmann von Venedig – die Tragödie des Juden Shylock', *Deutsches Volkstum* (1933): 962–5.

[10] Heinrich Heine, 'S's Mädchen und Frauen' (1838), *Sämtliche Werke* (Winkler Verlag, München, 1972), vol. 3, p. 652.

with greater or less damage to the main argument. In the case of Günther's lecture, for instance, the restatement of the wedding celebrations that normally end a romantic comedy in terms of eugenics is merely quaint to the Shakespeare critic, but alarmingly important to the historian of Nazism. In the case of Lang, the damage done by removing the anti-Semitic digression is negligible, and his main argument is an account of Renaissance political thinking that the majority of historical scholars would find quite acceptable, even perceptive. 'Shakespeare carries on tiptoe his burden of Renaissance thought', says Philip Brockbank of this play,[11] and though Lang's formulation ('Die angebliche jüdische Tragödie ist eine bezaubernde Komödie von unvergleichlicher politischer Kraft und theologisch verlkärter Schönheit') may be less elegant, his point is essentially the same. The analogy with music (seeing both human society and God's universe as a harmony), and the claim that the play is a romantic comedy whose conclusion is meant to emerge from the resolution of earlier conflicts: all this is what any responsible literary historian would tell us. S is a playwright who loves to build wholes out of contrasting and interrelating parts, and Heine's humane and sympathetic interpretation would make nonsense of the whole of the last act: to attribute a sour taste to the serene ending of this enchanting comedy would be merely perverse.

Does this mean that the W S of our thought experiment, who wrote 400 years ago, clearly wrote an anti-Semitic play? If we can establish that Elizabethan society was anti-Semitic, then since the play is by an Elizabethan it too must be anti-Semitic. That is precisely the kind of simplistic argument that the New Historicism has set out to subvert. If historical scholarship is a matter of uncovering the tensions and contradictions of past societies, then literary history must expect to find these tensions reproduced in the texts produced by those societies. And even if we claim to find in the homilies and sermons of Renaissance England a clear attempt

to pin down these shifting contradictions in unambiguous assertions, we can still say (with the New Historicism) that to read such homilies in depth is to see that the pinning down does not ever quite succeed, or (with the more traditional literary critic) that whatever may happen in sermons, drama does not pin down, and to reduce *The Merchant of Venice* (or any other play by W S) to a homily is to ignore what makes it a great play, even what makes it a play.

I return now to the 'trial' of the play after it was produced in Palestine in 1936. The prosecution charged that the play failed to admit that the responsibility for turning Jews into usurers rested with Christian society 'because you never let us survive in any other way: you have turned us into usurers and profiteers'. This is the most interesting form of the indictment I have come across, since it raises the question of what a play can and cannot say. Certainly there is no awareness *in Shylock* that Christian society is responsible for forcing him into a degrading profession; on the contrary, he seems to embrace it with gusto, citing his Old Testament precedents for 'thrift' with a chuckle of pleasure:

> When Jacob grazed his uncle Laban's sheep –
> This Jacob from our holy Abram was,
> As his wise mother wrought in his behalf,
> The third possessor; ay, he was the third –
>
> (1.3.70–3)

Shylock is pleased both at his own knowledge of Scripture and at the way it confirms him in his profession; and he then proceeds to tell a story that demonstrates Jacob's thrift and shrewdness, concluding, in reply to Antonio's objection (a medieval commonplace) 'Is your gold and silver ewes and rams?', with a further chuckle at his own financial acumen: 'I cannot tell, I make it breed as fast.' Shylock, clearly, is a moneylender to the core.

---

[11] Philip Brockbank, 'S and the Fashion of these Times', *Shakespeare Survey 16* (1963), p. 40.

But is that incompatible with the view that society is responsible? Once the Jews have been driven into money-lending, there is no reason why they shouldn't do it well, and even enjoy doing it. Awareness of the social explanation does not need to be part of the consciousness of the individual money-lender.

Does it then need to be part of the consciousness of the play? That is trickier. Certainly it does not need to be explicitly said in the play: for that purpose we would need a chorus, or a perceptive observer among the characters who would point out (cynically or sorrowfully or even appreciatively) the mechanisms in Venetian society that were keeping Shylock down. That would be one kind of play, but not the only kind, and not the kind that S writes.

But are there not subtler ways of conveying such awareness? One suggestion that has often been popular with directors and critics is that Shylock really meant the bond to be a merry one, and was only goaded into revenge by his daughter's elopement. Tyrone Guthrie, who also (in 1959) produced the play in Israel, held this view:

It is my view that Shakespeare's portrait is not anti-semitic, that the pound of flesh wager was entered upon as a jest, and only turns to vengeance after Shylock has been robbed and his daughter abducted by young Venetians of Antonio's set.[12]

This is attractive, not only to liberal critics but also to directors, since it suggests a tableau that was introduced notably by Henry Irving in his Lyceum production, and has often been repeated, the return of Shylock at the end of Act 2 Scene 6 to find the house empty, his daughter gone, and (perhaps) the shutters flapping in mockery.[13] But attractive as it is, this interpretation seems refuted by the text for two reasons: first, that Shylock's aside on his first appearance ('I hate him for he is a Christian') suggests that the bitter hostility to Antonio was there from the beginning, and second that Jessica tells us quite explicitly 'When I was with him' (that is, before the elopement)

> I have heard him swear
> To Tubal and to Cush, his countrymen,
> That he would rather have Antonio's flesh
> Than twenty times the value of the sum . . .
> (3.2.282–5)

Yet although this disposes of Guthrie's reading, it does contain a tiny verbal detail that reveals a good deal about how Venetian society treated Shylock: that is Jessica's use of 'his'. Tubal and Cush were, after all, her countrymen too, but she has now identified herself completely with the Christian shutting out of Shylock. The ease with which Jessica changes sides, like her stealing of his ring and selling it for a monkey, aligns her with Christian exclusiveness and frivolity, and if we had pointed it out to Heine's 'schöne blasse Brittin' it would surely have strengthened her feeling that the poor man is wronged.

Not of course that we need hunt for such tiny verbal details in order to see how Venetian society excluded Shylock. It mocked him, cruelly and grossly: most famously in the parody by Solanio and Salerio of his grief when his daughter has run away:

> I never heard a passion so confused,
> So strange, outrageous, and so variable
> As the dog Jew did utter in the streets.
> 'My daughter! O, my ducats! O, my daughter!
> Fled with a Christian! O, my Christian ducats!
> A sealèd bag, two sealèd bags of ducats,
> Of double ducats, stol'n from me by my
> daughter!' (2.8.12–18)

Mockery as crude as this would goad anyone to wanting his pound of flesh. It does not matter that Shylock doesn't hear this speech, just as it doesn't matter that he doesn't hear his daughter say 'his countrymen': he must have

---

[12] Tyrone Guthrie, *In Various Directions: A View of Theatre* (1965); quoted by Oz, 'Transformations of Authenticity', p. 172.

[13] John Gross, *Shylock: Four Hundred Years in the Life of a Legend* (London, 1992), discusses this, amid much else of relevance to the present essay.

caught that tone in her voice when she was still with him, and he must have heard mockery like Solanio's a hundred times ('Many a time and oft/On the Rialto you have rated me'). This is a glimpse of the endemic anti-Semitism of the Venetians, and can easily be interpreted as an explanation for Shylock's lodged hate and certain loathing of Antonio.

But it is also a comic speech, which must have been thoroughly enjoyed by the original audience. The alliteration of ducats and daughter is brilliant: the two losses are, to him, equivalent, and the equivalence is reproduced in the signifiers. The same effect recurs in more complex form in 'double ducats', where the relation between form and meaning becomes a kind of tautology: money is twice as important as people realize, and to express this we use both the word 'double', and an act of doubling. The speech is a perfect mimesis of the fury of the comic villain whose thoughts are fixated on money.

Mimesis? Or caricature? A representation of the crude greed of the Jewish usurer, or of the crudity with which the Venetians perceive him? Is the speech anti-Semitic, or a representation of anti-Semitism? Again, this raises the question of what dramatic representation can and cannot do. The question whether the play shows any awareness of the social explanation for Shylock's greed is unanswerable, because plays do not show that kind of awareness directly. A play is a representation of social behaviour, not an explanation of it. Of course representation can imply explanation (ideology, as the point might now be put, is unavoidable), but not in any simple, monocausal fashion: explanation results from the interaction between play and audience, and the audience will decide whether anti-Semitism is being expressed or caricatured – not because all meaning is indeterminate, but because audiences fit meaning into an ideological framework. The original audience may have identified with Solanio and roared with delight – both original audiences, Shakespeare's Elizabethans and Wilhelm S's Nazis. But a different audience (you and I, reader) will laugh uneasily, or feel indignant, or praise the author for his exposure of Solanio's crude mockery. And audiences are not uniform: there could have been someone in 1597, and there almost certainly was someone in 1939, who had a Jewish friend, or for any reason felt uneasy about the ideological demands made on him, who did not laugh either. It is even possible that Shakespeare did not laugh.

PILGRIMS OF GRACE: *HENRY IV* HISTORICIZED

TOM McALINDON

PAST AND PRESENT

R. G. Collingwood once remarked that all historical writing is a selective process governed by a sense of contemporary relevance.[1] Most historical critics who have sought to interpret Shakespeare's interpretation of the past in *1* and *2 Henry IV* seem to have been in agreement with this view. There has, however, been remarkable divergence among both recent and not-so-recent historicists on how the play (I shall use the singular term for convenience's sake) connects with sixteenth-century practice and ideas; on how, in other words, we should define the context (or larger 'text') which makes most sense of its conceptual orientation. E. M. W. Tillyard tied the play to the Tudor, providentialist philosophy of history focused on the Wars of the Roses and the birth of the Tudor dynasty. But he saw in it nothing more specific to sixteenth-century political experience than a large, approving picture of Elizabethan England, rendered vivid by its social and topographical detail. Like Tillyard, Lily B. Campbell read the play as an uncomplicated endorsement of Tudor political orthodoxy; she was much concerned, however, to establish a central analogy with the Northern Rebellion of 1569–70 (an idea first advanced by Richard Simpson in 1874), as well as a number of politically significant parallels between some of the *dramatis personae* and contemporary individuals.[2]

The two most self-consciously historicist among recent critics of *Henry IV* have constructed interpretative frameworks which also differ strikingly from each other. For Stephen Greenblatt, the dynastic conflict between the houses of Lancaster and York in fifteenth-century England makes most sense when seen in relation to the treacherous methods used by the Elizabethan ruling classes in securing control over the trusting natives of Virginia and the vagabonds and thieves of the domestic underworld. Graham Holderness shares Greenblatt's preoccupation with power, domination, and class conflict as the key to social and political history, but denies this play any important connection with sixteenth-century politics; instead, he sees in it a genuinely historicist concentration on the contradictions of fifteenth-century feudalism.[3]

---

1 *The Idea of History* (Oxford, 1961), p. xi; cited (approvingly) in Paul Q. Hirst, *Marxism and Historical Writing* (1985), p. 44.

2 Tillyard, *Shakespeare's History Plays* (1944); Campbell, *Shakespeare's Histories: Mirrors of Elizabethan Policy* (San Marino, California, 1947); Richard Simpson, 'The Political Use of the Stage in Shakespeare's Time', *New Shakspere Society Publications*, series 1, no. 2, part 2 (1875): 371–95. Simpson's claim was casually anticipated by Sir Cuthbert Sharpe in his *Memorials of the Rebellion of 1569* (1840), p. 336.

3 Greenblatt, 'Invisible Bullets: Renaissance Authority and Its Subversion, *Henry IV* and *Henry V*', in *Political Shakespeare: New Essays in Cultural Materialism*, ed. Jonathan Dollimore and Alan Sinfield (Manchester, 1985), pp. 17–47; Holderness, *Shakespeare Recycled: the Making of Historical Drama* (1992).

The limitation of Tillyard's history-of-ideas approach is not just that it constructed a monolithic Elizabethan world-picture, but that it seems to have distracted his attention from the material realities of sixteenth-century political history. So too the interpretative frameworks created by Greenblatt and Holderness, by excluding the high politics of Tudor England, seem initially implausible and leave an impression of contextual mislocation. Campbell's approach (utilized by Alice-Lyle Scoufos in her study of the Falstaff-Oldcastle problem),[4] although unduly speculative in its pursuit of topical allusions, and insensitive to Shakespeare's political scepticism, seems to me to have pointed in a direction which has not been adequately explored. For as I hope to show, *Henry IV* is shaped by certain patterns of thought, action, and characterization which suggest deep affinities between Henry's reign and the religio-political and cultural experiences of sixteenth-century England. Shakespeare was here viewing the rule of Henry and the rise of Hal through the lens of a century when, in one complex process, the English Reformation was coercively established and the crown finally centralized (and 'southernized') power by subduing the Catholic leaders of the North; and when, too, the Renaissance ideals of civility were enthusiastically embraced by gentry and Court. The basis for this interpretation lies in the play's constellation of motifs and historical analogies centred on a complex theme of immense importance in the sixteenth century, that of grace.

REBELLION

A major historical analogy, as I hope to show, is one linking the rebellions of *Henry IV* with the Northern Rebellion of 1569–70 and, more importantly, with the earlier northern rebellion known as the Pilgrimage of Grace (1536). The latter was the first and most dangerous of the Tudor rebellions, 'the archetypal protest movement of the century'.[5] It acquired its paradoxical name because its leaders wished to emphasize its religious and essentially peaceful nature and their willingness to disband if the King redressed their grievances. Although these grievances were a mixture of the economic, the political, and the religious, recent historians have tended to acknowledge that the major source of discontent was Henry VIII's attack on what was soon to be called 'the old religion'.[6] The religious motive was famously declared in the rebels' banners and badges, relics from a recent crusade against the Moors on which were painted the Five Wounds of Christ.[7] The rebels were presenting themselves as crusading defenders of a wounded Christian nation.

The Pilgrims were defeated in a notorious piece of treachery.[8] Heavily outnumbered by the rebels, Henry's deputy followed his master's advice and temporized with politic promises

---

[4] Scoufos, *Shakespeare's Typological Satire: a Study of the Falstaff-Oldcastle Problem* (Athens, Ohio, 1979).

[5] Penry Williams, *The Tudor Regime* (Oxford, 1979), pp. 316–17. Scoufos (pp. 125–6) briefly notes a parallel between Henry VIII's suppression of the Pilgrimage of Grace and Prince John's handling of the rebels at the end of *2 Henry IV*. She assumes (wrongly, I believe) that John's treachery is presented in an uncritical fashion.

[6] C. S. L. Davies, 'The Pilgrimage of Grace Reconsidered', *Past and Present*, 41 (1968): 54–75; J. J. Scarisbrooke, *Henry VIII* (1968), pp. 338–9; Scott Michael Harrison, *The Pilgrimage of Grace in the Lake District* (1981), pp. 1–3, 132–6.

[7] Edward Hall, *Chronicle Containing the History of England During the Reign of Henry IV and the Succeeding Monarchs to the End of the Reign of Henry the Eighth* (1548–50; 1809 edn), pp. 322–3; Raphael Holinshed, *Chronicles of England, Scotland, and Ireland*, 6 vols. (1587 edn rept. 1808), vol. 3, p. 800. See also Madeleine Hope Dodds and Ruth Dodds, *The Pilgrimage of Grace 1536–1537 and the Exeter Conspiracy*, 2 vols. (1915), vol. 1, pp. 19, 239.

[8] For evidence of contemporary criticism of Henry's treachery, see William Thomas, *The Pilgrim: A Dialogue on the Life and Actions of King Henry VIII* (1546), ed. J. A. Froude (London, 1861), pp. 11, 50–1. Tudor apologists imputed the bloodless suppression of the rebellion to 'the kynges wisedom and . . . discrete counsayle'. See John Hardyng, *The Chronicle. Together with the Continuation by Richard Grafton* (1543), p. 605; and cf. Hall, *Chronicle*, p. 823.

during his two conferences with their leaders at Doncaster. The rebels disbanded and Henry invited their trusting captain-in-chief, Robert Aske, to London, where he was warmly entertained and honoured with a chain of gold; but within months Henry found a pretext for arresting Aske and the other rebel leaders and executing them on a charge of treason. Among those executed was Sir Thomas Percy, the most warlike member of a family which troubled Henry VIII and Elizabeth I almost as much as it did Henry IV (it was Thomas Percy, seventh Earl of Northumberland, who was to lead the Northern Rebellion of 1569). After the Pilgrimage, there were four more rebellions of substance in the sixteenth century, and the one 'clear theme of national significance' running through them was opposition to the Reformation.[9] Thus the banner and badges of the Five Wounds were used again in the Western Rebellion of 1549 and the Northern Rebellion of 1569, with the addition in the latter of the crusaders' red cross.[10] Because of this recurrent theme and symbolism, the Pilgrimage of Grace understandably acquired archetypal status both in the popular imagination and in the historical thinking of government propagandists.

It might seem implausible to claim that in 1596–8 Shakespeare could rely on his audience recognizing inexplicit allusions to the rebellion of 1569;[11] and much less likely that he could expect anyone to recall the Pilgrimage of Grace. But the facts suggest otherwise. The continuing relevance and essential identity of the major Tudor rebellions was hammered into the consciousness of the Elizabethan citizen; it was intrinsic to the state's self-justifying and self-protective version of history. That most popular of Elizabethan histories, John Foxe's *Acts and Monuments*, included an indignant account of the Pilgrimage of Grace that strongly influenced later propagandists.[12] In Richard Norton's *A Warning against the dangerous practises of Papistes, and specially partners of the late Rebellion* (1569), King John's troubles with

the papacy, the overthrow of Richard II (allegedly caused by the Archbishop of Canterbury), the Pilgrimage of Grace, the Western Rebellion, and the contemporaneous rebellion in the north, are all linked in immediate sequence as part of the long history of papal incitement to rebellion against lawful rulers in Europe.[13] So too in the 1570 *Homilie agaynste disobedience and wylful rebellion*, subsequently to become the last and longest in the Book of Homilies ('to be read in euerie Parish Church'), a sweeping history of papally inspired rebellions passes from France and Germany to England, where an account of John's struggle with pope and cardinal proceeds to 'matters of later memory': the rebellions 'in the North and West countries' against Henry and Edward, in Ireland against Elizabeth (1566–7), and 'yet more latelie' among 'Northen borderers'.[14] Wilfrid Holme's lengthy narrative poem on the Pilgrimage of Grace, *The fall and euil successe of rebellion*, although written shortly after the event, was not published until 1572, when it had acquired the merit of underlining the repetitive pattern of history. No doubt this aureate composition was gathering dust when *Henry IV* was first staged. Like the Book of

---

9 Antony Fletcher, *Tudor Rebellions* (1968; 3rd edn, 1983), p. 101.

10 Frances Rose-Troup, *The Western Rebellion of 1549* (1913), p. 128, 257, 411–14; R. R. Reid, 'The Rebellion of the Earls', *Transactions of the Royal Historical Society* (1906): 171–203.

11 Irving Ribner, *The English History Play in the Age of Shakespeare* (London, 1957; revd edn, 1965), p. 182; David Bevington, *Tudor Drama and Politics: a Critical Approach to Topical Meaning* (Cambridge, Mass., 1968), p. 20.

12 Edn of 1583, pp. 1086–7.

13 *All such treatises as haue been lately published by Thomas Norton* (1569), sigs. D5v–C1r. Norton's pamphlets were drawn on by other polemical writers throughout the remainder of the Elizabethan period. See James K. Lowers, *Mirrors for Rebels: a Study of Polemical Literature Relating to the Northern Rebellion of 1569* (Berkeley: Calif., 1953), pp. 36, 55, 64.

14 *The Two Books of Homilies*, ed. J. Griffiths (Oxford, 1859), pp. 594–5.

Homilies, however, the popular sermons of the Marian martyr, Bishop Hugh Latimer, were not. They were reprinted four times between 1575 and 1596, and in the last as in the earlier editions the opening sermon was one devoted to the Pilgrimage of Grace.[15]

We have good reason to believe that this Henrician sermon, like the last in the Book of Homilies, was felt to have continuing relevance in the late 1590s. The missionary work of the Jesuits and seminary priests was defined by law as treason, seditious and rebellious in intent;[16] thus it was common for trial judges to compare the priests' 'traitorous' activities with those of the northern rebels decades earlier.[17] The mounting sense of political insecurity which afflicted England in the nineties was due almost entirely to a perceived threat from Catholic forces at home and abroad.[18] From 1595 the Irish earls and bishops were in rebellion and receiving help and encouragement from Philip II, who complimented them on their defence of Catholicism; in 1598 they scored a major victory over the English forces, and in 1599 humiliated Essex. There was constant fear of a Spanish invasion, direct from the peninsula, or from Calais (which fell to Spain in 1596), or from Ireland. When Sir Francis Knyvett wrote his *Defence of the Realm* in 1596, advocating compulsory military training for all men aged between eighteen and fifty, he could not have assumed that the expected Second Armada would, like the first, be scattered by storms (as was the case); and in fact organized defensive measures against invasion were in operation throughout the country until the end of the century. Although inspired by the 1569 rebellion, the final sermon in the Book of Homilies, with its systematic linking of past and present, would not have seemed quaintly out of date in these years; much less would its concluding prayer of 'Thanksgiving for the Suppression of the Last Rebellion'.

It is thoroughly characteristic of Tudor politics that in the great body of propagandist writing denouncing actual and potential rebellion there is an insistent attempt to demystify the religious language and symbolism used by the major rebel movements and to dismiss it as an ideological cloak for political ambition and economic discontent designed to ensnare the ignorant populace. The name of the Pilgrimage of Grace, and the insignia copied from it by the later rebellions, were construed as epitomizing the very nature of papistry. For Foxe, calling insurrection 'a holy pilgrimage' and painting Christ and his wounds on streamers and banners was true to the nature of devilish hypocrisy.[19] For Norton, the rebels' self-presentation was all 'shewes and color' – 'plaine coun-

---

15 *Sermons*, ed. G. E. Corrie (Cambridge, 1844), pp. 25–32 (the Elizabethan editions were entitled *Frutefull Sermons*). Concerning the 1536 rebellion, George Whetstone says in *The English Myrrour* (1586): 'It is yet within the compasse of oure memorie' (p. 167). He gives an account of this and later rebellions and conspiracies against the Tudor monarchy (pp. 24–68).

16 See the Acts of 1585 and 1593 against priests and recusants, rept. in G. R. Elton, *The Tudor Constitution: Documents and Commentary* (Cambridge, 1960), pp. 424–32.

17 Richard Verstegan (c. 1550–1640), *Letters and Dispatches*, ed. Anthony Petti (1959), p. 145 (trial date, 1593; Catholics and Brownists both likened to 'the rebelles in the northe'; their 'diabolicall perswasions tendeth to plaine insurrection and rebellion . . . clooked under the face of religion'); Christopher Devlin, *The Life of Robert Southwell, Poet and Martyr* (1956), p. 305 (trial date, 1595: 'The Rebellion in the North, by whom was it stirred but by . . . Jesuits and Priests?').

18 J. B. Black, *The Reign of Elizabeth, 1558–1603* (Oxford, 1936; 2nd edn, 1959), pp. 406–18. Fletcher, *Tudor Rebellions*, p. 100, notes that the years 1595–8 – within which period *1* and *2 Henry IV* were probably written – were arguably 'one of the most insecure periods of Tudor government'. In addition to the political-religious threat, there was widespread rioting over enclosures and dearth.

19 *Actes and Monuments* (1583), p. 1087; he is echoing Hall (*Chronicle*, p. 823), who is copied by Holinshed, *Chronicles*, 3, 800. Cf. the Act of 1593 on 'rebellious and traitorous subjects . . . hiding their most detestable and devilish purposes under a false pretext of religion and conscience' (Elton, *Tudor Constitution*, p. 428).

terfeit color'.[20] As a translator of Calvin he was especially offended by the claim to 'grace', insisting that papist rebels were instruments of the Pope's political ambitions and adherents of a religion which draws 'the redemption and iustification of man', which is 'God's greatest honor and dignitie', from 'God to man, from grace to workes . . . denying his graciousness therein'.[21] Echoing Norton, and playing on the different senses of the word 'colour' (a military ensign, a painting, a fraudulent appearance), the homily *Against Disobedience and Wilful Rebellion* declaims: [whereas] 'redress of the common-wealth hath of old been the usual pretence of rebels . . . religion now of late beginneth to be a colour of rebellion'; 'though some rebels bear the picture of the Five Wounds painted in a clout . . . by some lewd painter', yet they know not 'what the cross of Christ meaneth' and march 'against those that have the cross of Christ printed in their hearts'. Even a mixture of good and bad motives is never conceded: idealistic claims are all 'feigned pretence'; pur-ported 'reformation' of religion and country is actually 'deformation';[22] grace is disgrace.

GRACE

From a Shakespearian perspective, the name of the 1536 rebellion must have seemed both ironic and prophetic, since the Reformation and the Renaissance combined to create a cul-ture in which everyone was a pilgrim of grace in one or more senses of the word. Grace as the divine gift which redeems sinful mortals, making them pleasing in the eyes of God, was, as Norton sharply implied, a distinguishing and proprietorial concern of Reformation theol-ogy. And everything required by Castiglione and his like from the gentleman seeking grace and favour at court – eloquence, wit, versati-lity, *sprezzatura*, modesty, and an unfailing sense of fitness or propriety – was comprehen-ded in that one word: 'every thing that he doth or speaketh, let him doe it with a grace'.[23] Thus in Elizabethan usage the spiritual and the socio-

aesthetic senses of this unusually polysemous word tended to reinforce each other so as to make it an index of supreme value.

Not surprisingly, 'grace' is a conspicuous idea in a number of Shakespeare's plays. It is most obvious in those which concentrate on the nature of kingship and 'the Lord's anointed'. In *3 Henry VI* (in the characterization of Edward), in *Richard III*, and in *Richard II*, the word 'grace' functions primarily as an ironic index of the ruler's unfitness for his office and of a more general sense of lost excellence – honour, civi-lity, moral integrity – in the nobility and the nation at large. The word actually occurs more often in *Richard III* than in *1* and *2 Henry IV*; but as a theme the notion of grace is much more deeply embedded in the two-part play. This is due in the first place to the fact that Shakespeare is here concerned not only with loss and decline but also with the struggle for personal and national renewal (redemption, reformation); and in the second to the way in which he has complicated the meaning of grace by tying it to the notion of rebuke or censure, thus drawing upon a central feature of Calvinist spirituality. Indeed with its complex vision of grace in all its senses and associations – socio-aesthetic, spiritual, and political – *Henry IV* becomes something like a dramatic encapsulation of the Tudor century.

Intimately connected, the concepts of grace (with its antonyms 'disgrace', 'shame', and 'impudence') and rebuke (with its synonyms

---

[20] *To the Quenes Maiesties poore deceiued Subiectes of the North Country, drawen into rebellion by the Earles of Northumberland and Westmerland*, in *All such treatises* [n. 13 above], sigs. A3v, B1r. The figure of the rebels' deceitful 'colours' is used repeatedly in this pamphlet.

[21] *To The Quenes Maiesties poore deceiued Subiectes*, sig. C4v.

[22] *Two Books of Homilies*, ed. Griffiths, pp. 579, 581–2.

[23] *The Book of the Courtier*, trans. Sir Thomas Hoby (1561), Everyman edn (1966), p. 42. The nature of grace, and the means by which it is achieved, preserved, or lost is the subject for discussion in the central part of the book (pp. 42–184).

'check', 'rate', 'chide', and 'upbraid') dominate dialogue and action in both parts of the play. Since disgraceful conduct invites rebuke, the connection is instantly intelligible; but the prominence and full significance of the twin motif can only be understood in relation to Augustinian and Calvinist theology.

Dealing in the *Institutes* (II.v) with objections to his teachings on grace, free will, and predestination, Calvin refers to the claim that if men are predestined to be saved or damned, then 'exhortations are vainely taken in hande . . . the use of admonitions is superfluous . . . it is a fond thing to rebuke'. Augustine, he replies, wrote his book *De Correptione et Gratia* (*On Rebuke and Grace*) in answer to this objection; and he proceeds to summarize an argument on 'the medicine of rebuke' to which Augustine often returns in his anti-Pelagian writings. When addressed to the reprobate, rebuke beats and strikes their conscience in this life, and renders them more inexcusable on the judgement day. When addressed to the elect, 'if at any time they be gone out of the way sith they fell by the necessarie weaknesse of the fleshe', it avails much 'to enflame the desire of goodnesse, to shake off sluggishnesse, to take away the pleasure and venimous swetnesse of wickednesse'. It 'stirreth them to desire . . . renuing', prepares them 'to receiue . . . grace', and 'maketh them a new creature'. Thus the prophets, Christ, and the apostles never ceased to 'admonishe, to exhorte and to rebuke'.[24] Preliminary reflection alone would suggest that all of this resonates through *Henry IV*, a play whose seemingly reprobate and much censured hero was fixed in history as one of the elect. But in order to appreciate just how deeply embedded is this play in the culture of its time, one must note that Calvin's discussion of rebuke and grace is really a preamble to his exposition of church discipline (II.xii), 'whereof the chiefe use is in the censure and excommunication'. This provided the theological foundation for what was arguably the best-known feature of Tudor Puritanism: its censoriousness.

Fired with a 'white-hot morality', the Puritan saw himself as 'a prophet in his generation, one who freely rebuked both high and low alike'.[25] Why the Puritan preoccupation with grace-and-censure should have coloured the whole of *Henry IV* has to be ascribed ultimately to Falstaff's uncensored identity as Sir John Oldcastle or Lord Cobham, the Lollard burned for heresy by his friend Henry V and revered by Puritans as a heroic martyr. Much as Falstaff dominates many a performance of *Henry IV*, so Oldcastle dominates John Foxe's 'ecclesiasticall historie' of Henry V's reign: for him, that was the time when a synod was called 'to represse the growing and spreading of the Gospell, and especially to withstand the noble and worthy Lorde Cobham', chief favourer of the Lollards.[26] Oldcastle, however, was the subject of religious controversy in the sixteenth century and had a dual identity as reckless profligate (the Catholic version) and repentant sinner-turned-saint (the Protestant).[27] Shakespeare's comic debunking (and final 'excommunication') of the Protestant hero counterbalances whatever

---

[24] *Institution of the Christian Religion*, trans. Thomas Norton (1582), pp. 96–8 (II, v. 4–5). For Augustine's *On Rebuke and Grace*, see *The Works of Aurelius Augustine*, ed. Marcus Dods, vol. 15, *The Anti-Pelagian Works*, vol. 3 (Edinburgh, 1876), pp. 68–117.

[25] M. M. Knappen, *Tudor Puritanism* (Chicago, 1939), p. 344. Cf. Patrick Collinson, *The Elizabethan Puritan Movement* (1967), pp. 41, 100–2, 346–7, *The Religion of Protestants* (Oxford, 1982), pp. 105–8, 111.

[26] *Actes and Monuments* (1583), p. 557.

[27] Wilhelm Baeske, *Oldcastle-Falstaff in der englischen Literatur bis zu Shakespeare*, Palaestra 50 (Berlin, 1905); Scoufos, *Shakespeare's Typological Satire*, pp. 44–69. In 'The Fortunes of Oldcastle', *Shakespeare Survey 38* (1985), pp. 85–100, Gary Taylor contends – wrongly, I believe – that because of the name-change forced on Shakespeare (by the Elizabethan Cobhams) when he came to write *Part 2*, Falstaff of the second part is a different character to the re-named Oldcastle of *Part I*. Taylor's reference in the course of his argument (p. 93) to 'the original name of Shakespeare's most famous comic *character*' (my emphasis) indicates how difficult it will be for this view to win acceptance. It has been rejected by the editor of the New Cambridge *Part 2*

anti-Catholic attitudes might have been read into his presentation of northern rebellion; and the ideas of sin, rebuke, repentance, and grace which are intrinsic to the fat rogue's characterization are gravely relevant to the uncomic characters on both sides of the political divide.

Examination of the ways in which *Henry IV* is shaped by ideas of grace and rebuke, so that an earlier age seems to disclose the major patterns of Tudor experience, must begin with the associated ideas of pilgrimage, crusade, and reformation. The chroniclers mention that Henry had plans at the end of his reign to go on a crusade to recover Jerusalem from the infidels. Shakespeare seizes on this idea, makes it frame the whole of Henry's reign, and gives it the character of a pilgrimage. Henry's motives in this project combine and confuse the political and the spiritual: he would busy restless minds with foreign quarrels, and he would expiate the murder of Richard II, a shared guilt which he never explicitly acknowledges until the end. Henry's sense of guilt and shame, his feeling that present and impending troubles are retribution for past mistreadings, seems to involve the whole nation, so that his postponed pilgrimage effectively symbolizes a general quest for redemptive grace. As in Holinshed, whose favourite rendering of *anno domini* is 'in the year of our redemption', and above all as in St Paul, who urges the Ephesians to put off the unregenerate old man, 'redeeming the time: for the days are evil' (Ephesians 5.15–16), history here is time conceived as a quest for liberation from the sins of the past and the present. Falstaff, the sensual, time-wasting 'old boar' who feeds 'in the old frank' with pagan 'Ephesians . . . of the old church' (2:2.2.111–14), personifies (among other things) the unregenerate order.[28] It is that order which Hal must reject if he is to redeem time past and present and crown the future with a glittering 'reformation' (1:1.2.201–5), thus fitting the role, given him by the chroniclers, of a madcap prince who miraculously became 'a new man'.[29]

The idea that England is almost hopelessly seeking to recover lost grace is posited in the opening scene of *Part 1*. Westmoreland discloses that Council had to 'brake off' its 'business for the Holy Land' on hearing that 'the noble Mortimer' and his men had fallen into 'the rude hands' of 'the irregular and wild Glendower', and that the corpses of his butchered men suffered 'Such beastly shameless transformation . . . as may not be / Without much shame retold or spoken of' (1.1.38–46). Henry complains that 'riot and dishonour stain the brow' of the heir apparent and that the pride and malevolence of his erstwhile friends compel him to 'neglect / Our holy purpose to Jerusalem' (lines 84–101).

Although the word itself is not introduced until 1.2, this opening scene begins to suggest the wide spectrum of meaning in 'grace'. Initially there is grace in the religious sense, and it refers primarily to the process by which military-political aggression is given supreme justification. In *Part I* the Percys make much of the fact that the 'noble prelate well beloved', the Archbishop of York, 'commends the plot' to overthrow Henry: 'it cannot choose but be a noble plot', concludes Hotspur (1:3.265, 277; 2.3.19). Gadshill's comment on the parallel action to rob royal officers and pilgrims reflects ironically on the northern prelate's blessing (while hinting perhaps at the historical parallel in a characteristically ambivalent manner): the

---

(below, n. 29) and strongly contested by Jonathan Goldberg: see his 'The Commodity of Names: "Falstaff" and "Oldcastle" in *1 Henry IV*', in *Reconfiguring the Renaissance: Essays in Critical Materialism*, ed. Jonathan Crewe (London and Toronto, 1992), pp. 76–88.

[28] J. A. Bryant Jr, 'Prince Hal and the Ephesians', *Sewanee Review*, 67 (1959): 204–19.

[29] Hall, *Chronicle*, p. 4; Holinshed, *Chronicles*, 3, 61. Shakespearian references in this article are to *Henry IV, Part I*, ed. David Bevington (Oxford, 1987) and *The Second Part of King Henry IV*, ed. Giorgio Melchiori (Cambridge, 1989); and (for other plays) to *The Complete Works*, ed. Stanley Wells and Gary Taylor (Oxford, 1988).

involvement in the action of the 'nobility and tranquillity' – who 'pray continually to their saint, the commonwealth, or rather . . . prey on her' – serves to 'do the profession [of high-waymen] some grace' (1.1.69–78). It is only in *Part 2*, however, that 'The Archbishop's grace of York' (1:3.2.119) becomes actively rebellious. Without him, the people could never have been persuaded to rise with the Percys a second time. 'The gentle Archbishop', reports Morton to Northumberland, binds his followers because he 'Derives from Heaven his quarrel and his cause', 'Turns insurrection to religion', and arms himself with a holy relic, 'the blood / Of fair King Richard, scraped from Pomfret stones' (2:1.1.189–206). That this speech is given in the opening scene to a character called Morton (who never appears again) is adroit. There is no comparable character, and no one of that name, in any of the sources, but it was well known that the Northern Rebellion of 1569 was stirred up by Dr Nicholas Morton, an exiled priest and former Prebendary of York sent by Pius V to foster Catholic resistance to Elizabeth.[30] When the rebels confront the King's deputy at Gaultree, and are defeated in the most elaborately treacherous manner, the word 'grace', both as honorific and as abstract quality, will ring through the dialogue no less than nineteen times; for the historically minded, the Pilgrimage of Grace is vividly anticipated. But Morton's name and role ensure that the insurrection in *Part 2* is implicitly paralleled with the other major rebellion of the Tudor period as well. As we have seen, Shakespeare's audience was familiar with complex historical parallelism of this kind.

The role imputed to the archbishop concurs nicely with the demystifying polemics of Tudor orthodoxy. But of course the eye of the demystifier has settled also on the monarchy from the start, and never leaves it until almost the end. Henry's habitual self-righteousness, his proclaimed desire to 'draw no swords but what are sanctified' (2:4.2.4), Gadshill's 'graced'

attack on the pilgrims, and 'his grace' Prince John's smug claim at Gaultree that 'God, and not we, hath safely fought today' (2:4.1.142, 266, 280, 349) complete the picture of a political world where all claims to moral authority must be scrutinized with the utmost care. This is Tudor England as many Protestants and Catholics must have seen it.

Converging on grace in the religious sense is the notion of grace as the quality and title of true royalty: kings being sacramentally exalted, appointed 'by the grace of God', and expected like Him to be bountiful and forgiving as well as just and firm. The 'title of respect' which Henry (in his opening speech) complains he is denied by the Percys (1:1.3.8) is possibly 'Your grace', the honorific first used in England in royal address during the reign of Henry IV.[31] Henry's loyal followers readily grant him this title; in fact Westmoreland, engaging with the Yorkist Mowbray in a bout of partisan historic-izing, claims that in Richard's time the people's prayers 'were set on Hereford, whom . . . they blessed and graced indeed more than the king' (2:4.1.136–40). But the key question is whether Hal deserves this title. Symptomatically, Falstaff denies this, dis-gracing the Prince in their first scene together: 'God save thy grace – majesty I should say, for grace thou wilt have none . . . not so much as will serve to be prologue to an egg and butter' (1:1.2.15–20). But it is noticeable that when Falstaff has spoken 'vilely' of him in *Part 2* ('a good shallow young fellow, a would have made a good pantler'), both Doll and Mistress Quickly show a conspicuously different attitude: 'O, the Lord preserve thy grace! By my troth, welcome to London. Now the Lord bless that sweet face of thine' (2.4.193, 236–7). Henry himself endorses

---

[30] William Cecil, Lord Burghley, *The Execution of Justice in England* (1583), ed. Robert Kingdon (Ithaca, N.Y., 1965), pp. 14, 16; George Whetstone, *The English Myrrour*, pp. 141–2.

[31] William Camden, *Remains Concerning Britain*, rept. from the 1674 edn (1870), pp. 169–70.

this attitude in his dying advice to the Prince's brothers. Although 'being incensed, he is flint', Harry 'is gracious if he be observed', having 'a tear for pity, and a hand / Open as day for meting charity'; they must not 'lose the good advantage of his grace' by ignoring or alienating him (2:4.2.28–33).

Henry's advice introduces the kindred notion of royal 'grace and favour' and what it entails in terms of generosity and indulgence. His politic withdrawal of such from the Percys, his 'first and dearest . . . friends', is a major cause of the civil war. In the parleys at Shrewsbury, Worcester complains that Henry 'turn[ed]' his 'looks / Of favour' from 'all our house' (1:5.1.30–1); Hotspur that he 'disgraced me in my happy victories' (4.3.97). But it is in Falstaff's relationship with the heir apparent that this issue becomes one of major importance, both dramatically and politically. Far from being a herald of democratic republicanism, as Graham Holderness has claimed,[32] Falstaff is from the start wedded in soul to the idea of a monarchical order in which royal grace and favour is entirely at his disposal, to be enjoyed, dispensed, and denied by him as he pleases. In the same opening dialogue where he denies Hal 'his grace', Falstaff (with graceful wit) pleads for the titles of respect which will grace and 'countenance' – the word signifies both favour and patronage as well as pretence – his own and his friends' disreputable activities: 'Marry, then, sweet wag, when thou art king, let not us that are squires of the night's body be called thieves of the day's beauty. Let us be Diana's foresters, gentlemen of the shade, minions of . . . our noble and chaste mistress the moon, under whose countenance we steal' (1.2.22–8). At Shrewsbury, Hal magnanimously accedes in part to this request, allowing Falstaff to steal the credit for killing Hotspur: 'if a lie may do thee grace, / I'll gild it with the happiest terms I have' (5.4.152–3). So Falstaff expects 'to be either earl or duke' (line 158); but *Part 2* tells the familiar tale of court preferment endlessly deferred. On his first appearance here he

huffily admits (in effect) that he is now out of favour with Hal: 'He may keep his own grace, but he's almost out of mine, I can assure him' (1.2.20–1).

But he sees himself too in the role of patron. He has his own realm where hopefuls like Justice Shallow believe that 'a friend i' th' court is better than a penny in purse', and where servants like Davy complain that 'a knave should have some countenance at his friend's request' (2:5.1.25–6, 36). Hopes for Falstaff and his followers soar with news of the old King's death. He thinks of himself instantly as 'Fortune's steward'. Pistol he will 'double charge with dignities' and 'Lord Shallow' can choose what office he will: 'I will make the king do you grace . . . do but mark the countenance he will give me' (5.3.102–7; 5.5.5–7). The key to his failure lies in the way he approaches the new King. Arriving travel-stained and sweaty to stop the coronation procession with 'God save thy grace, King Hal, my royal Hal' (5.5.36), he publicly dis-graces Henry V and presumes to appropriate his royalty. Falstaff's quest for grace is hilarious to begin with and pathetic in conclusion; but its negative underside has been made clear: in the King's fears that Hal's reign will reenact that of Richard II, when 'sage counsellors' gave way to 'apes of idleness' (4.2.249–51); in Falstaff's promise of revenge on the Chief Justice (5.3.113); and in the conviction of Warwick, Clarence, and John that no one in office can now be 'assured what grace to find' unless he is prepared to abandon his principles and 'speak Sir John Falstaff fair' (5.2.30–3).

Falstaff's performance at the coronation procession is a highly theatrical and 'jocoserious' example of social impropriety: of disregard, as Castiglione would express it, for the circumstances of time, person, and place;[33] he is rebuked at this point in just such terms by Hal,

[32] *Shakespeare Recycled*, pp. 159–60, 167.
[33] *The Book of the Courtier*, pp. 85, 93–5.

and earlier by the Chief Justice (2:5.5.44, 2.1.49–50). The dazzling verbal dexterity with which he entertains his prince and fits his holiday mood make him in one sense the perfect Renaissance courtier; but his decline and fall are defined in terms of the courtly code which justifies his 'graceful recklessness'.[34] Even in *Part 1* his sallies can displease because mistimed ('is it a time to jest and dally now?' (1:5.3.54)). In *Part 2* the sheer impudence in his responses to rebuke precludes 'the right fencing grace' to which he still lays claim (2.1.151). His perpetual fooling seeks to impose the timeless world of holiday (where disregard for 'the circumstances' is the norm) upon the timebound world of politics, and to collapse the difference between himself and youth and royalty. Applied thus, the courtly code of social grace is inseparable from a philosophy of natural order and a sense of historical necessity. It is the same philosophy which tells us in *Twelfth Night* that there are times when a joke is not a joke (3.1.59–67), and that the rain it raineth every day.

In the wider perspective, the play's concern with grace in the socio-aesthetic sense seems to reflect a self-conscious, Tudor-establishment contrast between medieval and modern, North and South. The contrast is dramatized in the rivalry between Hal, 'king of courtesy' (1:2.4.10), and 'that same mad fellow of the north, Percy' (lines 324–5) – noble and lovable in his way, but more 'rude', 'irregular and wild' than his Welsh allies. His 'dearest grace', as his uncle perceives, is his outspoken contempt for falsity; but too often this declines into frenetic bluntness and crude philistinism; and his response to tactful criticism is itself graceless: 'Well, I am schooled. Good manners be your speed!' (3.1.177–85).

Hal by contrast proves himself to be the complete Renaissance man.[35] Witty, eloquent, and adaptable as well as valiant, he is obviously schooled in both 'arts and martial exercises' (2:4.2.203). He is eloquently modest as well as concerned to save lives when he issues his challenge to Hotspur, chiding 'his [own] truant youth with such a grace' as 'became him like a prince indeed' (1:5.2.60–2); and with equal grace he relinquishes the name of victor to Falstaff. There is nothing fraudulent in these gracious gestures; no hint of an unfit relationship between what he seems and what he is. His 'fair rites of tenderness' and 'courtesy' when alone (as he believes) with the dead Hotspur (5.4.93, 97) are one of several indications that he is not the coldhearted 'princely hypocrite' imagined by some critics.

Grace in *Henry IV* also means honour, the respect due to those who live by the knightly code whose cardinal values are valour and fidelity.[36] What most stains Hal's honour in his father's eyes is his surrender of military glory to Hotspur. But although Hal's redemption in *Part 1* depends on his defeat of Hotspur, the value of supreme importance in both parts is not valour but truth. Hal's triumph at Shrewsbury is less crucial as a martial achievement than as the fulfilment of a solemn promise (that he would 'redeem' all his shames by killing the rebel leader or dying in the attempt); it accords with his awareness that 'redemption' also means 'fulfilling a promise' (OED 2), and with his self-conception as 'the Prince of Wales who . . . never promises but he means to pay' (1:3.2.132–59, 5.4.41–2). Feudal England celebrated the verbal pledge of trust as the foundation of society; thus as J. Douglas Canfield has argued, the word as bond and the contest between

---

[34] 'Recklessness' is Hoby's translation of Castiglione's *sprezzatura*, signifying the impression of naturalness and careless ease. 'Recklessnesse . . . is the true fountaine from which all grace springeth' (p. 48; cf. p. 99). Somewhat pertinent to Falstaff's decline is Castiglione's remark on the 'noysome sawsinesse' of strained and untimely humour: 'thinking to make men laugh, which for that it is spoken out of time will appear colde and without grace' (p. 93).

[35] Cf. Tillyard, *Shakespeare's History Plays*, pp. 278–80.

[36] Sidney Painter, *French Chivalry: Chivalric Ideas and Practices in Mediaeval France* (New York, 1940), pp. 28–30.

fidelity and betrayal are central to the representation of conflict in literature from *Beowulf* to Dryden.[37] But this contest acquired a singular intensity and painfulness in the sixteenth century with the coming of the Reformation and the disputes about royal sovereignty and succession. The anguish of conflicting loyalties and mutually contradictory vows is vividly registered in the historical documents of the major rebellions. Precisely the same experience is dramatized in that most overtly topical of Shakespeare's plays, *King John* (probably written just before *Henry IV*), where the conflict between Pope and King intensifies the succession dispute and forces conscientious subjects into humiliatingly repetitive changes of allegiance: setting 'oath to oath', making 'faith an enemy to faith' (3.1.189–90).

In *Henry IV* this characteristically Tudor trauma is echoed in the representation of a crumbling society where the very basis of personal loyalty has been undone, and the original and continuing sin is betrayal, perjury, and a total devaluation of the word: 'What trust is in these times?' (2:1.3.100). Mutual accusations of treachery and perjury, and consequently flawed attempts to claim the moral high ground, characterize the relations of Henry and the rebels in *Part 1*. The first rebellion is motivated by anger and fear; but another motive is the Percys' desire to 'redeem' their family honour and erase from 'chronicles in time to come' the 'detested blot' of regicide in which Bolingbroke's broken vow implicated them (1.3.153–82; 4.3.52–105). Distrust bred by Henry's original 'violation of all faith and troth' (5.1.70) prompts Worcester to lie to Hotspur about the King's conciliatory offer at Shrewsbury. By his stress on location Shakespeare connects this distrust with an archetypal historical event, the treachery practised on the Pilgrims at Doncaster in 1536.[38] Rebuked by Henry for having 'deceived our trust', Worcester insists on the King's perjury as the source of dissension, saying: 'You swore to us, / And you did swear that oath at Doncaster ... Forget your oath to us at Doncaster' (lines

41, 58). The parallel is sharpened by the fact that the offer which is distrusted is four times defined as 'grace, / Pardon, and terms of love' (5.5.2–3; cf.4.3.30,50,112; 5.1.106). What redeems Shrewsbury from the taint of dishonour which the remembered past introduces is the Prince's fulfilment of his promise, and his closing gesture of freeing 'ransomless' his most valuable prisoner: 'I thank your grace for this high courtesy' (5.5.32).

Part 1's pattern of treachery is re-enacted in *Part 2*. Having broken his word to Hotspur by failing to support him at Shrewsbury, Northumberland now resists the pleas of his wife and Lady Percy to absent himself from the planned uprising, arguing that his 'honour is at pawn' and that 'nothing can redeem it' but his going. But he is induced to betray his friends by the accusing argument of Lady Percy ('new lamenting ancient oversights') that it would dishonour Hotspur's name if his father were to keep his promise to others now (2.3.7–47). Northumberland is trapped by his disgraceful past.

But Northumberland's infidelity cannot match that of Prince John at Gaultree; not even in *King John*, which rings with indignation against 'perjured kings' (3.1.33), is there anything comparable to this act of royal treachery. 'His grace's' offer of pardon and redress is buttressed with oaths by the honour of his blood and upon his soul to boot; and it is solemnized by the public ritual (proposed by himself) of drinking and embracing together in token to the assembled armies of 'restorèd love and amity' (4.1.281–93). This studied act of treachery endows the breaking of the verbal bond with the quality of sacrilege.

Apart from royal treachery and the nineteen uses of the word 'grace', there is much to bring

---

[37] Canfield, *Word as Bond in English Literature from the Middle Ages to the Restoration* (Philadelphia, 1989).

[38] Dodds, *The Pilgrimage of Grace*, II, pp. 1–25.

the fate of the Pilgrim leaders to mind and generally stimulate the historical sense. Mowbray predicts that Henry will not forget what they have done and will soon find some trivial cause to exact his vengeance on them (precisely what Henry VIII would do); the prelate responds that Henry, knowing that such executions are always remembered by 'the heirs of life', will rather 'keep no tell-tale to his memory / That may repeat and history his loss / To new remembrance' (lines 200–4). As if predicting the way in which the sons and nephews of the leading Pilgrims (Percys, Nevilles, Nortons, Tempests) would rise again in the rebellion of 1569, Hastings warns that, if the rebels fail, 'heir from heir shall hold his quarrel up / Whiles England shall have generation'. The young Prince retorts that Hastings is 'much too shallow / To sound the bottom of the after-times' (4.1.276–9).

REBUKE

Prince John foregrounds the play's censorious mode. 'Monsieur Remorse', the play's mock-Puritan, points to its theological matrix with pious remarks on 'the spirit of persuasion', the 'ears of profiting' (1:1.2.106, 143–4), and the need for 'the fire of grace' if one is to be properly 'moved' (2.4.370–1). What one should be moved to by rebuke is confession, contrition (asking pardon), and 'a good amendment of life' (1.2.97). But as Calvin acknowledged in his discussion of rebuke and grace (*Institutes*, II.v.5), and as Falstaff habitually demonstrates, evasion is a common response. It is characteristic of the endemic dishonesty of Henry's unregenerate world that almost everyone responds to rebuke by denial, obfuscation, and retaliation in kind. The dialogue of the play, both comic and serious, is substantially built on rebuke, evasion, and counter-rebuke.

Rebuke and evasion explode in the third scene of *Part 1* when Henry berates all the Percys for his 'indignities', and Hotspur in

particular for withholding his prisoners. Although he still refuses to surrender them, Hotspur protests in the most tortuous manner that he made no such refusal at all. Henry treats this evasion with contempt, a fierce quarrel erupts, and the scene ends with the Percys planning rebellion. On the battlefield, the initial pattern of rebuke and evasion becomes one of rebuke, evasion, and counter-rebuke. Henry lectures Worcester on his betrayal of trust and on the impropriety of old friends and old men confronting each other in 'ungentle steel' (5.1.9–21). Worcester responds at greater length, blaming the present conflict on Henry's violation of all faith and on his 'ungentle' treatment of his former allies (lines 30–71). Loftily dismissing this justification of rebellion, Henry employs a familiar Tudor discourse:

> These things indeed you have articulate,
> Proclaimed at market crosses, read in churches,
> To face the garment of rebellion
> With some fine colour that may please the eye
> Of fickle changelings and poor discontents,
> Which gape and rub the elbow at the news
> Of hurly-burly innovation.
> And never yet did insurrection want
> Such water-colours to impaint his cause . . .
>
> (lines 72–80)

Consistently with this discourse, however, Henry presents himself as the instrument of both grace and rebuke, offering pardon and redress if the rebels disarm: 'take the offer of our grace . . . if . . . not . . . rebuke and dread correction wait on us' (lines 106–11). Educated by history, Worcester distrusts his grace's word, lies to Hotspur, and the battle takes place. But Worcester is subjected to another homily on the point of execution: 'Thus ever did rebellion find rebuke. / Ill-spirited Worcester, did we not send grace, / Pardon, and terms of love to all of you? / And wouldst thou . . . Misuse the tenor of thy kinsman's trust?' (5.5.1–5). While there is no suggestion here that rebellion is justified, the ironic inappropriateness in the given circumstances of the King's anti-rebellion rhetoric is un-mistakable.

From the start, Falstaff's relationship with the Prince is governed by the same dynamics as that between Henry and the men who had and lost his favour. Most of Hal's speeches to the fat knight are either hilariously devastating criticisms of his self-indulgence and deceit or attempts to make him tell truth and shame the devil. And Falstaff's responses characteristically slide from evasion to counterattack. Hal's opening tirade on Falstaff's time-wasting is dissolved in sinuous wordplay leading to the Puritan-sounding lament that Falstaff himself has been corrupted by Hal's company: 'O, thou . . . art indeed able to corrupt a saint. Thou hast done much harm upon me, Hal, God forgive thee for it' (1.2.87–9). His superb escape from the charge of 'open and apparent shame' after Gad's Hill is followed by his warning that Hal should prepare to be 'horribly chid' (2.4.360) by his father. By playing the part of the rebuking king much to his own advantage, Falstaff provokes the exchange of roles which brings upon Hal and himself a thunderous royal rebuke: 'Swearest thou, ungracious boy? . . . Thou art violently fallen away from grace. There is a devil haunts thee in the likeness of an old fat man . . .' Falstaff's 'fencing' pretence of innocent and polite incomprehension is perfect: 'I would your grace would take me with you; whom means your grace?' (lines 429–44).

Very different is Hotspur's churlish reply in the next scene to his uncle's kindly rebuke ('You must needs learn, lord, to amend this fault'). And different to both is Hal's response in the ensuing scene to Henry's overblown, self-righteous condemnation of his 'rude' and 'degenerate' behaviour (3.2.14, 32, 128). The scenic juxtapositions are pointed, as is the nodal position given to the father-son encounter in the play's structure; for Hal's reaction to rebuke is designed (like his attitude to promises) to distinguish him from everyone else, marking him out as the figure of redemption and reformation, a man of grace. He is most respectful to

his irate father ('my thrice gracious lord'); and while pleading that he is in part the victim of newsmongers, confesses that his 'youth / Hath faulty wandered and irregular', and so begs 'pardon'. Moreover, in making his solemn promise of amendment – that he 'will redeem' his 'shames' by defeating Hotspur – he acknowledges that success will depend on divine grace: 'This in the name of God I promise here, / The which if he be pleased I shall perform' (lines 26–8, 132–3, 144, 153–4). Since the defeat of the rebels effectively depends on the fulfilment of this promise, Calvin's teaching on the benefits of rebuking the elect when they 'be gone out of the way by the necessarie weakness of the fleshe' has been fully justified.

In keeping with its graver mood, *Part 2* shows an extraordinary intensification in the spirit of rebuke. In addition to present rebukes, future rebukes are anticipated (4.2.37–41; 4.2.105–21), and past ones are remembered. Northumberland (says Henry) 'checked and rated' Richard II, who rebuked him and Henry in turn (3.1.67–70). Henry 'had many living to upbraid' his way of gaining the throne (4.2.320). Since Shrewsbury, Hal has fallen from grace again and suffered accordingly – as he recalls in his tactical rebuke of the Chief Justice: 'What! Rate, rebuke, and roughly send to prison / Th' immediate heir of England?' (5.2.69–70). Mistress Quickly too has been reproved by the law – 'Master Tisick the debuty' – for keeping uncivil customers (2.4.68).

In her response to rebuke ('You would bless you to hear what he said') the hostess set an example which Falstaff, 'deaf . . . to the hearing of anything good', conspicuously fails to follow (2.4.68–76; 1.2.54–5). He is now being reproved by everyone, from his tailor and his whore to Hal, John, and his dedicated moral 'physician' (1.2.100), the Chief Justice. Falstaff's pretended deafness with the latter emblematizes his chronic problem but is also symptomatic of his new impudence. However, the old tricks of sanctimonious reversal, pious pretence, and righteous indignation are in evidence too: it is not he who has misled Hal but Hal who misled him; he has 'checked' the 'rude Prince' for striking the Justice 'and the young lion repents' (lines 115, 153–4); his replies are not impudent sauciness but honourable boldness (2.1.97); if his manners are foolish and become him not he was a fool that taught them him (lines 150–1); abusing the prince behind his back was the part of a careful and true subject, designed to protect him from the love of the wicked (2.4.259–63); he 'never knew yet but rebuke and check was the reward of valour' (4.1.382–3).

As in *Part 1*, the most entertaining dialogue is woven around Falstaff's evasions. However, the volume and severity of the criticisms, and the waning of 'the right fencing grace' to which he still lays claim (2.1.151), anticipate the moment when he prepares to move from tavern to court, only to be fiercely rebuked ('Make less thy body hence, and more thy grace') and resolutely denied the opportunity to 'Reply . . . with a fool-born jest' (5.5.48, 51). The puritanical harshness of Hal's final rebuke may or may not be justified in the circumstances; but the significance of certain obvious facts is too often ignored. Falstaff's banishment (or 'excommunication') is the fulfilment of a promise ('I do, I will'), and it is not absolute: its harshness is moderated by the promise of a pension designed to keep Falstaff out of mischief and to help him 'reform' and so expect 'advancement' (that he is most unlikely to reform and seems deaf to what has been said is beside the point) (lines 64–6).[39] Hal's promise of a pension is a notably solemn one too: in his very last utterance, he emphasizes his own self-conception as defined at Shrewsbury: 'Be it your charge, my lord, / To see performed the tenor of my word' (lines 66–7). As for Falstaff's subsequent sending to the Fleet by the Chief Justice, that accords with Hal's public recognition that the Justice was right to 'rate, rebuke, and roughly send to prison' the heir-apparent, and with his assurance that he would never interfere with the decisions of this 'bold, just,

and impartial spirit' (5.2.115). It has been intimated throughout that if anything will redeem England it will be a strong leader who keeps his word and so inspires trust and loyalty. Thus it can be argued that the nature and circumstances of the final rebuke contribute to the conception of Hal as a redeemed and redeeming prince, one who possesses the major *king*-becoming graces. Clearly, however, the scene is intrinsic to a comprehensive structure of thought founded on Calvin's twin Augustinian themes.

The same thematic twinship governs the two other most important scenes in *Part 2*: Prince John's encounter with the rebels, and the King's with his socially rebellious son. Here too the rhetoric of a censorious throne is turned against those who are thought to threaten its survival; and here too the nature and reception of the rebuke deserve scrutiny. Soundly rated by both Westmoreland and the Prince for taking up arms, 'his grace of York' passes lightly over the motive of personal revenge which initially inspired him to rise against Henry; instead, he justifies his action by reference to unspecified common grievances and in particular to the pressures of 'the time misordered' (4.1.70–85, 261). Quite unlike Northumberland, who declared himself committed to anarchy and bloodshed (1.1.154), he repeatedly insists that he is bent, not on conflict, but on securing a genuine peace. His accent is that of confused sincerity, his manner dignified, and his attitude to his opposites trusting and half-apologetic. All of which serves to intensify the unsettling aspects of the criticism to which he is subjected. What is remarkable in the first place is that he is rebuked at length, in the most orotund manner, and twice over: first by Westmoreland, and

---

[39] Even when rebuke and censure lead to excommunication, says Calvin, 'such seueritie becommeth the Church as is ioyned with the spirit of mildnes'; 'punish them that are fallen, mercifully & not to the extremitie of rigor . . . hoping better of them in time to come than we see in time present' (*Institutes*, trans. Norton, II.xii.8–9).

later by the youthful Prince: the artifice and the doubling intensifies the sense of hollowness and duplicity. Even the argument is the same in both rebukes: a variation on Henry's attack on Worcester in *Part 1*, suitably adapted to the person addressed, and evocative of the great historical paradigm and all the indignant eloquence it spawned. Both men expatiate on the horrible impropriety of a man of God dressing 'the ugly form / Of base and bloody insurrection' with 'the fair honours' of his calling, perverting 'the grace, the sanctities of heaven', and employing 'the countenance and grace of heaven' in 'deeds dishonourable' (4.1.39–41, 249–54). Given his treacherous intent, the Prince's preachifying shows that he has wholly appropriated 'the counterfeited zeal of God' (line 255) which he imputes to the bishop: an appropriation which sharply interrogates official Tudor attacks on 'the counterfeit service of God', the 'false pretences and shews', whereby the various rebel leaders purportedly deluded their gullible followers.[40]

Henry's 'dear and deep rebuke' of Hal two scenes later is comparable to John's in its excess, and mistaken in its view of Hal as a 'rebel . . . spirit' in deep 'revolt' (4.2.195, 300); but it is at least sincere in its anger and its care for the commonwealth. What matters, however, is Hal's response. He is here reduced to tears by his father's words. When he speaks, he begins with the words, 'O pardon me', explains himself, and eloquently communicates feelings of filial love and duty. The effect of this response, like its counterpart in *Part 1*, is all-important: not, this time, for the commonwealth, but for the King. Reconciled and at one with Hal, Henry confesses his guilt for the first time, and begs pardon. Echoing his earlier and entirely characteristic, 'God knows, I had no such intent / But that necessity so bowed the state / That I and greatness were compelled to kiss' (3.1.71–3), he now says: 'God knows, my son, / By what by-paths and indirect crooked ways / I met this crown . . . How I came by this

crown, O God forgive' (4.2.311–12, 346). He then learns that he has been resting in the Jerusalem Chamber, and he is satisfied: 'In that Jerusalem shall Harry die' (line 367). Some critics read this detail as a final sign of Henry's insufficiency. I take it as evidence that his pilgrimage is over; that he has, through his son, found grace. Unlike Falstaff and others, he has stopped wrenching the true cause the false way, has told truth and shamed the devil.

PARDON

The analogies adumbrated by Shakespeare between the reign of Henry IV and the Tudor period indicate that his interpretation of English history is here affected at every level by ideas derived from the major political and cultural experiences of his own time, as well as by notions of historical recurrence long established in western historiography.[41] In particular, those analogies intimate that the bitter intestinal divisions of the later period, with their conflicting loyalties and mixed and confused motivations, contributed much to his sense of the tortuous relationship in political affairs between right and wrong, justice and injustice, morality and expediency, freedom and necessity, present and past. Neither the rebellious bishop nor the regicidal King in *Henry IV* is blameless, but both claim with some sincerity and truth that the strong necessity of the times – the accumulated pressure of events – compelled them to do what they did not want to do. Elizabeth might have said the same about the execution of her Catholic cousin, Queen Mary, and of the eight

---

[40] *The Two Books of Homilies*, ed. Griffiths, p. 579 ('Against Disobedience and Wilful Rebellion').

[41] See G. W. Trompf, *The Idea of Historical Recurrence in Western Thought: From Antiquity to the Reformation* (Berkeley, California, 1979); Achsah Guibbory, *The Map of Time: Seventeenth-Century English Literature and Ideas of Pattern in History* (Urbana and Chicago, 1986).

hundred northerners who supported Mary and 'the old religion'.[42]

For Shakespeare, it would seem, the nature of politics is such that most leaders will necessarily do things they would rather have withheld from 'chronicles in time to come'. But if they are to make peace with themselves and posterity, they must confess and beg pardon and not wrap themselves in the rhetoric of righteousness and evasion. And since no one else is guiltless, they may, if they are lucky, be forgiven. Hardly a theme (either political or literary-critical) for our time; but it was probably Shakespeare's intended, final message from the stage. In the epilogue to *The Tempest*, Prospero, the all-powerful but less-than-perfect ruler, addresses the audience in language of moving simplicity. Like his rude and rebellious subject, Caliban, he humbly 'seek[s] for grace'

(5.1.299), reminding the audience of its own faults, echoing the Lord's prayer, and gently recalling the old religion's overly indulgent attitude to forgiveness and redemption:

> And my ending is despair
> Unless I be relieved by prayer,
> Which pierces so, that it assaults
> Mercy itself, and frees all faults.
> As you from crimes would pardoned be,
> Let your indulgence set me free.

---

[42] I have side-stepped in this article the possibility – persuasively argued by E. A. J. Honigmann in his *Shakespeare: the 'Lost Years'* (Manchester, 1985) – that Shakespeare was brought up as a Catholic and spent his 'lost years' before 1592 working as a schoolmaster and player for a wealthy Catholic landowner in Lancashire. If correct, the argument would certainly be relevant to my interpretation of *Henry IV*.

HOLY WAR IN *HENRY V*

STEVEN MARX

Joel Altman calls *Henry V* 'the most active dramatic experience Shakespeare ever offered his audience'.[1] The experience climaxes at the end of the final battle with the arrival of news of victory. Here the King orders that two hymns be sung while the dead are buried, the 'Non Nobis' and the 'Te Deum'. In his 1989 film, Kenneth Branagh underlines the theatrical emphasis of this implicit stage direction. He extends the climax for several minutes by setting Patrick Doyle's choral-symphonic rendition of the 'Non Nobis' hymn behind a single tracking shot that follows Henry as he bears the dead body of a boy across the corpse-strewn field of Agincourt. The idea for this operatic device was supplied by Holinshed, who copied it from Halle, who got the story from a chain of traditions that originated in the event staged by the real King Henry in 1415. Henry himself took instruction from another book, the Bible.[2]

The hymns which Henry requested derive from verses in the psalter. 'Non Nobis' is the Latin title of Psalm 115, which begins, 'Not unto us, O lord, not unto us, but unto thy Name give the glory . . .' This psalm celebrates the defeat of the Egyptian armies and God's deliverance of Israel at the Red Sea. It comes midway in the liturgical sequence known as The Egyptian Hallelujah extending from Psalm 113 to 118, a sequence that Jesus and the disciples sang during the Passover celebration at the Last Supper and that Jews still recite at all their great festivals.[3] Holinshed refers to the hymn not as 'Non Nobis' but by the title of Psalm 114, 'In exitu Israel de Aegypto' ('When Israel came out of Egypt').[4] The miraculous military victory commemorated in the 'Non Nobis' is the core event of salvation in the Bible, the model of all God's interventions in human history. That event is recalled and recreated in other psalms, in accounts of military victories like Joshua's, David's, the Maccabees', and archangel Michael's, and in stories of rescue from drowning like Noah's, Jonah's, and Paul's. Most scholars agree that the original source of these tales of deliverance is found in what they identify as the earliest biblical text, 'The song of the Sea' in Exodus 15: 'I will sing unto the Lord, for he hath triumphed gloriously . . . The Lord is a man of war, his name is Jehovah. Pharaoh's chariots and his host hath he cast into the sea . . . Thy right hand Lord, is glorious in power: thy right arm Lord hath

---

1 '"Vile Participation": The Amplification of Violence in the Theatre of *Henry V*', *Shakespeare Quarterly*, 42:1 (Spring 1991): 2–32; p. 2.

2 Citations in this essay are from *The Geneva Bible: A Facsimile of the 1560 Edition* with an introduction by Lloyd E. Berry (Madison, Wisconsin, 1969). I have modernized spelling.

3 Referred to by Matthew (26.30) and Mark (14.26) as 'The Passover Hymn'.

4 Holinshed, Raphael, et al., *The Chronicles of England, Scotland, and Ireland*, 3 vols. in 2, 1587; ed. H. Ellis, 6 vols., 1807–8, p. 555, reprinted in *Shakespeare's Holinshed*, ed. Richard Hosley (New York, 1968), pp. 133–4.

bruised the enemy.'[5] Like 'The Star Spangled Banner', this song defines national identity by commemorating a miraculous underdog battle victory.

The place of the Agincourt story in Shakespeare's English history cycle resembles the place of the Red Sea victory in the Bible: it fixes the central moment both remembered and prefigured: 'Just as the first tetralogy looks back to *Henry V* as emblem of lost glory that shows up the inadequacy of his son's troubled reign, the second looks forward to his glorious accession ... The progress of the two tetralogies, then, is a progress back in time to a dead hero ...'.[6] Agincourt creates a national hero like Moses, but more importantly it testifies to the intervention of God on our side: 'O God thy arm was here, / And not to us, but to thy arm alone, / Ascribe we all ... Take it God, / For it is none but thine' (4.8.106–12), says Henry, once again quoting scripture: 'For they inherited not the land by their own sword: neither did their own arm save them. But thy right hand and thine arm ...' (Psalm 44, 3–4). Under penalty of death, all the euphoria and relief of victory must be channelled toward God: 'be it death proclaimèd through our host / To boast of this, or take that praise from God / Which is His only' (4.8.114–16).

Henry is known as both the most religious and the most warlike of English kings. In this essay, I will explore some of the relationships between war, religion and politics that connect Shakespeare's play to the depiction of holy war in the Bible. After a discussion of Henry the Fifth's pious fashioning of foreign policy from biblical models, I will examine Shakespeare's treatment of Henry's Machiavellian uses of religion to gain political power. Then I will reconcile the contradiction between pious and cynical understandings of holy war with references to Machiavelli's own interpretation of biblical history and politics. I will go on to show that this reconciliation stems from the inner holy war in Henry's personal relationship with God, a conflict illuminated by the notion of the Mystery of State developed by seventeenth-century French apologists for Machiavelli. I will conclude by comparing the rhetorical strategies of biblical and Shakespearian holy war narratives and their effects on later audiences.[7]

Alone in prayer, Henry addresses his deity as 'God of battles' (4.1.286). In the Hebrew Bible, God is referred to more than fifty times with the formula, 'Yahweh Sabaoth', the Lord of Hosts. This title was derived from earlier Canaanite and Babylonian deities who were described as leaders of battalions of followers warring against enemy gods or monsters to bring forth creation. Biblical usage of 'Lord of Hosts' at some times refers to God at the forefront of troops of angels and at others as the chief of the armies of the Israelites.[8] Yahweh's

---

[5] See Gerhard von Rad, 'The Form-Critical Problem of the Hexateuch', in *The Problem of the Hexateuch and Other Essays* (New York, 1966), pp. 1–78, also Martin Noth, *The History of Israel* (New York, 1960), and G. E. Mendenhall, *The Tenth Generation. The Origins of the Biblical Tradition* (Baltimore, 1973).

[6] Phyllis Rackin, *Stages of History: Shakespeare's English Chronicles* (Ithaca, 1990), p. 30.

[7] Much attention has been paid to biblical references in Shakespeare, most recently in a three-volume series, *Biblical References in Shakespeare's Comedies, Biblical References in Shakespeare's Tragedies* and *Biblical References in Shakespeare's Histories*, by Naseeb Shaheen published by the University of Delaware Press. But very little scholarly study is available on the literary relationships between biblical and Shakespearian works. One notable exception is an address by James Black entitled '"Edified by the Margent": Shakespeare and the Bible', issued by the University of Alberta Press. I have yet to find a scholarly treatment of the manifold connections between biblical and Shakespearian historiography and politics.

[8] See Patrick D. Miller, *The Divine Warrior in Early Israel* (Cambridge, Mass., 1973), pp. 154–5. In *Yahweh Is a Warrior: The Theology of Warfare in Ancient Israel* (Herald Press, Scottdale, Philadelphia, 1989), Millard Lind points out that the identification God, king and general was a common ancient near east convention, as witnessed in a proclamation by Assurbanipal, King of the Assyrian empire 'Not by my own power / not by the strength of

war god manifestations range from miraculous interventions as a destroyer of Israel's enemies to mundane advice on logistical procedures.

In the latter four books of the Torah, God functions as the king of the emergent Israelite nation and is so addressed. In the later books of Samuel and Kings, the role of kingship descends to anointed human rulers like Saul, David and Solomon. Yet in the language of address and in the manifestations of royal behaviour, the demarcations separating these two levels of kingship are often blurred. No matter what level, the essence of kingship is sovereignty or rule, and rule is conceived as the exercise of military power. 'King' is synonymous with 'general' or 'warlord'. Yahweh's power is established by his victory in battle.

Miller, following von Rad, labels this underlying principle of biblical holy war as 'synergism': 'at the center of Israel's warfare was the unyielding conviction that victory was the result of a fusion of divine and human activity . . . while might of arms and numbers were not the determining factors . . . It was yet possible for the people to see themselves as going to the aid of Yahweh in battle (Judges 5: 23). Yahweh fought for Israel even as Israel fought for Yahweh . . . Yahweh was general of both the earthly and the heavenly hosts.'[9] Shakespeare's opening chorus proclaims this elision of god, king and general in a blithely syncretic mixture: 'O . . . should the warlike Harry, like himself, / Assume the port of Mars, and at his heels, / Leashed in like hounds, should famine, sword and fire / Crouch for employment' (1.0.1–8). The chorus specializes in such rhetoric of deification, referring to Henry as 'The mirror of all Christian kings', suggesting a 'King of Kings' godlike supremacy and instructing us to 'cry, "Praise and glory on his head."' Exeter employs similar hyperbole when he warns the French King of Harry's approach, 'in fierce tempest is he coming, / In thunder and in earthquake, like a Jove . . .' (2.4.99–100). Mixing pagan and biblical references to a storm

god, Exeter here alludes to the Yahweh of Psalm 29: 3–5: 'The voice of the Lord is upon the waters; the God of glory maketh it to thunder . . . the voice of the lord breaketh the cedars.'

In addition to being Godlike, like Moses or Joshua or Saul, the King claims God's authorization and backing for what he does. The Archbishops assert that 'God and his angels guard your sacred throne.' As opposed to the French who only use God's name to swear, Henry continually invokes His help and blessing, and his war cry in battle is 'God for Harry! England and St George!' (3.1.34). Specific biblical references and proof texts are offered as justification for his decisions. The Book of Numbers, the only biblical text mentioned in all of Shakespeare, provides support for the priests' interpretation of the Salic Law, and the rules for siege warfare in Deuteronomy 20 provide the guidelines for Henry's threat against and subsequent treatment of Harfleur.[10]

The attack against France is by implication a substitution for his father's oft-repeated intention to lead a holy crusade to liberate Jerusalem from the Turks. Crusade is a form of holy war that involves a different variation of the synergistic collaboration between God and humans. Rather than manifesting God's support of man, it is the human enactment of God's will on earth. Crusade undertakes to right wrongs, re-establish justice, punish evildoers and express God's wrath through human agency. It is waged by the faithful against those who have

---

my bow / by the power of my gods, / by the strength of my goddesses / I subjected the lands to the yoke of Assur', p. 30.

[9] Miller, p. 156.

[10] 'When thou comest near unto a city to fight against it, thou shalt offer it peace. And if it answer thee again peaceably and open unto thee, then let all the people that is found therein, be tributaries unto thee and serve thee. But if it will make no peace with thee . . . thou shalt smite all the males thereof with the edge of the sword.' (Deuteronomy 20: 10–13).

rebelled against God.[11] In addressing the French king, Exeter casts Henry in this role of God's agent: 'He wills you, in the name of God Almighty, / That you divest yourself and lay apart / The borrowed glories that by gift of heaven, / By law of nature and of nations, 'longs / To him and to his heirs, namely the crown . . .' (2.4.77–81). 'Henry Le Roy' represents the King this way to Williams, Bates and Court: 'War is his [God's] beadle. War is his vengeance. So that here men are punished for before-breach of the King's laws, in now the King's quarrel' (4.1.167–70). His war is holy not only because it collectively punishes his evil-doing opponents, but because it individually mortifies his sinful subjects. This notion of war as the Scourge of God justifies unlimited brutality against those who resist but insists on mercy to those who accede and beg mercy. It is this principle that not only authorizes but requires Henry's cruel threats to French noncombatants in his initial declaration of war and at Harfleur.

However, though the King insists that the victory of Agincourt is not his but God's, Shakespeare's depiction of Henry and of the way events unfold suggests otherwise. Henry follows his father Bolingbroke's footsteps in thinking and behaving as if the outcome of events is decided by his own courage and cleverness. The elder Henry plans a holy war against the Turks as a means to quell civil war at home and to ease his conscience for usurping the throne, and his dying words include the advice to his son to 'busy giddy minds with foreign quarrels' to solidify his shaky régime (2 Henry 4 4.3.342–3). And immediately following the Chorus's opening invocation of Henry's divine mission, we eavesdrop on a backroom conversation revealing that he has secured the Archbishop's sanction for the invasion of France in return for his agreement to block the bill in Commons that would force the church to pay taxes to support the sick and indigent.

Incidents like these suggest that Shakespeare exposes holy war as a device manipulated by Kings for political ends, confirming what Stephen Greenblatt calls '. . . the most radically subversive hypothesis in his culture about the origin and function of religion'.[12] That hypothesis was formulated by Machiavelli in his account of the ancient Roman practice of securing popular support for the state with the pretence of piety. The wisest leaders, Machiavelli claimed, are those who 'foster and encourage [religion] even though they be convinced that it is quite fallacious. And the more should they do this the greater their prudence and the more they know of natural laws.'[13]

The most popular critical solution to the apparent contradiction between Henry as holy warrior and as Machiavellian Prince is what Harry Berger labels 'the historico-political approach'. This explains Henry's manipulation of religion as the outcome of '". . . a passage from the Middle Ages to the Renaissance and the modern world", . . . the familiar story of disenchantment in which religious attitudes toward history and politics give way to secular and humanistic attitudes . . . a fall from sacramental kingship to a Machiavellian conception of kingship . . .'[14] But as Berger points out, such a reading fails to take account of the genuine spiritual conflicts and concerns experi-

---

[11] See Roland Bainton, *Christian Attitudes toward War and Peace: A Historical Survey and Critical Re-evaluation* (Nashville, 1960), pp. 44–50 and David Little, '"Holy War" Appeals and Western Christianity: A Reconsideration of Bainton's Approach', in *Just War and Jihad*, ed. John Kelsay and James Turner Johnson (New York, 1991), pp. 121–41.

[12] 'Invisible Bullets: Renaissance Authority and its Subversion in *Henry IV* and *Henry V*'. In *Political Shakespeare: New Essays in Cultural Materialism*, ed. Jonathan Dollimore and Alan Sinfield (New York, 1985), p. 2.

[13] D.I.12.3, p. 244. Citations of Machiavelli as follows: D = Leslie J. Walker trans. and ed., *The Discourses of Niccolo Machiavelli*, 2 vols. (London, 1950); P = *The Prince. A New Translation with an Introduction* by Harvey C. Mansfield Jr (Chicago, 1985).

[14] 'On the Continuity of the Henriad'. In *Shakespeare Left and Right*, ed. Ivo Kamps (London and Boston, 1991), p. 229.

enced by Henry – and, one might add, by his father, by Falstaff on his deathbed, and by all of those who continued religious warfare throughout the seventeenth century. Rather than demonstrate opposing biblical and humanist perspectives in *Henry V*, it may be more instructive to show how the Bible itself provided both Machiavelli and Shakespeare with a model for ambivalent attitudes toward holy war, kingship and the relationship between politics and religion.

Like *Henry V*, the biblical text is itself a 'site of contestation'.[15] The God of Deuteronomy through 2 Kings rewards those who obey His commandments and punishes those who don't. The God of Job states that assuming this, as the comforters do, is punishable heresy. Jesus states we should turn the other cheek, but also that he comes to bring the sword. Such inconsistencies are largely attributable to conflicting outlooks of previous 'traditions' or documentary sources of the final canonized text: priestly vs. prophetic, tribal vs. centrist, rural vs. urban, Northern vs. Southern Kingdoms.[16] Similarly, Shakespeare's histories are redactions of layers of documentary sources from Froissart to Halle to Holinshed, each the expression of different ideologies.

One of the contradictions most relevant to Shakespeare's histories is the Bible's dual view of kingship. The Henriad alternates between propounding the Tudor myth of divine ordination and royal infallibility and acknowledging 'that the crown is always illegitimate, that is, always an effect of social relations and not their cause, and therefore must (and can) endlessly be legitimated by improvisations of each wearer'.[17] Likewise, in the Bible, the institution of kingship was a gift of God to the Israelites – 'I will send thee a man . . . to be governor over my people Israel, that he may save my people out of the hands of the Philistines: for I have looked upon my people and their cry is come unto me' (I Samuel 9: 16) – or an expression of the people's rebellion against God: '. . . they have cast me away, that I should not reign over

them . . .', a rebellion in face of the warning that the king will exploit and manipulate them for his own purposes: 'He will take your sons, and appoint them to his chariots and to be his horsemen . . . he will appoint him captains over thousands and captains over fifties; and to ear his ground and to reap his harvest and to make his instruments of war . . . And ye shall cry out that day because of your King whom ye have chosen and the Lord will not hear you at that day' (I Samuel 8: 7–18). And like all of Shakespeare's kings, the individual kings of the Bible are portrayed under profoundly ambivalent judgement. Saul is a charismatic general who succeeds in securing territory by uniting the tribes against the Philistines, but he arrogates too many powers to himself and is driven insane. He is succeeded by David, God's favourite and beloved by the people, but after displaying the self-abnegating loyalty to his master, the brilliance in battle, and the genius in diplomacy to build a great empire, he is punished for betraying God and his subjects in a scandalous sexual intrigue. David's son, Solomon, builds on his father's achievements and attains distinction as the wisest of men, turning the Empire into a showpiece of wealth and culture, but his glory is eclipsed when his sons once again divide the kingdom and plummet it into civil wars which eventually result in

---

15 For a discussion of the ways conflicting perspectives and attitudes are juxtaposed in Shakespearian texts, see Louis Adrian Montrose, 'The Purpose of Playing: Reflections on Shakespearean Anthropology', *Helios*, n.s. 7 (1980): 50–73. For a discussion of the debate between pacifist and militarist politics in *Henry V*, see Steven Marx, 'Shakespeare's Pacifism', *RQ*, 45, Spring 1992.

16 See W. Lee Humphries, *Crisis and Story: An Introduction to the Old Testament* (Mt View, California, 1991), pp. 50–3, 120–1 and Baruch Halpern, *The First Historians: the Hebrew Bible and History* (San Francisco, 1988).

17 David Scott Kastan, '"The King Hath Many Marching in his Coats", or What Did You Do in the War, Daddy.' In *Shakespeare Left and Right*, ed. Ivo Kamps (London and Boston, 1991), p. 256.

foreign conquest. An analogous reversal is reported in the epilogue of *Henry V*:

> The star of England. Fortune made his sword,
> By which the world's best garden he achieved,
> And of it left his son imperial lord . . .
> Whose state so many had the managing
> That they lost France and made his England
> bleed.   (6–12)

The approach to Shakespeare's histories with a providential-historical or religious-secular dichotomy also breaks down when one notes how Renaissance humanists discovered that the Bible contained a political history as rich and revealing as those written by Romans and Greeks. Machiavelli himself found a precedent for his own remorseless value judgements in the Bible's often brutal portrayal of authority, rebellion and war. In the Moses of the Pentateuch, Machiavelli discovered an ideal hero, a model of the qualities that inhered in those who founded durable institutions: 'Of all men that are praised, those are praised most who have played the chief part in founding a religion. Next come those who have founded either republics or kingdoms.'[18] Moses was the only one in Machiavelli's history who did both. 'But to come to those who have become princes by their own virtue and not by fortune, I say that the most excellent are Moses, Cyrus, Romulus, Theseus and the like . . .' In common with all those political leaders who form new states, Moses faces a dual challenge: he must defeat enemies and maintain unity and support among followers. This is foreshadowed in the biblical story of Moses killing the Egyptian taskmaster who was beating a Hebrew slave (Exodus 2: 11–14). Next day, when he returned to try to get two Hebrews to stop fighting each other, they denied his authority and asked whether he planned to kill them as well. The only way that Moses can take control to achieve God's purpose of forming a nation strong enough to beat the Egyptians and conquer their own territory is by producing belief – in enemies, credibility; in followers, faith. This is also the task of Henry

the Fifth as he takes the throne in an England on the edge of invasion and civil war, and reluctant to accept his rule. The means to succeed in this endeavour are enumerated both in the works of Machiavelli and in the Bible.

One such means is to supply legal justification for the appropriation of territory. This is provided to the Hebrews by the contractual agreement Moses reports that God made with their forefather Abraham to grant his seed the promised land. The Archbishops provide Henry with a similar covenant in 'the Law Salique', which 'proves' that he can 'with right and conscience make this claim' (1.2.96) of the territory of France. Such legal justification is largely for home consumption, since it is unlikely to be persuasive to those who presently occupy the land, but the next means – that of intimidation – is addressed equally to followers and opponents. Threats must be rendered convincing with terror tactics, both to weaken enemy morale and to buttress one's own side's confidence. God tells Moses to punish Pharaoh with plague after plague to demonstrate the strength of the Israelites and he repeatedly hardens Pharaoh's heart to make him responsible for the suffering of his own people: 'Then there shall be a great cry throughout all the land of Egypt, such as was never one like, nor shall be. But against none of the children of Israel shall a dog move his tongue neither against man nor beast, that ye may know that the Lord putteth a difference between the Egyptians and Israel' (Exodus 11: 6–7). After justification, Henry also resorts to intimidation, in a series of threats against the French which emphasize the suffering of noncombatants. First he instructs the ambassadors to '. . . tell the pleasant Prince . . . his soul / Shall stand sore chargèd . . . for many a thousand widows / Shall this his mock mock out of their dear husbands, / Mock mothers from their sons . . .' (1.2.281–6). Through Exeter he bids the French king 'in the

---

[18] D. I.10.I, p. 236.

bowels of the Lord, / Deliver up the crown . . . take mercy / On . . . the widows' tears, the orphans' cries, / The dead men's blood, the pining maidens' groans . . .' (2.4.102–7). And finally he utters directly to the citizens of Harfleur the familiar litany of lurid atrocities which brings about the town's surrender (3.3.7–43).

Brutalizing of one's opponents like this also addresses the problem of 'murmurings' among one's followers that constantly troubles Moses – the 'lukewarmness' that Machiavelli observes in citizens of new states. Henry also uses intimidation among his own men to enforce discipline, letting them all know that he is willing to hang his former friend Bardolph for unauthorized plundering, and at the same time claiming that such rigour is mercy rather than cruelty: 'We would have all such offenders so cut off . . . none of the French upbraided or abused in disdainful language. For when lenity and cruelty play for a kingdom, the gentler gamester is the soonest winner.' (3.6.108–14) The king agrees with Machiavelli who insists that cruelty is merciful: 'A prince . . . so as to keep his subjects united and faithful, should not care about the infamy of cruelty, because with very few examples he will be more merciful than those who for the sake of too much mercy allow disorders to continue . . .'[19] Rather than contrasting this cynicism with biblical morality, Machiavelli substantiates his claims with the example of Moses: 'He who reads the Bible with discernment will see that, before Moses set about making laws and institutions, he had to kill a very great number of men who . . . were opposed to his plans.'[20] Here he refers to incidents of rebellion, like worship of the Golden Calf, or Korah's revolt which Moses responded to with mass executions. It is these God-sanctioned actions that validate the Machiavellian maxim that the end justifies the means.[21]

One of the most effective of such means is dissimulation: 'The princes who have done great things are those who have taken little account of faith and have known how to get around men's brains with their astuteness . . .

it is necessary to know well how to . . . be a great pretender and dissembler.'[22] The Bible approves countless examples of such shifts: Abraham and Isaac's deception of Pharaoh and Abimelech, Jacob's deception of his father and uncle, Joseph's protracted deception of father and brothers, Ehud's assassination of the Moabite King, Eglon, David's feigned insanity, Nathan's entrapment of David into confessing his own guilt. Jesus himself tells his disciples they must proceed with the wariness of serpents (Matthew 10: 16) and constantly dissimulates his own weakness. Trickery is a skill that Henry learns from both his father figures, Bolingbroke and Falstaff. Henry IV feigns loyalty to the king he deposes and then solicitude for the one he executes, and he triumphs over his enemies in battle not by valour but with the stratagem of dressing many in the king's coats. Falstaff is the father of lies and disguises. Likewise, just as he robs the robbers and confuses his father's spies, Hal deceives the whole kingdom both with appearances of prodigality and of holiness.

Dissimulation serves to disorient and confuse those over whom one wishes to gain power, but it also serves as a device to gather intelligence. Moses is commanded to send spies into the promised land to report on enemy strength; Joshua sends spies into Jericho to recruit Rahab to spy for them; David constantly spies on Saul, and his general Joab maintains surveillance in all camps. God spies on his enemies in Babel and Sodom and on his subjects, like Adam and Eve, Abraham, Jacob and Job, as he tests their loyalty with temptations and ordeals. So Henry V spies on his subjects in the Boar's Head

---

[19] P. XVII, pp. 65–6.

[20] D. III.30.4, p. 547.

[21] 'Reprehensible actions may be justified by their effects . . . when the effect is good, . . . it always justifies the action . . . I might adduce in support of what I have just said numberless examples, e.g. Moses, Lycurgus, Solon, and other founders of kingdoms and republics . . .' D. I.9.2–5, p. 235.

[22] P. XVIII, pp. 69–70.

tavern, on his captains and foot soldiers on the night before battle, and on his close friends, Cambridge, Scroop and Grey, at the outset of the French campaign.

According to Machiavelli, to produce the belief required for political rule, it is as important to be sceptical oneself as to manipulate the faith of others. Religious deceptions are required because most people are not rational enough to accept the real truths which such deceptions support: 'Nor in fact was there ever a legislator, who in introducing extraordinary laws to a people, did not have recourse to God, for otherwise they would not have been accepted, since many benefits of which a prudent man is aware, are not so evident to reason that he can convince others of them.'[23] Though it is his intelligence system that has discovered the plot against him, Henry construes his rescue as miraculous evidence of God's special protection and parlays that evidence into a morale-raising prediction of future success in battle: 'We doubt not of a fair and lucky war, / Since God so graciously hath brought to light / This dangerous treason lurking in our way . . . Then forth, dear countrymen. Let us deliver / Our puissance into the hand of God . . .' (2.2.181–7) Here he follows Machiavelli's advice about the efficacy of miracles in creating the 'synergistic' alliance between divine and human energies. Astute leaders will both try to create miracles and more important will reinforce faith in earlier miracles to buttress belief in their own miraculous powers.[24] In secret, the Archbishops admit that they no longer believe in miracles: 'It must be so, for miracles are ceased, / And therefore we must needs admit the means / How things are perfected.' (1.1.68–70) They nevertheless also construe Hal's conversion as a supernatural transformation: '. . . a wonder how his grace should glean it / Since his addiction was to courses vain' (1.1.54–5). Their wonder is the outcome intended by Henry's overall strategy of dissimulation. To frustrate expectation either by feigning weakness or bluffing strength is as strategic in politics as in

poker. Mystification and hiding is a rhetorical means of amplifying the power of revelation. God's obscurity in the Bible, his invisibility and remoteness, makes his voice that much louder when it speaks, whether in thunder on Sinai, out of a whirlwind in Job, or at those moments in the New Testament when he drops the disguise of mortal poverty and is suddenly recognized as a divine presence.

Such appearances and removals of disguise are experienced by the citizenry as another species of miracle. When Hal unmasks his own knowledge of the traitors' conspiracy, they admit their sins and condemn themselves to death. When he reveals himself after the robbery at Gad's Hill as one of the 'men in buckram', Falstaff manages to cover any trace of wonder, but when finally 'breaking through the foul and ugly mists / Of vapours that did seem to strangle him' (I Henry 4 1.2.199–200), Henry takes on the mantle of the true King at the last-judgement-like coronation, even the fat man responds by getting real religion. Both playful and awesome, these are the kind of tricks that Hal, like the God of the Bible, seems never to tire of playing.[25] Shakespeare himself also seemed never to tire of plot incidents about dissimulation and of power figures who use such deceptions to produce belief in order to rule others. Some practitioners of this art, like Iago and Edmund, are evil. But more often, the dissimulator adopts a benevolent stance to improve or educate those who are too corrupt

---

[23] D. I.II, p. 237.

[24] 'It was owing to wise men having taken note of this that belief in miracles arose and that miracles are held in high esteem even by religions that are false; for to whatever they owed their origin, sensible men made much of them and their authority caused everybody to believe in them.' D. I.12.3, p. 244.

[25] Only Michael Williams resists this form of Revelation trick. After the battle, when Henry tries to elicit his awe, repentance and gratitude by disclosing that the 'gentleman of a company' to whom Williams had expressed disbelief in the King was actually the King himself, Williams is not impressed.

or deceived or stupid to recognize the truth in its own terms. Ranging from Rosalind, Viola, and Paulina to Duke Vincentio and Prospero, what they all have in common, and what perhaps accounts for Shakespeare's fascination with them, is their theatricality, their association with himself as author and dramatist, a figure who like the author of the Bible is identified with the Word as creative principle, human protagonist, and book itself.

But Machiavelli's paradox about truth hidden in the lies of state religion hints at a conception of God richer than mere subterfuge. Though he rejects the Christianity of his own day as 'effeminate . . . due to the pusillanimity of those who have interpreted our religion', he affirms a religion like that of the Romans or Hebrews that 'permits us to exalt and defend the father land . . . and to train ourselves to be such that we may defend it'.[26] Machiavelli's own 'God-Talk' includes serious references to personalized cosmic forces – whether the seductive Fortuna of *The Prince* or the God who is a 'Lover of strong men', or the 'heaven' who involves himself in human history by choosing strong leaders.[27] Seventeenth-century commentators made much of this aspect of Machiavelli's writings, defending him as being a theologian of the Divine Right of Kings whose outlook was perfectly commensurate with the Bible's rather than an atheistic Machiavel.[28] Their interpretation links Machiavelli to the ancient and medieval doctrine of The Mystery of State – the notion that royal dissimulation is not only a requirement for rule but in itself a divine and divinity-generating activity. Kings are in possession of magic powers by virtue of their access to secrets and occult wisdom withheld from their subjects: 'It is specifically the violence, obscurity and ineffable quality of the gods that must be imitated . . . the coups d'état are princely imitations of all those attributes of divinity that were thought to be either beyond human power (like miracles) or beyond the laws and moral prescriptions that bound men but not God.'[29]

Although he practises dissimulation throughout the play, Henry's most sustained enactment of the Mysteries of State occurs during the moonlit scene before the final battle. The 'ruined band' of the 'poor condemnèd English', who 'like sacrifices, by their watchful fires / Sit patiently and inly ruminate / The morning's danger' (4.0.22–5) are experiencing the dark night of the soul which represents the 'original rendering of "holy war" in Christianity . . . the point at which the devotee is forced to fight with all his strength against despair, against creeping doubts concerning the meaningfulness of his past life and previous sacrifices'.[30] The king, in Godlike fashion, with 'largess universal like the sun . . . thawing cold fear' bestows comfort with 'a little touch of Harry in the night'. But after his morale-raising banter with the lords, Henry's warmth is shown to be a pretence when he asks Erpingham for his cloak and admits that he needs to be alone for a while before he can continue encouraging the other officers.

---

[26] D. II.2.6–7, p. 364.

[27] P. XXV, pp. 98–101 ('Fortuna'); Martelli *Tutti gli opera*, p. 626 cited by Anthony J. Parel, *The Machiavellian Cosmos* (New Haven, 1992), pp. 57, 56 ('Heaven'); D. II.29.1, pp. 444–5 ('Lover of strong men').

[28] Peter Donaldson, *Machiavelli and the Mystery of State* (New York, 1988). In his final chapter, 'Biblical Machiavellism: Louis Machon's *Apologie pour Machiavel*', Donaldson unearths and analyses an obscure seventeenth century reading of Machiavelli and the Bible. A work of close to 800 pages commissioned by Cardinal Richelieu, it defends those passages in *The Discourses* and *The Prince* most often attacked for impiety. 'One may cease to be surprised', says Machon, 'that I draw parallels between Holy Scripture and the works of Machiavelli and that I propose that his strongest and most formidable maxims were drawn from the book of books . . . if one considers that this sacred volume, which should be the study and meditation of all true Christians, teaches princes as well as subjects . . .' 1668 preface, pp. 1–2, trans. and cited by Donaldson, p. 188.

[29] Donaldson, p. 172.

[30] James Aho, *Religious Mythology and the Art of War: Comparative Religious Symbolisms of Military Violence* (Westport, Connecticut, 1981), p. 146.

The cloak's new disguise serves him in several ways. First he uses it to spy on the men, in order to determine the strength of their support and to root out their murmurings and weak morale. This he must do in mufti, for he knows that if he appears as himself, his subjects will tell him, like any higher power, only what they think he wants to hear. Eavesdropping on Pistol, Gower and Fluellen produces evidence of their full support, and so he moves on. The conversation between Court, Bates and Williams is less reassuring and requires intervention. He tries to counter their hopelessness with assurances of the King's exemplary valour and their cynicism with biblical parables and Jesuitical casuistry justifying the righteousness of the war, but none of these efforts works to produce belief.

This is the one time Henry fails, and he is so frustrated that he almost blows his cover with a threat against Williams (4.1.207). The frustration arises not so much from the inconsequential political setback, as from the failure of another motive covered by his cloak: he too needs a little touch of warmth. For Henry himself experiences an interior holy war, his own dark night of the soul. Upon leaving Erpingham, he had admitted that 'I and my bosom must debate awhile' (4.1.32), and to the soldiers he utters a lengthy description of the King's personal vulnerability: '. . . I think the King is but a man, as I am . . . when he sees reason of fears, as we do, his fears, out of doubt, be of the same relish as ours are. Yet, in reason, no man should possess him with any appearance of fear, lest he, by showing it, should dishearten his army' (4.1.101–12). The disguise here is thinning. Harry Le Roi speaks more frankly than Henry the Fifth ever could, but, ironically, the soldiers react to his plea for their support as if it were only manipulative dissimulation.

During the play's first scene, the Archbishops had used the language of holy war to describe Henry's earlier identity crisis as a scourging crusade: '. . wildness, mortified in him, /

Seemed to die . . . Consideration like an angel came / And whipped th' offending Adam out of him, / Leaving his body as a paradise / T'envelop and contain celestial spirits / . . . reformation in a flood . . . scouring faults; / . . . Hydra-headed wilfulness / So soon did lose his seat' (1.1.27–37). According to Canterbury, Henry's motivation and ability as a general/king/god was cultivated through his preparatory defeat of the forces of that Great Satan, Falstaff, in a coup d'état much like the one his father staged to topple Richard and his supporters. Developing the personality of a King required killing, whipping, and a scouring flood. But on this eve of battle we see his internal enemies not as wildness but as fear, doubt and guilt.

As he moves away from the soldiers to confront these opponents, Henry uncloaks himself fully. Heard only by the spying audience, in soliloquy he reveals the mystery of state. His royalty, his godlike divine right, is mere dissimulation performed by monarch-actor and applauded by subjects-spectators. His unceremonious encounter with Williams, Court, and Bates has taught him that he is nothing without ceremony, that ceremony itself is at once king and god, and that all are Baconian idols: 'And what have kings that privates have not too, / Save ceremony, save general ceremony? / . . . What kind of god art thou, that suffer'st more / Of mortal griefs than do thy worshippers?' (4.1.235–9) His acknowledgement resembles the tormented recognitions of other Shakespearian military leaders who have lost faith in their own self projections – tragic protagonists like Hamlet, Lear, Antony and Coriolanus – and it also alludes to the tragic portrait of the suffering servant in Isaiah and the Gospels, in particular the internal struggle of Christ during his vigil at Gethsemane. This identification is itself another Mystery of State, what Donaldson calls 'a royal kenosis':

The prince, imitating a divinity who put off his divinity in Christ in order to achieve the salvation of the world, puts off an ideal and otherworldly goodness in order to achieve the safety of the people, exchanging contemplative perfection for morally flawed action . . . the idea that the king is an imitator of God . . . includes mimesis . . . of those modes of divine action that entail a lowering of the divine nature . . . 'It is only a good prince who will hazard his own salvation to seek that of the subjects whom he governs'.[31]

Reconceiving his despair and weakness as itself an attribute of divinity, Henry can again dissimulate authority in a brief encounter with Erpingham, who interrupts him for a moment to remind him of his officers' need for the King's presence.

Alone once more, perhaps having returned the cloak to its owner, the King addresses God directly in a mode of discourse even less performative than soliloquy, prayer. We see him encountering the existential reality of God-in-the-trenches rather than projecting the ideological spectacle of 'God for Harry'. And yet what does he seek at this moment of truth? 'Steel my soldiers' hearts, possess them not with fear.' His request is for morale – the very thing that his own public performance is expected to produce, the very thing that the soldiers and the lords ask of him, and that he, as Harry Le Roy, has asked of them. His 'God of Battles' is imagined not as one who will bring victory through a miraculous defeat of the enemy, but rather as one who will succeed where Henry has just failed, in buttressing his men's courage and faith. As if to instruct God, he specifies the means by which this effect can be achieved: 'Take from them now / The sense of reck'ning, ere th' opposèd numbers / Pluck their hearts from them' (4.1.287–9). It is to blind them from the truth, to cloud their thinking, to reinstitute ceremonial dissimulation. This request for falsehood slides into another uncomfortable revelation of truth: 'Not today, O Lord, / O not today, think not upon the fault / My father made in compassing the crown' (289–91). He again begs God to hide the truth, but now from Himself. In other words, Henry prays that God will help him deceive his own

conscience, like the King in *Hamlet*, 'a man to double business bound' (3.3.41). But also like Claudius, Henry is again frustrated. Instead of being granted forgetfulness, he is further reminded of his guilt and failure: 'I Richard's body have interrèd new, / And on it have bestowed . . . contrite tears . . . / . . . I have built / Two chantries . . . / More will I do, / Though all that I can do is nothing worth, / Since that my penitence comes after ill, / Imploring pardon' (292–302). No matter how he tries to cover them, the King cannot escape the knowledge of the secrets he keeps. Sanctimonious action, whether in the form of daily penances of solemn priests or the holy war against France, fails to produce a feeling of innocence. Both God and King must rule by the art of dissimulation, and yet never be themselves deceived. This is the burden of the Mystery of State that will keep him forever imploring pardon. But simply setting it down for a moment in private allows him to gather the strength to carry it further. For that burden is also a magic instrument, an occult wisdom that gives him the sense of superiority over all other humans.

Machon illuminates the tension in the closing lines of Henry's prayer with this frank analysis of moral frailty and strength:

When I hide to attend to my natural functions, is this not to dissimulate the human weakness that is in me? When I do not speak all reveries that are in my mind and the extravagances that present themselves there without any consent, is that not to dissimulate, since my words are other than my thoughts and I reveal only the hundredth part of them? When I deny the vices I am accused of, hide my bad humor, am generous against my will, do not speak to women of the favors which in my heart I desire of them, forget myself before those to whom I owe respect, and since all my life, like those of other men is merely constraint, and ceremony, is it not to dissimulate, is it not in fact to practice what people want me to condemn in words? What would the world be

---

31 Donaldson, pp. 215–16 summarizing and citing Machon 1668, p. 778.

without dissimulation? What would become of prudence, shame, modesty, discretion, reserve, honesty, civility, pleasure, estimation, reputation, honor, glory, reward, love, clemency, compassion, good deeds and all the best virtues that temper our malice and cover up our infirmities and our faults?[32]

Like Machon's true confession that falsehood is necessary, Henry's honest acknowledgement of his secret guilt makes it possible for him to continue dissimulating. Now he can respond to his importunate brother Gloucester by saying, 'I will go with thee. / The day, my friends, and all things stay for me' (4.1.304–5).

The night-time victory in his inner holy war powers Henry's morning speech on St Crispian's Day. So effective is this in awakening faith and producing belief that the men express a sense of privilege in being able to participate in an engagement where they are five times outnumbered. In several ways that speech leads back to the original scene of holy war in the book of Exodus. Promising victory to the frightened Israelites on the night before their departure from Egypt, Moses delivers instructions for celebrating this as a feast day with a blood sacrifice and a shared meal that is to protect, mark and bond them:

Let every man take unto him a lamb according to the house of the fathers . . . then all the multitude of the congregation of Israel shall kill it at even. After they shall take of the blood and strike it on the two posts, and on the upper doorposts of the houses where they shall eat it. And they shall eat the flesh the same night . . .   (Exodus 12: 3–9)

Likewise, Henry proclaims that 'This day is call'd the Feast of Crispian' (4.3.40) and that '. . . he today that sheds his blood with me / Shall be my brother; be he ne'er so vile, / This day shall gentle his condition' (4.3.61–3). Both speeches prophesy the participation of future generations in the upcoming events by incorporating instructions for ritual commemoration of the event even before it happens. Thus Moses,

And this day shall be unto you a remembrance: and ye shall keep it an holy feast unto the Lord throughout your generations: ye shall keep it holy by an ordinance forever . . . for that same day I will bring your armies out of the land of Egypt: therefore ye shall observe this day throughout your posterity by an ordinance forever.   (Exodus 12: 14–17)

And thus Henry,

> He that shall see this day, and live t'old age
> Will yearly on the vigil feast his neighbors
> And say, 'Tomorrow is Saint Crispian.'
> Then will he strip his sleeve and show his scars
> . . .
> . . . Then shall our names . . .
> Be in their flowing cups freshly remembered.
>   (4.3.44–55)

Though embedded within their historical narratives, both speeches explain future ritual repetitions with reference to the tale that is about to unfold. Moses says,

And when your children ask you what service is this you keep? Then ye shall say, it is the sacrifice of the Lord's passover which passed over the houses of the children of Israel in Egypt when he smote the Egyptians and preserved our houses. Then the people bowed themselves and worshipped . . .
                                    (12: 26–7)

And Henry commands,

> This story shall the good man teach his son,
> And Crispin Crispian shall ne'er go by
> From this day to the ending of the world
> But we in it shall be rememberèd.   (4.3.56–9)

Such breaks of the narrative frame – endlessly repeated in the biblical accounts of the Exodus – anticipate what is to come, both within the stories themselves and in their later reception.

The anticipatory breaks in biblical and Shakespearian epics of holy war have complex functions. They recursively include readers and auditors as participants in past actions while at the same time instructing them how to make those actions come to pass in the present and stay alive in the future through imaginative reenactment. These functions are shared by Shakespeare's Chorus in its urgent direct addresses to the audience.[33] The Chorus insists that collaboration between author and auditor 'in the quick forge and working-house of thought' (5.0.23) is required to make the illusion real, thereby producing stronger belief, but also acknowledging the fictive nature of the history. The audience is thus both partaker and participant in the Mysteries of State that are enacted in the play. As opposed to the peasant slave whose 'gross brain little wots / What watch the king keeps to maintain the peace' (4.1.279–80), the 'discerning' reader of both the Bible and of Shakespeare is in on the secret and can share with Harry the power and the guilt of the holy war.[34]

---

[32] Machon 640–1, cited by Donaldson, p. 200.

[33] As Altman says, he 'extends the [participatory] relationship of prince and subject as portrayed in [*Henry V*] so that it becomes a relationship between player/king and audience/subject . . .', p. 15.

[34] Both Greenblatt and Altman have drawn attention to some alarming implications of these converging suspensions of disbelief: '. . . the first part of *Henry 4* enables us to feel . . . we are . . . testing dark thoughts without damaging the order that those thoughts would seem to threaten. The second part of *Henry 4* suggests that we are . . . compelled to pay homage to a system of beliefs whose fraudulence somehow only confirms their power, authenticity and truth. The concluding play in the series, *Henry 5*, insists that we have all along been both colonizer and colonized, king and subject.' Greenblatt, p. 42. '. . . amplification ambiguously reassuring and threatening, which offers up images of rational accessibility juxtaposed with those of imperial closure . . . revelation and mystification, both the articulated and concealed forms – the exquisition of causes, of effects, and of parallels, the emblems and personifications – fill the imagination only to make more illustrious Harry's darkly enigmatic nature. One must always feel anxious about such a king, since one can never fully possess him . . . From dim and unexpected places he will make claims upon one's mind and body that cannot be eluded.' Altman, p. 24. I believe the mentally colonizing rhetorical strategies discovered by these scholars are modelled in the history of the Bible.

HAMLET AND THE ANXIETY OF MODERN JAPAN

YASUNARI TAKAHASHI

The context in which Shakespeare made his first appearance in Japan was a rather curious one. It was in connection with a most unlikely book called *Self-Help* by the Victorian moralist, Samuel Smiles. Published in London in 1859, and now read, I suspect, only by specialists on Victorian ideology, the book preaches through many an instructive episode the virtues of perseverance and self-help required for achieving the all-important goal of respectability in society. It was translated into Japanese in 1871, three years after the Meiji Restoration, and instantly became one of the best-selling books of the time.[1] Why this popularity of what seems to us one of the most boring specimens of Victorian didacticism? The reason was simple: the book answered, or so it seemed, the need of a nation which, after nearly three centuries of isolation, was eagerly seeking whatever was new and modern. *New* and *modern* of course meant *Western*. 'Westernize!' was the greatest, or indeed the only motto of the age. And people jumped at Smiles's collection of prosaic homilies as a display of information about Western manners and customs, as a text book of Western morality, and even as a guidebook on 'how to live' in a brave new world of *bunmei-kaika* (civilization and enlightenment) where anyone, irrespective of his (not *her*, of course) class, at least in principle, could make a successful career in life.

Smiles first mentions Shakespeare as an exemplary man of self-help, 'a hard worker' who made his progress from 'a very humble rank' to a successful playwright.[2] Then, as an epigraph to the chapter entitled 'Money – Use and Abuse', he quotes three lines from Shakespeare without naming the exact source: 'Neither a borrower nor a lender be; / For loan oft loses both itself and friend, / And borrowing dulls the edge of husbandry.'[3]

It was on this didactic and utilitarian note that the play *Hamlet* made its unidentified début in Japan. Such incongruities may often happen in early periods of any cross-cultural encounter, but one must feel particular irony in the possibilities that *Hamlet* may have played a role in the ground-laying process of modern Japan. For the Victorian moral code of frugality, which Smiles illustrated with those lines of Polonius, together with his exhortation of 'self-help' and 'hard working', was later incorporated into the imperial edict on educational and fundamental principles of morality, which, proclaimed by Emperor Meiji in 1890, is considered to have exercised great influence upon the formation of the consciousness of the developing nation.

---

[1] Samuel Smiles, *Self-Help; with Illustrations of Character and Conduct* (London, 1859), translated by Masanao Nakamura under the title of *Saikoku Risshihen* (Stories of Successful Lives in the West) (Tokyo, 1871). Strictly speaking, the first mention of Shakespeare's name was made in 1841 in a Japanese translation (via Dutch translation) of Lindley Murray, *English Grammar* (1808 edition).

[2] Smiles, *Self-Help*, p. 8.

[3] Ibid., p. 215.

Extract from the new Japanese Drama
Hamuretu san, "Danumarku no Kami", proving
the plagiarisms of English literature of the 16ᵗʰ
Century

Arimas, arimasen, are wa nan deska :—
Moshi motto daijobu atama nika, itai arimas
Nawa mono to ha ichiban naruk takusan ichiban
Arui ude torimas me narimendo koto wa,
Sooshte, bobbery itashimas o shimai?. Shindanji, ner
Mada;—sorekara, neru de hanashi mo yoroshi
Kotoro itai to issen mainichi bonkots
Uski ototsan arimas. sore wa dekimashta mono
Takusan shimashita, Shindanji;— neru;—
Neru' okata nese haikin; sayo achira stoch
serampan;
ᵗ wa ano chindanji no neru nani nui haiken
dec̄ mas
Tono nanga shindanji mono piggy shimashita,
Stoshi mata ceayo

————

Voi valete, et plaudite.
Amata sayonara, sooshte te pompon.

6 A sketch of the supposedly first (partial) performance
of *Hamlet* in Japan, published in *The Japan Punch* (1874).
The script beginning with 'Arimas, arimasen, are wa nan
deska' is a romanized translation of the first part of
Hamlet's 'To be, or not to be' soliloquy, which sounds
gibberishly colloquial. From Toshio Kawatake, *Nippon no
Hamuretto* (1972)

After that aridly moralizing exploitation of
'Hamlet without the Prince of Denmark', it is
with great relief that we come upon our second
document which deals with 'the thing itself',
the Prince himself, and moreover the performance itself of the play. Three years after the
translation of Smiles, an interesting picture was
published in *The Japan Punch*, a monthly
English journal edited by Charles Wirgman,
the English painter and correspondent of *The
Illustrated London News*, and circulated among
foreigners in Yokohama. It is apparently a
sketch by Wirgman of a scene from a certain
performance, depicting a samurai standing in a
meditative posture, with two Japanese words

vertically flanking the stage (the right-hand side
one meaning *playhouse* and the left-hand side
one *Shakespeare*). There is a four-line English
caption at the top saying 'Extract from the new
Japanese Drama Hamurettu san, "Danumarku
no Kami" (the Prince of Denmark), proving
the plagiarisms of English literature in the sixteenth century', and below the picture we see
what purports to be a Japanese translation in
romanized transcription of the first thirteen
lines of Hamlet's 'To be or not to be' soliloquy.

This may be no more than a simple cartoon;
in fact the Japanese translation of the soliloquy
sounds so *Jabberwocky*, that one is tempted to
take the whole thing as a joke or a riddle which
the cartoonist enjoys at the expense of some
foolhardy Japanese amateur company which
challenged the most difficult of Western plays.[4]
And yet, it looks to me as though it epitomizes,
in an embryonic form, the whole problematics
involved in my subject. Could it be that this
melancholy-looking samurai-Hamlet was pondering more than just a philosophical question
of 'to be or not to be'? Surely, prior to being
philosophical, the question for him must have
been theatrical: How do I speak these thirteen
lines? What do they mean? How should I play
this part? How should one put on this play
called *Hamurettu san*? Could one ever do it?
Indeed, to do it, or not to do it, that might very
well have been the question.

The question was compounded of many
dilemmas. It was clear that the cultural trans-
plant of drama required acclimatization of the
original work – or 'plagiarism', as the cartoonist
satirically called it in the caption. And that
would mean in this case adaptation of *Hamlet*
into *kabuki*. But then it was obvious that *kabuki*
in its existing form was far too old-fashioned to
appropriate *Hamlet*, or any Western play, for
that matter. If *kabuki* was not allowed to be an

---

4 See Toshio Kawatake's indispensable study, *Nippon no
Hamuretto* (Hamlet in Japan) (Tokyo, 1972), pp. 56–67.
Also useful is the same author's *Hikaku Engekigaku*
(Comparative Theatrology) (Tokyo, 1967).

exception to that grand rationale of modernization-as-westernization, it must be innovated to meet the demand of the age. And it fell to the lot of *Hamlet* to become a crucial site for this transformation to take place. Or more precisely, it was *Hamlet* as well as Japanese theatre that had to change in the process. And the whole labour of assimilating *Hamlet*, from the beginning down to the present day, could be seen as the mirror up to the nature of Japan's modernization since 1868.

At one end of the spectrum, we find a public or political dimension. In 1886, as part of the cultural policy of the Meiji Government a group of influential apologists for westernization from academic and political fields formed a body called 'The Society for Improvement of Theatre'. One of the first things it did was to deplore the low social status of actors and criticize the vulgarity of manners of the audience in kabuki playhouses. It proposed to replace *onnagata* (a male actor impersonating a female role) with an actress – not out of feminist concerns, of course, but simply because such a custom did not exist in the West. It argued for the abolition of musical performance accompanying the show as well as of *kurogo* (stage-hands in black visible on stage). It wanted to eliminate scenes which would seem too grotesque or cruel or erotic in the eyes of an enlightened audience. (It may be of some interest, by the way, to note that these strictures upon *kabuki* were couched in phrases that might faintly remind us of Hamlet's lecture to the players upon the standard of popular theatre.) The ultimate aim of the Society was to create on the model of the West a new form of 'national theatre' fit for a new age. Political implication was unmistakable in its appeal for the building of a new presentable playhouse which any civilized country should be equipped with for the purpose of entertaining important guests from overseas. In short, to 'make it new' meant to make it more 'rational' and more 'realistic'. At the worst, the urge for innovation in theatre became indistinguishable from the general cry for the nation-wide march towards the goal of 'materialistic civilization'.

The Society also encouraged the creation of new plays, but the only tangible result was a *kabuki* play based on historical facts. Predictably, it was a poor play, for it discarded what constituted the 'irrational' charms of *kabuki* without creating a new form of realism. After all, there was no denying that *kabuki* was a theatre form which, over the long period of national seclusion, had become the flesh and blood of popular culture. It was simply not possible to bring about a transformation overnight through a set of ideas conceived in the West-oriented brains of a few intellectuals and bureaucrats.

What would have happened, one wonders, if *kabuki* had attempted a foreign play, say, *Hamlet*? Let us picture to ourselves a seventy-year-old *kabuki* actor in a minor troupe who had been in the business for the last fifty years, i.e. from before the Restoration. And let us suppose that his favourite part was the character called Kudayu, a villain in the *kabuki* play *Kanadehon Chushingura* (or just *Chushingura* for short), the most popular piece in the whole repertory of *kabuki*. It is a story about forty-seven samurais who, despite all hardships and distractions, succeed in revenging their lord who was wrongfully forced to commit *harakiri*. What would happen if, as luck would have it, the old stubborn actor were assigned the role of Polonius in the first ever production of *Hamlet* in Japan around 1890? He would very probably refuse to play it on the ground that this chap Polonius didn't make sense to him, or (as a modern actor would say) that he just couldn't *relate to* the role. Then, how should one persuade him?

Perhaps by coaxing him into believing that Polonius does resemble Kudayu. In fact, this man is not unlike Polonius in being a petty plotting politician, who, after the lamentable death of his former lord, is now serving the enemy lord. Besides, both Polonius and Kudayu have a hot-tempered young son (Laertes and

Sadakuro). And if that is mere concidence, is it not significant that both die in a similar way? In Act 7 of *Chushingura*, Kudayu is stabbed to death by Yuranosuke, the revenger-hero of the play, when he (Yuranosuke) discovers him (Kudayu) hiding under the floor (though not behind the arras) to spy on the letter which Yuranosuke is reading.[5] It would be amusing to imagine the old actor being happily convinced, even to the point of declaring that this Western playwright named Shakespeare must have read *Chushingura* before writing *Hamlet*. He might have cried out, inverting the caption of the cartoon, '*Hamlet* is a plagiarism of *Chushingura*!' – It might have been only in some such manner that the old actor's mind and body would begin to respond to his new role.

There is, in fact, a sense in which *Hamlet* was less intractable a play than it would seem to those unfamiliar with *kabuki*. For 'revenge play' with complicated power struggles inside a big royal or ducal family was a genre so familiar to *kabuki* that people could be expected to accept without too much resistance what looked like its Western equivalent. Furthermore, similarities seemed to obtain not only at the narrative level but also in dramatic techniques. Shakespeare's un-classical, richly variegated dramaturgy, with its mixture of the poetic and the prosaic, the tragic and the comic, the rational and the irrational, looked, *mutatis mutandis*, rather amenable to *kabuki*'s own tradition which cherished a baroque profusion of scenes with ghosts, blood, suicide, pretended madness etc. Certainly, Shoyo Tsubouchi, the great Shakespeare translator, was right in emphasizing that the early seventeenth-century English playwright shared much more in common with Chikamatsu, the great *kabuki* playwright of the late seventeenth century, than he does with a modern European dramatist like Ibsen.[6]

Such similarities and accessibilities, however, were only half of the story. The samurai-Hamlet in the cartoon would not have looked so worried had there not been more serious and complex problems. Difficulties over adapting

Hamlet were manifest in the earliest full-scale attempt by Robun Kanagaki to introduce the play as a whole, published twelve years after the cartoon. Entitled *Hamuretto Yamato Nishikie* (The Story of Hamlet in Japanese Colour Wood-print), it was conceived as a totally traditional *kabuki* piece, as is clear from its sumptuous illustrations.[7]

Of course, there should be no need to object to the story being set in fourteenth-century Japan, or to the characters being given Japanese names. But a more serious kind of distortion occurred in the process of adaptation. For instance, filial duty forces 'Laertes' to avenge his father, but at the same time he knows that to kill the son of his (former) master would be a crime against fealty. This essentially static double-bind between two kinds of loyalties, a favourite theme of *kabuki*, is so much stressed that it must gravely alter the tragic ambiguity of the ending of the original play. At the end of the duel scene, 'Hamlet' commits *harakiri* after killing 'Claudius', and *then* (not *before*) the wounded 'Laertes' follows suit and takes his own life in the same way. This act, which is for him the only solution of the dilemma, is praised by the final chant of the chorus as 'the admirable pattern of loyal samurai'. This is a strange conclusion, one must say, to be drawn from *Hamlet*, but it is in perfect conformity to the feudalistic-Confucian ideology which defines the moral world of *kabuki*.

In terms of dramatic structure, this first adaptation of *Hamlet* succumbs to another weakness ingrained in *kabuki*, a strong penchant

---

5 For further similarities between the two plays, see Harue Tsutsumi, *Kanadehon Hamuretto* (Tokyo, 1993), an intriguing play set in a rehearsal scene of an imaginary might-have-been-the-first production of *Hamlet* in Japan.

6 Shoyo Tsubouchi, 'Chikamatsu versus Shakespeare versus Ibsen', *The Selected Works of Shoyo* (Tokyo, 1927), vol. 10, pp. 769–813.

7 The first Shakespearian play adapted into Japanese (*Julius Caesar*, 1884) and the first one performed (*The Merchant of Venice*, 1885) were both in *kabuki*-style.

7 Illustration to Robun Kanagaki's *kabuki* adaptation, *Hamuretto Yamato Nishikie* (1886), depicting Hamuramaru (Hamlet)'s encounter with his father's ghost

for independent scenic effects. This is geared to the taste of the audience which appreciates individual skills of main actors quite regardless of the logic of dramatic action. This *kabuki Hamlet* presents two scenes of pure spectacle where the mock-mad prince and the mad Ophelia perform typical *kabuki*-dances respectively. In the much-delayed first production of this adaptation seen in Tokyo and London in 1991, this indulgence in the spectacular at the expense of the dramatic was carried to an extreme by the directorial device of doubling the roles of Hamlet and Ophelia, which meant that the nunnery scene was impossible to play. And that meant the Prince had no chance to display an acerbic sense of irony, that inalienable hallmark of his character.

This leads us to the problem of actresses. The tradition of *onnagata* goes back far beyond 1629

when the Tokugawa Government banned the performances of female followers of Okuni, the legendary female originator of *kabuki*. *Onnagata* had been so long-established and so much taken for granted that the idea of actresses was not easily embraced even by the theatre innovators of the Meiji Era, some of whom just went on using *onnagata* in their new productions. The *kabuki Hamlet* we are talking about was no doubt written with *onnagata* in mind (and it was produced that way in 1991).

The first *performance* of *Hamlet* in Tokyo in 1903 was interestingly ambiguous in this respect.[8] This important event was particularly memorable for two reasons: firstly, the story

---

[8] There had been an earlier performance in Osaka the previous year.

8 Madame Sadayacco as Orieko (Ophelia) in the second full performance of the play (1903) which adapted the story to contemporary Japan

was set not in the past as in other adaptations but in contemporary Japan, and secondly, the part of Ophelia was played by an actress. The actress was Sadayakko, who had previously become internationally famous as 'Madame Sadayacco' during her American and European tours in 1899 to 1901. But even this production could not make a complete break with tradition. It made an odd compromise: Gertrude

was played by an *onnagata*; the cast was a mixture of actress and *onnagata*. Characteristically, the production was billed as *Hamuretto* (phonetically close to the English *Hamlet*) in order to make it sound new, but in actual performance the names of the characters were all 'Japanized'.

Another serious problem brings us back again to our cartoon, to the 'to be or not to be' soliloquy — or I should rather say, to its *absence*. For the soliloquy, and all the other soliloquies too, were completely cut in both the first adaptation and the first two performances of *Hamlet*. Another impossibility here: the Prince of Denmark without soliloquies. The cut cannot be attributed to the absence of soliloquy in the *kabuki* tradition, since *kabuki* does use soliloquy. The reason must be sought in the differences in the nature of soliloquy. In *kabuki*, soliloquy is often performed rather like an aria in opera, accompanied by musical instruments; the language, half-sung, is explicitly stylized; and its function is mainly descriptive and explanatory rather than expressive of the speaker's inner workings of thought. In other words, the kind of 'pure' soliloquy which characterizes Hamlet as an individual, as a self independent of the situation, in short as a typically modern thinking man, was something unknown to *kabuki*.

How painfully gradual the process of acclimatizing *Hamlet* had to be may be gathered from the fact that, in the first Tokyo performance, the first soliloquy ('O that this too too sullied flesh would melt . . .') was re-arranged into a dialogue with Horatio, and the 'to be or not to be' soliloquy, although it had been included in the play-script, was cut by the judgement of Otojiro Kawakami who produced the show. This notoriously inventive actor-manager and entrepreneur deserves great applause for rebelling against the *kabuki* tradition and attempting a Western-style dialogue drama. Ironically, however, his very aim put him at a loss as to how to deal with Hamlet's soliloquy, which seemed unrealistic (as all soliloquies are bound to seem a bit artificial). He would have liked to do it, had he been able to find the right way, but since he could not, and since he had disavowed the way of *kabuki*, the only thing he could do was to cut it. He could not see that *Hamlet* was not quite a 'realistic' play in the modern sense.

In this respect, we should acknowledge how singular our cartoon Hamlet is. Far from avoiding the soliloquy, he is seen grappling with it in sad earnest. The gibberishly literal and colloquial translation which is given him to speak sets it utterly free from the traditional archaism of *kabuki* language. Even in comparison with dozens of later translations, its experimental boldness is devastating and unmatchable; it sounds almost like a Dada poem. The rendition of the famously difficult first line into 'Arimas, arimasen, arewa nan deska' will be sure to make any Japanese today laugh for its literalism and for its vast difference from familiar translations. For the cartoon actor, however, it must have been no laughing matter.

Things look a little different if we glance away from the theatre world proper. In 1882, twenty years before the first performance of the adapted *Hamlet*, there was published a book of poetry entitled *Shintaishi-sho* (An Anthology of Poems in New Style), which sent a profound shock of the new into the hearts of young readers. It included two translations of the entire 'to be or not to be' soliloquy, which quickly became one of the best-known quotations of Western literature. Without the play's having been actually performed yet, Prince Hamlet became for the young literati what he had become for the European romantics a century before: a modern self, doubting everything, but true to its own doubting conscience, fiercely critical of the established order, lonely and vulnerable.

Among many who were inspired by the translations was a poet and would-be dramatist who, while recognized now as one of the most fascinating figures in early modern Japanese literature in his own right, can perhaps claim

the honour of representing the reception of *Hamlet* in Japan at its most radical level. This young man, Tokoku Kitamura by name, had a burning ambition to revolutionize Japanese drama. And the shadow of the Prince of Denmark is felt in many of his utterances on drama. He believed in drama as a mirror up to the age; he criticized *kabuki*-influenced contemporary drama for its lack of great themes such as the fate of man, the meaning of death, or the mystery of the universe; he defied tradition by claiming the sovereignty of author over actors; and he aspired to give theatrical expression to what he called in his celebrated essay 'the inner life' of modern self, which could have been an echo of what Hamlet had called 'that within which passes show'. In 1891, the twenty-two-year-old Tokoku wrote a verse play, *Horai-kyoku* (The Play of Mt Fuji), which revealed the influence of the 'new style poetry' translations of the soliloquy, although its hero had more affinities with Byron's Manfred and Goethe's Faust than with Hamlet. In both manner and matter, the play looked far too literary and cerebral, and Tokoku himself knew too well that there could be no way of getting it performed. Ultimately, the price he had to pay for 'the necessity of being absolutely modern' (in the phrase of his French contemporary, Arthur Rimbaud) proved high. Amidst the despair resulting from an amalgam of literary, political, and emotional frustrations, he committed suicide at the age of twenty-five in 1894.

Tokoku created what might be called a genealogy of 'literary suicide', the most famous case perhaps being that of a precocious seventeen-year-old named Misao Fujimura, who flung himself into a waterfall in 1903, leaving a kind of death-poem on the 'utter imponderability of life and universe', before which (the poem said) 'Horatio's philosophy is worth nothing.' The incident was construed at that time as symptomatic of the anxiety over the problem of self which had been accruing in the Japanese psyche underneath the rage for material prosperity ever since the Meiji Restoration. With the death-poem acquiring a fame comparable to that of the 'to be or not to be' soliloquy, the boy became a bit of a Hamlet-figure. A much later case is the double suicide in 1947 of Osamu Dazai, one of the best post-war Japanese novelists and the author of *Shin Hamuretto* (The New Hamlet) (1941). I wonder if our poor cartoon actor had any premonition that the character he was playing might come to cause such real-life tragedies. Surely, the author of *Self-Help* would have been the last man to admit responsibility, much less to smile.

Coming back to theatre, the too too solid bond of tradition was not to melt and thaw even in a production in 1907, perhaps the most significant one in our history. The man who masterminded this first production using a translated (not adapted) text was Shoyo Tsubouchi, professor of English at Waseda University, translator of the complete works of Shakespeare to be finished thirty years later, playwright in his own right, and undoubtedly the greatest figure in my subject. The production was the first to use fully Western costume, the first to name Hamlet Hamlet, Ophelia Ophelia, and the first to speak the 'to be or not to be' lines as a proper soliloquy.[9]

Even so, it failed to go the whole way. Gertrude was still played by an *onnagata*; there was still too much of a *kabuki* inflection in the language. Though the actors were consciously chosen from amateurs untainted by the professionalism of *kabuki* or *kyogen*, they were not able to create a fresh 'colloquial' and 'realistic' acting style. These contradictions were, in the last analysis, a reflection of the contradictions that were built into the personality of the great leader himself. Despite the fact that Shoyo realized the necessity of modernization of theatre more clearly than anyone else in the theatre world, his heart was obeying a logic which his mind did not know. His sensibility had been nurtured too deeply by the old *kabuki* tradition to allow him to be 'absolutely modern'. He was a living fissure between the old culture and the new.

To give one telling instance. Shoyo was enlightened enough to ask two English people ('Mrs Kate' and 'Mr Mackay', who had had dramatic training in England) to instruct the actors in vocal expressions and physical actions. Coming, however, to see a rehearsal three days before the first night, he caused havoc by requesting everything to be changed. He did not like the 'Western' acting style at all; he forced his own taste and interpretations on the company.

Four years later, in 1911 (which was the last but one year of the Meiji Era), Shoyo challenged the task yet again. He reshuffled the company, abolished *onnagata*, re-wrote the text so as to make it less archaic. And the venue could not have been better: the newly built Western-style theatre Teikoku Gekijo (The Imperial Theatre), the first of its kind. This was as 'complete' and 'faithful' a performance of *Hamlet* as anyone at the time could have possibly imagined. It had every right to be deemed the achievement of the grand aim towards which all the past renderings of *Hamlet* had been striving. One might have thought that the cartoon Hamlet had at last got all his problems solved and had been freed from that worried contraction of his eyebrows.

But not quite. The limitations discerned in the previous production remained unchanged, the contradictions unresolved. Commercially it was a big success, but it made 'the judicious grieve' (as Hamlet would say). In the 'censure' of one of the most redoubtable critics, Soseki Natsume, who had studied English literature for two years in London, it failed to reproduce 'that poetic beauty which Shakespeare created at the expense of realism', nor did it succeed in

---

[9] There had been previous productions using the original names of characters: *Julius Caesar* (1901) and *The Merchant of Venice* (1903, 1906). The credit for speaking the soliloquy for the first time in performance must go to the first kabuki-style adaptation which preceded Shoyo's production by a month (excepting of course the unverifiable production dealt with by the cartoon).

providing the audience with 'the pleasure of seeing a lifelike portraiture of ordinary men and women'.[10] Soseki is a novelist who is now considered the most important of modern authors for his insight into the problems besetting the identity of Japanese self after the encounter with the West. He perceived that Shoyo had failed to do justice to either of the two sides of Shakespeare's art, that is, his 'poetry' and his 'realism', and he judged, rightly I believe, that Shoyo had been hampered by his inveterate adherence to the old sensibility.

Nevertheless, there is no question but that it was a production marking a crowning moment. And as such, it dealt a death-blow to the already weakening fashion of adaptation, announcing the beginning of an age of faithful translation. But the irony of history was that what one would have thought a decisive step towards the greater popularity of Shakespeare turned out to be rather the opposite. The commercial success of Shoyo's *Hamlet*, with its reassuring remnant of *kabuki* elements, had the effect of alienating the intellectually advanced audience, confirming the impression that Shakespeare was 'old-fashioned'. Similarities between Shakespeare and Chikamatsu, emphasized by Shoyo, were taken to mean that the Renaissance dramatist was after all a 'classic' rather than an author of contemporary concerns.

Even within his own company, The Bungei Kyokai, young radicals revolted against Shoyo, anxious to do something more modern, that is, plays with more explicitly contemporary 'problems'. Shakespeare was overtaken and left behind by the mainstream theatre which was all too eager to 'make it new'. The dramatist who replaced him was Ibsen. Shoyo could not stop his company doing *A Doll's House* immediately after *Hamlet*. The actress Sumako Matsui who had played Ophelia a few months before now played Nora, and became a great star of the time. This might be regarded as the beginning of what is usually called *shingeki*, or 'new drama' (in Western-style), as distinguished from

kabuki and other forms of traditional drama.

And this also marks the end of the first period in the history of *Hamlet* in Japan, which coincides with the end of the Meiji Era. It was a period fraught with the excitement of trials and errors. In comparison, the second period, which extends from the beginning of the Taisho Era (1913–26) to the end of the Second World War, looks far more stable and consistent. The last ten years of the first period had seen a spate of twenty productions of *Hamlet*, whereas in the second period the pace was slowed down with about twenty productions spread over thirty-five years. There were virtually no adaptations any longer; all used more or less faithful translations and Western dress.

The real problem, from our point of view, is that *Hamlet* (or Shakespeare) ceased to be the battleground of creative experiment in theatre. The mainstream of *shingeki* was going through the whole gamut of European avant garde fashions, from Ibsenian realism to German or Meyerholdian Expressionism to socialist realism to Chekhovian psychological realism, while Japan as a country was making its way through a relatively liberal phase of the Taisho Era into the mad expansionism outside and the reign of militarist terror inside of the Showa Era – one of the disastrous conclusions of modernization. For the people of *shingeki* who were West-oriented, liberalist or leftist in political persuasion, the latter half of this period was a nightmare of censorship, arrest, torture, and forced conversion.

Hamlet was apparently outside all these labours and tribulations. It was performed in 1933 to celebrate the completion of Shoyo's revised tradition of Shakespeare's complete works, and the reason why *Hamlet* was chosen, according to the recollection of the actor who played the title role,[11] was because it was felt to

---

[10] 'Dr Tsubouchi and Shakespeare', *The Complete Works of Soseki Natsume* (Tokyo, 1966), vol. 11, p. 286.
[11] Kenji Usuda's memoir (*The Shingeki*, July 1964).

be the 'safest' play to avoid being targeted by the secret service police. One wonders if this was to be interpreted as a tribute to the innate ability of the play to escape ideological pigeon-holing, or as a sarcastic reflection on the obtuseness of Japanese thought police, or as evidence of the degree to which *shingeki* had allowed the play to lose its subversive edge on the stage.

The other side of this phenomenon was that *Hamlet* and Shakespeare became a subject of serious academic and critical study. The period saw publications of new translations, annotated academic editions, accessible text-books, and a number of critical essays. It was, for the play *Hamlet*, a period of intellectual retreat from the actualities of the theatre world, a time of reflective assimilation. Under the militarist régime during wartime, people could not talk about Shakespeare openly, along with other foreign authors. The hush was only broken when a fanatic right-wing professor of English echoed the imperialistic slogan, 'Charge and appropriate other Asian countries, they are ours!' by yelling, 'Charge and appropriate Shakespeare, he is ours!'

We must wait for Hamlet to make a comeback to the forefront of the theatrical scene until 1955, when Tsuneari Fukuda directed the first production of *Hamlet* after the War. This was a new milestone, marking not only the beginning of the third period of the play's reception but also an important turning point in the intellectual history of post-war Japan. As pointed out earlier, the pre-war *shingeki* started its course by criticizing Shoyo's compromise; it aimed at a complete break with the old tradition. Ibsen and Chekhov became sacred texts. There is a well-known episode about Kaoru Osanai, one of the founders of *shingeki*, paying a respectful visit to the Moscow Arts Theatre in 1912 to see plays directed by Stanislavski; he jotted down all the details of the productions, and came back to Japan to direct the same plays in almost the same way. *Shingeki* thus might be considered a

reductio ad absurdum of the categorical imperative of modernization-as-westernization, that dream which started with the Meiji Restoration.

Underlying Fukuda's production of *Hamlet* was a two-fold critique of the limitation of *shingeki* and, more broadly, of the modernity of Japanese culture. On the one hand, he saw through the insufficiency of modernization, the fragile fashioning of modern self in Japanese theatre and society. On the other hand, he was aware of the impasse that the modern Western self had reached over the centuries since Descartes (or Romanticism, if you like). The crisis created by rationalism, individualism, and the resulting solitariness of the modern self must be faced and overcome by the West as well as by Japan, a country which has had to live in a hundred years' time what Europe had experienced in three hundred years. And Fukuda claimed that theatre was a privileged ground to enact the process of criticizing, establishing, and overcoming modernity simultaneously.

That was why his Hamlet was witty, agile, and debonair. He saw to it that this hero was played as a man fully aware of reality, enacting all the rich spectrum of his personality, instead of indulging in romantic solitude or intellectual cynicism.[12] By directing the play with such an interpretative stance, Fukuda rescued Shakespeare out of the subordinate position in which *shingeki* had left him, reinstating him at the centre of Japanese theatre. *Shingeki*'s view of Shakespeare as an 'old-fashioned' dramatist was now proved to be itself old-fashioned.

But Fukuda's critique of the 'modern' ideology of *shingeki* does not mean that he reverted to Shoyo's style, nor does it mean that he became a champion of the 'post-modern'. On

---

[12] See Tsuneari Fukuda, 'Ningen Kono Getitekinarumono' (Man as Dramatic Being), *The Selected Essays of Tsuneari Fukuda* (Tokyo, 1966), vol. 2, and 'Kindai no Shukumei' (The Destiny of the Modern), *The Collected Works of Tsuneari Fukuda* (Tokyo, 1987), vol. 2.

the contrary, glancing back from the vantage-point of time, we see that Fukuda was himself one of the 'modernists', part of *shingeki* against which he battled with such perspicuity: his *Hamlet* was a perfection of modern *shingeki*-style rather than a new venture into a new age. It comes as a bit of bathos to see how his Shakespearian productions were always looking Westward for authenticity. Just as Osanai had gone to the Moscow Arts Theatre, Fukuda went to the Old Vic in 1954, where he was deeply impressed by Richard Burton's *Hamlet* directed by Michael Benthall. He made minute notes of the performance, which, together with Dover Wilson's rationalistic interpretation of the play which he greatly admired, had a decisive influence on his *Hamlet* in Tokyo. There is no disputing that Fukuda succeeded in making Shakespeare 'modern' more than anyone before him, but he did not make him 'contemporary'. Nor did he want to. It is hard to imagine that he liked Trevor Nunn's *The Winter's Tale* or Peter Brook's *A Midsummer Night's Dream*, both of which came to Tokyo (the former in 1970, the latter in 1973) and revolutionized the taste of Japanese theatre-goers, especially younger ones.

It was for these younger ones to deconstruct modernity in a way and to an extent undreamt of by Fukuda. And it was they who opened the fourth period of *Hamlet* and Shakespeare in Japan, a period in which we still find ourselves. Without going to London, they were convinced that there existed no model to be copied, no original to be faithfully reproduced, that one was free to do anything so long as one could make Shakespeare feel contemporary. Totally unshackled by the ideology and method of *shingeki*, they seemed to believe in the contemporaneity of Tokyo, London, New York, and any city on the earth.

One of them is Norio Deguchi who dedicated his small company to 'Shakespeare in jeans' (so nicknamed from its casual costume) and performed the whole dramatic canon of the Bard within six years (1975–81), using new translations by Yushi Odashima whose versions are now overwhelmingly popular among young actors and audiences. Perhaps the two most powerful directors of this generation are Yukio Ninagawa and Tadashi Suzuki, both of whom have created their own styles, in their efforts to go beyond modern psychological realism, by drawing upon the traditions of *noh* and *kabuki*. Neither of them, however, is a 'traditionalist', if the term means preserving traditions. Rather than obeying the existing forms of traditional theatre, they sought to tap the primeval energy which must have produced those forms originally. Typically of the generation of the sixties which carried out a radical critique of *status quo* in intellectual and artistic fields, they were 'deconstructors' of the traditional establishment (*noh* and *kabuki*) just as much as of the modern one (*shingeki*). They were seen as 'iconoclasts' from both sides. This ruthless radicalism applies even better to Suzuki than to Ninagawa, whose famous *Macbeth*, when we look back after a decade, may perhaps seem to have been in danger of too much aestheticizing, a little bit too 'Japanese'. Suzuki's transformation of the Shakespearian text is far more violent and far-reaching, going side by side with his breath-takingly stylized use of actors' bodies. His version of *King Lear* was highly talked of in America where it toured extensively in 1988, but one feels sure somehow that its scheduled production at the Barbican in London in November 1994 will provoke some critics to call it not a lawful 'exchange' or a permissible 'plagiarism' but an unforgivable 'robbery' of a Shakespeare play.

If Ninagawa and Suzuki keep creative tension vis-à-vis native tradition, and thereby succeed sometimes, as I believe, in achieving a certain universality, or an archetypal dramatic experience, there are still younger directors who are completely free from the anxiety of influence. Takeshi Kawamura remade Macbeth into a *yakuza* hero with outrageous freedom. Another remarkable director-playwright-actor, Hideki Noda, transposed *A Midsummer*

9 The last scene of *Hamlet in Asia*, directed by Sho Ryuzanji (1990). The story is set in a mafia-like world of an imaginary Asiatic town where complicated ethnic power struggles are brewing

Night's Dream into the world of Japanese cuisine business and *Richard III* into that of flower arrangement. Adept in the post-modern paradox of passionate nonchalance, Noda goes on playing games, not caring a straw about either Japanese or Shakespearian traditions. All in all, it looks as though the post-modern age we are in is a new period of Shakespearian adaptation a little reminiscent of what happened a century ago.

Since the Prince of Denmark would seem to be the most adaptable to their taste of all Shakespearian heroes, it may be ironic that none of the above-named directors have tried their hands at *Hamlet* so far, except Deguchi and Ninagawa (whose production, using the archaic Shoyo translation and the colloquial Odashima one in different scenes, must be counted as one of his not too rare failures). In fact, there have been countless productions of the play over the last two decades, of which I will here mention only one, probably the most ambitious of them all. *Hamlet in Asia*, billed as 'Ryuzanji *Hamlet*' after the name of the director Sho Ryuzanji, and performed in Tokyo in 1990, sets the story in an imaginary town on the Chinese coast where complex power struggles are brewing among residents of varied racial extraction. Resembling somewhat a hard-boiled action film, the play presents Hamlet, the son of the late Chinese tycoon and his Japanese wife, enacting the absurdly heroic fate of a 'Japanese in Asia'. This was a powerful though flawed work, forming a twin piece with the same director's previous adaptation of *Macbeth* into a kind of Vietnamese war.

If a definitive *Hamlet* has failed to come out of these people, one of the reasons must be because the play as created by Shakespeare is too richly ambiguous to be given quietus by a bare bodkin of directorial inspiration. And that is perhaps only another way of pointing to the complexity of *our* own problems. No one would be so simple-minded as to claim that, in Japan, or in any other country for that matter, the anxiety of modernity has been overcome by the 'ludic' spirit of post-modernity. A new Hamlet must and will keep emerging, embodying the perennial and specific anxieties of contemporary self. And it is doubtful if our cartoon hero will ever be able to stop worrying.

HAMLET'S LAST WORDS

TOM MATHESON

At least three interlocking applications of the word 'culture' are currently identified: first, a general process of intellectual and spiritual development, once conceived as a unilinear movement from innocence or barbarism to civilization; second, a particular way of life, specific manners, habits, practices located in a particular people, or period, or group; and third, the works and products of intellectual and artistic activity – music, literature, painting and sculpture, theatre and film – perhaps also philosophy and history.[1]

If, as seems appropriate, we regard culture as an active system rather than as a passive collection of disparate traits, then cultural exchange (or acculturation) is a necessary and inevitable condition of any kind of social existence: a continuous reciprocal contact between individuals, families, groups, classes, nations, and races; involving money, food, work, property, possessions, commerce, sex, and every kind of leisure and recreation, including literature and ideas. It is facilitated at every level by technology, education, communications, economic prosperity, and genuinely democratic institutions. The only naturally occurring barrier to cultural exchange is language; and even that can be overcome by translation. But it is restricted by the artificial barriers of economic, political, and ideological oppression. Governments anywhere may and do seek to regulate and control its operation; but by its nature it is spontaneous, expansive, and innovative, having the character and force of an evolutionary mechanism.

In this broadest of senses, the interlocking systems of European culture have thoroughly assimilated Shakespeare's works and are in turn significantly defined by them. They have become both instruments and beneficiaries of a continuous process of cultural exchange: adapted and appropriated; performed, parodied, plagiarized; re-presented, re-produced, re-written; translated, transformed, transposed, and sometimes transcended. They are enshrined in the National Curriculum of English education; Shakespeare's iconic portrait (usually in its Droeshout archetype) authenticates everything from T-shirts to teabags. Commercially the works may be used to promote Carling Black Label, the Royal Insurance Company, or Allied Domecq, along with cricket, football, snooker, and darts. They have become, if not quite bread and wine, at least food and drink.

Thus, an English play borrowed from Danish history, set in a Danish court; first published in 1603, the year that a Danish Queen

---

[1] Many of the examples of cultural exchange and intertextuality in this paper were first presented in a different form for seminar discussion at The Shakespeare Institute in Stratford-upon-Avon, to whose past and present members the author acknowledges a continuing debt. On the shifting definitions of 'culture', see, for example, Raymond Williams, *Keywords: A Vocabulary of Culture and Society* (London, 1976), or the articles on culture by Oliver Stallybrass, Barry Cunliffe, and Ronald Fletcher in *The Fontana Dictionary of Modern Thought*, new and revised edition by Alan Bullock and Stephen Trombley, assisted by Brude Eadie (London, 1988), p. 195.

ascended the throne of a united kingdom as the wife of King James I; moreover, a play whose second edition in 1605 may in parts omit speeches potentially offensive to her – such a play is already a significant model of cultural exchange.

As an example of the immediacy with which *Hamlet* was recognized as an accurate depiction of conflicting power within a contemporary state, the published account of Sir Thomas Smith's embassy from King James to the Emperor Boris Godunov in Moscow in 1604 and 1605 is relevant.[2] While Smith was there, in an atmosphere of diplomatic splendour and celebration, banqueting and exchanging gifts, news arrived that Dimitry Ivanovich, son of the late Emperor Ivan, had gathered an army of Poles and Cossacks and was set on regaining his inheritance and the kingdom from the former regent Boris.

This Dimitry was thought to be an impostor, the real Dimitry having died, possibly with Boris's connivance, during the reign of his feeble-minded brother Feodor, by falling on a knife during an apoplectic fit. Nevertheless, Boris sent an army of 200,000 soldiers to capture or kill him. But Boris himself died first. Two hours after a dinner, certified well by his attendant doctors, the Emperor suddenly felt heavy and pained in his stomach. He went to his chamber, summoned the doctors again, but was soon speechless and dying. Unconfirmed rumours reached the English ambassador that the Emperor had been poisoned; that the Prince his successor was imprisoned; and that the rebel Dimitry had been crowned.

In fact Dimitry, supported by the boyar lords, was holding the city under siege. After listening to a letter presenting Dimitry's claims, the commons as a mob rioted in the streets, and the Prince was advised either to leave the kingdom or to kill himself. Under the influence of his powerful mother, he decided to take poison, along with both mother and sister. The contemporary account reconstructs the scene:

The Princely mother began the health of Death to her noble Sonne, who pledged her with a hartie draught ... Yes hand in hand (as hart in hart) imbracing each other, they fell, and dyed as one, the Mother counselling and acting, whilst the child bethought and suffered ... the Princesse dranke, but like a Virgin temperatly. (L3)

Mother and son were found in each other's arms; the daughter was still alive, grovelling on the floor. Dimitry, when he read the Prince's last letter, is said to have wept.

The ambassador, as ambassadors do, reconciled himself to the new ruler, exchanged more gifts, and received letters of peace and amity for King James. However, by 1606, Dimitry had himself been murdered by the boyars. (Two other pretenders, False Dimitry II and False Dimitry III, met similar fates in 1609 and 1612.)

Obviously, these events cannot provide a source for *Hamlet*, although they do seem to offer several real-life analogies: the elaborate ceremonies and rituals of court life; its luxury, indulgence, and conspicuous consumption; the maintenance of power based on intrigue and physical violence; the conflict of claim and counterclaim to inheritance; the anarchy and instability of subjects, both aristocratic and common; private passions finding a public expression; the apparent suicide of a guilty ruler; a mother and son poisoned in each other's arms. Even the contingent sequence of voyages and journeys between Denmark, Poland, and England seems to echo the Shakespearian geography. And the arrival of Dimitry, with his band of Polish and Cossack lawless resolutes, might well be that of either Laertes or Fortinbras.

But the anonymous reporter, writing in 1605, himself makes the connection to a tragedy of *Hamlet* which is obviously fresh in his memory:

---

[2] *Sir Thomas Smithes voiage and Entertainment in Rushia* (London, 1605). The reference to a *Hamlet* play on I4v is noticed by A. M. Dunne, 'English Books and Readers 1605' (unpublished Ph.D. thesis, University of Birmingham, 1989), pp. 848–54.

This falling away of them, the State so greatly blinded upon ... with the many continually doubts of the issue, hastied the last breath of the once hoped-for *Prince*, as from him that (though an Emperor, was much hoodwinckt by his politique kinsmen [and] great counsellors) now might easilie discern these times to outrun his, and must notoriously know (though happely his youth and innocencie shadowed the reflection) that his Sonne was setting or beclouded at noonedayes, and that the right heir was (and would be when he was not) apparant; that his fathers Empire and Government, was but as the *Poeticall Furie in a Stage-action*, compleat yet with horrid and wofull Tragedies: a first, but no second to any *Hamlet*; and that now *Reuenge*, iust *Reuenge* was comming with his sword drawn against him, his royall Mother, and dearest Sister, to fill vp those Murdering Scenes; the *Embryon* whereof was long since Modeld, yea digested ... by his dead selfe-murdering Father: such and so many being their feares and terrours; the Diuell aduising, Despaire counselling, Hell itselfe instructing; yea, wide-hart-opening to receiue a King now, rather than a Kingdome; as *L. Bartas* deuinely sayth: *They who expect not Heauen, find a Hell euerywhere.* (I4v)

This recognition that the events at the court of Boris Godunov contain all the elements of a tragedy, together with the identification of that tragedy with an English play called *Hamlet*, seems a clear example of one kind of cultural exchange – as well as being one of the earliest possible allusions to Shakespeare's play. It was made in September 1605, in a pamphlet written anonymously and published only two weeks after Smith's expedition had ended, for the printer James Roberts – by coincidence also printer of the newly enlarged second quarto of Shakespeare's *Hamlet*.

From an example of *Hamlet* very specifically applied to contemporary Russian history to other more familiar examples from the modern Russian and European theatre, is not as great a distance as it might seem for a less universal play. The actor Simon Russell Beale, in Stratford in 1993 to play the part of Ariel, was asked at a question-and-answer session which Shakespearian role he most wanted to play. Not surprisingly, as an ambitious performer, he identified Hamlet. But he did so in an unusually indirect way. He said: 'I want to play the three great Hamlet parts before I'm thirty. I've already done two, and only Hamlet himself remains.'

By the 'three great Hamlet parts' Beale meant Shakespeare's Hamlet (which he still expects to play); Oswald in Ibsen's *Ghosts* of 1881 (which he played at The Other Place in Stratford in 1993); and Konstantin in Anton Chekhov's *The Seagull* of 1895 (which he played at The Swan in Stratford in 1990). His perception of a theatrical affinity between the three plays is not new, and there is already an extensive critical literature identifying and analysing the network of allusions and borrowings from Shakespeare by Ibsen and Chekhov respectively.[3] But

---

[3] See, in general: *European Shakespeares, translating Shakespeare in the Romantic Age*, edited by Dirk Delabastita and Lieven D'Hulst (Amsterdam, 1993). For examples in Ibsen criticism: David Grene *Reality and the Heroic Pattern, Last Plays of Ibsen, Shakespeare, and Sophocles* (Chicago, 1967); Inga-Stina Ewbank, '*The Tempest* and After', *Shakespeare Survey* 43 (1991), pp. 109–19; Errol Durbach 'Playing the Fool to Sorrow: "Life-Lies" and "Life-Truths" in *King Lear* and *The Wild Duck*', *Essays in Theatre*, 6(1), (1987): 5–17, and '*Antony and Cleopatra* and *Rosmersholm*: "Third Empire" Love Tragedies', *Comparative Drama*, 20(1), (1986): 1–16; Andrew Kennedy, 'Natural, Mannered, and Parodic Dialogue', *Yearbook of English Studies*, 9 (1979): 28–54. Accounts of Chekhov and Shakespeare include: Eleanor Rowe, *Hamlet: A Window on Russia* (New York, 1976); Patrick Miles, *Chekhov on the British Stage 1909–1987, an Essay in Cultural Exchange* (Cambridge, 1987); Verna A. Foster, 'The Dramaturgy of Mood in *Twelfth Night* and *The Cherry Orchard*', *Modern Language Quarterly*, 48(2), (1987): 162–85; Harai Golomb, 'Hamlet in Chekhov's Major Plays; Some Perspectives of Literary Allusion and Literary Translation', *New Comparison: A Journal of Comparative and General Literary Studies*, 2, (1986): 69–88; Charles J. Rzepka, 'Chekhov's *The Three Sisters*, Lear's Daughters, and the Weird Sisters: The Arcana of Archetypal Influence', *Modern Language Studies*, 14(4), (1984): 18–27; Alma H. Law, 'Chekhov's Russian Hamlet (1924)', *The Drama Review*, 27(3), (1983): 34–45; Robert Porter, 'Hamlet and *The Seagull*', *Journal of Russian Studies*, 41, (1981): 23–32.

the structural resemblances between all three plays are not commonly addressed. The director Jonathan Miller, at the Greenwich Theatre in 1974, did adopt what he called a structuralist technique of 'interpretation by superimposition', producing *Hamlet*, *The Seagull*, and *Ghosts* as a sequence of what were identified, alluding to Freud, as 'Family Romances'. The three plays were juxtaposed, the same actors playing corresponding roles from one night to the next, with the aim of revealing that beneath the surface totally different characters in different plays may be exercising identical functions. Writing about the experiment subsequently Miller observed: 'Now it may well be that as far as the audience was concerned the effects of the superimposition were not readily apparent in any one of the plays but if you saw all three together the salient structures common to each play were very prominent . . . It brought out features in each that would not have been visibly present had they been performed on their own or in a repertoire with other plays.'[4]

In what sense are *Ghosts* and *The Seagull* 'Hamlet' plays, and Oswald and Konstantin 'Hamlet' parts? And what is the significance, if any, in our perceiving them to be so?

Obviously, despite a considerable contextual cultural distance in time and place, all three characters are doomed, only sons, destroyed by the pressures, internal and external, exerted upon them by family and society. (Although neither Oswald nor Konstantin physically or psychologically dominate their respective plays as does Hamlet.) But there are other structural similarities. All three plays exploit the absence or death of a real father; all revolve around the formidable personality of a sexually conscious mother; all contain an actual or potential lover for that mother, threatening the position of the vulnerable son, who is himself alienated and anxious, oppressed with thoughts of death; all contain a nubile heroine, threatened with sacrifice by the dysfunctional family, either succumbing or escaping; all contain, in the person of an older male relative, a philosophical and crafty

counsellor who attaches himself to the principal characters – and so on. Like Shakespeare, Chekhov includes a play within his play, encouraging reflection on the relation between art and life. In *Hamlet*, the hero contemplates suicide, and dies in a duel; in *The Seagull*, the hero contemplates a duel, and dies by suicide.

The modes of assimilation from one play to another are different. Ibsen was familiar with Shakespeare's plays probably from the beginning of his professional career. He saw and read them: *Hamlet* he saw in Copenhagen and Dresden; he directed an adapted version of *As You Like It* in Bergen; he took the critic Georg Brandes to a meeting of the Dresden Literary Society for a lecture on Tieck's essay on the soliloquies of Hamlet; he himself lectured in Bergen on Shakespeare and his influence on Scandinavian Art (the lecture is unfortunately lost). Yet, writing to Gosse about the rejection of verse in his play *Emperor and Galilean* (1873), he said: 'We are no longer living in the age of Shakespeare . . . what I desired to depict were human beings' (that is ordinary mortals, as distinct from the extraordinary and god-like verse-speakers of Shakespeare's plays). Ibsen sought also to reject the artificial devices of plot (mistaken identities, overheard conversations, intercepted letters, and so on) conventionally associated with Shakespearian drama. He did not entirely succeed.[5]

Ghosts contains no direct references to *Hamlet* and Ibsen deliberately seems to challenge and invert the moral ordering of Shakespeare's play: the dead father (Alving) is not pure and virtuous, but sexually degenerate (although his degeneracy is traced back to the marital and

---

[4] Jonathan Miller, *Subsequent Performances* (London, 1986), pp. 154–5.

[5] The most accessible information in English about Ibsen's contacts with Shakespeare's works is in Michael Meyer *Ibsen*, 3 vols. (London, Rupert Hart-Davis, 1967, 1971); abridged in 1 vol. (London, Penguin Books, 1974). The letter to Gosse is cited in vol. 2 *Ibsen, The Farewell to Poetry 1864–1882*, p. 185.

social repression of what is called his 'joy in life'); the mother (Mrs Alving) is not seduced and corrupted, but driven stoically to endure a tragic destiny (also through the rejection and inhibition of *her* desires); the potential lover (Pastor Manders), nominally virtuous, is in fact ruined by cant, hypocrisy, and self-deception; the son (Oswald), no longer fierce and aggressive but a pathetic and petulant victim; the illegitimate heroine (Regina), no longer oppressed and persecuted, but finding in an escape from the family the only prospect of life, strength, and joy in the play, and even that is deeply ambivalent. The literal act of poisoning in *Hamlet* takes place before the play begins; in Ibsen, it will follow the end of the play, when Mrs Alving gives Oswald the morphine that will free him from the effects of tertiary syphilis. Shakespeare's onstage Ghost is transformed into an inherited disease and the oppressive burden of dead, outworn, unwholesome ideas from the past. In this reading, *Ghosts* demonstrates, both literally and metaphorically, the corrupting poison of lies and hypocritical self-deception in the family and in society. The extent of the debt to *Hamlet* is disguised; the characters and incidents radically transposed into the context of nineteenth-century Norway; but the tragic sense of ruined and wasted lives is equally intense. (Ironically, Ibsen's account of a dismal, guilty, and rain-sodden Norway, was composed in the sunlight of Rome, Ischia, and Sorrento – another kind of deliberate cultural exchange, in Ibsen's own perception.)

Hamlet is certainly not a source for *The Seagull*. As Hanna Scolnicov says: '*The Seagull* uses *Hamlet* as its "classical" form of reference. Shakespeare's play lends shape to Chekhov's naturalistic material, and provides it with a sense of direction and purpose'.[6]

Incidents from Chekhov's own life provided many of the characters and scenes of the play. Lydia Mizinova (or Lika) was a young teacher's assistant, in love with Chekhov, who treated her with irony, mockery, and evasion. In 1893,

at Chekhov's dacha, Lika, hoping to provoke him, flirted with another writer, Ignaty Potapenko. She became Potapenko's mistress, followed him to Paris, where he tired of her and returned to his wife. She remained in Paris and gave birth to a girl. She saw Potapenko again, but was deserted a second time. The baby died. The relationship of Nina in the play to Lika was apparent at its first reading, before friends. Indeed, those present drew a further parallel between the character of the actress-mother Arkadina and Potapenko's own wife.

Similarly, in 1895, Chekhov sent an inscribed copy of *Stories and Tales* to a married admirer, Lydia Avilova. She ordered a watch fob in the form of a book with 'Stories and Tales by A. Chekhov' engraved on one side and 'page 267, lines 6 and 7' on the other, a reference to a sentence from 'The Neighbours': 'If ever you have need of my life, come and take it.' Chekhov failed to acknowledge its receipt, and when she asked him about it at a masquerade party, he replied that she would find out in his play – where the episode is played out between Nina and Trigorin.

Even the actual seagull seems to have an equivalent in life. Isaak Levitan, a young Jewish landscape painter – rejected in love by Chekhov's sister Maria, often moody, melancholy, suicidal – was hunting in woods with Chekhov and winged a woodcock. Levitan couldn't bring himself to finish it off, finally persuading Chekhov to do so. Levitan, living with a rich, older woman (Anna Turchaninova) attempted to commit suicide after quarrels between the mother and her daughter over his favours. When Chekhov arrived to see his friend, he found him deathly pale, his head wrapped in a bandage – much as Konstantin is bandaged, after his suicide attempt, by his mother Arkadina. At the heart of all three

---

[6] Hanna Scolnicov, 'Chekhov's Reading of *Hamlet*', in *Reading Plays: Interpretation and Reception*, edited by Hanna Scolnicov and Peter Holland (Cambridge, 1991), p. 203.

plays is a recriminatory mother-son encounter.[7]

(The woodcock, incidentally, occurs twice in Shakespeare's *Hamlet*, along with a number of other birds: Polonius referring to Hamlet's vows to Ophelia as 'springes to catch woodcocks' (1.3.115) and Laertes' reference to his suffering a wound in the duel 'as a woodcock to mine own springe' (5.2.259). I am afraid that Chekhov missed a unique opportunity to bind his play forever to *Hamlet* by not calling it 'The Woodcock' instead of 'The Seagull' – although 'Missed Opportunities' itself might not be a bad title for any of Chekhov's plays.)

So much of the play does seem to reflect aspects of the daily life of Chekhov himself in the 1890s. Yet the structural resemblance to *Hamlet* is just as explicit, and fully signalled to the audience. In the first Act, just before Konstantin's play is about to be given its ill-received first performance, Arkadina quotes the instantly recognizable lines:

Oh, Hamlet, speak no more!
Thou turn'st mine eyes into my very soul;
And there I see such black and grained spots
As will not leave their tinct.

To which Konstantin, taking up the allusion, replies:

And let me wring your heart, for so I shall,
If it be made of penetrable stuff.

She believes herself to be joking: Konstantin knows he is not.[8]

The second allusion, in a play full of references to a wide variety of other texts, Russian and European – confirming Barthes' observation in 'The Death of the Author' that 'The text is a tissue of quotations drawn from the innumerable centres of culture . . . the writer can only imitate a gesture that is always anterior, never original. His only power is to mix writings, to counter the ones with the others, in such a way as never to rest on any one of them' – comes in Act 2.[9] Konstantin, leaving Nina, to make way for Trigorin, quotes Hamlet's reaction to Polonius (2.2.195):

Here comes the man with the real talent, entering like Hamlet, even down to the book. (*Mimics him.*) 'Words, words, words . . .'[10]

Chekhov uses the play explicitly here not because it was part of the educated apparatus of his class, in his time and place – although that is also a fact to be considered. In my judgement he uses it to authenticate, enrich, and confirm the contingent crises of everyday life from which his own play is drawn. *Hamlet* is never merely contingent. It is used not because it is famous, but because it is perceived to be true – the best account of the emotional structures of a family in crisis – and has been found to be so over many generations and across cultures. And, if *Hamlet* enriches the two modern plays; then a knowledge of Ibsen and Chekhov undoubtedly enriches our response to *Hamlet*. The exchange works both ways.

Yet there are dangers in this kind of analogue watch. The habitual analogue watcher is like a

---

[7] Biographical information on Chekhov is available in David Magarshak, *Chekhov: A Life* (London, 1952); Ernest J. Simmons, *Chekhov: A Biography* (Boston, 1962); Ronald Hingley, *A New Life of Anton Chekhov* (London, 1976); and Henri Troyat, *Chekhov*, translated from the French by Michael Henry Heim (London, 1987), from which details here are partly derived.

[8] Quoted here from Elizaveta Fen's translation (London, 1954), p. 128. The history in English translations of *The Seagull* of these *Hamlet* quotations (from 3.4 of the play) is interesting. Constance Garnett (1923) and Fen follow the original; Michael Frayn's translation of *The Seagull* (London, 1986), deliberately adds Gertrude's speech of invitation to Hamlet from the play scene ('Come hither, my dear Hamlet, sit by me', 3.2.104) as an introduction, and replaces Konstantin's original reply with a much more hostile and explicit insult from the closet scene ('Nay but to live / In the rank sweat of an enseamed bed / Stew'd in corruption, honeying and making love / Over the nasty sty . . .' 3.4.82–5).

[9] Roland Barthes, 'The Death of the Author', in *Image-Music-Text*, essays selected and translated by Stephen Heath (London, 1984), p. 146.

[10] Quoted from Frayn's translation, p. 28.

security surveillance video camera, endlessly sweeping the deserted and rubbish-strewn subways of derelict literature for the least sign of autonomous movement; often focussing on that ramshackle old shopping mall in downtown Thebes, known as The Oedipus Complex. Shakespeare, himself no mean analogue manipulator, was also aware of the dangers, as in *Henry V*:

I tell you, captain, if you look in the maps of the world I warrant you shall find, in the comparisons between Macedon and Monmouth, that the situations, look you, is both alike. There is a river in Macedon, and there is also moreover a river at Monmouth. It is called Wye at Monmouth, but it is out of my prains what is the name of the other river – but 'tis all one, 'tis alike as my fingers is to my fingers, and there is salmons in both. (4.7.22–30)

This certainly exposes the absurd dimension of analogue watching. And yet, there are significant ways in which all rivers resemble each other; as do all military conquerors, whether we consider them as Great or, in Fluellen's pronunciation, as merely 'Pig'.

The passage offers another useful lesson. Not only are some comparisons valid but insignificant, and therefore hardly worth pursuing; but even significant analogy may be exploited as much to differentiate the copy from the model as to imitate and resemble it. Irony, parody, satire, and dissent may motivate analogical rewriting as strongly as emulation. Further, the incorporation of one text into another cultural context is always and inevitably partial and selective. Ibsen and Chekhov seem to feel no sense of distance, difficulty, or strangeness in assimilating *Hamlet*: it is both fully accessible and fully intelligible. But they do domesticate the play, removing the motif of revenge, and reducing its central struggle for power and domination to what may well be its primary and natural location, the bourgeois family. In that respect, they seem not only to echo the relevant contemporary observations of Darwin and Nietzsche, but to anticipate Freud's *Interpretation of Dreams* by nearly twenty years,

Darwin, Nietzsche, and Freud providing a cultural context at least as relevant to any reading of the plays as Shakespeare.[11]

What has been left out is the state, politics, and government; the public arena in which private motives have their greatest consequences. For Shakespeare, political revolution in the state begins and ends the action: the play starts with the threat of war from Fortinbras, and ends with his bloodless assumption of power. Everything else exists within that framework. The question of who rules is inseparable from the question of who lives or dies in the play. The decision to place the whole action at the heart of an aristocratic ruling class is Shakespeare's, and no accident.

In over thirty years the only production I have seen which fully convinced me of the urgent relevance of the private passions of the play to their public setting was performed in Bucharest in 1989, shortly before the overthrow of the Ceausescu regime. The Bulandra theatre was packed, with the audience, mostly young people, in raked galleries on three sides of a large platform stage. I sat in the protocol box, surrounded by some of the officials and functionaries who had tried to prevent the production in the first place. The audience's concentration remained intense over nearly five hours of the performance; they responded with applause to familiar speeches, laughing aloud at Hamlet's jokes and sallies. In some respects the production itself was more absurdist than political: Hamlet was accompanied for much of the action by two painted clowns, one's white face a mask of tragedy, the other's of comedy; appearing at one moment as Rosencrantz and Guildenstern, at another as the Gravedigger and the Sexton.[12]

---

[11] See, for example, Brian Downs, *Ibsen, The Intellectual Background* (Cambridge, 1946).

[12] *Hamlet*, translated by Nina Cassian and others; first shown at the Bulandra Theatre in Bucharest in 1985; directed by Alexandru Tocilescu; with Ion Caramitru as Hamlet. Shown at the Lyttleton Theatre in London, 2–6 September, 1990.

What gave the production its relevance and topicality was precisely the audience's recognition, electric in its intensity, that the play's depiction of a state governed by a corrupt and tyrannical married couple and turned into a prison, policed by an army of spies and informers, was a depiction of their own situation.

According to report, after the actual revolution came, on 22 December 1989, the actor Ion Caramitru was recognized in the street by a General commanding a tank squadron. He was borne on the tank to the television station where the main battle was taking place. There he joined the small group announcing the overthrow of Ceausescu to the watching world. This is *Hamlet* rewritten by history: 'Claudius' is dead; 'Gertrude' is dead; but 'Hamlet' survives, escorted by 'Fortinbras' on his tank, to become, for a time anyway, a vice-president in the new government of National Salvation.

Not surprisingly, when the same production was brought to the National Theatre in London, its impact was aesthetic rather than political. The best productions, like the best plays, are conceived to work best at one time, and in one place. The appropriate audience to give it meaning was missing in London.

When, also in 1989, Ron Daniels' RSC production of *Hamlet* was taken to Broadmoor, Britain's main hospital for the criminally insane, the specialized audience of murderers gave it a significance it could never have in Stratford. Only the copious stage blood had to be omitted, in case it aroused traumatic memories and inflamed present passions among the spectators. But all the knives, foils, swords, and daggers had to be counted in; and had to be counted out again. These 'guilty creatures sitting at a play' wanted, on a subsequent occasion, to be given the chance to perform their own stories in front of the actors.[13]

At the end of Shakespeare's play, Hamlet, in his own last words, proclaims a perpetual silence:

> O, I die, Horatio!
> The potent poison quite o'ercrows my spirit.
> I cannot live to hear the news from England,
> But I do prophesy th'election lights
> On Fortinbras. He has my dying voice.
> So tell him, with th'occurrents, more and less,
> Which have solicited. The rest is silence.
>
> (5.2.304–10)

Quite apart from its appropriateness to the climax and conclusion of the play, the passage is interesting in sustaining a structural contrast which has operated throughout, between speech and silence. Existence itself in *Hamlet* seems to be equated with speech, and death with silence. Perhaps it isn't surprising that a dramatist, who by profession surrenders his own individual voice to those of his invented characters, makes 'voice' (and the permanent loss of it) the climax of the play. There may even be a pun, silence consisting, in Wittgenstein's formulation, of what we cannot speak about (here, the experience or sensation of death); as well as offering a rest or relaxation from the seemingly endless vocalizations of existence.[14]

As I've tried to show by my diachronically selected examples, in its subsequent history, *Hamlet* has been the *least* silent of any of Shakespeare's plays, continuing to speak across the boundaries of time, place, and culture. Paradoxically, the play, and not its principal character, will continue to have the last word – and even that is likely to be partial and provisional.

I therefore propose an emendation, bibliographically but not historically frivolous: that the last four words of any modern Hamlet ought to be replaced by the ominous prophecy

---

[13] See *Shakespeare Comes to Broadmoor, The Performance of Tragedy in a Secure Psychiatric Hospital*, edited by Murray Cox (London, 1992).

[14] Ludwig Wittgenstein, *Tractatus Logico-Philosophicus*, translated by D. F. Pears and B. F. McGuinness (London, 1961), Proposition 7, p. 74: 'What we cannot speak about we must pass over in silence'.

of an equally frustrated avenger, Arnold Schwarzenegger's 'Terminator', in the film of that name, a mythic and mysterious story about the destiny in the future of a mother and her son: not 'the rest is silence' but 'I'll be back!'[15]

15 *The Terminator*, American film directed by James Cameron, 1984. Curiously, an episode of another American product, the television sitcom *Boy Meets World*, transmitted in Britain in October 1994, presented a class of children divided in a choice of avenging roles for their school play between the passive model of *Hamlet* and the active model of *The Terminator*.

VENETIAN CULTURE AND THE POLITICS OF *OTHELLO*

MARK MATHESON

In *Othello* Shakespeare represents a society in many ways fundamentally different from his own, and rather than minimizing or obscuring these differences he explores them in a politically creative way. The play is a powerful illustration of his ability to perceive and represent different forms of political organization, and to situate personal relationships and issues of individual subjectivity in a specific institutional context. Here and in much of his other work Shakespeare displays what might be described as a sociological imagination. He portrays in *Othello* not a feudal monarchy or Renaissance court but an enduring Italian city-state, a republic which continued to survive despite growing Habsburg domination in the rest of the peninsula. Taken in the context of his career as a whole the play is a fascinating example of Shakespeare's interest in republicanism, which is evident from 'The Rape of Lucrece' to *The Tempest*. It provides clear evidence that he was neither an uncritical advocate of conservative Tudor ideology, as an older critical tradition maintained, nor a writer materially unable to think and imagine beyond the monarchical paradigm, as a more recent historicist criticism has sometimes suggested. In the English context the act of representing a republican culture was itself a progressive gesture, since Venice offered an existing and stable alternative to the 'natural' and 'eternal' order of monarchy. In addition to this, and to a degree not usually recognized, Shakespeare represents the city's institutions exercising a shaping influence on personal relationships and individual experience. These institutions inform and complicate the ongoing process of cultural exchange at the heart of the play, which is Othello's attempt to thrive in the foreign cultural world of an aggressive European power, and they also influence the representation of women's experience, which the play suggests would be different in a patriarchal but non-monarchical culture. The play is itself the product of cultural exchange, and Shakespeare's imaginative sensitivity to the ways of a different society generates political energies in the text which carry it beyond the ideological boundaries of official English culture.

The extent of Shakespeare's interest in the institutional life of Venice can be suggested by a comparison with contemporary playwrights. John Marston's *Antonio's Revenge* (c. 1600) is set in the city but offers little sense of its specific social and political practices. Jonson's *Volpone* (1605) reveals a much greater interest in particular Venetian institutions, and Daniel C. Boughner has argued that Jonson's research for the play was stimulated in part by Shakespeare's recent portrayal of Venice in *Othello*.[1] Shakespeare had probably read Lewes Lewkenor's *The Common-Wealth and Government of Venice* (1599), a translation of Contarini's laudatory

---

[1] Daniel C. Boughner, 'Lewkenor and *Volpone*', *Notes and Queries*, n.s. 9 (1962): 124.

exposition of the Venetian state.[2] Those who wrote dedicatory poems for this volume include Edmund Spenser, who praises not only the beauty of Venice but its 'policie of right', and John Harington, who compares it 'For Freedome' with the Roman republic.[3] Jonson read Contarini for *Volpone*, in which Sir Politic Would-Be reveals that he has hastily studied 'Contarene' in order to pass himself off as a Venetian citizen (4.1.40). Boughner has argued that in this play Jonson deliberately undercuts the idealized portrait of Venice in Contarini's work and Lewkenor's introduction. This is a plausible view, since the Venice of *Volpone* is a greed-driven city where predatory relations are the norm, where the citizens take a Machiavellian attitude toward religion (4.1.22–7), and where the supposedly democratic law courts are venues in which 'multitude' and 'clamour' overcome justice (4.6.19).

Shakespeare's more favourable representation of Venice may suggest an imaginative willingness to explore the strengths of a republican culture, and may also reflect a sympathy with the political interests of the Sidney and Essex circles, with which of course he had some connection. Members of these aristocratic circles were interested in the mixed government of the Venetian republic, and as Protestants they approved of its steadfast opposition to the authoritarianism of the Counter-Reformation. Some took a specific interest in the work of Lewkenor, who in his address to the reader describes the Venetian state as comprising monarchical, aristocratic, and democratic elements. The prince has 'all exterior ornamentes of royall dignitie' but is nevertheless 'wholy subiected to the lawes'; the 'Councell of Pregati or Senators' is invested with great authority but has no 'power, mean, or possibility at all to tyranize'; and a 'Democrasie or popular estate' is evident in the existence of a 'great councell, consisting at least of 3000. Gentlemen, whereupon the highest strength and mightinesse of the estate absolutely relyeth.'[4] Lewkenor's adverb in this final clause

demonstrates how terms usually associated with monarchy could slip from their ordinary usage in descriptions of a state with a mixed constitution, and his account is an example of how cultural exchange could destabilize and enrich conventional English political discourse. There is unquestionably a degree of idealization in Lewkenor's discussion of Venice, just as there is in the text of Contarini, but the enthusiasm he reveals is itself suggestive of the political interest the city was generating in England at the end of the sixteenth century.

The governmental structure of Venice may seem to be of only incidental importance to *Othello*, but in fact it is indispensable for generating the basic dramatic situation, and it influences every personal relationship in the play. In the first act Shakespeare offers a compelling representation of the city's political and cultural life, and his interest in its institutional structure is evident in a variety of ways. There is a notable shift, for instance, to a more explicitly republican discourse than he had used in *The Merchant of Venice*. In part this might be due to his intervening work with Roman republicanism in *Julius Caesar*, which seems to have influenced the later play. The councilmen who were simply 'magnificoes' (4.1.1 stage directions) in *The Merchant* have become 'Senators' in *Othello* (1.3.1 stage directions). Other traces of a discourse associated with republican Rome include Iago's early reference to 'togaed consuls' (1.1.24), with whom he compares Cassio for their common lack of military experience. Iago

---

[2] For discussions of Lewkenor as a source for *Othello* see Kenneth Muir, 'Shakespeare and Lewkenor', *Review of English Studies*, n.s. 7 (1956): 182–3; William R. Drennan, '"Corrupt Means to Aspire": Contarini's *De Republica* and the Motives of Iago', *Notes and Queries*, n.s. 35 (1988): 474–5; and David McPherson, 'Lewkenor's Venice and Its Sources', *Renaissance Quarterly*, 41 (1988): 459–66.

[3] Gasparo Contarini, *The Common-wealth and Government of Venice*, trans. Lewes Lewkenor (London, 1599), 3v, A4.

[4] Contarini, *The Common-wealth and Government of Venice*, A2v.

may be making a vague reference to classical culture, but he is probably referring instead to the current members of the Venetian council, as becomes clear in the next scene when Cassio uses the republican term 'consuls' for the senators who are meeting with the Duke (1.2.43). Iago's words may glance at Rome but can also be read as referring to a specifically Venetian practice. It was widely known that the members of the Venetian council had no military pretensions, and Lewkenor finds it extraordinary that these 'vnweaponed men in gownes' should give direction to 'many mightie and warlike armies'.[5] The practice of employing foreign mercenary officers and generals – by law no Venetian citizen could have more than twenty-five men in his command – was also based on republican principle. Contarini writes that Venetian leaders and armies involved in long wars on land would inevitably fall into 'a Kinde of faction' against the other 'peaceable citizens'. This could easily lead to civil war, and he notes in an analysis identical to Machiavelli's that this problem helped to undermine the Roman republic, since Caesar drew the loyalty of his men away from the state and to himself, and this permitted him 'to tyrannize ouer that commonwealth to which hee did owe all duty and obedience'.[6] The Venetian policy designed to prevent any conquering Caesar from turning against the republican state opened the way for men like Othello, and owing to its setting in this particular city the play has genuine plausibility.

Perhaps the character most clearly shaped by the institutional life of Venice is Desdemona. In part this influence is traditional, since Brabanzio's household functions on a typical patriarchal model. His rule seems to have been mostly benign, but a specifically political idiom emerges in his spontaneous laments over Desdemona's behaviour: 'O heaven, how got she out? O, treason of the blood!' (1.1.171). After he learns that she has willingly married Othello he employs the same political language:

> I am glad at soul I have no other child,
> For thy escape would teach me tyranny,
> To hang clogs on 'em.   (1.3.195–7)

Throughout Act 1 Brabanzio speaks the language of fatherly ownership with a frightening intensity, and he has inculcated in Desdemona obedience to the father's word. But Brabanzio's absolutist regime at home exists in tension with the government of the state, which as the council scene attests is based on debate and consultation. His household is built on the older political model of a *corpus*, of which he is unquestionably the head, but it exists within a larger political order based on the more progressive model of a *res publica*, whose participants are citizens rather than subjects, and whose leaders conduct affairs of state on a generally equal footing.[7]

In the council scene Brabanzio uses a kind of absolutist discourse in his address to Desdemona, asking if she knows where most she owes 'obedience', and she replies by saying that what she owes her father is 'respect' (1.3.179, 183). Desdemona's response represents a cultural shift away from her father's conception of the family, with her carefully chosen term 'respect' indicating in part the degree to which she has been shaped by the relatively liberal institutions of Venice. It seems to be a word in some ways specific to the republican context, where it characterizes the tenor of relations among members of the council, and this government has certainly made Desdemona aware of alternatives to the royalist doctrine of unquestioning obedience. Desdemona herself introduces the concept of a broader cultural order in her reply to Brabanzio before the senators, in which she makes repeated mention of her 'education'

---

[5] Contareno, A3.

[6] Contareno, pp. 130–1.

[7] For a discussion of these contemporary political models see J. G. A. Pocock, *The Machiavellian Moment: Florentine Political Thought and the Atlantic Republican Tradition* (Princeton and London: Princeton University Press, 1975), pp. 339 ff.

(1.3.181) – the only time this word appears in Shakespearian tragedy. This education is partly responsible for her independence, and for the verbal agility with which she disengages herself from the identities constructed for her by her father. The most striking line by which she accomplishes this is 'I am hitherto your daughter' (1.3.184), in which she brings out an instability in the word 'daughter' itself, using it to designate not the natural bond she refers to earlier when she says she is 'bound' to Brabanzio for 'life', but rather a relationship of power in which the daughter is the father's possession as guaranteed by a specific set of cultural arrangements. By using the word in this second sense she implicitly asserts the role of culture in establishing such identities, and thus disturbs Brabanzio's simple distinction between a nature which cannot 'err' and the supernatural order of 'witchcraft' (1.3.62, 64).

The problem for Brabanzio is that the progressive political and economic life of Venice is at work beneath his conservative ideology of gender and paternal relations, and Shakespeare's broad representation of Venetian political life makes Desdemona's capacity for independent judgement and action more convincing. A comparison with the sexual politics of *The Merchant of Venice* can be instructive here. As Walter Cohen has pointed out Belmont functions in that play as a 'green' world inhabited by a traditional landed aristocracy, who in the course of events are brought into contact with the commercial and urban world of contemporary Venice.[8] The central figure of this green world is Portia, 'a living daughter curbed by the will of a dead father' (1.2.23–4), and one who completely accepts that her father's word has taken away her choice in marriage. As witty and resourceful as she is Portia never contemplates the transgression of the patriarchal decree, and even allowing for the difference in genre her behaviour makes a notable contrast with that of the city-dwelling Desdemona, who does something incomparably more daring. It also happens that Portia is visited by

the Moorish Prince of Morocco, who comes in suit to her for marriage, and of whom she says 'If he have the condition of a saint and the complexion of a devil, I had rather he should shrive me than wive me' (1.2.126–8). The first thing Morocco says to her is 'Mislike me not for my complexion' (2.1.1), and when he has departed after failing to choose the correct casket Portia says 'Let all of his complexion choose me so' (2.7.79). Next to Desdemona's cosmopolitan open-mindedness Portia's response looks very provincial, a predictable reaction to cultural otherness from the daughter of a traditionalist aristocracy. Portia lives idly in her great house on inherited wealth, with perhaps the nearest neighbour a 'monastery two miles off' (3.4.31); by contrast Desdemona lives in the city which Contarini describes as 'a common and generall market to the whole world', its streets thronging with a 'wonderful concourse of strange and forraine people'.[9] In this setting the traditionalist gender and racial ideologies of Belmont are on rather more shaky ground, subjected as they are to the pressures of a society moved by the concerns of commercial exchange and with a practical-minded government ready to reward merit rather than birth.

Shakespeare thus represents Desdemona's

---

8 Walter Cohen, '*The Merchant of Venice* and the Possibilities of Historical Criticism', *ELH* 49 (1982): 777. Cultural historians have pointed out that in contemporary Italy the countryside became a prime area for the investment of urban capital, and this was especially true of the region around Venice. Powerful families who made their fortunes in banking or trade bought estates in the country, and city interests dominated the rural economy. Partly as a result there was a revival of the pastoral genre and older aristocratic ideals, a 're-feudalization' similar in some respects to what was happening elsewhere in Europe. Cohen is right to stress the conservatism of aristocratic culture in the 'green' world of the play, though in actual historical terms it was often an instance of the 'new' traditionalism. See Lauro Martines, *Power and Imagination: City-States in Renaissance Italy* (Harmondsworth: Penguin, 1979), pp. 221–9.

9 Contareno, *The Common-wealth and Gouernment of Venice*, p. 1.

self-confidence as partly a product of the progressive Venetian culture he portrays in the play. Othello comes to this culture as an outsider, and his association with the city is based on both the government's republican principles and its readiness to seek out those with merit and to pay for their services. Much of Othello's relationship with Venetian culture is determined by the racial prejudice (like Portia's) he encounters there, which Shakespeare makes a deliberate point of portraying in the opening scenes of the play. This prejudice surfaces repeatedly, as in Brabanzio's insistence that the case be heard that very night:

> For if such actions may have passage free,
> Bondslaves and pagans shall our statesmen be.
>
> (1.2.99–100)

This is one of the earliest recorded uses of 'statesmen', a noun which evokes the republican setting of the Italian city-state. (Jonson had used it a few years earlier to name a category of men typified by Machiavelli.)[10] The limits to popular participation in contemporary republican government are abundantly clear in Brabanzio's speech, in which he apparently alludes to the period when Othello was 'sold to slavery' (1.3.137). He also leaves little doubt about his view of Othello's conversion to Christianity, which he evidently regards as a flimsy overlay for an essentially pagan nature. It seems to be Shakespeare's imaginative sympathy for the experience of the cultural outsider, particularly in the hostile environment often created by natives like Brabanzio, which enables him to move beyond the stereotypical images of Moorish people retailed in plays and pageants in England throughout his lifetime.[11] He created this highly original character by imagining Othello in a concrete social situation, and by permitting him to bring to Venice an ideological orientation formed under a different set of cultural institutions.

If one judges this orientation in the context of the Venice Shakespeare represents, Othello emerges as arguably the most conservative character in the play. The rich portrayal of his conservative sensibility seems to be generated in part by Shakespeare's interest in liberal Venetian institutions, and in the contrasts which accordingly emerge as Othello's relationship with Venice unfolds. He finds a model for his personal and political relationships in the tradition of monarchy, and in his first appearance he offers an indication of the degree to which his sense of self has been shaped by this tradition: 'I fetch my life and being / From men of royal siege' (1.2.21–2). Among the things to which Othello will later bid farewell is 'the royal banner' (3.3.358), a detail suggesting once again his experience of a political order remote from the republican institutions of contemporary Venice. Othello's language before the council in Act 1 tends to obscure the economic basis of his relationship with the state, which is accurately described by Iago's reference to their employment in 'the trade of war' (1.2.1).[12] Othello has a more nearly feudal conception of this relationship, which he speaks of in terms of duty and religious devotion. He conveys this in his first address to the senators – 'Most potent, grave, and reverend signors, / My very noble and approved good masters' (1.3.76–7) – where his devotional attitude contrasts with the practical tone of the council's deliberations. Othello positions himself here in the role of devoted

---

[10] See *Every Man Out of His Humour*, 2.6.168.

[11] For discussions of the representation of Moors and other non-Europeans in contemporary English culture see Samuel C. Chew, *The Crescent and the Rose: Islam and England during the Renaissance* (New York: Oxford University Press, 1937); Eldred Jones, *Othello's Countrymen: The African In English Renaissance Drama* (London: Oxford University Press, 1965); and Geoffrey Bullough, *Narrative and Dramatic Sources of Shakespeare*, vol. 7 (London: Routledge and Kegan Paul, 1973), pp. 207ff.

[12] Barbara Everett has noted the conflict between Othello's romanticized view of war and the fact that he is paid to fight by a city known for commerce and secularism. See her '"Spanish" Othello: The Making of Shakespeare's Moor', *Shakespeare Survey* 35 (1982), p. 112.

servant, and interestingly to the men themselves rather than to the state as an institution. His sense of his relationship with Venice as a personal tie rather than a contractual agreement is also evident when he prefaces a request to the council with 'Most humbly therefore bending to your state' (1.3.234), where 'state' slips from its usual sense of designating the Venetian republic and refers instead to the personal status of the senators. At one point he likens their council to the judgement seat of the Christian God:

> as truly as to heaven
> I do confess the vices of my blood,
> So justly to your grave ears I'll present
> How I did thrive in this fair lady's love,
> And she in mine.   (1.3.122–6)

Some have read this as an ominous passage, as perhaps revealing an unconscious identification in Othello's mind between sexual vice and his love for Desdemona,[13] but more plainly it indicates the hierarchical understanding he has of both political and religious institutions. The deep identification Othello makes in these lines would seem to be between Roman Catholicism and political absolutism, a conceptual integration roughly on the Habsburg model.

The council acts in a way which contrasts sharply with the political world as understood by Othello. Shakespeare represents them as a functioning participatory government, with a large measure of equality among aristocratic peers. Brabanzio makes reference to 'my brothers of the state' (1.2.97), an unusual locution which recalls the republican rhetoric of *Julius Caesar*, in which the anti-imperial faction employs the metaphor of fraternity in regarding themselves as the true sons of Rome. The members of the council make no sweeping ideological claims about what is at stake, but engage instead in a business-like attempt to calculate the number of ships in the Turkish fleet. In denying the accuracy of a certain report the First Senator says ''tis a pageant / To keep us in false gaze' (1.3.19–20), which suggests the

deliberative nature of their government, and their ability to see through theatrical displays of power associated in contemporary culture (and in present-day criticism of Renaissance texts) with imperial and absolutist governments. The practical-mindedness of the council was objected to in the late seventeenth century by Thomas Rymer, who found that Shakespeare's presentation lacked sufficient nobility:

By their Conduct and manner of talk, a body must strain hard to fancy the Scene at *Venice*; And not rather in some of our Cinq-ports, where the Baily and his Fisher-men are knocking their heads together on account of some Whale, or some terrible broil up the Coast.[14]

What Rymer sees as a fault (and exaggerates to make his point) can also be read in terms of Shakespeare's awareness of different political cultures. He may have thought it fitting that the senators of this commercial republic should be less concerned with shows of worldly greatness than with shrewd calculation and getting their figures right.

Certainly the religious character of Othello's devotion to the Venetian cause cannot be found among members of the council, who make no plea of any kind for Christendom. In fact in the context of Venetian culture Othello's religious sensibility seems rather antiquated. More than any other character he invests the Turkish-Christian conflict with spiritual significance, as his attribution of the Turkish defeat to God's will and his plea for 'Christian shame' among the victors makes clear (2.3.163–5). His piety seems to belong more to the era of the Crusades than to the increasingly secular world of sixteenth-century politics, when the powers of Europe were sometimes willing to ally

---

13 See Stephen Greenblatt, *Renaissance Self-Fashioning: From More to Shakespeare* (Chicago and London: University of Chicago Press, 1980), p. 245.

14 From his *Short View of Tragedy* (1693); quoted in G. R. Hibbard, '*Othello* and the Pattern of Shakespearian Tragedy', *Shakespeare Survey 21* (1968), p. 41.

themselves with the Ottoman empire to gain an advantage over other Christian states. Desdemona's sensitivity to this aspect of her husband's character may emerge when she tells Emilia that instead of losing the 'handkerchief' she would rather have lost her purse 'Full of crusadoes' (3.4.26). This is Shakespeare's only reference to this coin, which was stamped with a cross and current in contemporary England, and its name evokes the larger context of religious war in which Othello is involved, and perhaps also his tendency to regard the Christian-Turkish conflict in heroic and romantic terms. Desdemona's reference to 'crusadoes' might thus be read as an involuntary testimony to her sympathetic understanding of Othello's motives.

The character most aware of how Othello's traditionalist perspective makes him vulnerable to exploitation in Venice is Iago. Shakespeare makes a point of emphasizing Iago's role in the Venetian army, whose rigidly hierarchical relations contrast markedly with those within the state government, where the rule is consultation among equals rather than a structure of command and obedience. Like Brabanzio's household, the army and the martial law government in Cyprus have absolutist associations. Marguerite Waller has pointed out how Iago derives a sense of his own value from the military hierarchy – 'I know my price, I am worth no worse a place' (1.1.11) – and that what he regards as the intrusion of Othello and the Florentine Cassio helps to create the 'obsessive energy' with which he plots their ruin.[15] Othello and Cassio are also incorporated into the structure of the army in a way which shapes their subjective experience, but their concept of this institution lacks the commercial connotations of Iago's view. Both tend to regard the army as an instance of the organic community envisioned by the ideology of contemporary monarchy, and the politicized language of love which typifies political discourse in absolutism comes easily to them both. Cassio reveals this in his fall from Othello's favour, particularly in his request to Desdemona to intercede on his behalf:

> I do beseech you
> That by your virtuous means I may again
> Exist and be a member of his love
> Whom I, with all the office of my heart,
> Entirely honour.   (3.4.108–12)

Cassio's identity is dependent on his place within the institution, though he figures this not in practical political or economic terms but in the language of love, with the term 'member' recalling the traditional monarchical rhetoric of the 'body' politic and the organic community. Shakespeare may represent Cassio in this way partly because he is a product of the absolutist government of Florence, which had reverted from its earlier republicanism to the autocracy of the later Medici. In any case the crucial role played by the army in supporting Cassio's sense of self is evident in his use of the surprisingly strong verb 'Exist', and in its prominent placement. The play offers an analysis of male identity within the army as profoundly dependent on place and hierarchical relations, and as being distinct in this way from the system of relative equality among members of the Venetian governing class. In the speech quoted above Cassio's discourse of love and duty is suggestive of the personalized politics of absolute monarchy, and at odds with the legalism and practical business relationships of Venetian society as a whole. As a product of this society Desdemona is influenced by these more progressive conditions, and the legal or contractual basis for relationships in the city is evident in her language. She tells Cassio 'If I do vow a friendship I'll perform it / To the last article' (3.3.21–2).

Othello prefers to conduct his political relationships in the older language of loyalty and loving service, and Iago plays on this

---

[15] Marguerite Waller, 'Academic Tootsie: The Denial of Difference and the Difference It Makes', *Diacritics*, 17.2 (1987): 17.

idealistic and somewhat dated vocabulary to exploit him. In the central scene of the play (3.3) he is attuned to Othello's habit of viewing power relations in terms of devotion and love. When Othello threatens to kill him he projects indignation at his general's ingratitude: 'I'll love no friend, sith love breeds such offence' (3.3.385). At this Othello retreats, and presently Iago swears himself to 'wronged Othello's service':

> Let him command,
> And to obey shall be in me remorse,
> What bloody business ever.
> OTHELLO   I greet thy love,
> Not with vain thanks, but with acceptance
> bounteous.   (3.3.470–3)

In the speech partly quoted Iago never mentions love, and that Othello interprets his promise of devoted obedience in this way reveals the politicized nature of 'love' in his discourse. The extent to which Othello's mind is imbued with the monarchical is evident in the despairing language he uses after falling to Iago's treachery. It emerges in his vow of revenge, 'Yield up, O love, thy crown and hearted throne / To tyrannous hate!' (3.3.452–3), in which Othello represents his own subjective world as an absolutist political order. The following image in which he compares his 'bloody thoughts' to the rushing Pontic Sea is a remarkable intensification of a conventional Renaissance metaphor for tyranny, in which the boundless ocean is used to figure engulfing despotism.

There is also a religious element in the political discourse Othello uses at this point in the play, as in his accusation that Desdemona's hand is 'moist':

> This argues fruitfulness, and liberal heart.
> Hot, hot and moist – this hand of yours requires
> A sequester from liberty; fasting, and prayer,
> Much castigation, exercise devout,
> For here's a young and sweating devil here
> That commonly rebels. 'Tis a good hand,
> A frank one.

> DESDEMONA You may indeed say so,
> For 'twas that hand that gave away my heart.
> OTHELLO
> A liberal hand. The hearts of old gave hands,
> But our new heraldry is hands, not hearts.

It is typical of Othello's deeply conservative notions of service and heroism that he praises the 'old' ways and speaks of infidelity in love in terms of the debasement of heraldic signs. His speeches here are an interesting mix of political and sexual discourse, in which he conflates the Venetian tradition of political liberty with sexual licence – another tradition for which the city was widely known.[16] Othello uses the term 'liberty' to imply sexual indulgence, and the remedy he prescribes is the very un-Venetian practice of authoritarian religious discipline, indicating once again the distance of his sensibility from the religion and politics of Venice.

One further aspect of Othello's ideological orientation needs to be mentioned: he has no conception of a world divided into public and private spheres. This is manifest when Iago impugns the fidelity of Desdemona, and Othello responds by bidding farewell to his career in war, uttering in a painful lament that his 'occupation's gone' (3.3.362). Michael Neill has noted Othello's tendency to make no distinction in his life between public and private roles, and that his reference to 'occupation' can be read at a variety of levels both political and sexual.[17] The play seems to suggest in fact that the domestic or private sphere is in the process of evolving as a practical and conceptual category within the broader institutional life of the Venetian state. Francis Barker has argued that a

---

[16] For a discussion of how contemporary observers of Venice found it difficult to distinguish between the political freedom fostered by the city's institutions and its reputation for sexual indulgence see William Bouwsma, 'Venice and the Political Education of Europe', in *Renaissance Venice*, ed. J. R. Hale (London: Faber, 1973), p. 461.

[17] Michael Neill, 'Changing Places in *Othello*', *Shakespeare Survey* 37 (1984), p. 127.

conception of the public and private as autonomous spheres developed mostly after Shakespeare's work in the theatre, and he cites the
second scene of *Hamlet* to support his point.[18]
He suggests that in that scene the looming war
with Norway, Laertes' intention to return to
France, and Hamlet's melancholy are all represented as continuous issues within a single conceptual and political order. The scene which
invites comparison in *Othello* is the gathering
of the council, in which the Duke responds
tellingly to the question of whether Desdemona
should be permitted to accompany Othello to
Cyprus: 'Be it as you shall privately determine'
(1.3.275). In *Hamlet* Claudius involves himself
much more conspicuously in the familial debate
over whether Laertes should return to France.[19]
What Shakespeare seems to suggest in *Othello* is
that the distinction between public and private
is more developed in the context of a commercial and republican society. If it is less evident in
Hamlet this is probably because in that play he
represents a monarchy in which the traditions
of feudalism continue to exert an influence. In
royalist countries the corporate ideology which
Barker finds in *Hamlet* may have inhibited any
sharp distinction between the domestic and
public spheres, but Shakespeare's treatment of
the issue in his play about Venice suggests his
ability to think beyond the social practices of
monarchy, and perhaps also his awareness of
how the conceptual order would be different in
a commercial state based on citizenship rather
than on the older notion of membership in a
body politic.

As the play develops Shakespeare shows an
increasing interest in the association of Venetian
women with the private sphere, and in the
different roles they play there. In part this seems
to be because the domestic sphere is charged
over the course of the play with the displaced
energies of state politics, and this politicizes the
language of this sphere and the actions and
speech of women to an unusual degree. The
relative equality of Desdemona and Othello in
their marriage is evident in the encounter when

she first pleads Cassio's 'cause', in which she
adopts the part of a 'solicitor' and establishes the
setting for debate and persuasion (3.3.27). Both
the legalism of Venice and its consultative
government are influences here, and Desdemona brings a consciousness shaped by republican traditions to both her marriage and
the more conservative institutional setting of
Cyprus. After speaking her mind freely
throughout this scene she exits telling Othello
'Whate'er you be, I am obedient' (3.3.90), and
thus uses a traditional discourse of submission
to male authority only when she has already
succeeded in creating a space for negotiation.
Much more oppressive is the marriage between
Iago and Emilia, in which the husband exerts a
despotic control over his wife's actions and
speech. In this relationship Shakespeare
portrays the private sphere as a place of priva-
tion, with Emilia deprived of any broader
agency or public role. Her plight reflects Iago's
virulent misogyny and his obsession with hierarchical relations, and perhaps also a contemporary republican tendency to masculinize the
state and to confine women exclusively to the
private order. That Iago believes Emilia has no
role in the public world is evident in his rebuke
to her for suggesting that some 'villainous
knave' is poisoning Othello's mind: 'Speak
within door' (4.2.148). But Shakespeare also
shows an interest in the private order as the

---

[18] Francis Barker, *The Tremulous Private Body: Essays on
Subjection* (London and New York: Methuen, 1984),
pp. 30ff.

[19] The practice of Shakespeare's own culture was closer to
that represented in *Hamlet*. On 29 June 1601 William
Herbert, third earl of Pembroke, asked the queen
through Robert Cecil for permission 'to go abroad to
follow mine own business'. He was still asking for this
permission two months later. At Elizabeth's court such
royal control over the travels of the nobility was the
general rule, and Shakespeare was thus departing from
the custom of his own society in imagining a different
political practice for contemporary Venice. See
'William Herbert, third Earl of Pembroke', *Dictionary of
National Biography*, vol. 9, p. 678.

place of women's collective experience, and this is most clearly evident in the 'willow' scene (4.3). Desdemona and Emilia experience solidarity and freedom of speech in this setting, and in the absence of male controls they touch issues of power and desire beyond the range of ordinary discourse.[20] Shakespeare represents them developing a collective consciousness by quietly exploiting the limited freedom of the private sphere, and this scene clearly generates some of the political energy Emilia displays in the final act.

In the last scene Othello is moved not only by his desire for revenge but by what he regards as the requirements of 'Justice' (5.2.17). As it opens he is still the military governor of Cyprus, and he evidently believes the murder of Desdemona to be within the purview of his powers under martial law. Dedemona may refer to his status as the ruler of the island when she says 'O, banish me, my lord, but kill me not' (5.2.85). Othello is thus guilty not only of murder but of the arbitrary exercise of power, and Shakespeare represents his actions as both morally wrong and tyrannical. Othello has himself been tyrannized by Iago, and the character responsible for overthrowing both these tyrannies is Emilia. That Shakespeare chose her as the agent responsible for breaking her husband's domination can be regarded as the fulfilment of a certain logic in the play in which a relationship develops between the women of Venice and the city's tradition of political liberty. The aspect of this tradition focused on in the text is the idea of free speech, which is defined not in terms of modern liberalism but in the contemporary context of monarchical and patriarchal restrictions on utterance, an absolutist context in which political speech is made 'tongue-tied by authority' (Sonnet 66). Desdemona's candid political and sexual discourse before the council is the first evidence of this relationship between women and the city's traditions, and she is associated with such discursive freedom repeatedly in the play, as when Othello says (approvingly) that his wife is 'free of speech' (3.3.189), and when she later tells Cassio that she stands in the

blank of her husband's displeasure for 'my free speech' (3.4.127).

In the final scene Emilia uses much the same discourse to bring down the tyranny of her husband. Shakespeare's interest in Emilia in the context of the relationship between Venetian women and political speech emerges much earlier in the play. When Iago implies in Act 2 that his wife is a scold Desdemona defends her by saying 'Alas, she has no speech!' (2.1.106). This is a rather unusual phrase for making the point, and its oddity signals the gradually developing connection between the women of Venice and political expression. When Emilia's speech threatens him at the end of the play Iago tries to return her to the private sphere: 'I charge you get you home' (5.2.201). Having already spoken without male permission in interrupting Montano's address to Othello, Emilia asks the representatives of the Venetian state for 'leave to speak':

> 'Tis proper I obey him, but not now.
> Perchance, Iago, I will ne'er go home.
>
> (5.2.203–4)

What Emilia announces in these lines is a political revolt: in this context 'going home' has both its literal meaning and the political sense of returning to a state of complete subordination. Emilia's disobedience of her husband's authority will likely have radical consequences, as she is well aware. When Iago again tells her to be silent she again rejects him:

> 'Twill out, 'twill out. I peace?
> No, I will speak as liberal as the north.
> Let heaven, and men, and devils, and 'em all,
> All, all cry shame against me, yet I'll speak.
>
> (5.2.225–8)

---

20 Carol McKewin has noted that the women's friendship in this scene is an 'implied rebuke' to relationships between men in the play. See her 'Counsels of Gall and Grace: Intimate Conversations between Women in Shakespeare's Plays', in *The Woman's Part: Feminist Criticism of Shakespeare*, ed. by Carolyn Ruth Swift Lenz, Gayle Greene, and Carol Thomas Neely (Urbana: University of Illinois Press, 1980), p. 128.

In Emilia's use 'liberal' is completely without the sexual connotations it had in Othello's discourse, and suggests a freedom exercised with great effort in the face of traditional male authority. Her image of the north wind for the force of a woman's speech in the public sphere summons up other Renaissance usages in which storm and tempest are metaphors for political upheaval and revolution. And the emerging emphasis late in the play on the solidarity of women makes it possible to take her reference to 'men' as designating not humankind but the ruling gender. Like the Venetian woman she serves Emilia seems to be an agent for realizing the city's political ideals of justice and liberty. Her last words are 'So, speaking as I think, alas, I die' (5.2.258), a line which foreshadows Edgar's closing speech in *King Lear*, in which he says that the witnesses to the catastrophe must 'Speak what we feel, not what we ought to say' (5.3.300). Emilia's words endow what Edgar says with a significance more clearly political, and they may suggest that Shakespeare regarded such speech as a recourse against both loss and tyranny.

Critical awareness of Shakespeare's interest in fundamentally different forms of social organization allows this kind of political content in his work to emerge more clearly. Certainly this interest informs *Othello*, and the tension between monarchy and republicanism charges its language with nuance and political significance. Shakespeare's representation of a non-European's life in Venice and of women's experience in the city is creatively influenced by his awareness of these different systems, and his encounter with the foreign political culture of Venice produces a play that explores and at times subtly endorses ideological perspectives outside the framework established by the monarchical and patriarchal traditions of contemporary English politics.

'MY MUSIC FOR NOTHING': MUSICAL NEGOTIATIONS IN *THE TEMPEST*

PIERRE ISELIN

In an early scene of *Henry VIII* (or *All is True*), while denouncing the 'spells of France' displayed at the Field of the Cloth of Gold, and the extravagant vanities imitated from the French, Sir Thomas Lovell rejoices in the recent prohibition of these foreign customs and deplores their efficacy in the form of a local 'O tempora, O mores', which is not altogether devoid of personal frustration or innocent of erotic meaning:

LOVELL   The sly whoresons
Have got a speeding trick to lay down ladies.
A French song and a fiddle has no fellow.
SANDS The devil fiddle 'em! I am glad they
    are going,
For sure there's no converting of 'em. Now
An honest country lord, as I am, beaten
A long time out of play, may bring his
    plainsong,
And have an hour of hearing, and by'r Lady,
Held current music, too.

                    (*Henry VIII* 1.3.39–47)

The characteristic reduction of music to an object of discourse, the use of the musical *double entendre*, with the implicit equation of music and love making, and the superior efficacy of French – and now fortunately illicit – music as erotic recipe, thus estrange the musical material in a threefold manner, making it simultaneously improper, foreign, and alien. Music's potential for seduction is held dangerous to courtiers and puritans alike, and its Trojan horse status, on the stage and elsewhere, raises issues of limits and transgression, both semiotic and ideological, not to mention the Mercurial

roles of spies, plotters, ambassadors, messengers, regularly ascribed to musicians in the court and on the stage.[1] Whether it is performed by an aerial spirit acting as informer or by a man of mode, music has a taste of the foreign. Is not Sir Andrew Aguecheek one who 'plays o' th' viol-de-gamboys, and speaks three or four languages word for word without book' (*Twelfth Night* 1.3.23–4)?

More often than not ridiculed as inappropriate and ineffectual – not to say incongruous – stage music is also the butt of institutional criticism in the Puritan attacks on entertainment. An extreme version of artistic 'abuse', the former constitutes a territory hardly defensible even to the warmest apologists of art and music. This, *The Praise of Musicke* – one plausible reply to *The Schoole of Abuse* (1579) – posthumously[2] and anonymously published in Oxford seven years after Gosson's tract, makes a single passing remark

---

[1] For the roles of the musicians William Kinlock and James Lander in Scotland, see Helena Mennie Shire, *Song, Dance and Poetry of the Court of Scotland under James VI* (Cambridge University Press, 1969), pp. 71 and 77; for those of William Byrd, Alfonso Ferrabosco and Thomas Morley in England, see Alan Haynes, *Invisible Power: The Elizabethan Secret Service, 1570–1603* (Alan Sutton Publishing Limited, Phoenix Mill, 1992), pp. 12, 71, 79, 84.

[2] The text of *The Praise of Musicke* (anon., Oxford, 1586) is presented by its publisher, Joseph Barnes, as 'an Orphan of Musickes children', a statement which, in the absence of contrary evidence, must allude to the death of its author.

on what is presented as the object of an ethically, culturally, and politically heated debate. In non-committal, rather cautious terms, the hybrid, 'depraved' form of art – to follow Quintilian[3] – is rhetorically given up through paralipsis and ideologically held at a distance, in order not to contaminate more respectable and safer grounds:

For I dare not speak of dauncing or the theatrall spectacles, least I pull whole swarms of enimies upon me [. . .] I confesse I am accessory to their injurie against Musick in bereaving it of these so ample, notable provinces, because I doe not by open resistance hinder their riot. For howsoever obscenity may bring the stage in suspicion of unchasteness and incontinency, make dauncing disfavorable and odious, I am sure that neither of them keeping themselves under saile, that is not overreaching their honest and lawful circumstances, can want either good groundes to authorize them, or sufficient patronage to maintain them.[4]

The vocabulary of war, of territorial loss, confirms that in the period's controversy over art and entertainment in general, music in the theatre is a fragile, nearly untenable outpost. This indeterminacy of strategic status may partly account for its interstitial, front-line position in the field of theatrical representation and inscribes it in the topography of warfare. The military metaphor is not fortuitous, as is evident in the notions of 'penetration' and 'appropriation', two neoplatonic concepts central to the definition of music's efficacy. Not only the power of music *per se*, but also the comparative power of music and drama are at stake in this cultural confrontation. It is no accident that *The Tempest* – a play itself largely concerned with issues of power(s) – makes several species of power, the musical, the magical and the political, coalesce in the character of Prospero, conferring on him a complex status as artist, magus and ruler through the unifying discourse of myth, and that of praise, the epideictic.[5] A song, even if not sung in parts, may thus be viewed as a virtual cultural polyphony, a potential form of debate.

In the Shakespearian canon, a significant change may also be traced in the clearly discernible shift from verbal allusion and complex musical polysemy to a more and more abundant inscription of actual music and songs in the plays; this possibly reflects the growing expectations of the audiences in terms of stage-music, making the latter an economic as well as an artistic stake in the commercial rivalry between the theatres and the dramatists. It is significant, for instance, that the play in the canon in which most is said about music, *The Taming of the Shrew*, is paradoxically one in which the scanty stage music holds very little meaning.[6] Conversely, *The Tempest* represents the *terminus ad quem* of an evolution and has the position of an ultimate crossroads of dramaturgical and musical channels, with a considerable amount of music and song, quite a few significant verbal commentaries on the music actually heard on the stage, and few – altogether commonplace – conceits of musical tenor. The inclusion of music and song can therefore be seen as part of an implicit cultural and economic transaction between the dramatist and his audience.

Concluding her study of the singer's voice in Elizabethan drama, Elise Bickford Jorgens develops this idea of an implicit polyphony contained in any stage music:

in these songs, the singer's voice provides us with many voices, carrying on, at several levels, the period's cultural debate about the physical, spiritual, emotional, and moral efficacy of music. The voice of the dramatic character, [. . .] the voice of the playwright [. . .]. And beneath these a multitude of other voices from the culture sing out: the Gossons and the Cases, the Mulcasters and the Elyots and the Lodges and the Brights, and the members of the audience

---

[3] Quintilian, *De institutione oratorica*, I.x.9–33.

[4] *The Praise of Musicke*, pp. 79–80.

[5] In this connection, see Donna Hamilton, *Virgil and* The Tempest: *The Politics of Imitation* (Ohio State University Press, Columbia, 1990), pp. 7–10.

[6] See T. M. Waldo and T. W. Herbert, 'Musical Terms in *The Taming of the Shrew*: Evidence of Single Authorship', *Shakespeare Quarterly*, X (1959): 185–200.

who – whatever their private response to the songs they heard from the stage – were all in some way party to the debate.[7]

Even though *The Tempest* does not characteristically echo the debate raging in the late 1580s, as the play is – even if problematically – related to the Jonsonian Court masque[8] and the sphere of private theatres, still it will be shown how the praise of music constitutes a discursive pattern, 'un schème de culture' in Jean Jacquot's words,[9] which has late representatives at the beginning of James I's reign,[10] and above all which is contrapuntally related to another discourse of encomium, the panegyric of the Prince. In the discursive polyphony on the theme of power, musical myth and political allegory will thus be shown to represent two closely connected parts in *The Tempest*.

Inherent in stage music is therefore a set of discourses making up an implicit system of exchange, one obvious aspect of which is the variety of the responses of stage audiences, in the form of verbal commentaries, and those of the paying audience more or less ironically anticipated or echoed on the stage. Nevertheless, the polyphony is not only to be construed as the superposition of voices of varying actantial relevance, but also as a dialectical relationship of mutual framing – the coalescence/confrontation of two mutually dependent sign-systems –, since on the one hand music *is* the indispensable gambit of theatrical representation, on the other no musical piece is left unframed by language, the variety of these verbal commentaries and responses inducing in turn one more polyphonic construction to the whole.

A crossroads of media, verbal and non-verbal, the theatre is also a crossroads of discourses. For the isle in *The Tempest* is not only 'full of noises', as Caliban has it, but also full of voices and discourses. Variously defined in the text as manipulative, civilizing, maddening, magical, rapacious – like Prospero-as-ruler – music has a particular significance in *The Tempest* as it features as a metonymic version of Prospero's power, while at the same time it is also the figure of the challenge to this very power in its discordant, anarchic dimension. Its plural meanings in the play do but reproduce its contested meanings in the culture of the period, and *The Tempest*'s music(s) may thus be said to articulate several discursive voices: those of myth and praise, that of *furor*, but also those of disruption and scepticism.

The isle appears as a nautical magnet and a place full of acoustic oddities even before the landing of Prospero; the transaction between Ariel and the wrecked magician has immediate acoustic resonances: the groans of the imprisoned spirit, which 'Did make wolves howl, and penetrate the breasts / Of ever-angry bears' (1.2.288–9) are turned to playing and singing throughout the play. Musical (ex-)change in politics has become a trope with the usurping brother Antonio, who, 'having both the key / Of officer and office, set all hearts i'th' state / To what tune pleased his ear' (1.2.83–5). Both categories of subjects therefore comply musically with their respective prince's likings. In the economy of power, music regularly appears as an asset, an object of implicit or explicit transaction, as well as a tool of metamorphosis and manipulation. Prospero promises a musical show to reward Ferdinand's

---

7 Elise Bickford Jorgens, 'The Singer's Voice in Elizabethan Drama', in *Renaissance Rereadings, Intertext and Context*, ed. M. C. Horowitz, A. J. Cruz and W. A. Furman (University of Illinois Press, Urbana and Chicago, 1988), p. 45.

8 The many parallels between Shakespeare's play and Jonson's Masque of Union, *Hymenæi*, performed on the fifth of January 1606 to celebrate a dynastic marriage, are numerous and clear enough not to necessitate a full-length demonstration here.

9 Jean Jacquot, '*L'éloge de la Musique*: grandeur et décadence d'un schème de culture', *Revue Belge de Musicologie*, XX, 1–4 (1966): 91–110.

10 See in particular *The Praise of Musicke and the profite and delight it bringeth to man [. . .]*, Ms. Roy. 18 B XIX, British Museum, which was written in the very first years of James I's reign in an attempt at praising both music and the monarch for the sake of corporative interests.

chaste resolution – and possibly, as will be seen, to cool the heat of physical desire; similarly, all the retributive and elective music in *The Tempest* is part of the political deal, when some are granted sleep through 'solemn music', and others given warnings; virtually an opiate for the people, the acoustic wealth of the isle is oneirically transmuted into 'riches ready to drop upon [Caliban]' (3.2.144–5). Another form of exchange takes place when Ariel amends the tune of Caliban's catch, learnt from Stefano (3.2.119–29), the 'three-men's song' literally becoming a 'free-men's' one. Another complex form of musical negotiation is reflected in Caliban's song of rebellion. 'No more dams I'll make for fish', which has been seen to contain a reference to those artificial fish weirs which were a traditional skill of the aborigines of Virginia, described by Ralph Lane on his visit to Virgina in 1586. These dams, whose construction was intricate enough, represented an important source of sustenance for the colonists – hence a fear that the Indians might destroy them.[11] Travel literature thus provides a credible context for Prospero's resigned confession to Miranda that, villainous as Caliban is (1.2.311), they 'cannot miss him', so indispensable are his practical skills – a discourse clearly resonant with colonial anxieties:

> He does make our fire,
> Fetch in our wood, and serves in offices
> That profit us.   (1.2.313–15)

It is not too far-fetched, I think, to see in Prospero's beast of burden a local version of Zethus, the more pragmatic of the two mythical twins, the one who *did* lift the stones to build the walls of Thebes, whereas the new Amphion, Prospero, can raise and dissolve in a single breath 'cloud-capped towers', 'gorgeous palaces', and 'solemn temples' to boot (4.1.152–3). The allusion to the wonderful musician is ironically made by the two usurping brothers, Antonio and Sebastian, while debunking the generous and visionary chattering of Gonzalo:

ANTONIO His word is more than the miraculous harp.
SEBASTIAN He hath raised the wall, and houses too.
ANTONIO What impossible matter will he make easy next?   (2.1.91–4)

Ironically enough, the powers thus derided by the two 'auro-sceptics' are effectively at work, much of the action in the play being attributable to the workings of the air and musical sound. The figure of the mythical hero is thus exploded into two *dramatis personae*, Prospero and Gonzalo; besides, the Amphion myth itself is fragmented and displaced, giving birth to the confrontation of two attitudes towards language, the magic and poetic view of the natural origin of language as opposed to its conventional definition. Characteristically, the usurpers and the boatswain question the magical and the tropical senses, deride their inconsistencies at a literal level, and use blasphemous idiom. In the initial scene, which stages an acoustic competition between Prospero's loudspeakers and the characters' voices, the boatswain exclaims: 'What care these roarers for the name of king?' (1.1.15–16). Here not only do the topical and the tropical meanings superpose – 'roarers' referring both to the billows and the street rioters – but while the name of the king proves an ineffective talisman to 'command these elements to silence, and work the peace of the present' (1.1.20–1), it is precisely not the name, but the word of 'wronged duke of Milan' that is commanding. The debate on the status of language thus seems to be ironically blurred by

---

[11] 'Thy Kynge [of the Indians] was disposed to have assuredly brought us to ruine in the moneth of March 1586. himselfe also with all his Savages to have runne away from us which if he had done wee coulde [not] have bene preserved from starving. For wee had no weares of fish, neither coulde our men skill of the making of them. [But finally we] wanne this resolution of him, that out of hand he should goe about, and withall, to cause his men to set up weares foorthwith for us'. *Hakluyt's Voyages*, ed. Hakluyt Society (1903–5), VIII, pp. 334–6.

dramaturgical strategies, or even truncated perspectives, as the irony only appears retrospectively, when we are told in the following scene that it was by his 'art' that Prospero 'put the wild water in this *roar*' (1.2.2).

Conversely, traces of verbal realism[12] or auralist magic are to be found among the other school of thought, the two attitudes being represented in Gonzalo's winning remark in the last scene:

> GONZALO   . . . Now, blasphemy,
> That *swear'st grace o'erboard*: not an *oath* on
>   shore?
> Hath thou no mouth by land?   (5.1.221–3)

or in Prospero's address to his brother:

> PROSPERO For you, most wicked sir, whom to
>   *call* brother
> Would even *infect my mouth*, I do forgive
> Thy rankest fault.   (5.1.132–4)

A burlesque, literalized, rendition of the cult of the word can be seen in the parody of a traditional scene of dubbing staged by the mock-usurpers, with Caliban kissing what Stefano blasphemously calls '*the* book'. The parallel with the serious magical attitude goes even further, as the object of their cult is unwillingly drowned in the pool, and this 'infinite loss' (4.1.210) operates a grotesque anticipation of the deliberate drowning taking place within a hundred lines, that of the instruments of the ritual, the staff and the book (5.1.54–7). The last page perused by Prospero may well have been concerned with musical charms as described by Ficino,[13] judging from the proximity of the two statements: 'when I have required / Some heavenly music [. . .], I'll drown my book' (5.1.51–7). This drowning, and its grotesque double, thus cast a problematical, fragmented, light on the mythical, unnamed, *exemplum* of Amphion. Disruption, construed both as interruption on the part of the Magus and as insurrection on that of the rebels, threatens the unifying discourse of myth, which happens to be equally that of empire, since the musical

powers of the hero are subservient to the political ambition to wall in the city of Thebes.

Another musical myth lurks beneath the surface of the text, as its hero tries to survive above the surface of water; one can catch a glimpse of the figure of Arion, one associated with theft, treachery and watery death, in Prospero's account of his voyage in exile:

> PROSPERO   There they hoist us,
> To cry to th' sea that roared to us, to sigh
> To th' winds, whose pity, sighing back again,
> Did us loving wrong.   (1.2.148–51)

Life does not depend here on the legendary dolphin charmed by the musician's valedictory song, but on the 'rotten carcase of a butt, not rigged, / Nor tackle, sail, nor mast' (1.2.146–7), a mere ruined barrel then, which had been 'prepared' for that purpose. The notions of premeditation, of nightly plotting and of political usurpation, the lexical oddity of 'butt' as an unrecorded trope for 'boat', and the merging of the discourses of statecraft and music already observed, may be seen to constitute a network of hermeneutic signs and suggest the palimpsest vision of a living monarch, equally 'rapt in secret studies' – a new Arion – who had recently been threatened by a plot involving gunpowder barrels in 1605.

An interesting verbal parallel can here be established between Ferdinand's commentary on the 'effect' of the isle's music,

> This music crept by me upon the waters,
> *Allaying* both their *fury* and my passion
> With its sweet air   (1.2.394–6)

and the Arion fable as told in the text of *The Praise of Musicke*:

---

[12] Other instances of verbal realism can be found in the play, in particular at 1.2.266–9, 2.1.112–13, 3.2.70–1 and 4.1.10–11.

[13] See his *De vita coelitus comparanda*, III, 21, 32, 42; the last two passages mentioned refer to the role of music in the evocation of certain demons and the spirits of the dead, which may represent aspects of Prospero's 'rough magic'.

Arion seeing no way to escape the *furie* of his cruel enemies, tooke his Citterne in his hand, and to his instrument sang his last song, wherewith not only the dolphines flocked in multitudes about the ship readie to receive him on their backes, but even the sea that rude and barbarous element, being before roughe and tempestuous, seemed to *allay* his choler, waxing calme on a sodaine, as if it had bene to give Arion quiet passage through the waves.[14]

Another evident association of Prospero with the arch-musician, Orpheus, may be perceived in the definition of iatromusic,

> PROSPERO A solemn air, and the best comforter
> To an unsettled fancy, cure thy brains,
> Now useless, boiled within thy skull.
>
> (5.1.58–60)

Perspective – a visual, elective device introduced into the dramaturgy of the court masque in 1605 by Inigo Jones, that creates 'another focus for the show of royal power'[15] – operates here: if one can see an Orphic magus and pedagogue in Prospero, then the same royal perspective makes it possible to

> Behold how like another Orpheus, Amphion, and Arion, he draweth to the true knowledge of God, very salvage Beasts, Forrests, Trees and Stones, by the sweet Harmony of his harp: the most fierce and wilde, the most stupid and insenced, the most brutish and voluptuous, are changed and civilized by the delectable sound of his Musicke.[16]

The epideictic discourse therefore seems to unfold an implicit two-part polyphony: the praise of art and music being the plain-song, the praise of the inspired sovereign the descant, with the addition of the discourse of disruption, a burden distinctly audible at times too.

The common denominator between the first two discourses is obviously the notion of 'power', which appears in the related form of 'effects'. In his *Apologia Musices* (1588), John Case, the Aristotelian scholar, declares he will refrain from resorting to mythology in his defence of music; still it is only a few pages later that he comes to list not only the classical

mirabilia, which are as many *topoi*, among which those 'nymphs Islands', in Lydia, 'which at the sound of the trumpet forthwith come into the middle of the sea . . .',[17] but also lists the modern analogues of acoustic *mirabilia* so as to establish the continuity between the classical and the contemporary worlds:

> [. . .] in the much renowned church of Winton, a choir – as it were – of the sweetest harmonies, with no human voice, was distinctly heard, and with no little admiration, for many years: [. . .] at the sepulchure of a Scottish nobleman dead for few years, some kind of music – shall I say celestial or terrestrial, doleful for sure – could be heard.[18]

The uncertainty Case identifies is probably of the sort expressed by Ferdinand, who wonders about the origin and the destination of this non-human harmony:

> FERDINAND Where should this music be? I' th' air, or th' earth?
> It sounds no more; and sure it waits upon
> Some god o' th' island. (1.2.390–2)
>
> This is no mortal business, nor no sound
> That the earth owes. I hear it now above me.
>
> (1.2.409)

But the discourse of myth, which articulates that of power, is here brought to its limits: the deceptive 'ditty' of Ariel's song does have political implications in that it furthers the dynastic premeditation of Prospero, but simultaneously

---

14 *The Praise of Musicke*, pp. 57–8.
15 K. R. McNamara, 'Golden Worlds at Court: *The Tempest* and its Masque', *Shakespeare Studies*, 19 (1987): 185.
16 George Marcelline, *The Triumphs of James the First* (London, 1610), p. 35, cited by Robin Headlam Wells, *Elizabethan Mythologies, Studies in Poetry, Drama and Music* (Cambridge University Press, 1994), p. 69.
17 John Case, *Apologia musices*, p. 3 [my translation].
18 Ibid., p. 4. J. Cardan similarly reports: 'In Caledony, a region of Scotland, on a hill called "mournful", one can hear by night voices sounding like those of tormented human beings – either demons or souls of the defunct.' (*De subtilitate*, *Opera omnia*, Lugd., 1663, p. 301) [my translation].

its potential for seduction and erotic allurement contradicts the father's anxious concern with chastity. In playing with music, Prospero more than once proves to be a sorcerer's apprentice rather than a full-fledged magus. He even seems to trap himself in his own stratagem when the beauty of the masque makes him forget the 'foul conspiracy of the beast Caliban', and causes the much debated 'interruption'. It is indeed through the channel of 'noises, sounds and sweet airs' that access is given to the 'artificial paradise' of golden dreams (3.2.138–46); yet the musical fable is unambiguously annexed by the theatre when musical transe becomes simultaneously a process both purifying and introspective – merging the characteristics of the two aristotelian notions of *catharsis* and *anagnorisis*:

> ALONSO   O, it is monstrous, monstrous!
> Methought the billows spoke and told me of it,
> The winds did sing it to me, and the thunder,
> That deep and dreadful organ-pipe, pronounced
> The name of Prosper. It did bass my trespass.
> Therefor my son i' th' ooze is bedded, and
> I'll seek him deeper than e'er plummet sounded,
> And with him there lie mudded.   (3.3.95–102)

Musical *furor* is here conducive to a forced *anamnesis*, a painful recollection, the *mise en scène* of guilt: it operates as an acoustic 'mirror of truth' held up to Alonso to purgatory ends. Shakespeare – or Prospero – here merges the two meanings Aristotle gives of *catharsis*, one referring to the tragic, the other to the musical experience.[19] The alchemical meaning of the word *tempest*, 'a boiling process which removes impurities from base metal and facilitates its transmutation into gold',[20] only adds a further symbolic significance to the process of change and exchange, metamorphosis and negotiation, at work in the play's musical dramaturgy. If music is a tool for political manipulation, it can be equally asserted that it is in turn the object of theatrical manipulation. For if music in *The Tempest* can be ascribed the two definitions of the Aristotelian *catharsis*, and if *nemesis* follows the path of forced recollection, *anamnesis*, still

this version of the musical *furor* is a downgraded one. To neo-Platonic philosophers, from Ficino to Parrizi, 'furor was nothing other than a forced anamnesis, a celestial *raptio*, by which individual planetary Muses recalled to themselves the souls most like them'.[21] In *The Tempest*, poetic justice has turned into musical retribution, the powers of music have become those of Prospero and these powers are precisely those of 'penetration' and 'appropriation', two notions which partake both of the aural and the political, two versions of *imperium* applied to the spheres of the physical body and the body politic. Plato's simple definition in *The Republic*,

> Rhythm and *harmoniai* penetrate most deeply into the recesses of the soul[22]

is extrapolated by Ficino, who gives of it a quasi-imperialistic definition in his commentary on the *Timæus*:

> Musical sound moves the body by the movement of the air; by purified air it excites the airy spirit, which is the bond of body and soul; by emotion it affects the senses and at the same time the soul; by meaning it affects the mind; finally by the very movement of its subtle air it penetrates strongly; by its temperament it flows smoothly; by its consonant quality it floods us with a wonderful pleasure; by its nature, both spiritual and natural, it at once seizes and claims as its own man in his entirety.[23]

Ficino here defines a form of prerogative that does not altogether differ from Prospero's virtually violent desire of aural appropriation of Miranda:

---

[19] Aristotle, *Politics*, 8.7.1841b37.

[20] John S. Mebane, *Renaissance Magic and the Return of the Golden Age: The Occult Tradition and Marlowe, Jonson, and Shakespeare* (Lincoln & London: Nebraska University Press, 1989), p. 181.

[21] Gary Tomlinson, *Music in Renaissance Magic: Toward a Historiography of Others* (Chicago & London: Chicago University Press, 1993), pp. 213–14.

[22] Plato, *Republic*, 401 d, A. Barker ed. (Cambridge University Press, *Greek Musical Writings*, 1984), vol. I, p. 305.

[23] M. Ficino, *In Timæum Commentarium*, Opera Omnia, Basileae, 1576, p. 1453 [my translation].

PROSPERO Dost thou hear?
MIRANDA   Your tale, sir, would
                             cure deafness.
                                        (1.2.106)

A run-of-the-mill version of 'furor' is offered in the scene where Ariel charms the three drunkards' ears only to drive them into a 'filthy-mantled pool', their quasi-'swinish' behaviour being reminiscent of Circe's metamorphosis of Ulysses' companions on the isle of Aeaea,[24] and of the German myth of the 'Rattenfänger von Hameln',

> ARIEL I told you, sir, they were red-*hot* with
>   drinking;
> So full of valour that they smote the air
> For breathing in their faces, beat the ground
> For kissing of their feet; yet always bending
> Towards their project. Then I beat my tabor,
> At which like *unbacked colts* they pricked *their
>   ears*,
> Advanced their eyelids, lifted up their noses
> As they smelt music. So I charmed *their ears*
> That calf-like they my lowing followed,
>   through
> Toothed briars, sharp furzes, pricking gorse, and
>   thorns,
> Which entered their frail skins. At last I left
>   them
> I' th' filthy-mantled pool beyond your cell,
> There dancing up to th' chins, that the foul lake
> O'er-stunk their feet.   (4.1.171–84)

Soul loss, '*alienatio mentis*' to use Ficino's phrase, is parodied here in grotesque manner, human beings being brought to the level of 'brutish beasts'. It is interesting to note that the exact tune of Stefano's catch played in tune – musical exact truth – deceives more than alcohol itself: the play literalizes and dramatizes the adage: 'musica multos magis dementat quam vinum'.[25]

This bacchic context seems to be poles apart from the discourse of praise. Nevertheless, Ariel's recital bears more verbal resemblances to Shakespeare's own version of the *encomium musicæ*, in *The Merchant of Venice*:

For do but note a wild and wanton herd
Or race of youthful and *unhandled colts*,

Fetching mad bounds, bellowing and neighing loud,
Which is the *hot* condition of their *blood*,
If they but hear perchance a trumpet sound,
Or any air of music touch *their ears*,
You shall perceive them make a mutual stand,
Their savage eyes turned to a modest gaze
By the sweet power of music.   (5.1.71–9)

The classical source for this *topos* is certainly Ælian,

But the mares of Libya . . . are equally captivated by the sound of the pipe [*aulos*]. They become gentle and tame and cease to prance and be skittish, and follow the herdsman wherever the music lead them; and if he stands still, so do they. But if he plays his pipes with greater vigour, tears of pleasure stream from their eyes.[26]

But the passage immediately following in Ælian is occulted in most texts of praise, as it describes the erogenous power of music – a moot point which encomiasts would rather not tackle. They would not readily cite *exempla* demonstrating the diametrically opposed effect of Dorian music, of which Clytemnestra's story is the paradigm:

Touching the first effects of musick we read that Agamemnon going to the war of Troy left behind him Demodocus, an excellent musician, skilfull in *Modo Dorio*, to keep chast his wife Clitemnestra, whom he nicely had in suspicion of wantonness and levity with Ægistus.[27]

One may wonder in this light if what Prospero calls a 'trick' of his, a 'vanity of [his] art' does not partake of this manipulative policy of desire which inscribes 'the contract of true love' in the frame of cultural, dynastic and erotic exchange. The masque, or rather the 'allusion' to it (in David Lindley's words[28]) – or the citation of it

---

[24] *Odyssey*, 10, 135 and 210ff.
[25] 'For many people, music inebriates more than wine.'
[26] Aelian, *On the Nature of Animals*, tr. A. F. Scholfield, 3 vols. (London: Loeb, 1958–9), XII, p. 44.
[27] *The Praise of Musicke*, p. 57.
[28] David Lindley, 'Music, Masque and Meaning in *The Tempest*,' *The Court Masque*, ed. David Lindley (Manchester: Manchester University Press, 1984), pp. 47–59.

10   Cesare Ripa, *Iconologia*, Les quatre ages

– thus seems to explore the limits of power at several levels: musical, mimetic, ethical and imperial. Its interruption, apparently due to local amnesia and the musical show's potential for seduction, might be seen as the term of a particular type of exploration, the 'artistic correlative' of the final drowning of the book.

Another instance of how myth, music and politics merge in the play's dramaturgy is the way musical messages are either semanticized, or de-semanticized: Alonso perceives the name of 'Prosper' in the thunderous celestial organ; conversely, Gonzalo recollects the awakening song (2.1.305–10), whose allegorical meaning is transparent ('Open-eyed conspiracy / His time doth take [. . .] Awake, awake'), as first a mere 'humming' (322), then a 'noise' (325) which obviously contrasts with the 'hollow burst of bellowing' that Antonio and Sebastian pretend they have heard. The inarticulate sound Gonzalo alludes to, and the visual spectacle of the two men with their swords drawn, looking 'aghast' (313), dramatically juxtaposed here, are evocative of another emblematic confrontation: if Gonzalo's 'humming' be construed as the sound of bees, then one is entitled to perceive in Gonzalo's acoustic reception the attributes of the Golden Age as represented by Cesare Ripa, an age 'without winter' in which 'pearls grew under the water'[29] (Malherbe), whereas the visual tableau of the 'false' brothers is characteristically that of the Iron Age, emblematized by a 'shield, in the midst of which fraud is represented in the figure of a monster with a man's head and a serpent's body, or, if you like, of a siren alluring passers-by to devour them.'[30] The allegorical reading of Ripa thus telescopes Ariel's discriminating, elective musical process: verbalizing one's response to music is tantamount to defining the symbolic age one belongs to. The co-existence of ages and their problematical dialogue is the emblematic version of the play's multidiscursive, polyphonic construction.

The 'noises' of the island, because they are perceived in such an individualized, differentiated manner, and induce such discordant commentaries, contribute to the æsthetic uncertainty of the play, and to the spectator's own doubts as to the validity of his or her own experience. The efficiency of music, represented verbally and dramatically, is indeed regularly 'taken over' by that of the theatre. Not a single musical citation is innocent of a *mise-en-scène* in the play – possibly except Ariel's last song: 'Where the bee sucks . . .', which nevertheless is to be found in the vicinity of a highly theatrical scene of magical dressing. In the musical utopia of *The Tempest*, music can hardly be said to be given 'for nothing': the terms of the exchange, if implicit, are made clear by the action of the play itself. Not only does music give access to the intimate theatre of the self, or such experiences as dream, trance, phantasm, madness, sleep or traumatic recollection, but it can be said to be an actual agency.

The general tenor of this paper is that the play may be viewed as a series of dramatic variations on and explorations of the limits of authority. The following remarks are a tentative attempt at mapping the discursive 'maze' of the play, and the problematical inscription of music in its economy. Translated into musical idiom, it is the notion of 'effect' which is at issue for at least six reasons.

(1) The notion of effect, and its extreme form, that of '*furor*', is distanced, not to say alienated on the stage by its individualized, highly differentiated, reception. For instance, Ferdinand perceives the first song as 'music', the second one as 'ditty', though *we* have heard both as songs; Gonzalo is the only one to perceive Ariel's song, but does not understand or remember its verbal message.

---

[29] L'on n'avoit plus d'Hyver, le iour n'avoit plus d'ombre,
     Et les perles sans nombre
   Germoient dessous les Eaux au milieu des graviers.
   (M. de Malherbe, cited in Ripa, II, p. 43)

[30] Cesare Ripa, *Iconologie où les principales choses qui peuvent tomber dans la pensée touchant les vices sont representées*, trans. J. Baudoin: 1643 (repr. Paris: Aux Amateurs de Livres, 1989), II, p. 44.

(2) The Ficinian definition receives both a serious treatment and a farcical, grotesque one. This contrapuntal development is itself complicated by its correlation with the notion of power. It is in the course of an insurrection that musical dissonance appears in the form of the drunkards' canon. If the catch is a regular emblem of inebriation on the stage, here the song becomes a song of a free thought, as its burden claims, as well as a failed attempt at perfect equality – the three voices being in perfect imitation. It is probably far-fetched to read a precise ideological or allegorical meaning into this scene; still the exclusion of this part from Prospero's harmonious scheme is precisely the cause of its failure. As Yves Peyré suggests in his brilliant analysis of Ariel's masques, 'the final chord of *The Tempest* integrates wrong notes: it depends on the lucid integration of the discordant elements, not on their exclusion'.[31]

(3) The musical 'effect' is regularly distanced or even undermined by the recurrent allusion to the illusory and transient status of the representation. The staging of musical deceit partakes of this strategy, whether the text of a dirge convincingly tells lies, or the right tune of a song allays the drunkards' fury only to deceive them the better. Musical truth may thus turn to dramatic lie. The contest between the two media turns to a spectacular encounter.

(4) Owing to the fickle nature of music, the 'furor' theme receives an all but univocal treatment. The discourse of praise, which extols the power(s) of music, is debunked by the numerous Circean, Siren-like episodes which the play offers, as if to warn against the excess of power. The discourse of abuse paradoxically surfaces here.

(5) Music is not only an agency; it operates in the play as correlative of other discourses, those of desire and authority being the most prominent.

(6) The final remark far exceeds the scope of this discussion and is utterly tentative: can one not see in the fragmented discourse of effect and its correlates the unstable interplay of two orders of knowledge at a particular moment of history, the shift from magic, auralist thought to a more analytical, visualist type of representation, which the final 'vision' of the two young princes 'playing at chess' may emblematize? The drowning of the book, which a long tradition has made to mean the poet's farewell to the stage, might thus be viewed as a farewell to a particular approach to poetics.

---

31 Yves Peyré, 'Les Masques d'Ariel: Essai d'interprétation de leur symbolisme', *Cahiers Elisabéthains*, 19 (1981): 65.

THE TEMPEST AND CULTURAL EXCHANGE

JEAN-MARIE MAGUIN

Looking at commercial exchange may prove a convenient way of approaching the problem of cultural exchange in general, for commerce is steeped in all sorts of constraints and traditions and, pragmatic though it appears, still measures desire as much as reason, and reflects an estimated balance of power between seller and buyer. The proverb 'exchange is no robbery' (Heywood, 1542) is significant of a conceptual impediment. No less significant is the adjectival crutch it often uses in order to reassure itself and us that 'a *fair* exchange is no robbery'. Yet what is a 'fair' exchange? At one end of the scale, exchanging or bartering one necessity for another – so long as the need for the things exchanged is similarly pressing for both parties – may in all likelihood be accounted fair. At the other end of the scale, trading one luxury for another may be found fair as long as it suits the whims and plans of the exchanging parties. The trickster king, Richard III, exclaims 'A horse! A horse! My kingdom for a horse' (5.7.7). It is Shakespeare who adds the exchange suggestion. All that the source (Hall) says is that when they see that the battle is lost, the king's party 'brought to hym a swyfte and a lyght horse to convey hym awaie'. Are we to understand that Shakespeare's Richard is pinning a low price on his kingdom and a high price on a horse? As we laugh at Richard's desperate offer, are we to ponder also over the well-known fact that 'necessity's sharp pinch', according to Lear's phrase (*King Lear* 2.2.384), works a strange arithmetic or that need, as Lear puts it more

generally some time later (438), is simply not to be reasoned at all? The truth here is more simple. Richard is trying to barter what is no longer his for what may still save his life. Here is the disproportion that goads the audience into smiling or laughing. In this battle scene, poles apart from epic or tragic grandeur, the cheekiness of the character, drawing close to his last gasp, is still in the spirit of farce, but his ultimate deceitful offer, though repeated (5.7.13), will not save him from death.

Less pragmatic, though hardly less artful in its desire to move the listener, is Richard II's exchange programme, carefully built on the rhetorical pattern of *gradatio*:

> I'll give my jewels for a set of beads,
> My gorgeous palace for a hermitage,
> My gay apparel for an almsman's gown,
> My figured goblets for a dish of wood,
> My sceptre for a palmer's walking staff,
> My subjects for a pair of carvèd saints,
> And my large kingdom for a little grave.
>
> (3.3.146–52)

Apart from the revealing – nay, poignant – symbolism of each proposition, the general truth applies to the beginning of the wars of the Roses as it did to the end of them at Bosworth: lost kingdoms go cheap enough.

All exchanges are marked by a triple uncertainty. They bow to circumstances that may suddenly transform a needle into the most precious thing on earth. They defer to subjective preferences whatever those may be. They reflect cultural traits. No two cultures rate their values according to the same scale. The scarcity of a particular product is a local factor and unless it proves a common denominator between the exchanging parties – which virtually precludes exchange of that product – it will lead to mutual misapprehension. To exchange a handful of glass-beads for an ingot of gold arguably sets up each party of that exchange as the other's laughing-stock, if the respective cultural backgrounds are not thoroughly known and mastered. In this respect, all exchanges, commercial bargains included, are coloured by culture.

As a story of visitors setting foot successively on an inhabited island, albeit singly, *The Tempest* addresses very plainly the problems that arise from cultural difference, and influence exchanges between men, and also, as it turns out, exchanges with supernatural entities. Although the story line adopted by Shakespeare does not appear indebted to any main narrative or dramatic source, *The Tempest*, for all its low level of intertextuality, still manifests a diversity of cultural exchanges. There is what Stephen Greenblatt has described in terms of 'negotiation'. To quote him, 'works of art, however intensely marked by the creative intelligence and private obsessions of individuals, are the products of collective negotiation and exchange'.[1] The formula is deceptively unassuming and one immediately thinks this is nothing but the foreseeable return of a once fashionable socio-historical approach. And it is, in a way. Yet everything in Greenblatt's successful analysis is idiosyncratic, and, in the case of *The Tempest*, the measure of his mastery is demonstrated in proving – odds-against, as far as I am concerned – that the play is partly the result of a negotiation between representatives of two London joint-stock companies with Shakespeare standing for the King's Men's venture and Strachey for the Virginia company. The substance of the fascinating demonstration need not be summed up here; I shall accept it as defining a new type of cultural exchange, infinitely more subtle and important than the commercial negotiation whose pattern I initially borrowed to explore the concept of exchange.

While in material and commercial exchanges we can always trace a cultural element, in the cultural negotiation or exchange there is no swapping of objective goods, neither need there be an awareness of mutual enrichment on the part of the participants. Cultural exchange is primarily communication but this need not be reciprocal, and certainly not so *hic et nunc*. What did Shakespeare give Strachey, a friend of friends and a Blackfriars neighbour, in exchange for the yet unpublished account of his shipwreck and of the state of the Virginia colony? Put in this way, the question is badly formulated. What did Strachey receive in exchange for his information? Only Strachey knows. Perhaps nothing that he was conscious of, bar the pleasure he must have felt as a keen follower of the stage, of making conversation with the greatest dramatist in London – that is, assuming that the two men communicated verbally. Shakespeare may simply have read a copy of Strachey's manuscript letter, if the letter was circulated in this form, as we think it was. Even in this form, cultural exchange did take place. In exchange – but by now it is plain that strictly measured reciprocity and mutual advantage are no longer defining features – Strachey, like ourselves, received *The Tempest*. Adaptation, appropriation, deviation according to whatever set of pressures is at work on the body and the mind that receive the cultural implant take precedence as far as the literary scholar is concerned. The phenomenon is still akin to intertextuality even though the hypotext may not be a text at all. None of those who imitated, adapted, or stole from Homer could repay him, naturally. The type of cultural exchange I am describing is no longer reciprocal but one-sided and outward bound. Its progress is comparable to that of wine in a still.

---

[1] Stephen Greenblatt, *Shakespearean Negotiations* (Oxford, 1988), p. vii.

Substantial changes take place in the process. 'Exchange' and 'change', understood as 'transformation' become equated (as in the *Oxford English Dictionary*, 'exchange' 1.1.6.)

The play's plot successively portrays two pseudo-colonial situations, the first with the relationship between Prospero and Miranda on the one hand and Caliban on the other, the second between Stefano and Trinculo on the one hand and Caliban again on the other. No structure could invite us more clearly to establish comparisons than does this parallel between two separate and successive representations of inter-cultural exchange. Such are the givens of the dramatic work that we are made to react to situations in different and often contradictory ways according to whether we pay attention to macro- or micro-elements in the play's structure. The parallel instituted between the three sets of pseudo- or would-be planters (Prospero, Gonzalo, and Stefano) depends on macro-elements. While keeping them separate until the very end in order to allow independent and sharper focus, the play reflects here the contacts established between Europeans and Indians in the new world since the end of the fifteenth century. The spectrum of European society is reduced to its two extremes with at one end the gentility of the prince and his fair daughter, or the political philosophy of Gonzalo, and, at the other end, the vulgarity of the jester and the drunken butler. On the indigenous side, Shakespeare simplifies the social picture by giving us only one savage. Caliban's singularity possibly emblematizes an undifferentiated European vision of the savages as 'other'. Gonzalo and Caliban never meet to talk but exchanges between savage and prince, savage and rag-tag crew members pass through two distinct and opposed phases of friendship and hatred. The prince's gift of language and amity is reciprocated by the savage's gift of knowledge of the isle and worship. I stress *knowledge* of the isle for it seems to me that Caliban's gift is not simply practical. He has shown Prospero 'all the qualities o' th' isle, / The fresh springs, brine-pits,

barren place and fertile' (1.2.339–40). The proposition he makes later to Stefano, while starting more or less in the same fashion, soon bottoms out with mere ancillary services:

I'll show thee every fertile inch o' th' island,
. . .
I'll show thee the best springs; I'll pluck thee
berries;
I'll fish for thee, and get thee wood enough.
. . .
I prithee, let me bring thee where crabs grow,
And I with my long nails will dig thee pig-nuts,
Show thee a jay's nest, and instruct thee how
To snare the nimble marmoset. I'll bring thee
To clust'ring filberts, and sometimes I'll get thee
Young seamews from the rock . . . (2.2.147–71)

In this passage are found micro-elements whose presence, as they raise echoes, modifies the more immediate response to macro-structural features. We are referred to an earlier moment when Caliban nostalgically remembered how, in the friendly phase of their relationship, Prospero would reward him by giving him 'Water with berries in't . . .' (1.2.336), a diet whose simplicity is reminiscent of the golden age. Not so the diet Caliban is planning for Stefano in exchange for wine from the wicked, inexhaustible bottle. Amongst the nuts and berries, there lurks food of the iron age. The flesh of the marmoset testifies to competition between the species and brings feeding disturbingly close to cannibalism since the victim belongs to the animal family closest to man. Are we to understand that the more varied and sanguinary diet is innate, that Caliban did all these things for Prospero too, and from the first, though we are not told in so many words, or are we to believe that Caliban's fishing and hunting skills grew from Prospero's teaching? The question obviously cannot be answered but the difference between the two discourses on food, the allusive and the detailed, is sufficiently marked to arrest us in this exploration of cultural exchange. From the innocence of water and berries we have passed to wine – the imported curse of colonized New-World

populations – and blood, an ominous association. Caliban's other intended gift to Stefano is
also stained with blood. It is political power in
exchange for the killing of his present tyrant.

The second phase in each relationship is one
of hatred. Slavery and incarceration are the
price paid by Caliban for his attempted rape on
the person of Miranda. In exchange for this
hardship, all he can repay Prospero and his
daughter with are the curses which witness to
his acquired linguistic capacity. This new type
of exchange, using the word in the flattest sense
of 'reciprocal giving and receiving' (*Oxford
English Dictionary*, 1.1.d), has two main characteristics: (a) unbalance resulting from Prospero's position of power, and (b) the fact that it
is no longer intercultural but becomes intracul-
tural. Slavery and curses, meaningless in
Caliban's original isolation on the island, are
two evils that belong in Prospero's world.
What Caliban has lost is a capacity to exchange
with his visitor, and now master, anything of
his own tradition. He is the exemplary subject
of violent and total assimilation. The second
phase of the relationship between the two
drunkards and Caliban is also placed under the
auspices of contempt, and curses are exchanged.
While the balance of power is in this case
satisfactory, Caliban is still shown wanting, as
he was in his later dealings with Prospero and
Miranda, in anything original to exchange.

It seems important not to restrain the
meaning of Caliban's remark 'You taught me
language, and my profit on't / Is I know how to
curse' (1.2.365–6) to something which one
could gloss as 'and now I am capable of verbal
violence or vulgarity'. The play's strategy
encourages such a limitation, in a sense, since
a curse in the most common acceptation of
the word is made to follow immediately: 'The
red plague rid you / For learning me your
language!' (366–7). Caliban's own account of
the initial teaching process – he learned to name
the sun and the moon – suggests that 'your
language' does not mean the play's English,
or its Milanese referent, but 'that thing which

you call language'. In Prospero's laboratory an
extraordinary experiment has therefore been
attempted which consisted not so much in
teaching someone to speak as in humanizing a
'freckled whelp' (1.2.284), a less than human
creature accidentally found in the natural environment. In his original state, Caliban is like
Chaos, which is not the world at all, but capable
of becoming the world if it meets its god. What
Prospero and Miranda teach Caliban is to conceptualize, and whether or not Caliban is 'A
devil, a born devil, on whose nature / Nurture
can never stick' (4.1.188–9), Caliban is stuck
with language, or more essentially, as intimated
earlier, with the power to conceptualize without which misery is nothing but an experience
of the moment, and with which misery and loss
of liberty become subjects of endless woeful
meditation that aggravate the fate of the suf-
ferer. What Caliban chiefly deplores is the step
he was made to take into the human condition.
He was taught language and the only profit he
finds is a capacity to curse his fate.[2]

The Tempest is a play which capitalizes on
contradiction, and commentary is bound to
reflect this. Thus do I follow Shakespeare's
example in simultaneously setting up Caliban as
subhuman – therefore as incapable of culture –
and analysing his initial exchanges with Prospero as evidence of an original culture. We
should be careful, however, of possible dangers
arising from the fact that our notion of culture
is quite different from the Elizabethan concepts
of the development of mental faculties, of manners, or education. Although the *Oxford English
Dictionary* records one occurrence of the word

---

[2] In 'Learning to Curse: Aspects of Linguistic Colonialism
in the Sixteenth Century' (Freddi Chiapelli, ed., *First
Images of America: The Impact of the New World on the
Old*, 2 vols. (Berkeley, 1976), vol. 2, pp. 561–80),
Stephen Greenblatt appears fleetingly to move towards
this conclusion but the problematics of his paper work
against it since, rejecting the animal-man dichotomy
which I retain as one of the issues here, he chooses to look
instead at multiple degrees of humanity, as they seem to
emerge from the discourse of some of the early colonists.

'culture' in the modern sense about 1510, all other illustrations are post-Shakespearian. Shakespeare never uses the word either in this sense or any other. Modern usage has certainly stretched the concept to take in manifestations which, even recently, ethnocentric prejudice would have pushed far below the level of the cultural. No matter how ferocious the contempt of the conquistadors for the people whose lands they were taking over, the very ferocity of their persecution is proof that, in most if not in all cases, they were eliminating a recognized competitor. The ardour to Christianize the savages meant that although occasionally deemed not to own a soul, they were thought capable of acquiring one through the mystic operation of baptism, just as subhuman Caliban is capable of receiving the language of man. When and where the indigenous populations were thought to be the children of the devil this did not preclude conversion. Their barbarity was only strangeness, pleaded some humanists and a few, like Montaigne, radically deconstructed the prevailing contempt for the savages by holding them up as an enviable cultural model. They formed a society closely mirroring the famed Golden Age which we could describe through an oxymoronic phrase as a 'natural culture'. This paradox, or seeming paradox, is not the product of modernity. It is embedded in the very myth of the Golden Age where Saturn gives man a sickle, a symbol that the natural fertility of the soil can still be improved. In the Judeo-Christian world, the garden of Eden has pitfalls of its own but no agricultural implements.

There are two main borrowings from Florio's translation of Montaigne's essays in *The Tempest*. They concern Gonzalo's daydreams about a Utopian government of the island (2.1.149–70) inspired by Montaigne's essay 'Of the Caniballes', as well as Prospero's statement that 'The rarer action is / In virtue than in vengeance' at the beginning of Act 5 (5.1.27–8).[3] Montaigne's influence on the latter passage was identified by Elizabeth Prosser in

1935.[4] It poses little or no difficulty. Shakespeare simply makes Prospero adopt, in his renouncing vengeance, Montaigne's sentiment that flawless and unshakeable goodness is as unheroic as it is incomprehensible, and that the voluntary domination of his passions and overcoming of temptation is a rarer virtue. The flow of moral philosophy from Montaigne to the play's character-philosopher is straightforward and unencumbered. The problem offered by Gonzalo's Utopian enthusiasm is different. Although it is well known I shall cite the passage in full since I intend to scrutinize it. I omit the courtiers' quizzing interruptions:

GONZALO (*to Alonso*)
Had I the plantation of this isle, my lord, –
. . .
I' th' commonwealth I would by contraries
Execute all things. For no kind of traffic
Would I admit, no name of magistrate;
Letters should not be known; riches, poverty,
And use of service, none; contract, succession,
Bourn, bound of land, tilth, vineyard, none;
No use of metal, corn, or wine, or oil;
No occupation, all men idle, all;
And women too – but innocent and pure;
No sovereignty –
. . .
All things in common nature should produce
Without sweat or endeavour. Treason, felony,
Sword, pike, knife, gun, or need of any
   engine,
Would I not have; but nature should bring
   forth
Of it own kind all foison, all abundance,
To feed my innocent people.
. . .
I would with such perfection govern, sir,
T' excel the Golden Age.   (2.1.149–74)

---

[3] On these, and other similarities in thought and phraseology which he identifies, Arthur Kirsch comments in 'Montaigne and *The Tempest*' (in Gunnar Sorelius and Michael Srigley, eds., *Cultural Exchange between European Nations during the Renaissance* (Uppsala, 1994), pp. 111–21).

[4] 'Shakespeare, Montaigne, and the "Rarer Action"', *Shakespeare Studies*, 1 (1965): 261–4.

This, now, is how Florio translates the imaginary conversation carried out by Montaigne with Plato about the population discovered by Villegagnon in 'Antartike France':

It is a nation, would I answer Plato, that hath no kinde of traffike, no knowledge of Letters, no intelligence of numbers, no name of magistrate, nor of politike superioritie; no use of service, of riches or of povertie; no contracts, no successions, no partitions, no occupation but idle; no respect of kindred, but common, no apparell but naturall, no manuring of lands, no use of wine, corne, or mettle. The very words that import lying, falshood, treason, dissimulations, covetousnes, envie, detraction, and pardon, were never heard among them.[5]

Montaigne had introduced this description by deploring the fact that neither Lycurgus nor Plato could know of the existence of such peoples:

for me seemeth that what in those nations we see by experience, doth not only exceed all the pictures wherewith licentious Poesie hath proudly imbellished the golden age, and all her quaint inventions to faine a happy condition of man, but also the conception and desire of Philosophy.[6]

Shakespeare appears to be working with Florio's Montaigne at his elbow and reproduces the list of twelve or thirteen characteristic features whose lack negatively defines the state of happiness experienced by these Antarctic populations. Illiteracy and lack of political hierarchy, which take second and third places in Montaigne's list, are quoted in reverse order in The Tempest. Lack of occupation and lack of metal, respectively number seven and number twelve of Montaigne's declension are switched about and figure as number nine and number seven in Shakespeare. Lack of corn and wine are given a higher priority in the play, figuring as number eight instead of number eleven in Montaigne. The prohibition of weapons is original to Gonzalo's speech, and he is made to interject a remark about the innocence and purity of women which is perhaps an interpretation of Montaigne's statement of the fact that

'the women lie from their husbands'[7] and that the husbands are constantly reminded to observe 'an inviolable affection to their wives'.[8] None of these differences however are very significant, apart from the emphatic ban on arms, and they would pass unnoticed in the theatre by anyone who does not happen to know Florio's text by heart.[9] The manipulation lies elsewhere and is most evident whatever the capacity of one's memory.[10] Whereas Montaigne is indirectly describing a state of affairs existing in the new world, Gonzalo is talking about (re)creating such a state of affairs: nature and lack of artifice on the one hand, artifice in imposing a return to nature on the other. Gonzalo is running head first into the perverse old paradox of pacifism and tolerance only ever enforceable by dint of war and intolerance. The best of intentions are often the nearest way to the devil. In this connection Gonzalo's most reassuring quality is his ineffectuality for we have met such fundamentalists before. Jack Cade and his crew are against possessions,

---

[5] 'Of the Caniballes', The Essayes of Michael Lord Montaigne, translated by John Florio, 3 vols. (London, 1904), vol. 1, p. 245.

[6] Ibid., p. 245.

[7] Ibid., p. 246.

[8] Ibid., p. 247.

[9] In '"The Picture of Nobody": White Cannibalism in The Tempest', David Lee Miller, Sharon O'Dair, Harold Weber, eds., The Production of English Renaissance Culture (Ithaca and London, 1994), pp. 262–92, Richard Halpern, also attentive to alterations of Montaigne's thought and phraseology by Shakespeare, sees a major instance in Gonzalo's use of the word 'plantation' 'which unambiguously signifies an exclusively European colony. Hence the "innocent and pure" subjects of Gonzalo's imagined polity are not Montaigne's Indians but white Europeans who now somehow occupy an American Indian arcadia' (p. 268). The whole essay contributes to greater awareness of multiple and subtle forms of cultural manipulation in The Tempest.

[10] In Shakespeare and Ovid (Oxford, 1993), Jonathan Bate claims that 'Sixteenth-century models of reading were always purposeful' (p. 9) rather than mere stylistic imitations and therefore meant to be noticed. The problem is an interesting one.

partitions, and the knowledge of letters, and the rope and knife make short shrift of lawyers and schoolmasters. The courtiers are quick to underline the contradictions in Gonzalo's speech: 'GONZALO No sovereignty – SEBASTIAN Yet he would be king on't.' (162). Although the courtiers are cynical villains this does not detract from the fact that their logic is not only valid but establishes the truth. Although the fact that they are right does not make them better characters in the appraisal of the spectators, the effective invalidation of Gonzalo's reasoning by an arrogant couple of blackguards seriously undercuts the attraction of his Utopian zeal.

The question that interests us here is whether the manipulation of Montaigne's essay by Shakespeare is made solely at the expense of Gonzalo or also at the expense of Montaigne's philosophy. The answer is not easy to determine. It remains a general truth that the ridicule of the exponent of a theory – here Gonzalo – will, up to a point, rub off on the theory itself and its original proponent. Nowhere is Gonzalo more ridiculous or naive and unrealistic than in the introduction of his argument when he announces that his commonwealth would do 'all things by contraries'. We are free to imagine what Swift might have constructed on the basis of such an extreme proposition. Nowhere is Gonzalo less convincing than in the summation of his argument when he smugly remarks that he would govern with such perfection 'T' excel the Golden Age'. The statement is markedly different from Montaigne's. The French writer uses the regular contempt of the philosopher for poetic imagination to announce to the world that the blissful state of existence of the savages actually outdoes all those excessive accounts of the Golden Age found in poetic tradition. He then proceeds to hoist himself with his own petard by furthermore assuring the reader that the savages have actually outdone 'the conception and desire of Philosophy'. Two things here would have ruffled Shakespeare's sense of the relative and

his spirit of tolerance: (a) the philosopher's bad faith in accepting poetic symbols literally, and (b) the excessive claim in making experience the be-all and end-all, feigning thus to put matter so much over mind only to validate paradoxically what remains an *intellectual* operation, his philosophizing. In *Shakespeare and Ovid*, Jonathan Bate makes the point that 'Shakespeare denies the myth of the Golden Age restored in a New World peopled by noble cannibals',[11] and that Caliban's fallen state, whether innate or not, is apparent in his claim of the island as his heritage. I fully concur in this judgement and refer here to the Golden Age as a myth respected as such by Shakespeare but rather affectedly spurned by Montaigne in a conventional instance of philosopher disparaging poet. The confrontation between Shakespeare and Montaigne, as I see it, is anything but a head-on collision. It is rather in the nature of an abrasion of Montaigne's philosophy by Shakespeare concerning the point of knowing whether the savages' existence is perfect or not. At first sight, we might have thought primarily of Gonzalo as a man hopelessly exposed, a sort of *enfant perdu* shot at by his own camp, by the Antonios and the Gonzalos. Instead we discover that Gonzalo is, practically speaking, a mask from behind which Shakespeare is vigorously teasing Montaigne for his radicalism.

The last manipulation relevant to the problem of cultural exchange that I wish to look at here is apparent in Miranda's famous appreciation of the men she discovers: 'O wonder! / How many goodly creatures are there here! / How beauteous mankind is! O brave new world / That has such people in't!' (5.1.184–7). The traditionally observed inadequacy of the remark can hardly be overrated, Miranda looking as she does upon usurpers and would-be murderers. Although Shakespeare is not above a joke at the expense of his characters, I do not

---

[11] Bate, p. 257.

think irony *ad feminam* to have been his main motivation in this case. The colonial analogy developed in the play with varying degrees of accuracy and varying urgency, seems to take over here. We have hundreds of accounts by Europeans of Europeans discovering 'savages', but how many accounts do we have, recorded by savages themselves, of their discovery of Europeans? By the time Miranda discovers the Neapolitans, we have already seen Caliban, the play's single aborigine, worship a couple of newly arrived drunken aliens, a mistake he readily acknowledges and one that is a repeat of his initial adulation of Prospero. Miranda, since she has only a few memories of Milan, could almost be considered as a near aborigine, but is the category admissible at all? It is clear that the education received at the hands of her father disqualifies her as a 'savage' commenting on her discovery of a new race of men. Why then does Shakespeare choose her to repeat Caliban's mistake in a register totally different from the grotesque farce of Prospero's slave? Beyond the comedy of misplaced praise, the pressure of contemporary colonial history introduces graver and disturbing echoes in her words of welcome. They ring with the fatal error made by all the New-World people who judged us on our fair looks and declared good intentions only to be rapidly subjected or wiped out by alcohol, disease, and main force. In the circumstances, Prospero's warning to Miranda ''Tis new to thee.' (187) is one of those hushed, subdued asides that hold the promise of ulterior explanations ('Can't tell you now, not in this company'). The shift from 'savage' to 'civilized' is momentous. It implies that the error of the 'savages' in welcoming the colonists is not, as might have been thought, the unavoidable fault of brutish brains, a natural defect. European culture, represented in Miranda, is prone to a similar failure. The parallel between Caliban and Miranda is Shakespeare's deft way of putting the New World on the same fragile

footing as the Old. Humanity is shared equally between them because both worlds are shown to have an identical potential for erring in judgement.

Curiously, Miranda's exclamation about that 'brave new world' is close in sentiment to a Latin quotation added in the 1595 posthumous edition of Montaigne's *Essays* – the one that Florio translates – and omitted in the English translation. In the French book it occurs rather awkwardly just before another Latin quotation from Virgil's *Georgics*, already present in the 1588 edition. The Latin phrase that Florio leaves out is taken from Seneca's 'Epistle XC': *viri a diis recentes* (men fresh from the hands of the gods). Montaigne applies the phrase to the savages, Miranda's salutation is aimed at the sophisticated, and perverse Old-World race as it appears before her. Could Shakespeare have had access to a copy of the 1595 edition of Montaigne's *Essays* in French? If he knew Florio personally – as it is quite possible he did since the two men shared the same patron in Southampton – he could have looked at the copy from which Florio translated. Would the difference, would the omission have caught his eye? It is impossible to say. The beautifully clipped Latin phrase has a magic appeal and would understandably invite memorization and re-use or adaptation in a different cultural environment.

There is on the periphery of any critical problem a zone of grey shadow whose status is ambiguous and uncomfortable for while it still invites attention and probably belongs to the ground explored, analysis seems to lose its leverage here, and demonstrates its power of persuasion. One should not be shy of stepping into this area but retreat should always be kept in mind. In this last instance, we are perhaps facing no more than the ghost of cultural exchange and must perturb the spirit no further, but rest content with the more corporeal instances previously encountered.

CALIBAN AND ARIEL WRITE BACK

JONATHAN BATE

It is no coincidence that the now hugely influential reading of *The Tempest* in the context of 'the discourse of colonialism' began for the purposes of the Anglo-American academy with Stephen Greenblatt's essay 'Learning to Curse', published in 1976, in a book called *First Images of America: The Impact of the New World on the Old* which explicitly marked – in troubled fashion – the bicentenary of the American Declaration of Independence. As was the case more recently in Australia, official celebrations of a young nation's coming to the age of two hundred released an anguished cry from the liberal intelligentsia as they came to full realization of the exploitation and oppression on which their nation was built. Fashionable criticism is interested in assuaging the guilt of empire by making the author of *The Tempest* a scapegoat. But I find it mildly ironic that very few of the 'radical' critics of the 1970s and 1980s have acknowledged that a revisionary reading of *The Tempest* had already been undertaken in the 1950s and 1960s by non-white non-Europeans. I have to admit to my shame that I have been much longer familiar with the 'new historicist' readings of anguished Stefanos like Stephen Greenblatt, Stephen Orgel and Steven Mullaney than with the remarkable creative work done a generation before them by self-proclaimed Calibans like George Lamming, Edward Kamau Brathwaite, Aimé Césaire and Roberto Fernández Retamar.

The introduction to Stephen Orgel's 1987 Oxford edition of the play, which has already become as influential for its generation as Frank Kermode's Arden edition was for the previous one, is typical. It twice mentions Mannoni's pioneering interpretation of the play in relation to colonialism, but on each occasion passes straight from it to a liberal white interpreter. First: 'The most important treatments of the relevance of colonialism to the play are Octave Mannoni's *Psychologie de la colonisation* (1950), published in England as *Prospero and Caliban*; Stephen J. Greenblatt's brilliant 'Learning to Curse' . . .'[1] And secondly: '[Jonathan] Miller, in a 1970 production at the Mermaid, based his view of the relation of Prospero to Caliban and Ariel on Octave Mannoni's metaphorical use of these figures in his analysis of the revolt of Madagascar in 1947, *La Psychologie de la colonisation*' (p. 83). For a good liberal who is manifestly troubled by the white tradition's silencing and marginalization of blacks, Orgel is here remarkably adept in his own silencing of the major – 'brilliant' indeed – black interpretations of the two decades between the publication of Mannoni's book and the readings of Miller and Greenblatt. Typical, too, is Eric Cheyfitz's *The Poetics of Imperialism: Translation and Colonialization from 'The Tempest' to 'Tarzan'*: the author claims that Frantz Fanon is his 'immediate inspiration for reading *The Tempest*', then remarks that 'his name should remind us that Shakespeare's play is the possible prologue

---

[1] *The Tempest*, ed. Stephen Orgel (Oxford, 1987), p. 24n.

not only for the literature of the United States, but for a significant body of Caribbean literature'[2] – yet the rest of the book has nothing to say about that body of literature.

A handful of articles by less well-known critics, together with some pages in the Vaughans' book on the cultural history of Caliban, have begun to break this silence, but the Caribbean appropriation of *The Tempest* still remains unknown to many. The first part of this paper is accordingly devoted to a fine example of it.

Edward Brathwaite, who was born in Barbados in 1930, went to university at Cambridge and is published by Oxford. His work is written in a distinctively Caribbean voice, but it reconfigures rather than entirely rejects the 'high' English cultural tradition that is epitomized by Oxbridge. Unlike certain younger black poets, such as Michael Smith and Linton Kwesi Johnson, whose work relies entirely on the oral and vernacular traditions of reggae and rap, Brathwaite moves between jazz or folk rhythms on the one hand and 'traditional' allusion and diction on the other. His work thus enacts a passage between the old world and the new; his own passage into the tradition is a sometimes liberated, sometimes uneasy, reversal of the 'middle passage' of his forebears into slavery. The three volumes of his 'New World Trilogy' are called *Rights of Passage* (1967), *Masks* (1968) and *Islands* (1969).[3] They are triangulated upon the Atlantic slave trade: in both style and reference they move between England, Africa and the Caribbean. The overall structure of the trilogy proposes that after the passage to slavery in the plantations, it becomes essential for the black to wear masks. To begin with, he or she will inherit alienated western man's mask-making, inauthentic and associated with social roles (the black personae such as Uncle Tom being subservient). But by making the passage in reverse, returning to Africa and recovering its traditions – the animism, the rituals and the rhythms of the Ashanti nation – a more creative, spiritual use of masks can emerge. The mask becomes that of the god. It is

then possible to make the islands of the Antilles a place of grace and beauty, not of oppression.

The classic literary-dramatic role for Brathwaite, as for Fanon and Lamming before him, is Caliban. His poem of this title occupies a pivotal position in the collection *Islands*, which itself works through a development similar to that of the trilogy as a whole – its five sections are entitled New World, Limbo, Rebellion, Possession and Beginning. 'Caliban' is in the middle of Limbo, but within the poem 'limbo' brings a glimpse of freedom.

My description of *Islands* is misleading, insofar as it implies a sequential, historical narrative. Part of Brathwaite's project is to collapse different historical moments, to read the present by making the past simultaneous with it:

It was December second, nineteen fifty-six.
It was the first of August eighteen thirty-eight.
It was the twelfth October fourteen ninety-two.

How many bangs how many revolutions?

The poem begins in Castro's Havana, but it views modern Cuban history through the longer perspective that reaches back to Columbus' first sighting of land on his voyage in 1492. Brathwaite is himself a learned historian of the Caribbean, and such elisions are marks of an historical-artistic technique and attitude remarkably similar to those of Renaissance humanism. So too is the opening stanza of 'Caliban', with its holding together of prophets past and present, its sense that everything is already known but is always having to be learned again:

Ninety-five per cent of my people poor
ninety-five per cent of my people black
ninety-five per cent of my people dead
you have heard it all before O Leviticus O
    Jeremiah O Jean-Paul Sartre

Sartre is there because he wrote the preface to

---

[2] *The Poetics of Imperialism* (New York and Oxford, 1991), p. 23.
[3] Published together as *The Arrivants* (Oxford, 1973).

Fanon's *Wretched of the Earth*, but the voice who is speaking these lines is not that of the European prophet. The latter's empathetic voicing with the wretched could not but itself be a form of colonialism, of Prospering – I, Jean-Paul Sartre, great white French intellectual, speak with and hence for the 'other'. But when Brathwaite replies, the white man is not the subject: he is addressed with an 'O', he becomes the other. This change from object to subject is crucial to the creative renewal of the once oppressed – hence the witty title of the New Accent study of postcolonial writing, *The Empire Writes Back*.[4]

When it is Caliban who writes back, as in this poem, the voice is multiple. 'Caliban', after all, is the creation of another great white European. The Cuban revolutionary writer Roberto Fernández Retamar argued that the position of Caliban is the only available one for the 'new world' writer: he has no choice but to use the tool – the language – bequeathed to him by Prospero. At school in Barbados, Brathwaite had to read Shakespeare, Jane Austen and George Eliot: 'British literature and literary forms, the models which had very little to do, really, with the environment and the reality of non-Europe'.[5] He seized on Caliban because Caliban *could* be read as having a great deal to do with his own environment and reality, because (as Lamming did) he found in Caliban a prophecy of his own historical situation. It is a usable prophecy exactly because – unlike Sartre's – it is not directly couched as such. There is a certain scepticism in the attitude to Jean-Paul Sartre since he comes, as Retamar puts it, from the 'elsewhere' of the European metropolis, 'the colonizing centers, whose "right wings" have exploited us and whose supposed "left wings" have pretended and continue to pretend to guide us with pious solicitude'.[6] It is different with Shakespeare. Because of what Keats called his negative capability, because he was not trying to guide Retamar's and Brathwaite's 'us' with pious solicitude, they have no compunction about adopting one of his voices.

The process of writing back necessitates the creation of a new style, and here too Caliban can help. Brathwaite says of the English poetic mainstream: 'the pentameter remained, and it carries with it a certain kind of experience, which is not the experience of a hurricane. The hurricane does not roar in pentameters. And that's the problem: how do you get a rhythm which approximates the *natural* experience, the *environmental* experience?' The answer is in '*nation language*, which is the kind of English spoken by the people who were brought to the Caribbean, not the official English now, but the language of slaves and labourers'. The language, that is to say, which binds, indeed works to create, the black nation; this language and this nation initially cannot help but be parasitic upon the colonizing language and nation, as Caliban is upon Prospero, yet as they develop they take on their own identity, their own freedom.

How does nation language sound? It is 'the *submerged* area of that dialect which is much more closely allied to the African aspect of experience in the Caribbean. It may be in English: but often it is an English which is like a howl, or a shout or a machine-gun or the wind or a wave.' Many of Brathwaite's poems move between the voices of the English tradition and of nation. In his lecture *History of the Voice*, from which I have been quoting this account of nation language, Brathwaite cites John Figueroa's 'Portrait of a Woman' as an example of double-voiced West Indian poetry: 'the "classical", even *Prosperian element* – the *most* part of the poem – is in English. The marginal bit, that of the voice and status of the domestic helper, Caliban's sister, is in a nation but a

---

[4] Bill Ashcroft, Gareth Griffiths and Helen Tiffin, *The Empire Writes Back: Theory and Practice in Post-colonial Literatures* (London and New York, 1989).

[5] Brathwaite, *History of the Voice: The Development of Nation Language in Anglophone Caribbean Poetry* (London and Port of Spain, 1984), p. 8.

[6] Retamar, 'Caliban', *Massachusetts Review*, 15 (1974): 7.

nation still sticky and wet with the interposition of dialect.'[7] Section one of 'Caliban' is in traditional English: 'Ninety-five per cent of my people poor' is a pentameter. But in sections two and three Caliban speaks in the rhythms of nation:

> And
> Ban
> Ban
> Cal-
> iban
> like to play
> pan
> at the Car-
> nival;
> pran-
> cing up to the lim-
> bo silence
> down
> down
> down
> so the god won't drown
> him
> down
> down
> down
> to the is-
> land town

The allusion here is of course to 'Ban, Ban, Ca-Caliban' in *The Tempest*'s song of rebellion, 'No more dams I'll make for fish'. Caliban expresses his freedom by deconstructing the name that Prospero has given him; the vigorous rhythm of his song is an affront to Prospero's rod-like pentameter world. It may be imagined as a rudimentary form of nation language. For Shakespeare's Caliban, 'Freedom, high-day!' is an illusion: he has merely exchanged one master, one god, for another. Brathwaite revises the situation by combining Caliban's anthem of freedom with Ariel's song of watery metamorphosis, 'Full fathom five'. When the Caribbean Caliban bends his back and passes beneath the limbo stick, the music and dance transform him: because he has gone

> down
> down
> down
>
> he can rise
>
> up
> up
> up

A note in Brathwaite's glossary reminds us that 'limbo' is not only a state of spiritual darkness and exclusion, it is also

a dance in which the participants have to move, with their bodies thrown backwards and without any aid whatsoever under a stick which is lowered at every successfully completed passage under it, until the stick is practically touching the ground. It is said to have originated – a necessary therapy – after the experience of the cramped conditions between the slaveship decks of the Middle Passage.[8]

The limbo is first performed with

> eyes
> shut tight
> and the whip light
> crawl-
> ing round the ship
> where his free-
> dom drowns.

But it becomes a means to freedom and celebration:

> sun coming up
> and the drummers are praising me
>
> out of the dark
> and the dumb gods are raising me
>
> up
> up
> up
>
> and the music is saving me

[7] *History of the Voice*, p. 38. Previous quotations from pp. 10, 5, 13.
[8] *The Arrivants*, p. 274.

In Ariel's song, Alonso has gone down, down, down, but as the play unfolds we watch his soul rise up, up, up. From recognition of sin in act three,

> Methought the billows spoke and told me of it,
> The winds did sing it to me, and the thunder,
> That deep and dreadful organ-pipe, pronounced
> The name of Prosper. It did bass my trespass.
>
> (3.3.96–9)

he passes to penitence in act five: 'Thy dukedom I resign, and do entreat / Thou pardon me my wrongs' (5.1.120–1). In Brathwaite's poem, Caliban follows a similar course – down, then up – by means of the limbo dance.

The key difference is in the kind of god. Alonso's is a high Renaissance Christian God, reached through the linguistic formality of confession. The Caribbean Caliban is raised by gods who are dumb save in the music; as Brathwaite puts it in 'The Making of the Drum', a poem of great importance in *Masks*,

> God is dumb
> until the drum
> speaks

In each case, human art – Prospero's magic, the drummer and the dancer – brings about a perception of something named as divine. But where the hurricane of Alonso's god roars in pentameters, Brathwaite's Caliban finds a god of his own environment and culture. It is a defining characteristic of Shakespeare's Caliban that he hears the music of the isle, and that Prospero's failure to understand this must vitiate any monovocal Prosperian reading of the play; the music of the isle is the key to Brathwaite's poetry, too. But he makes a different music, that of his own isles, of Afro-Caribbean culture.

That culture is seen to be close to nature in a way that has been renounced by western man. The 'modernization' (westernization, Americanization) of Havana described in the first part of 'Caliban' is decadent ('the police toured the gambling houses / wearing their dark glasses / and collected tribute'). That modernization is also an assault on nature. Where Ariel's song imagines a creative transformation from dead bone to living coral, economic progress is conceived here as the destructive transformation of living coral into dead concrete:

> out of the living stone, out of the living bone
> or coral, these dead
> towers; out of the coney
> islands of our mind-
>
> less architects, this death
> of sons, of songs, of sunshine;
> out of this dearth of coo ru coos, home-
> less pigeons, this perturbation that does not
>   signal health.

When Caliban finds the god in the dance, what he is really achieving is a reunification with nature. The movement is the same as that in Aimé Césaire's adaptation *Une tempête*, where Prospero is anti-nature and Caliban's freedom means a unification of his voice with those of the birds and the surf. For Brathwaite, the legacy of European and American empire in the Antilles is the death not only of sons of Africa, but also of songs, of sunshine, of birds, of coral.

The hyphen across the stanza ending passes judgement on western man. Economic development, high-rise apartments resembling rabbit hutches, come 'out of the coney / islands of our mind' – but the 'mind' is transformed into 'our mindless architects'. As Robert Pogue Harrison has demonstrated in his remarkable book, *Forests*, imperialism has always brought with it deforestation and the consuming of natural resources. Since the Enlightenment privileging of 'mind', western man has mapped his own place in the world so as to justify this:

In his *Discourse on Method* Descartes compares the authority of tradition to a forest of error, beyond which lies the promised land of reason. Once he arrives in that promised land, Descartes redefines his relation not only to tradition but also to nature in its totality. The new Cartesian distinction between the *res cogitans*, or thinking self, and the *res extensa*, or embodied substance, sets up the terms for the objectivity of science and the abstraction from historicity, location, nature, and culture. What interests us about Descartes in this context is the fact that he sought to empower the subject of knowledge in such a way that, through its application of mathematical method, humanity could achieve what he called 'mastery and possession of nature'.[9]

Brathwaite's turn of 'mind' to 'mindless' is a rebuke to the *res cogitans* for its quest to master nature.

The poem 'Caliban', then, is not only about culture against culture, white against black, European against African ways of seeing; it is also about culture against nature. This raises doubts about the New Iconoclast assumption that *The Tempest* must be read only in terms of cultural confrontation. Readers of the play in relation to the 'discourse of colonialism' focus on Prospero and Caliban because their troubled relationship seems to encourage talk of hostile exchange between culture and culture. Such readers have political reasons for denying the possibility of exchange between culture and nature; nature, they say, is just someone else's culture. Eric Cheyfitz is typical when he writes in *The Poetics of Imperialism*: 'In *The Tempest* nature is not nature but culture.'[10] Césaire's and Brathwaite's linking of Caliban with nature proposes something very different. It seems to me that in our current ecological crisis, questions of culture's relationship to nature are of as great importance as questions of 'multiculturalism'. There are, however, problems with a model which praises black culture for being in touch with nature in a way that white culture isn't, for if imported into 'our' way of thinking it runs the risk of retaining the image of black traditions as 'other' – only this time a desirably primal, earth-true other. So in thinking about a rereading of *The Tempest* in terms of culture and nature, I shall follow an alternative track and consider an improvisation on the voice of Ariel – a voice which has been oddly silenced by recent criticism's obsession with Caliban.

In 1822, the last year of his life, Percy Bysshe Shelley wrote a group of lyric poems to his friend Jane Williams. One of them is called 'With a Guitar. To Jane'. It begins

> Ariel to Miranda; – Take
> This slave of music for the sake
> Of him who is the slave of thee.[11]

Written in the same tetrameter as Prospero's epilogue, it is a kind of second epilogue to *The Tempest* from Ariel's point of view. Jane is Miranda, her husband Edward Williams is Ferdinand, and Shelley himself, Ariel. The poem is a 'token / Of more than ever can be spoken'; it lightly and touchingly mediates Shelley's admiration for Jane through the fantasy of Ariel being silently and unrequitedly in love with Miranda. Shelley's ideal or intellectual love finds its analogy in Ariel's nature as a disembodied spirit of fire and air; the impossibility of that love's realization in the material world is expressed in an image suggestive of Ariel's fate at the hands of Sycorax: 'And now, alas! the poor sprite is / Imprisoned for some fault of his / In a body like a grave'. The elegant conceit which allows the poet/lover out of his bind is that the spirit of his art will be held in the guitar which he gives Jane together with the poem, and that when she plays it he will be able to continue serving her as she makes music out of him.

But where does the guitar come from?

> The artist who this idol wrought
> To echo all harmonious thought
> Felled a tree, while on the steep
> The woods were in their winter sleep
> Rocked in that repose divine
> On the wind-swept Apennine.

[9] Harrison, *Forests: The Shadow of Civilization* (Chicago and London, 1992), pp. 107–8.

[10] Cheyfitz, *The Poetics of Imperialism: Translation and Colonization from 'The Tempest' to 'Tarzan'* (New York and Oxford, 1991), p. 26.

[11] The poem was first published in 1832; I quote the text based on the original manuscript, repr. in *Shelley's Poetry and Prose*, ed. Donald H. Reiman and Sharon B. Powers (New York, 1977), pp. 449–51.

To make a guitar, you must fell a tree; to harness the power of Ariel, you must split open a pine. Shelley's poem claims that because it was felled while sleeping in winter, the tree 'felt no pain' and that now it is a guitar it is living 'in happier form again'. In the light of Shelley's neo-platonism, the latter phrase may be presumed to imply that in its guitar-form the tree transcends its original particular Apennine hillside and makes a music which holds together

> all harmonies
> Of the plains and of the skies,
> Of the forests and the mountains,
> And the many-voiced fountains,
> The clearest echoes of the hills,
> The softest notes of falling rills,
> The melodies of birds and bees,
> The murmuring of summer seas,
> And pattering rain and breathing dew
> And airs of evening.

In this account, art — the music of the guitar which is metonymic of the poem itself — offers the ideal or intellectual form of nature. In *The Tempest*, it is in response to Stefano and Trinculo's hearing of Ariel's music that Caliban speaks of how he has sometimes heard something which a Renaissance audience would have thought of as approximating to the music of the spheres. So here, the Ariel music of the guitar knows

> That seldom heard mysterious sound,
> Which, driven on its diurnal round
> As it floats through boundless day
> Our world enkindles on its way.

In another sense, however, this music does not constitute nature perfected. Early in each of the poem's two verse-paragraphs there is a noun which questions the status of the guitar. In the first, it is a 'slave': Prospero uses that word of Ariel, but does so more frequently of Caliban. In the first chapter of *A Philosophical View of Reform*, Shelley had described the struggle for liberty in terms of the abolition of slavery and the enfranchisement of poetry; the presence of the word 'slave' here, with its Calibanesque

undertow, suggests that poetry may nevertheless be dependent on certain enslavements of its own. And in the second verse-paragraph there is a suggestion of Bacon's term for false mental images: 'The artist who this *idol* wrought'. The apparently ideal may in fact be an idol. The premise of Ariel's unrequited love for Miranda and the positioning of the poem as a second epilogue to *The Tempest* establish a sense of loss, an elegiac tone, that cannot be unwritten by the gift of the guitar. 'Slave', 'idol' and 'felled' break up the harmonious movement of the couplets; 'wrought', twice used of the making of the guitar, suggests a beating into shape, the hard working of iron as well as wood. If something has to be wrought, resistance is implied.

> — and so this tree —
> O that such our death may be —
> Died in sleep, and felt no pain.

That the tree died in sleep and felt no pain implies that a tree might be killed while awake and feel pain; an optative like the parenthetic 'may' in these lines is always provoked by fear of its forceful opposite.

The price of art is the destruction of a living tree. You can't have music without dead wood; you can't have poetry without paper. You create culture by enslaving nature. Prospero makes gape a pine and threatens to rend an oak in order to display his power; in this, he is anti-nature. His technology is an image of that 'mastery and possession of nature' which Descartes believed was within the grasp of *res cogitans*, the mind of man. Shelley was an inheritor of Cartesian dualism — his neo-platonism was an attempt to get round it — and it does seem to me that at a profound level his poem registers the irony of our post-Cartesian condition. What are the highest things that the guitar tells of? They are *res extensa*: plains, skies, forests, mountains, birds, bees, seas, rain and dew. Art is an attempt to recover the very thing which has been destroyed so that art can be made.

Nevertheless, the end of *The Tempest* is still there as an image of the possibility of renunciation of the claim to mastery and possession of nature. We don't know where Caliban goes at the end of the play, but we do know that Ariel is free and that the island will be his again. In a general sense, *The Tempest* continues to function as an exemplary humanist text because it is a vehicle through which later cultures can reflect on pressing contemporary concerns. Formally speaking, it achieves this through its multivocality: it does not offer the sole voice of Prospero, it also enables poets like Browning, Brathwaite and Césaire to think as Caliban, Shelley to think as Ariel and even as the tree in which Ariel was confined. In a particular sense, *The Tempest* was and remains an exemplary humanist text because it is set on an island that is its own place. In the sixteenth century, the imaginary island was a place in which one could reflect upon the ideal society in the manner of More's *Utopia*. In the twenty-first century, we will need to imagine an island which Prospero has left, an ecosystem which man must be content to leave alone. We have gone quite a long way towards recognizing the rights of Caliban. Next we will need to set Ariel free.

SHAKESPEARIAN RATES OF EXCHANGE IN CZECHOSLOVAKIA 1945–1989

ZDÉNĚK STŘÍBRNÝ

Thanks to Karl Marx the value of Shakespeare was never called into question even by the most dogmatic Communists in Czechoslovakia and other countries of the former Soviet Bloc. Practically everybody, including the Stalinist cadres, knew about the high esteem in which Shakespeare had been held by Marx and his family. Marx's and Engels's appreciative views of Shakespeare and the whole age of the Renaissance were available in their collected works and special volumes devoted to Marxist theory of art. Yet while the value of Shakespeare remained undisputed, his rates of exchange were fluctuating considerably and sometimes quite dramatically with the changes in political climate. My reference to Malcolm Bradbury's novel *Rates of Exchange* may seem trendy but I believe that it can be both amusing and illuminating. At least I can promise that my story will be nearly as rich in ironies and paradoxes as Bradbury's East European fiction.

The first paradox consists of the fact that theatres were rather generously subsidized by Communist authorities but, at the same time, more or less strictly controlled. In the course of permanent negotiations between political power and artistic creativity, a precarious socio-cultural contract was being reached, giving the theatres economic freedom in exchange for political loyalty. Theatres could engage in artistic experiments released from commercial pressures on condition that they put up with political control. This control tended to be oppressive in the periods of revolutionary fervour and severity but could become quite challenging for directors, actors, and playwrights during the spells of political thaw.

In Czechoslovakia, the number of theatres increased threefold after World War II and, in spite of the competition from films and television, most of the more than sixty professional companies were full of energy.[1] The quality of acting, directing, and stage designing was also improving, mostly as a result of the education offered by the new theatre arts schools with university status founded after 1945 both in the Czech Lands and Slovakia. Almost all companies included Shakespeare regularly in their repertories because, since the national revival of the nineteenth century, Shakespeare has represented the highest artistic value in all foreign and native drama. He came to be considered the ideal playwright to reach both sophisticated and popular audiences and to bridge the gap which had often developed between modern art and the common man. Moreover, right after 1948, when the Communist Party of Czechoslovakia acquired practically all political and economic power in the state, Shakespeare's work was seen as a source of great spiritual vigour which supported the building of socialism.

---

[1] Cf. Jaroslav Pokorný, *Shakespeare in Czechoslovakia* (Prague, 1955), pp. 51–2; Břetislav Hodek, 'International Notes', *Shakespeare Survey 5, 8, 9, 10, 11, 12, 13,* and *18* (Cambridge University Press, 1952, 1955, 1956, 1957, 1958, 1959, 1960, and 1965).

A more or less official critic wrote in a pamphlet entitled *Shakespeare in Czechoslovakia* and published in English in 1955: 'Shakespeare has the gift for tragedy on the heroic scale and for laughter that frees the spirit. His positive heroes with their optimism and enthusiasm, their vitality and courage, make a direct appeal to a youthful and vigorous society which is transforming the lives of its people on the basis of a rational system of planning.'[2]

Shakespeare's comedies, especially *The Merry Wives of Windsor*, *The Taming of the Shrew*, *A Midsummer Night's Dream*, *Much Ado About Nothing*, *As You Like It* and *Twelfth Night* were produced in hundreds of performances not only in Prague, Bratislava and other large towns but also in much smaller places where they were brought by several touring companies of the so-called Village Theatre and introduced to audiences to whom Shakespeare had been almost all Greek before. The response to his humour, both popular and refined, was often enthusiastic. Even the rather wistful final song of Feste in *Twelfth Night* acquired a confident ring at that time. In the inventive translation of Erik Saudek, Feste's last stanza was slightly changed, apparently for the sake of rhyme but also to give it a more vigorous ending. Instead of

A great while ago the world begun,
With hey ho, the wind and the rain, (5.1.401–2)

Czech audiences were encouraged by the image of a world standing 'like a rock'.[3] Let me add that, characteristically, one of the popular songs of the period enthused with supreme self-assurance: 'We will command the wind, the rain.'

Considerable attention was turned to Malvolio who was explicated as a careerist devoid of genuine feelings and unable to enjoy life and love, an incipient Puritan, anticipating further developments of acquisitive drives in the island pharisees. His final threat to the worshippers of merry old England, 'I'll be revenged on the whole pack of you' (5.1.374), was felt to be a desperate cry of a nascent man of property who was doomed to historical failure.

Among the tragedies, *Romeo and Juliet* and *Othello* attracted special attention. The tone of heroic pathos verging on bombast and militancy, exacerbated by the tensions of the Cold War, was especially resonant in the production of *Othello* at the Prague National Theatre in 1952. It was presented as a black-and-white conflict between the humanistic ideals of the noble Moor and the inhuman, selfish, money-obsessed intrigues of Iago who was meant to represent the earliest historical stages of that social corruption which reached its climax in the ideology and practice of fascism. Moreover, it was suggested that the corruption did not disappear with the defeat of German and Italian fascism but was living on, in modified forms, in the profit-seeking societies of Western capitalism. Accordingly, particular stress was laid on Iago's acquisitiveness, crystallized in his favourite, reiterated slogan 'Put money in thy purse.' When his alarmed wife Emilia asked heaven to put a whip in every honest hand

To lash the rascals naked through the world,
Even from the east to th' west! (4.2.147–8)

heavy emphasis was put on the West.

Gradually, however, the cultural climate was changing, as the Cold War was becoming too exhausting and the realization of brutal Stalinist crimes of the recent past was harshly intruding upon the ideals of more equal and more human social relations. The translator Erik Saudek, reading a paper in Stratford-upon-Avon during the 1961 International Shakespeare Conference, entitled it significantly 'Endeavours for Fidelity'. He was intent on stressing, with all the weight of his dynamic personality, that

---

[2] Pokorný, *Shakespeare in Czechoslovakia*, p. 65.

[3] A certain justification for Saudek's optimistic rendering was supplied later (1968) in the New Penguin edition of *Twelfth Night* by M. M. Mahood, who added the following commentary to Feste's song: 'Modern actors of Feste like to sing it with pathos, but probably it was intended as a "jig" or cheerful conclusion to a comedy.'

'Shakespeare does not need any spurious actualizing or even adapting to appear the thoroughly modern author he has never ceased to be.' The translator's highest goal was stated by him simply but forcefully: 'To express the truth and nothing but the truth of the original.'[4] The conflict between fidelity to Shakespeare and loyalty to the prevailing Communist cultural politics was becoming more and more acute in Eastern and East-Central Europe as the years went by.

It should also be remembered that a number of East European scholars and translators never accepted either Marxist theory or Communist practice and continued their traditional work, sometimes under very difficult conditions. To give one telling example, Professor Otakar Vočadlo, who returned from the Buchenwald Nazi concentration camp in 1945 to resume his classes at Charles University in Prague, was dismissed by the Communists after 1948. Never despairing, he started to prepare a scholarly edition of *The Complete Works of Shakespeare* in classical Czech translations which were finally published with his prefaces and thorough commentaries in six volumes in the years 1959–64.[5]

Side by side with traditional scholars, some younger Marxists were feeling the need for radical reforms of Stalinist Communism and were developing the concept of socialism with a human face.

Another paradox was emerging. The new generation of actors, directors, and playwrights who were raised in the spirit of Communism and were expected to carry out the principles of socialist realism, were not shaping up to the expectations of the ruling party. In the late 1950s and early 1960s, when the breezes of the Prague Spring were starting to blow gently, such surprising individuals as Václav Havel were appearing from behind the scenes. Coming from a rich bourgeois family, Havel was first not allowed to enter a university but, at the turn of the 1960s, he was enrolled in the Prague Drama School as an external student and employed as a stage-hand in the new experimental theatre On the Balustrade (in Czech Na Zábradlí). At the same time, he started to write plays which deviated from the expected line and, biting the hand that fed him, approached the Western wave of the drama of the absurd.

A similar slackening of strict Marxist principles could be observed in the interpretations and productions of Shakespeare. Two completely different horizons of expectation were being raised by Shakespeare in the Communist authorities on the one hand and, on the other, in the audiences who were looking for scenes and images of corrupted power, of 'the law's delay, / The insolence of office' (3.1.74–5). *Hamlet* was becoming again the central play.

The most influential *Hamlet* production opened at the Prague National Theatre at the end of 1959 and remained in repertory until 1966. The atmosphere pervading those performances was a far cry from the militant bravado of *Othello*, produced by the same company in the early fifties. Instead of wielding a whip, Hamlet was smarting under 'the whips and scorns of time' (3.1.72). His part was taken by a sensitive and thoughtful actor who, as a religious man living in a predominantly atheistic society, considered his hero to be heaven's 'scourge and minister' (3.4.159), fully prepared to lay down his life for his revenge. His final act of killing Claudius was carried out in an elated peace of mind as a kind of ritual.[6] Throughout the play, he pronounced his lines very distinctly but without the slightest pose. His restraint, bursting into coarseness and obscenity rather than histrionic bombast evoked a ready response, especially among young audiences who empathized with him as with their fellow student from Wittenberg. They were eagerly

---

[4] Quoted from Saudek's typescript of his Stratford lecture which has not been published so far.

[5] Professor Vočadlo read his paper at the quatercentenary Shakespeare Conference at Stratford-upon-Avon in 1964.

[6] Radovan Lukavský, *Být nebo nebýt* (To be or not to be) (Prague, 1981 and 1985), p. 197.

looking for hidden meanings and messages in his ironies, puns, and other wordplays. There was especially one passage which usually triggered a burst of laughter. It was in Act 4, Scene 3, after Hamlet's unfortunate killing of the spying Polonius and Claudius' angry questions as to where the dead body was. When Hamlet replied that a 'certain convocation of politic worms are e'en at him' (20–1), the audiences took it as a glorious gibe at the Communist Party's obsession with political meetings and congresses.

One of the most important centres of the new artistic and political ferment was forming steadily in the theatre On the Balustrade. Václav Havel's progress from stagehand to playwright was accompanied by other remarkable events. The production of his first full-length play *The Garden Party* in 1963 was followed by Jarry's *Ubu Roi*, Ionesco's *La Cantatrice Chauve* and Beckett's *Waiting for Godot*, all three of them premièred during the single year 1964. A memorable dramatization of Franz Kafka's *Trial* was first produced here in 1966.

After the Soviet-led invasion of 1968, when all absurd plays were banned and Havel himself was either closely watched or put in prison, his theatre had to use indirect and subtle ways of pursuing their aims. In 1969, *Timon of Athens* was presented as Shakespeare's 'most satirical and, in his own way, most absurd play', 'the tragedy of lost illusions and abysmal disillusion'.[7] Without toning down Marx's favourite passages on the corrupting, poisonous power of gold (4.3.25–45, 384–94), the chief corruption was seen in the betrayal of friendship which, after all, is the essential theme of the play:

> Breath infect breath,
> That their society, as their friendship, may
> Be merely poison! (4.1.30–2)

After decades of Communist propaganda extolling Soviet–Czechoslovak friendship in innumerable speeches and pamphlets, these words were blowing on the audiences like a spine-chilling Siberian wind. To point out the protest against the tanks imposing order on the whole of Czechoslovakia, a rhymed couplet was added to Flaminius' lines at the end of Act 3, Scene 1:

> Those that have power to hurt and smother
> Will heap one injury upon another.

In 1978 the Balustrade Theatre introduced their absurd version of *Hamlet*. Convinced that the best acting text for a small experimental company was offered by the First Quarto of 1603, director Evald Schorm used the first Czech translation of it to turn the shortcomings of the garbled text and the small stage into striking effects. The first surprise came with the Ghost whose creaking armour and heavy bandages soaked in blood pointed to a travesty of the Elizabethan 'bloody tragedy'. This impression was strengthened by the setting of white panels spattered with blood. Gradually it dawned upon the audiences that the whole play was meant to oscillate between the extremes of farce and tragedy, approaching the modern genre of tragic grotesque, which had become one of the hallmarks of the Balustrade Company's artistic vision and expression.

Young Hamlet, with blackened eye sockets and in black jeans and sweater, behaved in a rather cool manner but he spoke daggers most of the time. His final act of revenge appeared as a kind of pre-programmed wild justice: during Hamlet's duel with Laertes, Claudius was tossed back and forth by the gravediggers and finally presented to victorious Hamlet as an easy target. The whole closing spectacle was arranged by the gravediggers who, from their first appearance, were marked like modern circus clowns in white face, with red plastic balls for noses, wearing black rubber boots and gloves and the long rubberized aprons of a sanitation unit. Now one of them dragged the

---

[7] Programme of the Theatre on the Balustrade, first night 31 January 1969.

bodies of Ophelia and Polonius back on to the stage, adding them to the corpses of the King, the Queen, Laertes and Hamlet himself. The other gravedigger pulled down a military camouflage net, which had been suspended above the stage from the beginning, and spread it over all the dead bodies, sprinkling them with chlorine powder. He did all this with evident malicious relish which was finding a vent in his soft whistling and humming to himself. Here the tragedy of the great and the mighty was seen, with devastating effect, from below, as from a frog's eye view. The final arrival of Fortinbras, for whom the gravediggers did not give a fig, could not alleviate the shock we had received from the image of a disinfected mass grave.

There was no upward turn, no hope. Shattered as we left the performance, we were still feeling a strange relief, some kind of modern absurd catharsis. Only years later, this complex and perplexed feeling was illuminated for me by the words of the master absurdist Václav Havel at the opening of the Salzburg Festival in 1990 when, by another paradox, he was no more dissident but President: 'Who knows whether hopelessness is not the innermost source of real human hope and whether without experiencing the absurdity of the world one can anticipate, look for and find its sense.'[8]

Toward the end of the Communist régime, Shakespeare's comedies were gaining ground again. Their productions, however, were turning out very differently from the confidently optimistic, energy-raising performances of the 1950s. By yet another paradox, their jubilant enthusiasm was changing into subtle forms of dissent. As observed by Martin Hilský, my younger colleague and Shakespearian translator, the attempts to appropriate Shakespeare ideologically were successful to some extent in the 1950s but became practically impossible in the 1970s and 1980s.[9]

To see the best productions of the comedies after 1968 one had to go as far as the North

Moravian mining and industrial centre Ostrava or the North Bohemian chemical and textile town on the Elbe Ústí nad Labem (German Aussig). In both towns, the director Jan Kačer was active in the 1970s because he was banished from his Prague experimental theatre called Drama Club (Činoherní klub) and allowed to direct only in the provinces for a whole decade. Perhaps the most innovative were Kačer's three productions of *Twelfth Night*, and I propose to discuss them briefly in conclusion.

The first opened in Prague where Kačer got a short-time engagement in 1980. The unconventionality of the production was indicated by its very title: instead of *Twelfth Night*, it was called *Carnival Comedy* (Komedie masopustu). The programme note explained that the shift in calendar time was called for by the fact that in Czechoslovakia there is no tradition of feasting on Twelfth Night, whereas carnival is generally associated here, as elsewhere on the Continent, with the kind of winter feasting and frolicking that in Shakespeare's England included the twelve days of Christmas.

The general carnival atmosphere was enriched by special Czech folklore features, including songs, dances, and masquerades. Feste, whose name was changed to Carnival (Masopust), became the chief cheerleader, directly opposed to Malvolio, whose evil will was emphasized by an elaborate parallel between his puritan humourlessness and the pagan idea of lifelessness that has been embodied, from time immemorial, in the mythic Slavonic figure of Morana (meaning Plague and implying Winter and Death).

The whole production opened and closed with two striking scenic images: the image of Olivia's brother being struck by the plague and the image of Malvolio carried out from the stage in a large white sheet as the Plague itself –

---

[8] Václav Havel, *Lidové noviny* (Prague, 27 July 1990), p. 4.
[9] Cf. Martin Hilský, 'Shakespeare in Czech, An Essay in Cultural Semantics', in *Shakespeare in the New Europe* (Sheffield Academic Press, 1944).

like Morana being thrown out of the village at the end of Winter.

The second version of the *Carnival Comedy* was produced in the North Bohemian industrial town Ústí nad Labem in 1981. It went even farther in superseding the conventional romantic interpretations of the play. In Prague, Viola's emergence from the tempestuous Illyrian sea was inspired by Botticelli's mythological painting *The Birth of Venus*: Viola was carried by two robust sailors on a huge shell. In North Bohemia, Viola emerged from behind a large wooden country tub. The same tub was used for lovelorn Orsino in the opening scene, when he bathed his feet in it, and finally for Malvolio. This unusual scenic metaphor was used to remind the characters of the play and the audience that we all need to be plunged into cold water from time to time to wash off our follies and passions. Another significant sign of the North Bohemian production was a death-bell, which was gripped by Malvolio in the opening carnival dance and rung violently now and then to make us wonder for whom the bell tolls. A high gallows stood at the left front stage throughout the whole performance to provide another *memento mori*. The whole production brought out the polar tensions between love and death, wild merry-making and deep melancholy, violent action and sober reflection. It was very different from the easily optimistic productions of the 1950s when the world seemed solid and firm like a rock. Now, director Kačer was revealing much deeper layers in Shakespeare's festive comedy: not only its Renaissance vigour but also its *rigor mortis* and all its amazing complexity and contrariety of dramatic modes, its fusion of comic, tragic, grotesque, saturnalian and carnival elements in an all-embracing vision of life.

In December 1987, Kačer's third version of *Twelfth Night* was introduced in an off-centre Prague theatre called the Atrium. It is a small, intimate building which was converted to its present use from an old baroque chapel. The whole production was adapted to the ambience of the former religious shrine. The sets were very simple: just white tablecloths and large white draperies covering the walls of the chapel except for an old mosaic which stood out in subdued contrast. In the opening scene, the audience was greeted by all the actors, whose number was reduced, with the help of doubling, to the biblical magic number of twelve. They came from the back of the hall through the crowded audience towards a large table standing across the whole space of the small stage and sat down as if to the Last Supper. Instead of eating bread and drinking wine, they started to sing Feste's final song which both opened and closed the play. It was not as carefree and cocksure as it used to be in the fifties. Surprisingly, it was supplemented by an old Czech Christmas carol, announcing the birth of Christ the Saviour. After four decades of persistent antireligious propaganda, the carol sounded as a note of defiance, both piously humble and brave.

As a whole, this third production of *Twelfth Night* was not so radically antiromantic as the second version but it kept, and sometimes enhanced, director Kačer's vision of Shakespearian comedy as an exciting and disturbing mixture of love and hatred, life and the suppression of life, boisterous drinking songs modified by a religious Christmas carol, wild carnival abandon and topsy-turvy reversal of all values opposed by harsh commands of denial or prohibition administered by killjoys.

This time, Malvolio was not thrown out as a pest, as the Plague, but was left on the stage at the end as a living threat. His distorted face and bellowing voice, when he roared his final 'I'll be revenged on the whole pack of you', sounded like a menacing, if rather desperate and spasmodic effort of a dogmatic cadre to terrorize all those who were yearning for a life-giving Spring overcoming deadening Winter.

My final paradox is this. After the November 1989 revolution, our theatres have been liberated from political control. They are free but now they are exposed to the pressures of the free market. As in the recent National Theatre production of *The Winter's Tale* (premièred 1992), we have a 'pedlar at the door', Autolycus, 'littered under Mercury', who sells 'ribbons of all the colours i' the' rainbow' and 'points more than all the lawyers in Bohemia can learnedly handle' (4.4.182, 4.3.25, 4.4.205–7).[10] Our actors who were, along with the students, the driving force of the Velvet Revolution, have to fight for survival. Only step by step are they asserting artistic values against the wholesale devaluation brought by a flood of commer-cialized culture. Fortunately, they can face the competition by offering such mystery thrillers as *Hamlet* or *Macbeth*, such love stories as *Romeo and Juliet*, *Twelfth Night* or *Othello* and such miraculous romances as *The Winter's Tale* or *The Tempest*. In different ways, Shakespeare is as vitally important for us today as he has always been in his 'fair Bohemia' (4.1.21).

---

[10] The production of *The Winter's Tale* at the National Theatre in Prague was directed by Jan Kačer in the new translation of Martin Hilský (first night 12 November 1992).

'ARE YOU A PARTY IN THIS BUSINESS?' CONSOLIDATION AND SUBVERSION IN EAST GERMAN SHAKESPEARE PRODUCTIONS

MAIK HAMBURGER

Looking back upon what was for forty-five years a self-contained historical unit closed at both ends, it is easy to fall into the trap of pat generalizations. In retrospect, the East German story seems to telescope to fit neatly into a small red case. Literary and cultural evaluation of this era is reduced, even by generally discerning critics, to moral judgements about alleged support of or opposition to the repressive régime.

Reality was, indeed, much more complex. Perhaps it is too early for any clear and objective assessment of cultural processes, even in a matter somewhat remote from more sensitive political issues, such as the reception of Shakespeare on the East German stage. However, theatrical events may prove particularly revealing as the theatre was on the one hand respected by the authorities as a pillar of cultural prestige, but on the other hand was the genre least harassed by them because of its ephemeral nature and its relative insignificance vis-à-vis the printed word or the mass media. Furthermore, a classical text could hardly on the surface of things be considered subversive; and more than any other writer Shakespeare was part of the cultural heritage dear to socialist *Kulturpolitik*. Besides, the concept and manner of a theatrical presentation was difficult to pin down and it was still more of a problem to harness the communicative energies of an actor relating to his audience.

I propose to consider a number of stagings of Shakespeare in the early period ranging from 1945 to about 1970 to provide some insight into the role played by Shakespeare in the cultural processes of the time. I hope it will become clear that relations between political, social and artistic discourses were not rigid but evolved in phases, each phase itself enlivened by interaction of various currents. Similarly subversion of dominant structures and ideas was not always a given, readily recognizable entity in art. Some productions acted subversively without appearing to be so, others adopted a subverse pose but were, in effect, consolidating, and others again actually combined subversion with reinforcement. I finally propose to introduce the concept of 'integrative subversion' as a form feasible up a certain historical point. I shall be talking from first-hand experience, having actually witnessed all productions mentioned hereafter except for the first one.

It should be borne in mind that in the period under consideration the frame of discourse was predominantly some order of humanistic mimetic realism. Subversion mainly occurred at this level, although occasionally deconstructive elements did creep in.

The beginning of the era was marked by an important production of *Hamlet* at the bombed out Deutsches Theater in the Russian Sector of Berlin. The première on 11 December 1945, just six months after Germany's unconditional surrender, reflected the cultural confusion after a point of national disruption. The play was directed by Gustav von Wangenheim, a Communist returned from Russian exile. His dramaturg was Armin-Gerd Kuckhoff, whose father Adam Kuckhoff had been executed in 1943, just a couple of years before, for his resistance to Nazi rule. It is of some interest just to look at the cast. Hamlet: Horst Caspar, a beautiful actor with a mellifluous voice, who had been a leading Juvenile and as such almost a cult figure during the Nazi period. Fortinbras: Heinrich Greif, a powerful actor who had also been in Russian exile as a Communist. Polonius: Paul Wegener, a renowned character actor under Reinhardt from 1906 on, who had tried to keep clear of Nazi involvement but did come to act in chauvinistic films like 'Der große König'. Gertrude: Gerda Müller, formerly a leading actress in the expressionist Centre of Frankfurt, who had refused to set foot on the stage during the Nazi dictatorship.

Here was a mingle-mangle indeed! People who had been involved in the most varying degrees in consolidating, subverting or opposing the Fascist regime joined in a theatrical venture in the Eastern Sector of Berlin to help ring in a new, post-Nazi era.

Wangenheim's concept, closely geared to the historic situation, aimed at awakening new hopes for the future and spurring people to activity. He addressed an audience that was, according to Kuckhoff, 'ready, but often not yet capable to go along in the establishment of a humanistic order'.[1] Everything was attuned to highlight Hamlet's will to change historical circumstances by action. The active, forward-looking elements of the Danish Prince were emphasized. Horst Caspar, although an inspired artist, was hardly the actor to fulfil these political demands. The actress Inge von Wangenheim describes him as a genius with unique endowments; but she goes on to say that his 'apparently self-imposed limits were that he did not have an organ for the extraordinary historical moment he was living in, for the decisive revolution in German conditions which was taking place before his eyes'.[2] In contrast to Caspar, the committed actor Heinrich Greif brought his political awareness to his interpretation of Fortinbras, who was depicted in a

glorious finale as carrying on Hamlet's historical mission. Curiously enough, the Russian cultural officers were not at all keen to see the Communist Greif in leading parts;[3] they preferred the aura surrounding the well-known traditional actors – maybe partly because during exile in Moscow, Greif had been typecast as the Nazi in Russian plays and films.

The unique circumstances of this production, its anomalies, its position at a turning-point of history and its intended message were ignored by most of the reviewers. A leading critic, Friedrich Luft, wrote: 'This is a new Hamlet, whipped and hunted and driven through the Acts by a passionate restlessness. An overslender black flame, purity incarnate, that looks shudderingly into a stinking world around him.'[4] This was, of course, time-old idealistic language repressing any awareness of the political situation. In contrast, Wangenheim himself, at a meeting with young members of the audience, urged them to 'be radical, be radical like Hamlet. We know the objective of our struggle. We are happier than Hamlet-Shakespeare because we know. If we are real men, we are not alone. That gives us the strength and the wish to live!'[5] Hamlet-Shakespeare is here set up as a figurehead for a hoped-for emergent culture.

From the start, this *Hamlet* disclosed a cultural dichotomy: on the one hand, the wish to

---

[1] Armin-Gerd Kuckhoff, *Das Drama William Shakespeares* (Berlin, 1964), p. 695. All translations from the German in this paper are by the author.

[2] Inge von Wangenheim, 'Horst Caspar', Michael Kuschnia (ed.), *100 Jahre Deutsches Theater Berlin. 1883–1983* (Berlin, 1983), p. 143. A different view is taken by another Marxist critic in: Paul Rilla, *Theaterkritiken* (Berlin, 1978), pp. 44–6.

[3] Cf. Kurt Seeger, 'In memoriam Heinrich Greif', Kuschnia (ed.), *Deutsches Theater*, p. 144.

[4] Friedrich Luft, 'Berliner Theaterbrief', *Deutsche Nationalzeitung*, 17 December 1945.

[5] Gustav von Wangenheim, 'Über meine Hamlet-Inszenierung. Ansprache an die jugendlichen Zuschauer', *Shakespeare Jubiläum 1964* (Weimar, 1964), 45–62; pp. 61f.

pick up the threads of liberal discourse of the 1920s, as though nothing had occurred in between; on the other hand, the desire for a radically new start with a socialist perspective. Although this *Hamlet* did not and could not live up to the political ambitions of its director, it was at the same time highly moving theatre of humanist restoration.

Restoration of humanist values on a rationalist, atheist basis was, in fact, the main concern of subsequent Shakespeare productions in East Germany through the 1950s. This made for clear, intelligible stagings that swept the dust off the classics and did away with late bourgeois mystification. Occasionally, as under Wolfgang Langhoff at the Deutsches Theater, these productions reached a high standard of excellence within the given aesthetic. However, Bertolt Brecht was already at work in the wings on a far more fundamental concept of non-illusionistic, non-cathartic theatre, that was deeply to affect Shakespeare productions, too.

Gradually two new approaches crystallized out of the given ideology and its declared historical perspective. These were social analysis on the one hand and what I would call the 'Renaissance syndrome' on the other hand.

Under the impact of the Marxian definition of classes, directors made a closer scrutiny of social relations in Shakespeare's plays and thus achieved a much clearer delineation of plebeian figures which had often enough been somewhat summarily treated as trivial comic relief. Over and above that, surprising new configurations were discovered. In the *Othello* at the Deutsches Theater in 1953, directed by Wolfgang Heinz, Iago was acted by Ernst Busch, the best-known proletarian actor and singer in Germany. Stemming from the Brecht company, his style of acting stood in contrast to the flamboyant art of mimetic metamorphosis practised by Willy A. Kleinau, the Othello. Ernst Busch's Iago considered himself Othello's friend and right hand, and as such he could not understand that the 'bookish theoric' prattling

Cassio should be preferred as lieutenant-general. To quote the programme notes:

He is unable to comprehend that Othello is doing him a favour when he promotes Cassio. A Lieutenant-General has diplomatic responsibilities, he has to carry on negotiations with the higher aristocracy of Venice. Othello did not want to expose the uncouth soldier Iago to ridicule in this office. But Iago feels this as a deliberate slight, as an insult, as an act of injustice, as an allusion to his low birth. That is the main motive for his revenge . . .[6]

Such a concept which socially underpins Iago's revulsion and renders Othello's continued trust in him credible, enabled Busch to bring his plebeian traits into the part for a uniquely compelling performance in a production that was otherwise unremarkable. Ernst Busch had never been assimilated by traditional culture and neither was his Iago. Kleinau, like Werner Krauss before him, was almost a generator of mimetic identification. His Othello was fully integrated in the given culture, except for the unfortunate circumstance of his being black. This clash between plebeian and upper-class cultures was not merely represented, it actually took place live in the view of the audience. It was marked by the encounter of two men who were incommensurable as to acting style, social rootedness and individual deportment. The conflict between them cut through the accepted order of representation and hinted at unknown crucial contradictions in the world order. Orthodox ideology was turned askew by the text of the playwright and the personality of an actor.

In a stage history some years later, one could discover a quixotic attempt to fit the production into the customary frame of discourse. Out-Marxing Marx, the authors declared: 'this Iago as an individual storms at class society, he begins to lie, to denounce, to kill, and thus his positive properties are perverted into negative

---

[6] Programme notes for Shakespeare, *Othello*, Deutsches Theater Berlin, Spielzeit 1952/53, Heft 9, pp. 9f.

ones'.[7] Reading this, we realize the benefit East German theatre enjoyed from cultural exchange: Shakespeare's 'positive properties' might be perverted into negative ones on paper but not so easily on the stage.

Some years later, a production of *Troilus and Cressida* in Dresden drew huge audiences mainly because of the vituperations of an incredibly impertinent Thersites. The staging was built around this character, many lines being rearranged to give greater force to his deconstructive clowning. There was no doubt that spectators construed his thrusts at authority as directed at their own rulers, at Party and Government functionaries. However, would-be censors were stymied, as this *Troilus* was quite honestly mounted as a vigorous anti-war play. To drive this point home, an enlarged replica of Picasso's *Guernica* was appliquéed on the stage curtain. Thus a genuine anti-war production consolidating dominant ideology gained a subversive twist through the deconstruction and partial dehistoricizing of its burlesque elements. In effect, this show deconstructed the official position which tried to justify social restrictions as the price the people must needs pay for their government's policy of world peace. It should be noted that a good part of the play's triumphal reception was due to the brilliant acting of Dresden's darling, Horst Schulze. The reviews were mainly enthusiastic. However, one commentator did remark sourly that the grotesque portrayal of the war-lords 'organised an uncritical sympathy towards this shabby hero' (meaning Thersites);[8] and an occasional term of disapproval such as 'pacifist tendencies' and 'superficial intellectual effects' betrayed a modicum of official discomfort.

In the early 1970s, another play demonstrated the adverse effect of well-intentioned but injudicious social bias. In the district capital of Halle, a city with a large working-class population, *The Taming of the Shrew* was presented under the title of *Love's Labour's Won*. Director Horst Schönemann hit on the notion that the principal bearer of plebeian ideas in this play was Christopher Sly. Consequently he devoted meticulous care to the staging of the Induction, bringing out a full-blooded, lovable Sly on whom his Lordship plays a dirty trick merely to relieve the boredom of aristocratic life. The central idea was to expose bourgeois wooing and marriage as mercenary transactions in contrast to relations among the common people, who have no fortune to woo for anyway. Sly was present as a spectator to the play within the play for the duration of the performance, at first watching attentively and occasionally going on 'stage' to rectify matters. Gradually, however, he nodded off under the influence of wine. Now the frame story was related with such vivacity and Sly acted so winningly that the audience were much more interested in him than in the rest of the action. As a result, when Sly dropped off to sleep, there was a disposition among the spectators to follow his example. Here, a production imputed a subversive force to Shakespeare that was not actually supported by the text.

By the 1960s, the Brechtian approach had after a struggle gained official acceptance in East Germany. This was inevitable, as no director of the post-war generation could avoid being affected by his innovations. But there were different ways of appropriating his precepts. Some regarded them in the way of an encouragement to be critical of prevailing opinions, to study life as well as art, to be creative out of a spirit of inquiry. Those who assimilated Brecht in this 'Socratic' manner, as it were – directors like Benno Besson, Adolf Dresen, the team Klaus Erforth and Alexander Stillmark – transcended the letter of his teachings but kept his spirit alive. In doing Shakespeare, they followed Brecht's opinion that the Globe actors 'were experimenting no less than was Galileo in Florence at the time or Bacon in London. One

---

7 Werner Mittenzwei et al., *Theater in der Zeitenwende*, 2 vols. (Berlin, 1972), vol. 1, p. 325.
8 Mittenzwei, *Zeitenwende*, vol. 2, p. 197.

therefore does well to stage Shakespeare's plays experimentally.'[9] One prominent example of this approach was Adolf Dresen's *Hamlet* which I will discuss in detail later. Other directors – particularly such as had actually worked with Brecht at the Berliner Ensemble – got more and more into the rut of theoretical doctrine. Paradoxically, their very theories of emancipation unwittingly led them to domestication. But sometimes their productions sparkled through the sheer vitality of the medium.

Two prominent productions explicitly based on Brecht were *Coriolanus* at the Berliner Ensemble (1964) and *Richard III* at the Deutsches Theater (1972). Brecht himself had reworked Shakespeare's Roman tragedy some years earlier. His adaptation dating from 1952/3 responded to the specific historical situation, when Adolf Hitler's rise and fall was still fresh in people's minds. As the critic Friedrich Dieckmann notes: 'with the experience won in vivisecting the jackal (i.e. Hitler, M.H.) Brecht now turns to disembowel the tiger (i.e. Coriolanus, M.H.) . . . an ahistoric venture . . . born from the desire to pursue the hated contemporary right into his last hideout and to rob him of his past as well as of his present'.[10] Brecht himself was not quite happy about his reductionist concept and believed people would soon be politically educated enough to enjoy and comprehend classics in their original form.[11] He delayed and eventually cancelled his staging of it.[12]

It was not until 1964, eight years after Brecht's death, that his followers Manfred Wekwerth and Joachim Tenschert put the play on. They readapted Brecht's adaptation, in many respects going back to Shakespeare. Their concept pivoted around the idea that a war expert like Coriolanus was indeed invaluable to Rome but the price society eventually had to pay for him was too high. In terms of theatrical presentation, this concept brought about one striking feature. To show General Coriolanus doing the work he was good at, the battle scenes had to be given greatest promi-

nence. These rhythmic, pounding clashes around the revolving gate, choreographed by Ruth Berghaus, have become part of the iconography of post-War Shakespeare productions.

Apart from that, the concept remained trapped within the categories of dominant ideology. Whereas Brecht had advocated experimenting with Shakespeare, the Wekwerth-Tenschert experiment was to look for the accepted social mechanisms within Shakespeare's play. 'Here the classes enter the scene unadorned and without any uniting ideals: their "naked" interests determine their ways of acting', Wekwerth says.[13] Considering that the production sacrificed the stature of Shakespeare's hero to a political rationale, it was disappointing to see that – despite brilliant effects – no innovative statement was in fact made. Shakespeare's material was not sharpened for a weapon but hammered out for sparks.

The production, it should be said, was a huge international success. However, some commentators did have reservations about the didactic approach, about 'a tendency to academic systematization', as one wrote.[14] Peter Brook, for whom the production was 'in most respects a triumph', pointed out 'a tiny defect' that became for him 'a deep, interesting flaw'. To uphold its social attitude, he thinks, the Berliner Ensemble was not able to accept 'the man-within-the-social scene'.[15] Now performances vary from one evening to the next. What

---

[9] Bertolt Brecht, *Schriften zum Theater*, 7 vols. (Berlin and Weimar, 1964), vol. 5, p. 133.

[10] Friedrich Dieckmann, '"Die Tragödie des Coriolan"', *Sinn und Form*, 17 (1965), 463–89; p. 471.

[11] Cf. Dieckmann, 'Coriolan', p. 467.

[12] Cf. Manfred Wekwerth, *Notate* (Berlin and Weimar, 1967), p. 122.

[13] Wekwerth, *Notate*, p. 117. Cf. also Käthe Rülicke-Weiler, *Die Dramaturgie Brechts* (Berlin, 1966), p. 147.

[14] Manfred Nössig, 'Die Tragödie des Coriolan', *Theater der Zeit*, 21 (Berlin, 1964), p. 7.

[15] Peter Brook, *The Empty Space* (Harmondsworth, 1980), pp. 91ff.

Brook probably did not see was a feature that evolved spontaneously, as it were, during the run. Coriolanus was played by Ekkehard Schall, who had risen to world fame a short while previously for his presentation of Arturo Ui.[16] All of a sudden, audiences *did* see him as 'the man within the social scene' in a most disturbing manner. Evidently drawing from his experience as Arturo Ui, Schall displayed an irrational, uncanny, self-destructive aggressiveness which at a moment's notice turned to whining self-pity. He overwhelmed the audiences with a vivid presentation of unholy hysteria often ascribed to Germans, which leaders like Kaiser Wilhelm II and Hitler had indeed managed to stir up in the German people with disastrous consequences. But Schall did not present this hysteria with a historical distance, he opened up a contemporary view that no longer legitimized the present order but rather included it in a highly disturbing world picture. This astonishing example of intercultural fusion was, as mentioned, a feature of the performed event, obviously not recordable by first-night critics. However, B. K. Tragelehn, a theatre director who had seen rehearsals and a preview, later wrote: 'I saw the staging again much later, and only then did Schall make a very great impression on me. The greatness and power of his gift, just to play a character divided into two, mother's pet and butcher, a very German metaphor, stood out far beyond the concept of the *mise en scène*'.[17] In a way, I suppose, Schall instinctively solved Brecht's problem on the stage and created a dictator who was both tiger and jackal at the same time – an image not inept for some functionaries produced by Stalinist hierarchy, either.

After Brecht, the greatest single influence on Shakespeare stagings in East Germany at the time was Robert Weimann's book on Shakespeare and the popular dramatic tradition.[18] Weimann showed that in the mingle-mangle of Elizabethan theatre there were many levels of aesthetic communication, that official discourses were being debunked just as much as upheld, and that techniques of spatial and verbal distancing were in force to contravene emphatic identification with any particular character. His stress on the plebeian dimension in Shakespeare helped an ongoing process of emancipating theatre both from classic and from socialist idealization.

The first production explicitly based on Weimann's research was *Richard III* at the Deutsches Theater, directed by Manfred Wekwerth. Weimann remarks that Richard Gloucester is represented as the formidable 'image of a royal person in history, but at the same time he remains the punning, self-expressive ambidexter directing, in continuous conspiracy with the audience, his own murderous rise to the throne'.[19] Wekwerth was intrigued by this resuscitation of the Vice-tradition and the opportunities it held for extensive audience-play. Following Weimann's textual analysis, he knew exactly at which point the actor had to come down into the auditorium for an eye-to-eye contact. Hilmar Thate, who had been Aufidius in *Coriolanus*, presented a versatile Richard Gloucester. Switching back and forth between a bloody tyrant and the audience's partner, he fully exploited all the theatrical effects available. But all the same, the performance was lacking in spice. Something was missing: Richard's impertinence did not draw any of its energy from the actual dissatisfaction felt by the man in the street. He did expose tyranny as a man-made net of dirty machinations, but in doing so he was not even obliquely inviting his audiences to take a critical glance at their own rulers. Here was an actor playing at being subversive instead of being a subversive actor.

---

[16] Also directed by Manfred Wekwerth and Joachim Tenschert, *Der aufhaltsame Aufstieg des Arturo Ui* by Bertolt Brecht had its première at the Berliner Ensemble on 23 March 1959.

[17] B. K. Tragelehn, *Theater Arbeiten* (Berlin, 1988), p. 109.

[18] Robert Weimann, *Shakespeare und die Tradition des Volkstheaters* (Berlin, 1967).

[19] Robert Weimann, *Shakespeare and the Popular Tradition in the Theater* (Baltimore, 1978), p. 159.

The audience-contact was encapsulated in historical discourse, it was thus historicized and bereft of its topical edge.

Wekwerth's production was a peculiar phenomenon: it certainly broke through the norms of current 'Kulturpolitik' with regard to style. Instead of single-level mimetic realism, it presented a differentiated repertory of theatrical means. But by *representing* forms that were originally non-representational, it was domesticating them. Wekwerth's stylistic irreverence was not kindled by irreverent ideas, it was a formal implementation of techniques expounded by Brecht and Weimann. Hence Clive Barker's critique that Wekwerth's *Richard III* was an example of 'the icy hand of the director's "concept" becoming the *raison d'être* of the production to the detriment of the ensemble playing of the actors'.[20] Although it severely shocked party functionaries who saw their beloved harmonic forms disrupted, it did not so affect audiences who could not sense any upsetting of prestabilized socialist harmony.

The terms subversion and opposition obtain tangible significance only within a concrete historical situation. There was no general impulse for out-and-out opposition to the East German state in the 1950s and sixties. The Government had the support of many artists, intellectuals, and sectors of the population for some of its policies, for example its social programmes, its commitment for peace, its anti-fascist stance and even for its attempt to implement a new social order under adverse circumstances. It was relatively easy to reinforce these objectives in theatrical discourse. But art always throws a spanner in the works, whether consciously or inadvertently. Consolidation not in one way or another conjoined with subversion of the country's rigoristic, undemocratic, man-deforming features, could not rise to any compelling artistic level.

In the period from the mid-fifties to the mid-sixties, years of great social tension, there was nonetheless a zest in artistic life that is difficult to convey in retrospect. The grandiose dreams and illusions of a younger generation of intellectuals were almost unbounded. A vague but optimistic feeling that after the dark ages of Nazi and capitalist rule, a new Renaissance was possibly emerging with new values and new humanist objectives led to an ahistoric fixation on the Renaissance as a social model. The future of socialism was to offset what was partly known and partly guessed at about its ugly past. And after all, had not the Elizabethan upheaval been accompanied by violent ideological struggles, by bloodshed and persecution? Frederick Engels' much-quoted characterization of the Renaissance as 'a time which called for giants and produced giants – giants in power of thought, passion and character, in universality and learning'[21] appeared, *mutatis mutandis*, applicable to the forthcoming time, too.

Theatre people felt they bore a responsibility to help evolve a humane socialist order: for them the stage held something like the opportunities of Schiller's 'Moralische Anstalt'. And their imaginations were fired by the idea of man developing limitless possibilities of self-realization; of future socialist giants with Gargantuan appetites and supreme capabilities.

Inevitably these lofty ideas often clashed with petty realities. Thus an odd thing happened in Greifswald when the director B. K. Tragelehn staged *Volpone* in this grandiose vein, showing the title character as a kind of superman of Rabelaisian dimensions. Fearing censorship, Tragelehn provided cover in the shape of profuse programme notes illustrating the stature of Renaissance personalities. Ironically, no one minded about the play, but the programme notes were banned, because of the nudes in them!

---

[20] Clive Barker, 'Theatre in East Germany', in Ronald Hayman, ed., *The German Theatre* (London, 1975), p. 199.

[21] Frederick Engels, *Introduction to Dialectics of Nature*. Quoted after Karl Marx and Frederick Engels, *Selected Works in One Volume* (London, 1968), p. 339.

Naturally the sense of affinity with the Renaissance led to a heightened interest in Shakespeare. There was considerable cross-textual influence between the Elizabethan and contemporary drama. Blank verse was at this time a living form on the East German stage – used by playwrights, not to emulate Shake-speare, but to provide an appropriate form to the magnitude of their concepts of Man. At the same time, new German translations of Shake-speare appeared which took into account the performative components, what Brecht called the 'Gestus' of his texts in place of the old, more literary renderings of the Romantics and their epigones. There was linguistic interplay be-tween new translations of Shakespeare (by Adolf Dresen, Maik Hamburger, Heiner Müller, B. K. Tragelehn, Eva Walch) and new verse drama being written by Volker Braun, Peter Hacks, Hartmut Lange, Heiner Müller and others. Shakespeare can be said to have strongly informed (and profited by) the lan-guage of contemporary theatre in East Germany.

The debate about the new emancipation of the individual was viewed with some concern in official quarters. The advocacy of strong-willed individualists making their mark in his-tory outside the guidelines set down by the party filled them with dismay. The authorities decreed that the aspirations of the giants of Humanism, be they characters in history or on the stage, were in fact being implemented under socialism; if not immediately then at least in the near future.

This theme pervaded East German celebra-tions for the Shakespeare Quatercentenary in 1964. The annual Conference of the Shake-speare-Gesellschaft in Weimar was extended to eight days instead of the usual three. Party leader Walter Ulbricht was present, the main lecture was given by Alexander Abusch, Deputy Prime Minister and former Minister of Culture, the ceremony was broadcast on radio and television nation-wide.

Abusch's speech in Weimar was unusual in that it gave a clear and reasoned line on what Shakespeare meant to socialist Germany and how he was to be validly interpreted. This was a far cry from the vituperations of Zhdanov or the diffuse, never convincing attempts to define 'socialist realism'. Abusch posited a continuity from what he defined as the ideals of the Renaissance, specifically those upheld by Shakespeare, and their realization within the evolution of socialist society. His disquisition found its full correlative in a *Hamlet* staged by Hans Dieter Mäde in the city of Karl-Marx-Stadt. Mäde's concept was in fact identical with Abusch's proclamation. Mäde's dramaturg Ulf Keyn gave a potted version of the Abusch-Mäde thesis when he wrote, characteristically equating the poet with his hero:

Hamlet-Shakespeare's ideal cannot find fulfilment in his reality. His bold notions of Man remain an ideal, whose translation into life was reserved for a later epoch . . . In our time, thinking and practical activity are in concord, the contradiction between the spirit and power (Geist und Macht) has been resolved. What was once a yearning in Shakespeare, a perspec-tive longed and hoped for, reaches our audiences today as a modern aim in life.[22]

Never in their wildest dreams could Commun-ist officials have wished for a more perfect congruence between ideology and cultural practice, between Party line and theatrical presentation. No matter that this accordance was itself a *mise en scène*, brought forth partly by directorial adroitness and partly by self-persuasive rhetoric. The director Mäde was the right man for the job, having risen rapidly on the politico-cultural ladder, at thirty-three al-ready Candidate of the Party's Central Com-mittee. To cement the status of his *Hamlet*, Mäde used a German text by translator-laureate Rudolf Schaller, officially approved by the Ministry of Culture and the Academy of Arts. Mäde presented his theoretical concept in a

---

[22] Ulf Keyn, 'Hamlet unser Zeitgenosse', *Theater der Zeit*, 8 (1964): 19–20; p. 20.

paper which latched on to Abusch's key-note lecture.[23] And most critics confirmed they had seen what they had been told to. Writing some years later, Armin-Gerd Kuckhoff approvingly noted: 'In view of frequent divergencies between directors' theses and the theatrical reality on the stage – not only in socialist countries – it should be explicitly stressed that Mäde's paper entirely corresponded with what was to be seen on the stage; it can thus be accepted as the reality of the Karl-Marx-Stadt production.'[24]

The extensive discussion of the various *Hamlets* of the year in the columns of *Theater der Zeit* (the GDR theatre periodical) was enlivened by one critic who played the part of the pike in the fishpond. Alexander Weigel boldly named a number of shortcomings of Mäde's production, accusing him of abstractly lifting the central conflicts out of the drama and displacing it into the present time.[25] The ruffled director responded with the remark that it was preposterous to accuse a member of the Central Committee of idealism![26]

Given the enormous claims made for it, the production itself seemed somewhat crude and full of clichés. One disturbing feature was the stylistic ambivalence in the handling of the open stage. With its apron jutting out into the auditorium, it was evidently borrowing from the Globe. Nonetheless, the director seemed unable to do without flats; as a makeshift, he used a rank of armed soldiers who walked over to wherever a 'wall' was needed to partition off a particular scene. This was of course the summit of insensibility. It was painful to have to watch an intimate scene in the Queen's closet being enacted in front of a dumb row of clods with pikes in their hands.

This coarse kind of aesthetic prevailed throughout the production. Its redeeming feature was the actor Jürgen Hentsch. Hypersensitive, self-doubting, he projected his inability to serve the concept into the part he was playing. He must have left some of the audience in some doubt as to whether they really were the right people to resolve this Hamlet's contradictions.[27]

Thus even this model of consolidation was partly subverted by human resilience.

Among the eighty productions of Shakespeare to mark the Quatercentenary, three further stagings of *Hamlet* achieved prominence. They testified to the fact that in spite of official pronouncements, a wide spectrum of concepts and aesthetic methods were being explored in East Germany at the time.

At the Deutsches Theater Berlin, the Grand Old Man of the theatre Wolfgang Heinz, a staunch Communist of many years' standing, a former member of the renowned emigré Company at Zürich, had his own views on how to politicize the play. To begin with, as an enlightened person and an atheist, he did not believe in ghosts and saw no sense in passing on such superstitions: he therefore had Hamlet's Father mimed by a small-part actor in armour while his lines were being spoken by Hamlet's voice on tape, i.e. as a projection of Hamlet's thoughts. This was not, however, just a gimmick: in the context of this staging it was important that the initiative came from Hamlet himself. Heinz's interpretation regarded the Prince as the potential reformer of a corrupt state who becomes socially guilty for not going through with his task. By failing to kill the King and seize power, he gambles away his opportunity to put his humanist views into practice and opens the door to Fortinbras, here represented as a far greater threat than Claudius, almost a proto-Fascist. The production hinged on the prayer scene, made more explicit

---

[23] Hans Dieter Mäde, 'Hamlet und das Problem des Ideals', *Shakespeare Jahrbuch*, 102 (1966): 7–22.

[24] Armin-Gerd Kuckhoff, 'Zur Shakespeare-Rezeption auf den Bühnen der DDR (1945–80)', *Shakespeare Jahrbuch*, 118 (1982): 107–19, p. 113.

[25] Alexander Weigel, 'Von der Schwierigkeit des Realisierung', *Theater der Zeit* 8 (1964), p. 20–2. Alexander Weigel, 'Von der Realisierung des Ideals', *Theater der Zeit*, 15 (1964):8–10.

[26] Communicated to the author by Alexander Weigel.

[27] Cf. Peter Ullrich, 'Erinnerungen an Hamlet', *Shakespeare Jahrbuch* (1994): 145f.

with the help of interpolations from *Measure for Measure* and elsewhere:

> Now might I do it pat, now a is a-praying,
> I do him right that, answering one foul wrong,
> Lives not to act another.
> And now I'll do it.
> That is to say: a villain murders my father,
> For that, I, his son do kill the murderer.
> Am I inhuman? [ein Unmensch]
> Has the world no other way than this
> Blood for blood, violence for violence?
> My mother stays.
> This physic but prolongs thy sickly days.[28]

The programme notes explain: 'Hamlet's new humanistic position poses him the question, whether force – which he has only experienced as an abuse hitherto – can be a legitimate means to implement new humane conditions. Hamlet cannot at first solve this great social contradiction ... His delaying prevents the crimes being halted and leads to his downfall. A true tragic conflict.'[29]

For Heinz, Hamlet's ideal would be realized one day, too, but that day lay far off. Hamlet's dying speech says in his version: 'But I do prophesy: the time will come / When man will be the master of his fate. / ... / This future era has my dying voice./ *(dies)*'[30]

This idiosyncratic product of a dogged Marxist was at odds with all current trends: neither did it affirm Abusch's official reconstruction of Hamlet's ideals, nor was it, with its call to arms, compatible with the principles of peaceful coexistence, then a bastion of official foreign policy. It was an erratic block in the Shakespeare-Anniversary, given due praise when it travelled to Weimar, but generally passed over and forgotten as soon as possible.

The most unencumbered *Hamlet* of the year was to be seen in Potsdam. In the hands of a group of stormy young actors under Peter Kupke, *Hamlet* almost became a thriller, telling the pathetic story of a youngster thrown into a world he cannot cope with. This young nobleman does not know what to do with all the wonderful theories he has brought with

him from Wittenberg. Given the practical task of avenging a murder, he cocks his sights at a higher aim, namely to put right the times that are out of joint. Trying to get on with this, he runs into difficulties and perishes.

Arno Wyzniewski, a slim, fragile, highly-strung actor, played the young Prince who becomes caught up in the meshes of intractable society. The most memorable scene was the duel: two youngsters in snow-white shirts, scarcely more than schoolboys, engaged in a furious fight to the death, complacently watched by a hard-boiled court which had prodded them into this situation. Here was a clear indictment of power politics crushing innocent, hopeful human beings between its jaws. The audiences could not help identifying with this youth and his untainted ideals, which would have been smirched by reality today just as they were then. Evidently, humanistic ideals were an anachronism in this society. As the authorities did not step in, no public sensation was caused and this little stab at current ideology went unnoticed by outsiders. The sum of thousands of such pinpricks probably played up the régime just as much as the limited number of sensational éclats.

The fourth and last staging of *Hamlet* to be discussed here came up in the northern town of Greifswald near the Baltic, a long way off from Weimar. The director Adolf Dresen later described his feelings when in 1964, then a newly appointed artistic director, he was entrusted with the task of honouring Shakespeare: 'I loathed this assignment, just as I loathed monuments. I proposed *Timon of Athens*, which at least was not famous. My proposal was not accepted. *Hamlet* was to be played, they said, because it was the best known play by Shakespeare.'[31] Dresen was not only sceptical about

---

[28] William Shakespeare, *Hamlet*, playscript Deutsches Theater Berlin, 1964, pp. 75f.

[29] Programme notes for Shakespeare, *Hamlet*, DT, 1964, p. 23.

[30] Shakespeare, *Hamlet*, playscript DT, p. 127.

[31] Adolf Dresen, *Siegfrieds Vergessen* (Berlin, 1992), p. 9.

official readings, he was also in an iconoclastical frame of mind towards the classics as such. Shakespeare's text seemed to him to abound with primitive flaws. It did not even live up to what one had been taught at school. Looking up what master Brecht had to say, he brightened up a bit; Brecht's Sonnett on *Hamlet* adopted a stance he could well follow: the intellectual who was being humane so long as he hesitated but who burst into bloody deeds when he launched into activity. Dresen found analogies to episodes of German history: after being, as Hölderlin had said, 'poor in deeds and rich in thoughts' ('tatenarm und gedanken-reich'), the Germans *had* become active with catastrophic results. He was reminded of Hein-rich Mann's dictum: 'Power was without spirit and the spirit was without power' ('Die Macht was geistlos und der Geist was machtlos'). There seemed to be a kind of dichotomy in German affairs that might possibly be traced back to a single root. Finally Dresen com-pressed his reflections into the slogan 'Buchen-wald is near Weimar', meaning that there was a connection between the non-performative, contemplative discourse of the German Classics (whose seat was in Weimar) and the gross inhumanity of Germans when they *did* resort to action (culminating in the atrocities of Buchen-wald concentration camp close to Weimar). This was not to be understood as some dubious revival of national psychology, rather as a result of historical processes for which Hamlet's story could serve as a paradigm: Hamlet, too civilized to kill one person, is in the end responsible for eight victims including himself. With this in mind, Dresen found the contradictions that had bothered him in the play suddenly became its key constituents.

Such a concept was easily transmutable into stage action: when Hamlet thinks, he cannot act, he *can* act when he is not thinking. Then of course his actions are blind. And finally he deliberately switches off his capacity to think ('And prais'd be rashness for it') and leaves everything to providence.

I had the privilege of being called in by Dresen for a scrutiny of the German texts. After some unsatisfactory attempts at touching up the classical renditions, we embarked upon a new translation which was able to profit from the enormous opening up of German performative language by Bertolt Brecht.

I've gone into the genesis of this production in some detail to show there was no deliberate intent of subversion. The director just followed his own trains of thought and made a discovery for himself – feeling, as he said, as exhilarated as Kepler might have done, only that he, Dresen, was merely rediscovering a discovery Shake-speare had made. He *did* feel he was making a valid contribution to Marxist discourse.

During rehearsals, Dresen had more to learn: namely that in practice, Shakespeare's text develops a tendency to override all concepts. The highly skilled Jürgen Holtz encountered difficulties in representing Hamlet critically. Dresen says:

Criticism presupposes distance, we were not able to keep at a distance, in the end it seemed unnatural and counter-effective [*wirkungswidrig*] and we realized: this play is not a parable but a tragedy, all criticism is contained in the tragedy . . . Everyone is in the right against everyone else, but their rights exclude one another – only then does the play become great . . . By and by we forgot about our 'concept', just as the masons forget about the scaffolding when the house stands. We had at least needed it, *not* to do all the wrong things that were in the air concerning this play.[32]

Thus any polemical impulses were sunk in Shakespeare's polyphonic discourse. In the event, Holtz gave a superb performance, run-ning the whole gamut from expressionist out-burst to representational finesse, switching at a moment's notice from a high-born Prince to a vulnerable intellectual, from a sensitive human-ist to a raving maniac. In the final duel, Holtz reliquished his rapier to bombard Laertes

---

32 Dresen, *Vergessen*, p. 15.

wildly with the chairs and tables of Elsinore. The staging incorporated any amount of clowning, burlesque and topsy-turveydom.

The show was a great success. It held audiences spellbound for four and a half hours; even rural subscription groups generally feared by theatres for their lack of cultural sophistication were enthusiastic. The staging combined philosophical depth with popular appeal, thus apparently ideally meeting the demands of socialist *Kulturpolitik*.

However, already before the opening, sinister rumblings could be heard in the wings. The *Generalintendant* suspected Dresen of deviating from orthodoxy and attempted to have the staging stopped before it opened. Paradoxically, the production was saved by the Party organization of the town of Greifswald. The local Party Secretary declared at a meeting he saw nothing wrong with the performance and despite pressure from above he did not intend to put any obstacles in its way. This courageous act did at least provide a breathing space for a number of performances.

However, the production *was* taken off after less than a dozen showings, without explanation and without fuss. The authorities were not at this point interested in an open confrontation which would have disturbed the harmony of the Quatercentenary. There was no public denouncing. The idea was to play down the whole embarrassing affair. This became evident when the most prominent full-length notice appeared in the satirical journal *Eulenspiegel*, of all places. It was penned by a man named C. U. Wiesner, an author unknown to Shakespearian criticism, whose usual routine was to compose chatty little pieces set in a barber's shop. From this lofty vantage point, he trimmed the 'young theatre revolutionaries' to size. He betrayed on whose behalf he was writing when he threw in a barely veiled warning to the theatre management: 'Now the theater's Intendant . . . is very much dismayed at this *Hamlet* farce and angry with its initiators. And rightly so. But he will have learnt for his future directorial career that

artistic talents . . . need to be cleverly and prudently guided.'[33]

Incidentally, there was only one ascertainable act of intervention by the State Security organs in this affair: they confiscated all negatives and prints taken by theatre photographers.[34] This was quite typical: the notorious 'Stasi' did not generally meddle in cultural discourse, but they *were* concerned with removing traces of a possible political scandal.

The new translation of *Hamlet* was also prohibited as part and parcel of an undesirable staging, also because its lower levels of vernacular subverted the sublimity of what was then taken to constitute a classical style. As officially no censorship existed, the banning was effected by simply not granting any publisher permission to duplicate the text, a legal requirement at the time.

It is not difficult to guess why Dresen's staging was dubbed subversive. It placed Hamlet's historical conflict squarely before the audience and made them feel social contradictions as something tangible, painful and potentially destructive, if unresolved. Not only did this protagonist undercut the dominant *Menschenbild* ('image of Man') but the whole production eluded orthodox criticism from a position of mimetic realism. Maybe for this reason the exponents of *Kulturpolitik* fought shy of confrontation.

The fame, or notoriety, of this production spread rapidly by word of mouth. The few performances allowed were seen by a good part of the country's theatrical élite including Benno Besson, Heiner Müller, B. K. Tragelehn and Wolfgang Heinz. Heinz immediately hired Dresen on the strength of his *Hamlet*, which was so different from his own. Heiner Müller tried in vain to have his appraisal of the translation and production published in *Forum*, a

---

[33] C. U. Wiesner, 'Theater-Eule', *Der Eulenspiegel*, 15 (1964): 30, p. 6.

[34] Communicated to the author by Wolfhard Theile, who was the theatre's graphic artist at the time.

lively weekly for young intellectuals. A television report incorporating excerpts from the production was disallowed. And there things rested for a while.

Again paradoxically, the *Hamlet* translation was rehabilitated nine years later by an academic reputed to be the most conservative member on the committee of the Shakespeare-Gesellschaft. In 1973, Anselm Schlösser wrote an appreciative report for the Henschel publishing house, on the strength of which it was finally permitted to disseminate playscripts. Before that, there had been one 'illicit' staging of the translation at Senftenberg, afterwards it was played by numerous theatres all over the country.

Dresen's *Hamlet* was to my knowledge the last Shakespeare production to be 'subversive by default' or 'naively subversive'. In a wider sense I would like to term this 'integrative subversion'. It was still possible to maintain a relaxed state of mind towards official communiqués, either ignoring them altogether or taking them as non-mandatory proposals for nation-wide cultural discourse. Dresen regarded his *Hamlet* as an integrative contribution to this kind of open discussion, being at first confirmed in this by the support of the local Party organization and of many personalities in cultural life. There was not yet the sense of schism between artists and rulers that was to develop later on. As Christa Wolf wrote in retrospect: 'only gradually did we come to realize that our hopes to help change this commonweal by means of art, by means of *critical* art, were doomed to failure'.[35] Integrative subversion would mean that production was not aggressive, it had no polemical edge, it did not try to squeeze some kind of *Tendenz* out of the play but delved into its full richness. The staging was also integrative inasmuch as it was intended for and accepted by wide audiences from all strata of society. It did not split its audiences. When animosities did develop, they originated in the party bureaux and not in the auditorium.

A year and a half on, late in 1965, things changed radically as the notorious 11th Plenary Session of the Central Committee marked a turning point in East German *Kulturpolitik*. Film-makers and writers were severely taken to task for alleged oppositional stances. A number of films were banned, novels censored. No one could fail to see the implications of this attack. It reinstituted a polarization of 'spirit' and 'power'. It was partially successful in driving a wedge between artists and other sections of the population. After this, an integrative approach in art was rendered almost impossible. That became evident when Dresen staged *Measure for Measure* at the Kammerspiele of the Deutsches Theater in Berlin in 1966. The production was in fact a commentary on the 11th Plenary Session: Angelo's fanatic zeal was associated with party dogmatism, it was counteracted both by the unruly rabble and the pragmatic, easy-going Duke. It was significant for the times that now the director had to keep his concept a secret and to adapt the play to fit his concept. Dresen did make a last, desperate attempt at an integrative production when he co-directed Goethe's *Faust 1* (with Wolfgang Heinz) in 1968. The result was a theatre-scandal of national dimensions, leading finally to the resignation of Wolfgang Heinz.

Henceforth, I believe, subversion, even under cover of Shakespeare, could no longer be naive or integrative in East Germany. As in Dresen's *Measure for Measure* and to a far greater degree in Benno Besson's *Hamlet* (1977), Alexander Lang's *Midsummer Night's Dream* (1980) or Heiner Müller's *Macbeth* (1982), subversion now implied a conscious thrust, an intended confrontation and a calculated selection – both as to the substance of the play and the audience to be addressed. This applied *a fortiori* to deconstructive stagings of the 1980s, like Martin Meltke's *Twelfth Night* in

---

[35] Christa Wolf, *Auf dem Weg nach Tabou. Texte 1990–1994* (Köln, 1994), pp. 63f.

Brandenburg (in which the most prominent prop was a lavatory bowl), Herbert König's *The Comedy of Errors* in Karl-Marx-Stadt and Frank Castorf's *Othello* in Anklam. These productions, totally off the mainstream, were undoubtedly highly subversive. Their oppositional stance was already manifest in their rejection of all traditional theatrical discourse, but under the given political conditions they could only reach a small intellectual clique and were easily suppressed by the authorities.

Aptly the last important Shakespeare production in East Germany was also *Hamlet*, directed at the Deutsches Theater by Heiner Müller in a conflation with his own play *Hamletmaschine*. During rehearsal, this staging was overtaken by subversion in action as the people of East Germany overthrew their Government and established a régime of parliamentary democracy. But although his opening unexpectedly took place in a democratic order, Müller was not over-optimistic about the outcome of contemporary developments. His Hamlet (Ullrich Mühe) repeatedly cites Müller's text: 'I was Hamlet, I stood on the shore and talked BLAH BLAH to the breakers, at my back the ruins of Europe . . .'[36] For Müller, Europe is today more completely and irrevocably in ruins than Berlin was in 1945. And today we may stand and wonder and ask ourselves with Autolycus: 'Are you a party in this business?'

---

[36] Cf. Maik Hamburger, '*Hamlet* at World's End: Heiner Müller's Production in East Berlin', in Tetsuo Kishi, Roger Pringle and Stanley Wells (eds.), *Shakespeare and Cultural Traditions* (Newark, London and Toronto, 1994), pp. 280–4. For a fuller discussion, see Maik Hamburger, 'Theaterschau', *Shakespeare Jahrbuch*, 127 (1991): 155–68, pp. 161–8.

THE MARTYRED KNIGHTS OF GEORGIAN SHAKESPEARIANA

NICO KIASASHVILI

The art of translation was known in Georgia from early times. Translations of the Bible appeared as far back as the fourth century. Practically all major Byzantine writings had been rendered into Georgian as early as the tenth and thirteenth centuries, the same being true of Eastern literature and lore. Incidentally, *The Wisdom of Balavar* or *Barlaam and Josaphat* legend was also translated by unknown translators into Georgian, and there is a remote and intriguing link between this translation and Shakespeare, however mysterious it may seem. The parable of the caskets could hardly have found its way into *The Merchant of Venice* unless the first Christian version of the legend had been available – I quote from the *Encyclopaedia Britannica* – '. . . from the Arabic by the Georgians . . . The Greek recension . . . which is a highly embroidered rendering of the Georgian, was made on Mt Athos by St Euthymius (d. 1028) the Iberian (that is Georgian), possibly in collaboration with Greek monks there . . . From the Greek came the Latin, Slavonic, Christian Arabic and other Christian versions.'[1]

Shakespeare himself was hardly aware of Georgia, a small country in the Caucasus of which the West learnt later.[2] And yet it is *The Merchant of Venice* in which we find these lines:

> . . . and her sunny locks
> Hang on her temples like a golden fleece,
> Which makes her seat of Belmont Colchis'
> strand,
> And many Jasons come in quest of her.
>
> (1.1.169–72)

Colchis here is the ancient name of Western Georgia (Cholchis) and the legend of the *Golden Fleece* is the story of *Jason*'s love for the Georgian princess *Medea*. And it seems symbolic that in Georgia Shakespeare was performed for the first time in 1873 in the village of Bandza, which is precisely in Cholchis, and that the amateurs performed no other play but *The Merchant of Venice*.

Shakespeare became known in Georgia only at the beginning of the last century and the Georgian translations began to emerge in the middle of it. Among the pioneers of Georgian Shakespeariana mention should be made of Dimitri Qipiani (1824–87), a prominent man of letters whose place among the predecessors of the famous translator Ivané Machabeli (1854–98) could be defined by paraphrasing what Somerset Maugham had to say about himself: Qipiani was the first among the second-raters. The first draft of his translation of *Romeo and Juliet* was considered to be lost, but recently it turned up in the collection of the rare books and manuscripts of Chicago University. Qipiani also translated and published *The Two Gentlemen of Verona* and *The Merchant of Venice*, and left an unfinished manuscript of *Much Ado About Nothing*.

---

[1] *Encyclopaedia Britannica*, vol. 3, 1968.

[2] *A King And No King* by Beaumont and Fletcher, the action of which is set in Armenia and Iberia (i.e. Georgia), could not be an authentic source of information on the history of Georgia, for the plot of the play does not contain real historical events.

Besides his literary activities Dimitri Qipiani was a well-known public figure as well. He became one of the founders of The Dramatic Society of Georgia and also published *The Modern Georgian Grammar*. In addition to its strictly practical and educational value, the book was of considerable political significance, for the Georgian language was brutally banished from schools. Qipiani's idea of the cultural and spiritual progress of Georgian people was expressed in his motto: 'Real progress can only be achieved by a nation that thinks and speaks in its native tongue.' But all this was not to the Empire's liking. And when the Exarch of Georgia Pavel Lebedev (incidentally, the Georgian Church by that time ceased to be autocephalous) anathematized the Georgian Nation, Qipiani wrote to him: 'Your Reverence, rumour has it that you have anathematized the country which you have been called on to guide spiritually and which looked to you only for love and grace. If all this is true, Your Reverence, the only way of rescuing the honour of your office is for the insulter to leave the insulted country forthwith.' The result was immediate and tragic: Qipiani was exiled to Russia (to Stavropol) where he was assassinated under mysterious circumstances.

Thus, Dimitri Qipiani became the first representative of Georgian Shakespeariana who finished his life tragically. Unfortunately he was not an exception as will be made clear later.

The Georgian theatre of the period had to rely on comparatively poor translations of Shakespeare. The prominent tragic actor Lado Meskhishvili (1857–1920), for instance, played Hamlet in Anton Purtseladze's (1839–1913) translation without apparent success. The imperfect translation naturally affected his interpretation of the character. In 1886 one of the Georgian reviewers remarked that Meskhishvili sometimes forgot that Hamlet was not mad, though in England they thought he was. Well, it is of some interest to recall Oscar Wilde's remark to his friend Ross approxi-

mately at the same time when the above critical remark appeared in the Georgian press: 'My next Shakespeare book will be a discussion as to whether the commentators on Hamlet are mad or only pretending to be.'[3]

But Meskhishvili's initial failure turned into a great success after Ivané Machabeli supplied him with his translation. Machabeli brought a high degree of professionalism into the translation and succeeded in making his rendering of Shakespeare's plays sound like original works of literature. The fact that he, together with the classic of Georgian poetry Ilia Chavchavadze (1837–1907), selected the most appropriate metre of Georgian verse, which perfectly conveys the sense and mood expressed by the iambic pentameter of the original, contributed a great deal to his success.

Rich material is available for the analyses of the problems the translator faced and the way he tackled them. I shall cite practically the only instance when Machabeli actually changes the accepted text and gives the Ghost's line 'O, horrible, O horrible, most horrible!' to Hamlet.

A careful examination of the sources of information available to Machabeli has convinced me that he could not have seen any Shakespeare publication in which these words are given to Hamlet. Even if he had read some commentary on the subject, still it must have been his intuition that gave him courage to alter the Shakespeare text itself. He must have felt the difference between the solemn narrative style of the Ghost's soliloquy and the state of Hamlet's mind at learning the 'most terrible' news and remaining silent all the way through the long narration. So, leaving aside for a moment all the scholarly arguments, the translator knew what the audience would expect Hamlet to do: he surely would utter or rather sigh out the doubt which arose in his mind. To put all this in the modern director's phrasing – the actor playing Hamlet professionally needs

---

[3] Richard Ellmann, *Oscar Wilde*, N.Y.: Alfred A. Knopf, 1988, p. 299.

to 'assess' what he hears. The line offers itself as Hamlet's obvious cue. And not for nothing, whoever left us the prompt book version (or whatever it is) of the first quarto (1603), interrupts the Ghost's soliloquy and, leaving only two 'O horrible's in the line, breaks it with Hamlet's 'O God!' The English original which was in Machabeli's possession has the translator's marginal note – HAMLET – across the words under discussion.[4]

As you may guess, I personally accept Kittredge's reading and Laurence Olivier's interpretation of the line.

Such feeling of the specific dramatic function of Shakespeare's poetic devices became organic for the Georgian public which by that time was already well adapted to similar theatrical subtleties. Incidentally, when in 1890 Ernesto Rossi brought his Shakespearian repertory to Georgia (Lear, Othello, Hamlet, Shylock, Romeo) he was deeply impressed by how sophisticated his audiences were in Georgia so far as their knowledge of Shakespeare was concerned.

The high regard which the British diplomat and translator of the works of Georgian literature Sir Oliver Wardrop (1864–1948), who, naturally, knew Georgian well, had for Machabeli's translations may be clearly observed in his correspondence with his Georgian friends. And in his letter (written in English) to Machabeli himself, Oliver Wardrop wrote:

Your translation of *Julius Caesar* is something to be proud of; it is a proof of your genius and of the wonderful wealth of your language. I have new French, German, Russian, Bulgarian versions of this play, but none of them seems to be as faithful as yours. You have done a work that progeny will admire, even if you do not get praise from your contemporaries. I hope you will gradually translate the whole of Shakespeare.

Machabeli's mysterious disappearance in 1898, which was a real tragedy for Georgian society (he left his house in Tbilisi and never returned) put an end to his work on Shakespeare.

Nine years later, the great Georgian poet and public figure Ilia Chavchavadze, the initiator of Machabeli's activity in translating Shakespeare and his co-translator of *King Lear*, was waylaid near his estate and killed by a gang from a Marxist organization which was displeased with the fact that the Georgian Prince, the Poet, was recognized by the Nation as its spiritual leader.

The Twenties of our century in Georgia were as Roaring as elsewhere. It was the time of the establishment of a new social order which my father's generation witnessed as the time of the creation of a terrible modernized Empire. And as part of the old Russian Empire from 1801, Georgia was destined to share the devastating seventy years of her subsequent history.

Even so, the early twenties showed a real flourishing of Georgia literature and arts, due to the fact that a number of Georgian writers, scholars and artists returned by that time from abroad. And the Prodigal Son of the Georgian Theatre Koté Marjanishvili, who had directed in numerous Russian theatres since the beginning of the century, also returned to his homeland, founded a new theatre in Tbilisi and in 1925 produced a *Hamlet* which is rightly considered to mark the birth of a new Georgian Theatre. Incidentally, as early as 1911 Marjanishvili assisted Gordon Craig and Stanislavsky who directed *Hamlet* for Moscow Art Theatre. In 1961, in reply to a letter from me, I received Gordon Craig's answer from Vence, France, confirming that Marjanishvili was a help in their work on *Hamlet*.

New translations of Shakespeare were undertaken in Georgia only in the 1940s. A new generation of translators (G. Gachechiladze, V. Chelidze and others) took over Machabeli's method, adjusting it to modern Georgian

---

[4] Michael Gizhimkreli, *Two Georgian Commentaries on 'Hamlet'*, Georgian Shakespeareana, vol. 2, ed. with Introduction and Notes by Nico Kiasashvili, Tbilisi, 1964 (in Georgian with English summary).

language standards. And in all these translations (including the Sonnets) the fourteen-syllable verse scheme has been retained.

By the way, *Shall I Die* was immediately translated into Georgian, thus actually becoming the first translation of the newly discovered poem into a foreign language. Notwithstanding the lively controversy over its authenticity, I have decided to include *Shall I Die* in our *Complete Works* (as Stanley Wells and Gary Taylor did for *The Oxford Shakespeare*).

Naturally enough, ideological regulation, strict control and supervision on the part of the Communist administration could not be applied so rigorously to translators. The case with the theatre was altogether different: those unreliable, vacillating directors and actors authorized to interpret and consequently add, figuratively speaking, some 'ideological gags' of their own, were so unpredictable – they had to be kept under constant and close observation! And as Dennis Kennedy notes: '. . . some of the most innovative and exciting productions of Shakespeare in the past twenty years come . . . from Europe . . . from Soviet Georgia and from Japan . . .' '[Shakespeare's] plays were used in postwar eastern Europe and the Soviet Union as dissident texts . . . producers are sometimes tempted to make the classics into coded messages about the present. Shakespeare thus became a secret agent under deep cover'.[5] Referring to Soviet Georgia, the author surely has Robert Sturua's production of *Richard III* in mind.[6]

And Sturua's second Shakespearian production is *King Lear*. The key episode for understanding Lear's character in this performance is his first entrance which is preceded by the longest theatre pause I have ever seen or read about. This masterfully created tension of the expectancy of the monarch's appearance (which for one moment has even a comic touch, when the Duke of Albany collapses and, having found his glasses, springs up to his feet again) and prepared the audience for seeing the despotic character not easily identified in the

weak posture of the old man carrying a birdcage in his hand. The same birdcage will be taken by Cordelia as her only dowry and will reappear at the end of performance to make Lear, who regains consciousness, feel, by the twittering of the real bird, his daughter's presence somewhere around the stage.

The striking finale of the production sums up the director's principal message. The set, which actually represents a kind of replica or extension of the spectators' hall, starts crashing down leaving the audience with the sense of cosmic catastrophe, while the figure of lonely Lear and Cordelia's body fill up the horrible emptiness of the Universe. Lear's final soliloquy is considerably cut and his much discussed words, last in this performance – 'pray you, undo this button', addressed to the dead Cordelia, add a final tragic touch to Robert Sturua's most original interpretation of the play.

Now I would like to share with you a piece of somewhat unusual yet important information on the period of Georgian history and culture which we always discussed with horror but actually knew little about.

After the Republic of Georgia attained full independence the archives of the KGB files became available to scholars.[7]

Something like a tragic farce was staged in 1937–8. Now we have the staggering statistics: in the period of this new era of Inquisition about 260 thousand were arrested, exiled or executed in a country with a population of only three million and a half.

Now we know that Sandro Akhmeteli, another prominent director was sentenced to death as early as 1924. Koté Marjanishvili, who was Akhmeteli's co-producer of *The Merry*

---

[5] A paper for the seminar at 25th International Shakespeare Conference. The Shakespeare Institute, Stratford-upon-Avon, 1992.

[6] Nico Kiasashvili, *A Georgian 'Richard the Third'*, *Shakespeare Quarterly*, 31, 3 (1980).

[7] Vassil Kiknadze, *Martyred Knights*, Tbilisi, 1992 (in Georgian).

Wives of Windsor in the same year, headed the campaign for his defence and succeeded, for it was not yet 1937. Akhmeteli even became the artistic director of Rustaveli Theatre. But in 1932 menacing charges were published in the press against Marjanishvili himself. In a couple of years any one of those accusations would surely have sufficed to have Marjanishvili sentenced to death, but he died within a year, leaving his disciple Sandro Akhmeteli alone to face Stalin-Beria revenge.

There are ten volumes of Sandro Akhmeteli's 'personal records' preserved in KGB files. Beria launched a new wave of assault against him. After its tremendous success in 1930 at the Moscow Festival, The Rustaveli Theatre was invited for a tour abroad. But in Beria's secret report to Moscow we read: 'We are strongly opposed to the idea of the Theatre's tour abroad. The main group of actors and the director Akhmeteli himself have been involved in anti-Soviet activities for many years.' And the most ominous part of the report was the conclusion which reads as follows: 'It seems necessary to carry out cardinal purges.' Neither should one rule out the 'sacramental' motto of the 'great leader of world proletariat' Lenin: 'We must encourage the demonstration of mass terror.'

The archival material gives a detailed account of the investigation of Akhmeteli's case. Within eighteen hours of his arrest he still seems strong, denying all the absurd accusations. But the file reveals the inhuman methods of investigation involved and at later cross-examinations Akhmeteli already admits – in fact mechanically repeats the accusations, though to all the questions referring to the possible involvement of other people, his replies are stereotypical – 'I do not remember.' The last entry in the files is dated 28 June 1937. Akhmeteli pleaded with his tormentors to preserve his life but the death sentence was carried out on the following day.

Another victim was Petré Otskheli, a young but already well-known artist and theatre designer, who did *Othello* for Marjanisvili's production. Being under the strict surveillance of Beria people in Georgia, he had to move to Moscow where another Georgian, Sergó Amaghlobeli, director of the Moscow Maly Theatre, took care of the young crippled fellow countryman. (Incidentally, Amaghlobeli tried to play a kind of mediator's role, though unsuccessfully, between Stanislavsky and Craig when the latter came to Moscow for the second time.) But soon both, Petré Otskheli and Sergo Amaghlobeli, were arrested. Later, Petré's father wrote to Stalin, asking him to help find out the whereabouts of his sick son. He received a reply from the KGB to the effect that Otskheli was exiled for ten years. Another cynical and sinister move on the part of Stalin and his KGB: Petré Otskheli, as we know now, had been executed four years earlier on 2 December 1937. Sergó Amaghlobeli was executed a year later . . .

And then – Vakhtang Garrick, a director, writer, translator and author of an original book on theatre, largely dealing with Shakespeare. Vakhtang Garrick was the pen and stage name of Vakhtang Vachnadze (a well-known Georgian aristocratic name, incidentally, used by Brecht in his *Caucasian Chalk Circle*). During the five days of the arrest he seemed to have been so thoroughly worked up that he started admitting what was demanded from him. But he was obviously leading the investigation to a nonsensical finale. And when all seemed to be over and his interrogator was close to attaining his goal, the accused all of a sudden declared: 'Well, but all this was a pack of lies!'

However, the defendant had to keep the Shakespearian and Kafka implication to himself. After his successful productions of *The Taming of the Shrew* and *Romeo and Juliet*, this seemed to be just another Shakespearian scene of his own creation, a kind of Epiphany in the form of a tragic farce, performed for a single spectator of his theatre, and the only spectator was Vakhtang Garrick-Vachnadze himself . . .

On 11 September, at 2.40 p.m. the so-called 'Troika' ('tribunal') – chairman Matulevich, members Zarinov and Zhigur, secretary Katiushko – conferred for twenty minutes, stating that the defendant pleaded 'not guilty' and passed the death sentence which was carried out on the same day . . .

I myself was only ten years old then, but I remember very vividly how my parents – both dramatic actors – used to say that my uncle was an innocent victim or mentioned the disappearance from their theatre of the gifted young stage designer, adding in a whisper: 'The boy may repeat at school what we say at home.' And it struck my imagination as they mentioned a tragic circumstance which could be worthy of Shakespeare's pen. I wondered what on earth Mr Shakespeare had to do with all that, for in my imagination he was strictly connected with my Mum and Dad on the stage as Lady Capulet and the Prince of Verona.

I hope this part of my paper will be accepted as I intended it . . . in the light of my main message: Shakespeare always helped us when we saw him as part of world culture and even more so when my nation went through the tragic stage of its history. And this reminds me of the often cited words of Anthony Burgess: 'Shakespeare remains for the modern writer, as for modern literate man in general, a standard for judgment of morality as well as of art. And, more than in the past, he is seen also as a fellow human being and a fellow artist.'

And I do not know whether it is proper on my side to do so, but I would like, if I may, to dedicate my modest survey of Shakespeare's fate in Georgia to the memory of those martyred knights of Georgian Shakespeariana for whom Shakespeare truly was 'a standard for judgment of *Morality* as well as of art'.

SHAKESPEARE PERFORMANCES IN ENGLAND, 1993–1994

PETER HOLLAND

Shakespeare productions intersect with many histories. When the Duke tells Angelo, 'There is a kind of character in thy life / That to th'observer doth thy history / Fully unfold' (1.1.27–9), he is probably as wrong about Angelo as commentators tend to be about any theatre production. Thomas Postlewait's brilliant analysis of the difficulties and contradictions of writing theatre history, using as his example the first London production of Ibsen's *A Doll's House*,[1] is as applicable to the problems of writing about a production one has seen as to the problems of recovering information about a production one has not. Yet only parts of the history can be unfolded and parts of a production's engagement with some of the interlocking patterns of history can be much more fully set out than others.

Productions intersect with the stage-history of the play, with the history of the theatre company, with the individual histories of all those associated with the development of the project (actors, director, designers). They set out, with more or less clarity, their engagement with specific historical moments: the moment of the play's first production, the moment of their own production, and the moments of history to which a production may allude. Their historical connections may interconnect with their geography, their place in the theatrical map as well as the places in which play and production are set: *Measure for Measure*'s Vienna means different things at different times and a production in Stratford-upon-Avon means something different from a production in Stevenage.

In reviewing productions, I feel different degrees of confidence that I can both define and communicate the historical patterning that a production seeks to define or engage with. In some cases, the production will make abundantly clear its relationship to particular histories. In many cases, my own perception of the histories involved seems an attempt to uncover a process of which those involved in the production seem less apparently aware. In all cases, the presentation of some of those histories, whether set out by production or reviewer, will occlude the presentation of links to others. Writing a survey like this one is only a partial view; a complete history is always a mirage. Let me set out the materials for this year's history: I shall be considering fourteen productions, seven by the Royal Shakespeare Company, two by Northern Broadsides and one each by the Royal National Theatre, Cheek by Jowl, Talawa, English Touring Theatre and Birmingham Old Rep Theatre.

HISTORY AND TRADITIONS

Richard Dreyfuss's production of *Hamlet* for the Birmingham Old Rep Theatre offered the spectators two criss-crossing perceptions of

---

[1] Thomas Postlewait, 'Historiography and the Theatrical Event: A Primer with Twelve Cruxes', *Theatre Journal*, 43 (1991): 157–78.

history. The attempt to locate the play at a precise historical moment had the surprising consequence of locating the production at an equally precise historical moment. Dreyfuss's vision of the play's world as a barbaric, violent society straight out of sagas, as if nothing much had happened to the fable in its transition from Saxo Grammaticus to Shakespeare, was fired by his commendable belief in the virtues of story-telling and by his bizarre belief that tenth-century Denmark was a culture that, as he was fond of saying in interview, was 'pre-fork and pre-Christian', the former as true as the latter false. The resultant design by Alice Purcell was full of wassailing, drinking horns and serving wenches, rough-woven tunics and anglo-saxon necklaces. The resultant performance style seemed to be strenuously eschewing anything that might remotely suggest poetry, imagination or complication.

A cynical response – and the reviewers competed with each other for the most acerbic mockery – might see this as an attempt to turn *Hamlet* into some version of Hollywood epic, Dreyfuss inappropriately importing his own experience as a film star. But the effect was rather more strongly to reveal the connections between film and nineteenth-century theatre. George Bernard Shaw, reviewing a production of *Hamlet* in 1897, began wryly:

The Forbes Robertson Hamlet at the Lyceum is, very unexpectedly at that address, really not at all unlike Shakespear's [sic] play of the same name. I am quite certain I saw Reynaldo in it for a moment; and possibly I may have seen Voltimand and Cornelius; but just as the time for their scene arrived, my eye fell on the word 'Fortinbras' in the programme, which so amazed me that I hardly know what I saw for the next ten minutes.[2]

At the Old Rep there was no sign of Voltimand or Cornelius. The Reynaldo scene was present but the character renamed Osric, at the expense of the metre. I should have guessed what the end would be like after Fortinbras was missing in Act 4: the play ended, as it nearly always did in nineteenth-century productions, immediately

after 'flights of angels sing thee to thy rest' (5.2.313) as the stage darkened leaving a spotlight picking out Hamlet cradled in Horatio's arms. Film is a medium that cannot tolerate much spoken language.

But, if the text seemed brutally cut in a style appropriate both to film and to performances before Forbes Robertson's, Dreyfuss's production eliminated the lure of the heroic poetic delivery that productions of the type Shaw usually saw indulged in. Instead the play rattled by, even the soliloquies passing lazily and choppily, with emotional disturbance defined only by Russell Boulter's insistence, as Hamlet, in cutting lines up with pauses that registered neither syntax nor metre. Yet, as the music swelled up under the speeches (for instance at 'within a month' in Hamlet's first soliloquy or at 'What a piece of work is man!' in 2.2), it suggested both the prevalence of film-music, literally to underscore emotion, and the source of such pervasive accompaniment in the incidental music of nineteenth-century theatre.

Only with the Ghost did another voice enter the play. On stage an actor clad in visor and armour postured and emoted while lip-synching to a tape (Dreyfuss's film experience came in useful here). The tape itself carried the sound of Steven Berkoff playing with each word in a way that transferred the sufferings of Purgatory from the experience of Hamlet's father to that of the audience: his grotesquely elongated vowels and throat-destroying hoarse and guttural tones suggested camp extravagance far more than the ghost's pain.

No nineteenth-century actor would have tolerated the ineptitude of Dreyfuss's staging, for instance in the placing of Hamlet's near-rape of Ophelia in the nunnery scene on top of a gallery which left the action inordinately far from the audience and left Claudius and Polonius, standing under the gallery, twisting their necks to try to see what was happening. This

---

[2] George Bernard Shaw, *Our Theatre in the Nineties*, 3 vols. (London: Constable, 1932), 3.200.

11   *Hamlet*, 3.1, Birmingham Old Rep Theatre, 1994: Hamlet (Russell Boulter) and Ophelia (Daniele Lydon)

was doubly unfortunate since it was only the actors playing these roles – George Irving (Claudius) and Bernard Kay (Polonius) – who emerged from the general debacle with any credit.

Irving sketched a Claudius of surprising gentleness and intelligence, the latter particularly surprising in this vision of Elsinore. Comforting Hamlet in 1.2 by sitting beside him with an avuncular arm around him, Irving suggested no threatening villain but an efficient and rather decent ruler, tenderly in love with Gertrude and trying to be a good step-father. Even in private in 3.3, this Claudius' agony over the murder was that of a good man who had taken an appalling step out of a combination of

political necessity, fundamental decency and a need to resist an oppressive brother. The effect was intriguing, though nothing else in the production worked to support or justify the interpretation.

Kay's Polonius displayed the brutal authority more usually associated with Claudius. In 2.1 he had certainly not lost his way in giving instructions to Osric (Reynaldo) but held a knife to the poor man's throat as he checked that his orders were being attentively heard. Most strikingly, his difficulty in getting to the point in explaining the cause of Hamlet's madness in 2.2 was the product of his terror at explaining his own responsibility. Prostrate on the floor, Polonius had cautiously and apologetically to admit that the problem of the heir's insanity was a direct result of his orders to Ophelia to 'lock herself from his resort' (144). That she 'took the fruits of my advice' was a statement spoken with breast-beating self-accusation. Again, a different production could have made good use of such original playing. Instead, Kay's hard work stood out as an ill-fitting aberration when surrounded by so much stock, thoughtless and perfunctory acting. Only Daniele Lydon's Ophelia, self-mutilating in her madness in imitation of Hamlet, offered something powerfully imagined, if conventional.

Trapped in a time-warp, Dreyfuss's directing début seemed not to know that anything had happened to our perceptions of *Hamlet* in the last century of productions. Most revealingly, his quite reasonable anxiety about the reactions of hardened Shakespearians led him to wish for an audience of fourteen-year-olds while denying them any way of perceiving that Hamlet is not Rambo. Birmingham Old Rep is a theatre with its own rich history, even if the traditions of Barry Jackson's company have moved to a new theatre. Jackson would never have tolerated such an insensitive exploration of the play. *Hamlet* thus trivialized became a play hardly worth putting on, the production a historical curiosity which registered the huge gulf in Dreyfuss's skills as actor and director and the equally vast abyss between film and theatre.

Dreyfuss's own reputation ensured that the production was much hyped, the press full of ghoulish anticipation. Work like Stephen Unwin's *As You Like It* often barely raises an entry in the arts listings in newspapers. Unwin has worked hard to raise the profile of his company since he took over as Artistic Director of Century Theatre and renamed it more grandly as English Touring Theatre. Its commitment to touring classical theatre is impressive and it deserves every support for its willingness to bring professional Shakespeare productions to Barnstaple and Darlington, Crewe and Worthing. I only wish my admira-

tion for the company's principles could extend to this production.

Unwin's programme note promised much, for it would indeed be 'revealing to look at Shakespeare's comedy of unrequited love from a sociological, even agricultural perspective'. As Unwin recognized, the play touches 'on many of the great changes in the Elizabethan countryside'. But the possibilities of an approach strikingly aware of the play's own consideration of its historical moment that the programme explored seemed to have been an anticipation that never reached production and the programme's other suggestions, with provocative material on gender relationships, cross-dressing and Ted Hughes' theories of Shakespearian myth, were equally ideas not followed through to the stage. By comparison with Cheek by Jowl's brilliant production of the play, revived and on tour at the same time, English Touring Theatre's production seemed tame and conventional, as if the pressures of traditional Shakespeare production had proved too great for the excitement and experiment that the programme suggested. Even Kelly Hunter, an actor of imaginative power and exhilarating risk, turned in a Rosalind of tame predictability, avoiding the dangers the role offers.

Seen on a Saturday in Stevenage, this *As You Like It* seemed locked in a different historical time-warp, far less extreme than Dreyfuss's *Hamlet* but still a disappointingly long way either from the engagement with Elizabethan society or from an immediacy of production style and significance which Unwin's thinking about the play might have generated. The stage platform of a high-tech floor illuminated from below and the characters in their rich renaissance costumes were at odds, the former suggesting a modernity and starkness that the actors did not investigate. The set itself capitulated to tradition when, with the move to Arden, the rear doors parted to reveal a realist treescape counterpointed by an equally stagey moon and stars, or when Duke Senior's picnic was laid with extraordinary elaboration,

12 *King Lear*, 4.5, Talawa Theatre Company at the Cochrane Theatre: Gloucester (David Fielder) and Lear (Ben Thomas)

requiring masses of brocade cushions and a wide variety of foodstuffs, topped off with a sizzling stewpot. Such aristocratic playing at pastoral undercut any statement about the harsh life of exile and it might well have contrasted interestingly with a harsher reality for the workers in the woods, had not the traditional acting-style for Shakespearian rustics taken over. Even when the consequences of stag-hunting were played out, in 4.2, as the lords scraped hides and shaved horns, up to their elbows in blood, the effect was too performed, never taking on the force of reality.

Elsewhere there were sudden and jarring shifts of pace that were simply ineffective: Oliver's narrative of Orlando's finding him asleep (4.3.99–121) was taken with a slowness that seemed portentous, more emphatic than anything that had preceded it but without carrying its implications through the rest of the play. Odd moments suggested a more thoughtful production – like Jaques tenderly feeding and caring for Adam in 2.7 as if he were the troubling embodiment of the seventh age Jaques had just described – but they were too glaringly isolated. Overall, the production spoke eloquently of a tradition of easy, un-threatening Shakespeare in which the achieve-ment of the play's ending had far too few obstacles to overcome. Touring Shakespeare is a demanding proposition but the production must validate those demands, proving in some measure why the play matters; otherwise the performance risks being a trivial gesture to an establishment culture, as this *As You Like It* for the most part was, failing to make the intervention in the understanding of history that it aimed at.

The kind of intervention a production does make may have little to do with the play. Instead the theatre company may be making a statement about itself, seeking to rewrite a particular form of theatre history. That was certainly the case with Talawa Theatre Company's production of *King Lear*. Talawa is a black theatre company, the only British black company to have its own theatre, the Cochrane Theatre in London. Their *King Lear*, directed by the company's artistic director, Yvonne Brewster, starred Ben Thomas as Lear. All the publicity took as its keynote the statement that figured so substantially in the company's own press release: that Thomas was the first black actor to play Lear in a professional production in England for 135 years, since a performance by Ira Aldridge.[3]

There is of course no reason at all why a black actor should not play Lear, no reason why black actors should be restricted in playing Shakespeare to Othello, Morocco in *The Merchant of Venice* and Aaron the Moor in *Titus Andronicus*. Companies like the RSC now regularly include black actors and are developing the practice of what is known in America as 'non-traditional casting' and in England, more punningly, as 'colour-blind casting'. We have grown used to seeing siblings of different colour so that Cheek by Jowl's *Measure for Measure* (which I review below) had a black Claudio and a white Isabella, a step beyond Nicholas Hytner's production for the RSC when both Isabella and her brother were black. My own experience is that I have stopped worrying about the parents in such cases; I observe the performances without trying to view colour as realist, without wondering whether the Cheek by Jowl pair indeed have the same parents. The actor's skin colour becomes unimportant. The development of such equal opportunity casting has been gradual and largely successful. Alongside the ethnicity of Thomas, the publicity for Talawa's *King Lear*

also emphasized the broad multi-racialism of the company: 'never before has a *King Lear* been performed by such a culturally varied cast in Britain', including white, black, and Asian actors.

The production achieved one part of its clear aim: to be taken as a production of *Lear* to be judged like any other, a presentable example of the work of a company whose strength has been in the performance of new work and who now declared their interest in a major classical text. But precisely in the measure that the company achieved that aim they obscured any reason to foreground the ethnic identity of the leading actor or the multi-racial company. The company's own publicity emphasis was effectively denied by the conventional classicism of the physical movement of the cast and the Received Pronunciation of most of the voices (except David Webber's Kent when disguised as Caius and the occasional piece of rap from Mona Hammond's Fool or when Lear and Edgar shared 'Child Roland'). While the aim of the production was a deliberate intervention in the history of black actors in Britain, the success of the production was that it denied the force of that publicity, making it appear unnecessary special pleading, a suggestion of something more substantially different from what the company actually offered. One reviewer complained that, apart from the electronic music that the composer Matthew Rooke described as 'the pulse of Africa', 'there is little else directly African in this production'[4] but that was to miss the point.

The style of Talawa's *King Lear* fell in the category of 'traditional experimental', played on Ellen Cairns's set of hanging red ropes, a neon and plastic throne and a suspended white plastic sheet together with its electronic sound-score to convey 'the rhythm in this future world' (Rooke). The court costumes suggested

---

[3] On the history of black actors playing Shakespeare see Errol Hill, *Shakespeare in Sable* (Amherst, 1994).

[4] Mark Ford in *TLS*, 1 April 1994, p. 18.

North Africa while Kent as Caius became a guerilla fighter in bandanna and Fool's face was half-whited, half-gilded, a cross between clown and oriental statue. Some of the cast were simply not up to the demands of the language, particularly Thomas himself whose huge strong voice became increasingly irritating in its monotonous volume. There were odd flashes of imaginative originality in Brewster's production to set beside the generally lucid performances: David Harewood's strong and charismatically sexy Edmund was touchingly thrilled by Cornwall's praise (2.1.115–16) and moved to stand beside his father, arm casually resting on Gloucester's shoulder; as Gloucester carefully removed the hand, the action caught both Edmund's need for praise that Cornwall had momentarily fulfilled and the father's continual rejection of the illegitimate child. But again and again an idea was not followed through into a more substantial argument about the play. Nonetheless, the end was moving and powerful: Lear entered carrying Cordelia with her head cradled against his shoulder, leaving ambiguous whether she might be alive; as he announced 'She's gone for ever' (5.3.234), her head fell back unequivocally. Lear himself died smilingly, his body carried out by Kent and Edgar as the other dead (Regan, Goneril, Edmund, Oswald, Gloucester) appeared with their backs to the audience, marking the play's body-count. At such moments the production could be easily admired for its straightforward emotional affect, the force of the play empowering the performance in a way that the politics of colour had not.

AN ALTERNATIVE HISTORY

It might appear by this point that I intend only to complain and carp about the forms of engagement with history that a production offers. But the work of Northern Broadsides continued to suggest a different and far more successful engagement with the historical struc-

tures of Shakespeare production than English Touring Theatre and Talawa managed to present. The company's commitment to freeing their actors' voices, allowing them to use their full vocal range by not constricting them to RSC-style, is combined with a freedom to be responsive to the nature of Shakespeare's language, vigorously and energetically pursued. As their publicity proudly proclaims, OED defines a broadside as 'powerful verbal attack' and their approach to speech showed the definition has been taken to heart. Where Talawa's actors were confined by a notion of orthodox Shakespearian acting, Northern Broadsides' casts tackle plays with a relish and a pleasure that communicates to the audience with great immediacy. Confirmed (perhaps unfairly) in their belief that the national companies would never cast them in the kind of roles they can play for Northern Broadsides, the actors seize their chance. The heterodoxy of voice is also perceived by the company as a heterodoxy of style: not only the 'poor theatre' of minimal sets and simple costuming but also seeking to communicate the text, refusing to cover the play with the production. As an alternative to the perceived traditions, the company seems successfully to be maintaining its impact and its quality of work.

Northern Broadsides toured two productions: *The Merry Wives* in the autumn of 1993 and *A Midsummer Night's Dream* in the autumn of 1994. When the former arrived in London for a season at the Lyric Theatre, Hammersmith, the production sat oddly in the plush surroundings of the theatre but seen in a more appropriate venue it had all the élan and determination the company aimed at. There was no mention of Windsor. The 'wise woman of Brentford' had moved north to 'Bradford' and the cast had accompanied her. The play lost its connection with the court and castle, its sense of a noble world present in the same town and of London being only twenty miles away. It did not lose anything of the sense of a town community, a bourgeois world in which the

13   *The Merry Wives*, Northern Broadsides, 1993: Mistress Page (Polly Hemingway) and Mistress Ford (Elizabeth Estensen)

characters live. Dressed in modern costumes, the characters were placed with great exactness in their society: Conrad Nelson's Host, with shirt-collar up and buttons undone to reveal his gold chains, clearly ran Karaoke nights at the Garter and saw himself as a pop star manqué, Ishia Bennison's Mistress Quickly, in apron and with a duster always at the ready, earned her living as a cleaner and had ambitions to retire as a Blackpool landlady, Edward Peel's Ford, when metamorphosed into Brook, donned sandals, sleeveless sweater and flat cap, the archetypal put-upon husband of the seaside postcard. Even the 'foreigners' were precise manifestations: Lawrence Evans's Caius patriotic in his red, white and blue clothes with long shorts and knee-length socks with tricolour garter tabs, his catch-phrase 'By Gar' turning by the end of the play into a good Northern 'Bugger' (pronounced 'Booger'); David Crellin's Pistol a smooth customer in Italian shiny trousers and white socks. Most powerfully of all, Barrie Rutter's Falstaff, a tough figure in blazer and grey trousers, sported a variety of awful ties, ending up with an MCC tie to which he obviously had no right whatsoever.

Falstaff's aim here was purely financial. With boundless self-confidence he could assume the wives would fall for him. While he was happy to take the 'entertainment' (1.2.39) Mrs Ford offered, his motive was her 'rule of her husband's purse' (47–8) and his eyes grew as big as saucers at the sight of Ford's 'bag of money' (2.2.167), a silver suitcase full of neatly arranged bundles of notes, straight out of any gangster film. If later, disappointed at the failure of his amorous adventures, he became an overblown child, able to be pulled around by the women as a great soft baby and grinning sheepishly from ear to ear whenever either wife tickled his belly, the venom returned at the end when he seized on the failure of Mrs Page's plot for the marriage of her daughter, relishing seeing the biter bit as he directed 'I am glad . . . that your arrow hath glanced' (5.5.226–7) very sharply at her. Falstaff's relish of money took on distinctly

regional overtones, a man brought up in the belief that 'where there's muck there's brass'. This was no Londoner out of his depth but a Northern schemer with a firm conviction that there is such a thing as a free lunch.

But Rutter also played the comedy, using his size to fine effect, especially as he nearly crippled Mrs Ford by leaning on her knee to help get over a bench or when he attempted to get into a buck-basket that seemed impossibly small to contain such a bulk, and finally, unable to climb in, having to fall backwards into it with Mrs Page then jumping on top of him to squash him down. In these scenes he was aided and abetted by Elizabeth Estensen's Mrs Ford and Polly Hemingway's superb Mrs Page, in a purple suit with a tight skirt that always suggested a woman ready to burst out of her clothes. In the letter scene (2.1), this Mrs Page was amused but also genuinely intrigued by Falstaff's offer, only sure she would reject it when Mrs Ford's copy appeared. As sure of herself as Falstaff of his own abilities, Mrs Page's delight in the trickery was infectious, not least in her control of her diminutive husband. She was quickly reconciled to her final defeat, a supreme pragmatist enjoying her life.

Throughout, the production played the narrative with clarity, even managing to show what was happening in the revenge of Caius and Sir Hugh on the Host where the text is unhelpful and incomplete. Even the catechism of young William Page (4.1) worked, especially when I saw the production in Bangalore, India. As the legacy of colonialism ensures that Latin continues to be taught in all English-language schools attended by middle-class Indians, the scene could, for the first time in my experience, be properly laughed at for Mrs Quickly's mistakings. Even – or, perhaps, especially – in a production where Herne's Oak was a ladder and Falstaff's horns bicycle handlebars mounted on a colander, the production's energies were all generated by the company's pleasure in the text.

The same held true for Northern Broadsides'

14 *A Midsummer Night's Dream*, 4.1, Northern Broadsides, 1994: Titania (Ishia Bennison) and Oberon (Barrie Rutter)

A Midsummer Night's Dream. Rutter, as Theseus and Oberon, in particular, demonstrated a flexible and delicate response to the verse, allowing the rhythms of the lines to underscore meaning throughout with an attentiveness to the variation in the metrics of blank verse that was an object lesson. This *Dream* was especially full of doubles and mirrorings: not only the doubling in the casting (Theseus/Oberon, Hippolyta/Titania, Egeus/Quince, Robin/Philostrate), an approach that is by now almost a commonplace, but also the less common doubling of workers and fairies, a piece of theatrical thrift that was recommended for small-cast productions as early as 1661.[5] But Rutter's production also explored mirrorings of moves so that Hermia's running leap high in the air into Lysander's arms in 1.1 as they contemplated flight metamorphosed into the same move at the height of the confusions in the wood when he rejected her with 'Get you gone' (3.2.329) or

when the blocking for the workers' horror at Bottom's transformation into an ass was repeated and echoed in their joy at his return in 4.2.

It was also a world of music: Titania's lullaby became a big choral number with the other members of the cast, in costumes that had nothing to do with the world of the wood, reappearing to join in. Many of the actors displayed their talents as musicians when needed. But music and song were often the accompaniments to striking dance. Northern Broadsides' *Richard III* had used traditions of clog-dancing; in *A Midsummer Night's Dream*, the sources were more eclectic, including a dance of amity for Oberon and Titania to the

---

[5] In *The Merry Conceited Humours of Bottom the Weaver* (1661) the cast-list recommends that Snout, Snug and Starveling 'likewise may present three Fairies' (sig. [A]2ᵛ).

sound of gypsy music, suggesting the links between fairies and another race of travellers. Choreographed by T. C. Howard who also played an athletic dancing fairy, the performers danced and sang energetically and enchantingly, creating the music of the play. The dominant style in all of this was drawn from morris-dance with fairy king and queen wearing long coats covered in ribbons and the other fairies costumed in versions of male morris costumes, as if the production had deliberately misunderstood Titania's reference to 'the nine men's morris . . . filled up with mud' (2.1.98). Morris-dancing suggests a style of dance that is complex and formalized, an echo of the patterns and permutations which the characters go through in the course of the play. But it also, much more significantly for the production, recalls dancing as a genuine rural tradition, a major part of the history of popular music in England. This was not a nod to some weak version of Merrie England; instead the dance tradition offered a dignified resonance of a working-class form that commanded respect as well as nostalgia. It also allowed Andrew Cryer's Robin to carry echoes of the jester/fool of morris dancing into the cocky wide-boy conspiratorially engaging the audience in his perspective on the play.

From its first moments, Rutter's *Dream* showed deep affection for the play's depiction of a proletarian world more authentic, more in touch with truth than anything in the society of the play's aristocrats. The performance's prologue showed the Athenian workers hard at work but their tinkering and tailoring, weaving and carpentry turned into a combined and harmonious rhythmic tapping. Throughout, the workers were funny but never ridiculed. Their first scene (1.2) began, as in Peter Brook's famous production, with the sound of a factory siren (here a sound made by Roy North's Quince), so that the casting took place in a tea-break. In their overalls and their enthusiasm, these workers enjoyed the prospect of their amateur dramatics and we shared their

pleasure, without ever patronizing them. Each of them found new riches in the play's comedy: Flute rehearsing Thisbe with tea-towel round head and table-cloth round waist, Snug plainly terrified at the prospect of the long speech of explanation Bottom was composing for the Lion.

They were led by John Branwell as Bottom, a man of boundless confidence and down-to-earth good sense, clearly the star of the local working men's club where he spent most evenings. Abandoned by his friends, wearing an ass's head magically created by Robin by turning inside-out the cushion on which the sleeping Titania had rested her head, Bottom sang 'The ousel cock' (3.1.118–26) to the tune of 'On Ilkley Moor'. Titania was far from amused at being woken – 'What angel' (3.1.122) was snarled in annoyance, for Oberon's drug does not work on her hearing but her sight. Exiting with the fairies at the end of the scene, seated on the hospital trolley that was Titania's bower, his legs swinging, Bottom looked totally bemused, out of his depth, but also a man perfectly willing to try anything once and able to get used to the life of luxury with attendant servants that seemed to be on offer.

Precisely because these earnest workers had never been mocked by the production, their own play could modulate quickly and effectively from comedy to something unexpectedly moving, as, for instance, Thisbe's summoning of the 'sisters three' drew the three women on stage (Hippolyta, Hermia and Helena) tenderly towards him/her, finding their own sympathetic echoes in Thisbe's plight. Yet there was space for a fine wild bergamask.

Beside the energies of the music and the honest treatment of the workers, the lovers paled rather, not helped by their bland costumes of interchangeable clothes. But Rutter's minimalist approach to production was well accomplished by Jessica Worrall's set in which the transition to the wood was achieved by unrolling a long ribbon of green carpet and the return to Athens was defined by the workers, entering for 4.2, rolling the carpet back up again.

STRATFORD HISTORIES

If Rutter's production carried a few distant echoes of Brook's in 1970, the moment of the play's recent theatre history against which all productions now seem to be measured, that production is bound to be present with particular intensity for the RSC. All productions of the play in Stratford since Brook's have negotiated with it by defining their distance from it, defiantly taking very different approaches from the abstractions of Sally Jacobs's set, for instance. Adrian Noble's production this year chose instead with great boldness to confront Brook head on, allowing for the echoes of discoveries Brook had made or effects Brook's actors had brilliantly accomplished but choosing its own path to define a view of the play strongly placed adjacent to Brook's territory.

Certainly, from the first sight of the set, I could not get Brook's production out of my mind. Part of the cause lay in Anthony Ward's design. It was not so much the red room, strong central doorway and swing for the first scene – though they did of course seem like a dream-echo, a transformation and rethinking of Sally Jacobs's white box and trapezes for Brook. The echo was much stronger in the costuming, particularly of the lovers, where the strong colours and the indistinguishability of Lysander and Demetrius, differentiated only by a blue or green shirt over their white trousers, were extraordinarily like the earlier production.

But the resonance of Brook's *Dream* was much more crucially apparent in a number of other ways. First was the energy and athleticism of the lovers. As they careered over a bare stage, banging in and out of the line of doors at the back of the stage that appeared for the wood scenes or the two doors that could rise out of the floor unattached to any walls, their frenetic speed turned them into the puppets of farce, driven by the simplicity, the unidirectionality of the desire they happened to be feeling at any particular moment. It was both absolutely right and extremely funny, particularly the men shuffling around at high speed on their knees or leaving for their duel so literally 'cheek by jowl' that it looked as if they were about to tango. The lovers are puppets of their emotions, unable to do more than live out their feelings. What Noble perceived was something of the women's pain within this process; Hayden Gwynne's superb Helena had begun as the woman doggedly determined to win Demetrius by being submissive; a woman who announces 'I am your spaniel' (2.1.203) positively wants to be told to 'Stay' (2.2.93). But in the middle of the chaos of the chases of Act 3 she could not help the tears coming.

The lovers became mechanical creatures in a farce which, like all good farces, depended on doorways. But dreams have doors too and the worlds of the play here meet. I was perfectly happy to see Theseus and Oberon, Hippolyta and Titania and even Philostrate and Robin doubled yet again, for all that I yearn for a production that will explore the difference between the roles rather than their possible connectedness by using six actors rather than three. But it need not follow from the doubling that the events of the night are therefore a dream dreamed by Theseus and Hippolyta. Theseus comments on Pyramus' death, played here by Bottom so movingly that Hippolyta cries at the sight, 'he might yet recover and prove an ass' (5.1.305–6) and the last word triggers all the associations, all the echoes that riddle the play. But Alex Jennings's Theseus offered the line as a very deliberate nudge to Hippolyta, as if to say 'this is the man who was the ass in your dream' and Stella Gonet's Hippolyta later offered Bottom her hand at a moment of mutual recognition and shared memory of dream, suggesting that for them too, like the lovers, the convergence of dream, 'their minds transfigured so together' (5.1.24), is a happy

15   *A Midsummer Night's Dream*, 3.2, RSC, 1994: 'Two lovely berries moulded on one stem': Hermia (Emma Fielding) and
Helena (Hayden Gwynne)

memory. Theseus had to put himself rather
rapidly between them, for fear that the balance
of his marriage might prove fragile. Connecting
the world of the forest and the world of the
court in this way seems to me to diminish the
real power of the play, the presentation of
multiple mirroring worlds, the play's glorious
awareness of the parallel, usually unseen world
of the fairies.

Like Brook, Noble's *Dream* had a superb cast
and, like Rutter, that most unfashionable of
achievements, a real relish of the play's verse.
Memories of verse-speaking tend to be golden.
I remember well how Alan Howard, particularly early in the run of Brook's production, made the play's poetry sing. Alex
Jennings was, if possible, even finer. From the
first line, he allowed the language all its musica-
lity. He was given a good run for his money by
Stella Gonet, initially content, eyes closed in

sensuous anticipation of her approaching
wedding-night but, like Ishia Bennison for
Northern Broadsides, made furious by the
treatment of Hermia, storming off stage at
1.1.122 to leave Theseus following her rather
awkwardly. But Jennings maintained a command in his approach to the language that
echoed the command of his presence. For as
Theseus and Oberon he had an authority that
was both commanding and troubled.

Oberon seemed, in this production, oddly
isolated; the troops of fairies all belonged to
Titania. Only Barry Lynch's sexy little Robin
seemed to accompany Oberon, a wicked imp
who pulled down his trousers to be scolded by
his master, revealing a bottom covered with
shaggy hair from which Oberon pulled out a
handful. Jennings's Oberon began with a malicious glee, laughing outright at the news that
the changeling boy's mother died in childbirth

and enjoying his participation in the lovers' quarrels by tripping up Demetrius or stopping him exiting. But he was also capable of stroking Helena's hair caringly and later the malice was tinged by melancholy. The sight of Titania and Bottom filled him not with triumph but with pain. It was not the pain of the cuckold, though there was no question in this production but that Titania and Bottom have sex: the sight of Bottom's bottom bouncing rhythmically up and down on top of Titania as the inverted, cushion-filled, giant pink umbrella that represented the bower rose at the interval told as much; so too did Bottom's sexual exhaustion on his reappearance in 4.1 while the fairies giggled and smirked at every possible double meaning (like 'weapons' and 'nuts' 4.1.11 and 35) as they played at horse-riding – or rather ass-riding – and used their switches to poke Bottom or to waggle suggestively between his legs. Oberon's pain was instead a lonely exclusion from their happiness, an isolation of a man whose revenges had exacted a harsh price even as he gloried in his power.

Bottom's happiness was simple and fulfilled as in the broad grin with which he contemplated the pink brolly as he left the wood. Desmond Barrit's performance was controlled and brilliant clowning. He needed to be reminded that all Robin does is give him an ass's head: in this case the ass's ears seemed to have exploded through his motor-cycle crash-helmet with a newly hairy chinstrap while his false teeth made him into an asinine Ken Dodd. Robin has not endowed him with an ass's penis and the mournful gaze down the front of his trousers at 'Methought I had' (4.1.206) was a silly vulgarity. But the immense confidence – and everything about Barrit is bound to be immense – with which he took control of his first scene modulated superbly into the gormless vulnerability of the transformed Bottom later, nervously singing to himself in a 'monstrous little voice' at Titania's appearance. Moving and funny – a rare combination – this Bottom returned from the wood with much of his

bumptiousness gone. Barrit did not dominate the scenes more than Bottom does and there was ample space for Daniel Evans' touching Flute, Philip Voss's Quince, grinning contentedly to himself as his leading actor delivered his version of Ercles' vein rarely, Robert Gillespie's dapper Starveling, delighted to be trying on his dress as Thisbe's mother at the rehearsal, and Kenn Sabberton's Snug who had cut out photos of lions from the papers to help him with his make-up.

Noble, like Rutter, had doubled workers and fairies but Noble's worker-fairies were costumed with parodic echoes of their other selves: the Snug fairy with a lion's mane, Flute wearing a version of the little brolly he had worn in his hat in 1.2 and so on. But as their fairy alter egos, the workers moved with a new lightness and airiness appropriate to their new status as spirits of another sort. If this suggested that the worker-fairies are projections of Bottom's dream-imagination, it made no sense for them to be present in 2.1, before Bottom has entered the world of this dream, an unnecessary confusion of the dream-structures Noble was developing.

Noble is not naturally a director of comedy; his comic invention for *A Midsummer Night's Dream* was too often made up of very old pieces of comic business. But overall his control and imagination were confident and assured, matched throughout by the playing of his cast and the wondrously inventive imagination of Ward's design, especially in his creation of a forest of dangling light-bulbs or when the lovers' sleep left them dangling in cocoons, awaiting the sound of the hunting horns to bring them out of their chrysalises into a new world.

It seemed to be raining a lot in Noble's Athens. Though the weather cleared up by the interval, the workers arrived for their first scene to the sound of pouring rain and Robin and the first fairy descended into the wood of pulsing light-bulbs sheltering under green umbrellas. The effect was to make this Greek wood take on overtones of England, that dankness which Angela Carter so brilliantly ascribes to the play.[6]

This suggestion of a geographical transposition was much more strikingly dominant in Ian Judge's production of *Twelfth Night*. This was Ian Judge's third Shakespeare production for the RSC and I have not liked any of them. Paul Taylor, writing in *The Independent*, described this *Twelfth Night* as 'tourist-friendly' but its attractions were clearly wider than that: the full range of the extraordinarily eclectic Stratford audiences showed great delight at the production and I feel a bit like Malvolio in standing out against it. Talking to his cast, Ian Judge announced, according to the programme, 'When I look through the hedges of New Place or sit in the gardens of Hall's Croft, I understand Illyria', echoing J. B. Priestley's comments in *Seeing Stratford* (1927), also quoted in the programme. If the play's costumes were conventionally Elizabethan, a precise location of the play's history, Stratford was brought in by the presence on the horizon of a row of half-timbered houses, to which a church was added before the entry of Olivia and the priest in 4.3. The locale and the costumes made of the play's events an episode in the history of the town where the audience was watching the production, Illyria made a part of an immediate history, rather than the romantic otherness more usually identified in *Twelfth Night*'s location.

The storm has certainly brought a fair number of tourists to Shakespeare's Illyria, if not quite as many as Stratford in the summer. But the dark and troubling world of Shakespeare's play is not as reassuring either as the view through the New Place hedges or as Ian Judge's production made of the play. Russell Jackson, in a fine review in the *TLS* (3 June 1994), summed it up perfectly: 'the darkness of the play is made wistful, the cruelty muted, and the gender confusions are amusing and wittily set out – but not so as to cause undue apprehension'. This *Twelfth Night* was trying very hard to be charming and as a result it seemed to

me unpleasantly ingratiating, ironing out most of the dangers and troubles of the play, its ambivalences and irresolvable difficulties in search of an easier, glib response. The pleasures of this play should be hard-won, worrying, uncertain.

When Malvolio arrives to complain about the late-night drinking-party, 'My masters, are you mad? Or what are you? Have you no wit, manners, nor honesty, but to gabble like tinkers at this time of night?' (2.3.83–5), we should have some sort of sense that Malvolio is right, that there is here 'no respect of place, persons, nor time' (88). Olivia's is a house of mourning, a fact Judge defined through a dumb-show mourning ritual before 1.3, conducted in rain, as Olivia grieved at her brother's tomb, though it was too comically dominated by the disjunction between the enormous figure of Desmond Barrit's Malvolio and his tiny umbrella which could barely keep him dry, let alone Olivia. Sir Toby's carnival is both attractive and ill-mannered, selfish in its rejection of Olivia's grief. The ambivalences of rank present in Malvolio's calling this crew 'my masters' must carry a charge. But the party in this production was so tame, its threats so muted, even its singing so tidily harmonized with the interventions of the theatre's musicians, that all attention at this moment focused on Malvolio's excesses.

Of course, with Desmond Barrit as Malvolio excess was the order of the day. For some strange reason, Malvolio turned out to be Welsh; if the suggestion was that his puritanism is like Welsh chapel morality, it did not square with the way he crossed himself at every mention of Jove (e.g. 2.5.171). I shall long remember his desperate attempt to manoeuvre his mouth into a smile, the muscles making the lips twitch uncontrollably until his hands push them into a semblance of a grimace, but I am

---

[6] Angela Carter, 'Overture and Incidental Music for *A Midsummer Night's Dream*', in *Black Venus* (1985), pp. 63–76.

16 *Twelfth Night*, 5.1, RSC, 1994: 'the whirligig of time brings in his revenges': Feste (Derek Griffiths) and Malvolio
(Desmond Barrit)

afraid I shall remember equally long the over-done gag of his tongue waggling lasciviously as he pounced on Olivia or the moment when Barrit changed that error in Malvolio's reverie so that 'play with my – ' (2.5.58) was no longer the character's automatic reaction of toying with his steward's chain, a mark of office Count Malvolio would no longer wear, but instead became a hand toying with his genitals. At this point Barrit picked on a member of the audience, cast a disapproving glance at her and pointed with his parasol towards the exit. But the dirty mind was Barrit's, not ours, the line coarsened for a cheap laugh. Malvolio is not Frankie Howerd and the humour of *Twelfth Night* has nothing to do with the rather different culture of the English seaside postcard.

The sheer nastiness of Malvolio's torments

was properly in place in the scene in the dark house, with its spotlight through the trapdoor picking out a man literally at his wits' end who screeched in the agony of his mind as the trap closed and he was left in darkness again. But the terrible sight of a man trying to gather the last remnants of his dignity at his final exit was cheaply lightened again when, throwing down his ruff and boots, he arranged the last few long strands of hair over his bald pate before leaving. The gags, funny though they were, were working against our attempts to respond sympathetically to a man so deeply unsympathetic.

Derek Griffiths's Feste was cynical enough, Bille Brown's Sir Andrew fatuous enough, Joanna McCallum's Maria resourceful enough but Feste's sharp awareness of the risk of unemployment and poverty, Sir Andrew's exploitation by Sir Toby, and Maria's rise through marriage went for nothing. Tony Britton sketched in a potentially fine Sir Toby but the production left no space for the detailing. The play's awkwardnesses were ignored in search of general and genial good humour. All was just too reassuring, even at the end in the sight of the strung-out line of rejects (Sir Toby, Sir Andrew, Antonio) trudging through a thunderstorm ('With hey, ho, the wind and the rain') down the Stratford street before Feste was unceremoniously thrown out of the front door. This ending was much more restrained than Judge's normal way with the end of Shakespearian comedy. The image may have clarified but it also made too comfortably explicit the play's deliberate gaps, the disturbing way that at the ending of this comedy so many characters have vanished.

In the same way, Viola's anguish at her brother's loss was smoothed over by the sight, immediately after her rescue in 1.2, of Antonio carrying Sebastian safe to shore. But for the most part the love-tangles were more effectively in place than the rest of the play. Emma Fielding's Viola moved from a full-throated romanticism in the storm-scene, played against billowing sea-cloths straight out of any nineteenth-century production, to a boyhood that was deliciously troubling in its ambivalence. She was both the most convincingly boyish Cesario I have seen and by far the most attractive, the sexual charge lying not in androgyny but in her male beauty. No wonder that Cesario's grief made Orsino kiss him at the end of 2.4, one of a series of perplexing kisses that confused the couples. Sebastian's easy kiss of Antonio as they parted was met by an open homoerotic response from Antonio. Hayden Gwynne's Olivia was disturbed by Cesario's lips, half-suspecting the real gender of her object of desire. This Olivia, so confident and sure of herself early on in her grey and gloomy house, was thrown completely off-balance by her desire, a woman who has never before felt anything remotely like this.

The great strength here lay in Clive Wood's Orsino, a performance whose complexity was not diminished by the production's over-frequent recourse to sentimental music swelling up at each scene's end. At first Wood's Orsino, swooning on cushions in his dressing-gown and pyjama bottoms, languorously self-indulgent in the romanticism of the music, seemed of a piece with the genial sentimentalism of the production but the abrupt transition of 'Enough, no more' placed the excess. This Orsino, whose puffed-up chauvinist sense of the largeness of masculine emotion ('There is no woman's sides / Can bide the beating of so strong a passion / As love doth give my heart', 2.4.92–4) matches his confidently displayed hairy chest, was reduced by his perplexity to a threat of violence, brandishing a dagger at Olivia before turning it on Cesario where it was met by a wide-eyed masochistic hunger for the dominance of his love, a driven appetite that pushed Viola's body down into an animalistic crouch through its force.

There was here a violent, rather frightening emotion, unusual in a production whose usual care and tact seem mirrored by Malvolio's carefully practised dance-steps in the letter scene. But such disruptive emotional power was rare in a production typified by the way that Viola's new costume for the second half turned out to be identical to Sebastian's new costume when the latter has, as far as I can tell from the plot, not had a chance to go back and change.

Where Judge diminished *Twelfth Night*, not least by turning it into a piece of local history, Matthew Warchus turned *Henry V* into a complex piece of national history. Warchus' production received only lukewarm reviews but, by the time I saw it, it had become a thoughtful and demanding piece of work. It gained substantially from Charles Edwards's extraordinary lighting design, by far the most intriguing exploration of the main house stage's potential for many years, setting spaces and shadows, creating closed arenas with lowered spots and using much side-lighting to produce startling changes in the perspectives on the actors.

Warchus investigated the play as a series of overlays of history. Its opening and closing image, with Henry's red regal gown with a gold collar placed on a dummy, roped off like an exhibit in the Imperial War Museum, established a sense of royal myth surrounded by tall red poppies, the strongest modern symbol of the cost of war. Tony Britton's Chorus was an old soldier, in his military camel-coloured overcoat and his campaign ribbons; the poppy in his button-hole and his rich theatrical voice summoned up past wars. With the house-lights still up he strode to an electrical box onstage, turned the handle and put out the house-lights, taking the audience from his contemporary perspective on the history of war into the play's own sense of its own history. The action inverted the effect of Jacobi's Chorus in Branagh's film who turns a switch to illuminate the film studio. But Britton's Chorus was also a man who stood as a reminder of what will happen to the myth of Agincourt, so that in the middle of the battle, at Henry's lowest ebb, he could come forward to help the King to his feet, reassuring him of the outcome that the Chorus, the military historian of the future, already knew.

Chorus's perspective, both a connection to all past war but also the distance from it defined by a survivor, was set against the frequent appearances of a crowd of English non-combatants, principally women and children, dressed in 1940s costumes, both visitors to the 'museum' and a reminder of the civil cost of war. This was a less successful ploy, as was the return of the poppies, planted on the field of Agincourt: they became too obvious a symbol of loss, calling up a clichéd image of Flanders. The fertility of Warchus' imagination needed restraining at such moments, the search for an appropriate theatrical device too glib, as in the sleight-of-hand at Agincourt that draped the corpses of the murdered boys over the corpses of the French prisoners, offering again a rather too easy equivalence. But I could hardly complain about the decision to follow Gary Taylor's suggestion[7] of having the prisoners killed on stage when it produced a reaction of protest and horror from Clive Wood's Pistol, a coward forced to kill and loathing it, nearly vomiting after the killing, an unwilling participant in the actuality of the war off which he has been freeloading.

Occasionally hit and miss in its effects, Warchus' *Henry V* was also not helped by the unevenness of the cast. At time the players were simply getting lost under the exhilarating scale of scenic effect that Neil Warmington had designed. Some certainly seized their chances. Monica Dolan as Katherine, for instance, showed just how interesting the wooing scene can be. She found its comedy: when Henry mentioned 'armour' (5.2.138) she touched her arm, remembering one of the words she has learnt in her English lesson. But she also registered blank incomprehension as Henry went on and on in English, blithely unaware, as he started to enjoy his own rhetoric, that it was all passing her by. Even more effective was her hint that she suspected that Henry's ability to understand French was greater than he was letting on and hence that she dared not speak to Alice at all. It made of the scene something dangerous as well, even as she copied his gesture, holding out a hand for him to shake, learning the body language of the conqueror. And the scene modulated uncomfortably as the English nobles, returning to the stage, giggled at the very male sexual innuendoes the King's conversation with Burgundy (so often cut) conjured up (5.2.279–316). Characteristically of the production, this advantage was followed by an immediate regret as the transfer of the Dauphin's lines to Bourbon, following the quarto text, meant that there was no point in keeping Henry's final triumph over the Dauphin at the end of the play as the French

---

[7] *Henry V*, ed. Gary Taylor (Oxford, 1984), pp. 32–4 and 4.6.37.1.

17   *Henry V*, 4.4, RSC, 1994: Pistol (Clive Wood), Monsieur le Fer (Sean O'Callaghan) and Boy (Daniel Evans)

King is forced to disinherit his son and nominate Henry as his heir (330–9).

There were many such moments of uncertain gain and loss. I have never heard the listing of the dead at Agincourt spoken with such a sense of mourning, when even Davey Gam Esquire was well known to the survivors and his death a reason for grief, or the long roll of the French dead mounting slowly as a litany of the obliteration of the French nobility. Yet that list should have been balanced by the French King's listing of some of the same people earlier in the play (3.5.40–6), a speech Warchus cut. The balance and connection was not in place, the local effect powerful but insufficiently resonant.

But the local effects were powerful, especially the use of the upstage area to suggest tableau visions of a heroic version of the narrative, images from a Boys' Own history-book, particularly the icon of the defeated English yielding under the hooves of the French cavalry, the vision of what the French anticipate from the impending battle, the last image before the interval. Earlier, as the invasion fleet embarked, Henry was incorporated into a heroic tableau of the spirit of adventure, a photo-pose waiting for the court painter to capture it for posterity, and then, as the pose was held through the narrative of Falstaff's death, Henry turned out of the static image, glancing back at his old companions, a group he would never forget (as when for instance he explained the reason for Bardolph's execution for theft to the Boy, 3.6.108–14), an effect beautifully counterpointed by the way that, in 4.7, Fluellen cannot remember Falstaff's name. The tension here between the heroic and the personal was strongly underlined.

Other effects were similarly well-judged: having a female Governor of Harfleur feminized the city and provided a direct response to the horrendous threat of rape and murder that Henry had offered, his language and her body in direct connection and opposition. At other moments the large stage effect was differently undercut, as when the dawn at Agincourt, with its fiercely rising spotlight of the sun capturing Orléans' 'The sun doth gild our armour' (4.2.1), tipped the stage floor to a steep rake, revealing that the rake carries the dates 1387–1422, the limits of Henry's life, so that the battle was fought across his tomb.

The battle was fought under a collection of bits of armour hanging down on chains, no longer the set of swords that dangled down for the aristocrats to choose from at the announcement of the expedition at the end of 1.2, now an eerie reminder of Williams's warning about the king's reckoning, 'when all those legs and arms and heads chopped off in a battle shall join together at the latter day' (4.1.134–6). There was at moments like this a remarkable combination of performance and commentary, the play existing with different levels of response at once. If achieving effects like that meant one had to put up with silly costumes at the French court, it was a fair exchange.

Iain Glen's was the finest stage Henry I have seen. We have had enough for now of theatrical, rhetorical Henries, shouting the big speeches to the upper balcony. This Henry, needing to encourage his troops before the battle, did so quietly, allowing the lines to make small local points, refusing to let a rising tide and rising volume overwhelm meaning. At the end of the speech he could isolate words in a line, letting the audience hear the point of 'with us' in the conclusion: 'whiles any speaks / That fought with us upon Saint Crispin's Day' (4.3.66–7).

The renaissance calendar was, of course, far more aware of Saints' Days than we are but Henry's definition of the battle's day as the 'Feast of Crispian' had never seemed so right before. Glen's Henry was a deeply religious man. Others may talk of the reformation of the wild Prince Harry but this King Henry was born-again in a rather modern sense. Canterbury's assessment in the first scene, 'Never was such a sudden scholar made; / Never came reformation in a flood / With such a heady currance scouring faults' (1.1.33–5) was entirely accurate. Henry naturally turned to his books to remind the others of the threat from the Scots or knelt to the Archbishop and kept with him throughout the rest of the play the crucifix his spiritual father had given him, sitting down to listen to the Archbishop as a willing pupil. Every time he mentioned God he spoke in genuine humility. The scenes the night before the battle did not here show Henry 'Walking from watch to watch, from tent to tent' (4.0.30) but instead a man who desperately wanted to find a quiet place to pray and kept on getting interrupted. As Henry says 'I and my bosom must debate awhile' (4.1.32) and the line was not a pretext to allow a little surreptitious wandering around in disguise. The scenes built towards the prayer itself and, later, the deeply-felt tones of the culmination of this sequence, the last line before the battle, 'And how thou pleasest, God, dispose the day' (4.3.133).

The Non Nobis that Henry calls for after the victory became a large-scale choral number, giving the request an importance entirely in character for a King who would hand over the cause of victory to God. Serious-minded, sincerely religious, this Henry took his share of the work of war, often seen shouldering a huge pack like his troops. He was part of a band of brothers and was respected for it. Glen is a highly charismatic actor but his effects have nothing to do with his good looks. Instead there was an acute actor's intelligence at work here, thinking through the lines and the role, making the production cohere in the man whose life he charts.

Warchus explored the overlays of history, the historicizing of Henry and the Agincourt campaign into a peculiarly national myth. Katie Mitchell's production of *Henry VI Part 3* for the RSC's tour was a far more rigorous re-creation of a sense of history, a single-minded investigation of the possibility of creating a past world of ritual and gesture. The productions shared an interest in the motifs of religion but what had been restricted to the king in Warchus' work

now became a general truth, a continual counterpoint to the play's action.

This was the first time that *Henry VI Part 3* had been performed on its own in Stratford, though it has regularly been seen, heavily abbreviated, as a part of productions of the first history cycle. Not surprisingly, the RSC decided against using its usual title for a touring production. Mitchell retitled the play *Henry VI: The Battle for the Throne*, summing up her identification of the play's action as an endless series of battles unfinished by the end, with Richard of Gloucester a malevolent presence clearly outlining his future plans. Mitchell trimmed the text, eliminating or combining characters to fit the limitations of a fifteen-strong touring company, but the cutting and pasting was neat and efficient. The result was a bleak and unremitting exploration of the viciousness of human behaviour, a tense and intense vision of political brutality.

Mitchell was concerned to place the aristocratic ambitions, the squabbling and side-changing, the political manoeuvrings in a play in which, in a sense far removed from its modern meaning, the personal is political, as power is sought by hungry individualists. The framing of the action was achieved by three devices. The first was typified by the weather. Heavy rain, snow-storms and bright, falling autumnal leaves and clear dawn-light, the full gamut of the English climate was heard or seen. The production's meteorology was supported by hints of an animal world, bird-song and sheep bleating, sounds that were both reassuring in their normality and disturbing in their transformations into the sounds of horses in pain during the battles. There was too a reminder of a natural world in the bark that covered the stage-floor, as in Mitchell's production of *A Woman Killed with Kindness*, and in a pine-tree on the side of the stage from which Margaret tore a branch to serve as the mocking crown she put on the Duke of York before killing him in 1.4. It was echoed too in the rough crosses of twigs tied together that

18   *Henry VI: The Battle for the Throne*, 1.1, RSC at The Other Place, 1994: Henry VI (Jonathan Firth) swears an oath with Richard, Duke of York (Stephen Simms)

accumulated along the sides of the stage as the production unfolded. Above all, it was present in the white and red roses, the symbols of a natural world abused for human ends and civil war. It was there most exquisitely, to the accompaniment of bird-song and a babbling brook, in the tuft of feathers Henry plucked from one of the wings that dangled on the belt of a gamekeeper and blew into the air: 'Look as I blow this feather from my face, / And as the air blows it to me again' (3.1.83–4). Suggesting continuity in a world beyond the political, the device belittled the high terms which the characters invoke.

Their actions were also placed by the pro-

duction's borrowings, from *Richard II* and from *Gorboduc*, of lines defining the horrific impact of war on the state, spoken most often by characters marginal to the action, warning ineffectually of the consequences of the others' course of action: Exeter, borrowing the Bishop of Carlisle's words from *Richard II*, warns at the end of the first scene 'Disorder, horror, fear and mutiny / Shall here inhabit, and this land be called / The field of Golgotha and dead men's skulls.' (*Richard II* 4.1.133–5). It is a language of apocalyptic political prophecy substantially missing from *3 Henry VI*, a perception of implication that the characters of the play mostly lack. Like the language of pastoral, it was generated for the production by the emblematic scene that was the still centre of the performance, Henry VI's meditations at the battle of Towton and the grief of the two anonymous figures who define in their acute pain the impact of war on family, the Son who has killed his father and the Father who has killed his son, a scene taken with great intensity and glorious relish of its symbolic power. Characteristically the two soldiers bring in no corpses, finding the identity of their dead instead, in two roses they unwrap.

The third frame was a religious one, again a device Mitchell had explored in *A Woman Killed with Kindness*, an acute sense of the immanence of religious practice in renaissance culture. The stage was dominated by a picture of St George, the patron saint invoked in the play, an image often left spotlit on a darkening stage. Beside the double metal doors through which the various armies crashed was a medieval wooden statue of a pietà, before which characters often knelt muttering prayers, while yet another step in the faction-making and breaking unfolded and ignored them, as, for instance, the half-naked servant praying during the scene in the French court (3.3). Above the stage hung an immense bell whose sound resonated endlessly, a church bell pressed into unholy uses as when it was rung to summon the Duke of York's troops to compel Henry to nominate him his heir in the first scene.

Throughout, the action was punctuated by liturgical chant and procession. Over the corpse of the two slaughtered young men, Rutland and Prince Edward, a woman keened a miserere before the dead figure rose to be led out by the hand through the audience. More elaborate choral kyries marked the murders of the two most significant adults, the Duke of York and King Henry himself, the singing led by a woman holding the bloodied napkin and mocking crown for the former and a feather and rosary for the latter, as the smell of incense filled the theatre.

This framing was not just a reminder of the central importance of religious ceremony in medieval and renaissance life. It contrasted with the savage use of religious gesture by the warring factions: in the first lines of the production, as Warwick made a vow (1.1.21–5), he knelt to confirm the oath; a parley between the Yorkists and Lancastrians was preceded by all kneeling and crossing themselves; under the rusty, well-used armour, the men wore rosaries, a very visible mockery when in 3.2 the three York brothers, a distinctly unholy trio, ridiculed the prostrate form of the mourning Lady Grey, supplicating with her arms out-stretched. In a play of repeated oath and prayer, in a world in which the forms of religion are a conventional recourse to underline and validate all action, the echoes of a genuine religion in turn underlined the political manipulation of the divine for entirely worldly ends. Only 'the good King Henry the Sixth' seemed removed from it.

Unrelieved by much colour, Rae Smith's design was the perfect accompaniment for Mitchell's rigorous and demanding direction, demanding of actors and audiences alike. The cast was that rarest of Stratford visitors, a group of actors almost all new to the RSC. If Tom Smith's fine Richard of Gloucester, shaven-headed and with his withered arm strapped to his body by belts, always biting his nails, made the most of his amazed self-discovery of his potential for evil, the logical outcome for this frustrated child in an adult's body, he had an easier task. But Jonathan Firth's Henry VI, a young man who has been king from nine months old, coughing and red-eyed after long imprisonment, showed brilliantly the terrifying irrelevance of contemplative goodness in the play's politics, supported by Chris Garner's stammering Exeter. It did not help Ruth Mitchell's Margaret to be continually reminding us that she is French so that she spoke of 'Henri' and 'Edouard', and the only real mistake in the production was the bizarre decision to put the first half of the scene at the French court into French, forgetting Gower's advice in *Pericles* that 'we commit no crime /

19   *Coriolanus*, 1.1, RSC at the Swan Theatre, 1994: Coriolanus (Toby Stephens) watches cascading corn

To use one language in each sev'ral clime / Where our scene seems to live' (18.5–7). But Margaret's hard-driven energy survived the awkwardnesses of accent.

Early Shakespearian verse is not easy to speak but the unusually slow pace gave the actors every opportunity to find the possibilities within the style. A production as slow and unrelieved in its intensity as this was not easy to watch but the action was set out with exemplary clarity, making the programme's careful provision of a family-tree unnecessary. *3 Henry VI* may have seemed an eccentric choice for Mitchell's first professional Shakespeare production but the outcome was a superb justification, another mark of the high aims with which the RSC approaches its touring.

Where Warchus had spread his view of the play across its after-life in history and Mitchell had defined the play as a historic moment, David Thacker's *Coriolanus* took a more familiar route, the choice of a particular historical moment as analogy. But if the route is hardly novel, the choice here was and the results provocative and coherently pursued. This *Coriolanus*, played in the Swan Theatre, pinpointed the moment of the play as the *ancien régime* teetering on the brink of the French Revolution. The choice was immensely suggestive: a world of popular uprising against oppression, a revolution that was overtaken by a dictatorship, a world of ideals betrayed, above all a moment of historical possibility, 'a republican Year Zero whose future is a blank sheet' (Irving Wardle, *The Independent on Sunday*). Coriolanus became, from this perspective, a potential Napoleon and I thought I saw Toby Stephens's hand occasionally straying towards his belly, hinting at an imitation of Napoleon's most clichéd gesture.

Like the French Revolution, the threat to the future of Rome came both from within and without. Hence the exploded brick wall at the back of the set was ambiguous: has it been shattered from inside or out? Was the revolution exploding outwards or the threat of invasion from the Volsces exploding inwards? But, more significantly, the whole of the history of the Revolution could be seen as a series of attempts to become Rome, from the hairstyles and furniture (both seen onstage in this production) to the imperial dream. *Coriolanus* is set in a Rome that is still only a small republic city-state, not yet an empire, a Rome that is, in effect, not yet Rome, not yet the potent symbol it will become, as France is not the Rome its leaders so often wish it to be.

There were of course some imprecisions in the analogy. As Thacker made clear at the opening, the potential for revolution in Rome is the result of starvation, not solely of political oppression. The striking opening image of corn cascading into an open trap on the stage, watched by Coriolanus in supremely arrogant pose, set the tone for the opening crowd scene, full of plebeians who really were starving, picking over grains that missed the chute, rocking and staring, twitching and drooling. It was a moment counterbalanced by one after Coriolanus' banishment when the grainstores were open and the plebeians could collect corn by the bowlful. The people's tribunes, especially Linal Haft's Sicinius, were genuinely concerned for their charges. Yet, as the tribunes basked in the adoration of the crowd, it was easy to see why, for all their good intentions, these middle-class leaders, tightly buttoned-up over their well-fed bodies, could so easily become potential Robespierres.

Yet, again, their actions seemed far prefer-

able to Philip Voss's Menenius, a smug patrician whose whole attitude was typified in a remarkable moment of actor's invention, a single gesture on his first entrance: as the plebeians held up hands palms upwards beseeching him for food or money, he turned their hands and shook them, offering the politician's genial expression of solidarity and friendship but no act to relieve their suffering. I saw no finer performance than Voss's Menenius anywhere this year, a performance of consistent intelligence and subtlety, a superlative investigation of the language of the role to construct both the politician and Coriolanus' substitute father. Even the tribunes had to respect Menenius' perceptiveness; it was his warning about starting a process that one cannot control that made them realize the necessity of giving Coriolanus a second chance, particularly in the First Senator's lines, spoken here by Menenius: 'The other course / Will prove too bloody, and the end of it / Unknown to the beginning' (3.1.329–31). It was there too in the hint of nervousness around the fable of the belly, the awareness that this totally fallacious parable was not really working. By the end of the play, the hollow emptiness of his response to his rejection by Coriolanus, 'I neither care for th' world nor your general' (5.2.102), was devastating in its despair as well as fully justifying the guard's awestruck response, 'A noble fellow, I warrant him' (108). 'Noble' was now much more than a definition of social class, a powerful transformation of Menenius' earlier comment on Coriolanus, 'His nature is too noble for the world' (3.1.254), a line which Voss played for its laugh.

There was a problem in the analogy too over the backing image of the play, an unfinished sketch of Delacroix's 'Liberty Leading the People', for Delacroix's image was a response to the failed revolution of 1830, not the 1790s. But the potency of the image lay not only in the symbolism of the revolution in arms. What was so striking in connection with the production was the symbolic power Delacroix accords a woman; Delacroix's Liberty became, as it were, the iconic expression of the control over the political world that Volumnia would have wished to have. For, in this male world, female power is necessarily vicarious, indirect: Volumnia cannot go to war except through her son. At the end of the play she becomes the saviour of Rome – indeed she is dubbed 'the life of Rome' (5.5.1) – but at the point of her individual triumph, at the point where she was the centre of political activity in her own right, she could only wear an appalled mask of grief, even while Virgilia and Valeria were enjoying their own part in the procession and the crowd's response.

Contemplating Cecily, Lady Bracknell advises her: 'the chin a little higher, dear. Style largely depends on the way the chin is worn. They are worn very high, just at present'. Caroline Blakiston's Volumnia had clearly heeded the advice. If her voice lacked range and detail, her power was seen in the angle of her chin as a woman prone to looking towards the heavens in ecstatic anticipation of her son's triumphant return to Rome. At the Herald's announcement in 2.1, she alone looked out towards the audience, again her head held high. The distance from that to her lying prone at her son's feet, imploring him to give way, charted the immense changes in their relationship. Crucial here, too, was the entry of the three women to that final encounter with Coriolanus, all three in white robes with blood-stained hems, echoing the blood-stained banners displaying the slogans of the revolution hung around the auditorium. The women have clearly walked through blood to this meeting. But strikingly, after the wide differences of their costumes earlier, they were now indistinguishable. Coriolanus recognized each one but the audience could not; even Volumnia's individuality had been submerged into her status as one of the women of Rome, Rome's last chance.

But this was also a woman who loves her son; her one moment of a loss of control came after Coriolanus left Rome, a wailing, wild animal who was as mad as the rumour Sicinius reports (4.2.11). Her attack on Virgilia's grief, 'Leave this faint puling and lament as I do' (55), was a hysterical scream at a woman whose puling had the dignity that Volumnia had for the first time in her life abandoned.

Volumnia's rival in this production was not Virgilia but Aufidius. Barry Lynch offered Stratford audiences one of the most improbable doubles imaginable: Aufidius and Robin. His Aufidius was a subtle representation of the warrior as politician, a man who, from our first encounter with him, was in total control of events in Volscian power politics. It was only right that he was, in the second half of the play, always accompanied by the two spies, Adrian and Nicanor. His love for Coriolanus was epitomized in the caressing and stroking of his rival's body in their embrace at his house, as Coriolanus stood with his arms stiffly around Aufidius, unsure how to react. Lynch picked up the tremendous homoerotic charge in Aufidius' language, the man who compares Coriolanus' arrival to his own wedding-night. Yet the achievement of that love, the transformation of military rivalry into co-leadership, is Aufidius' crucial political misjudgement, love clouding his acuity, leaving him vulnerable to Coriolanus' charisma. In the final image of the production, Thacker resisted the last stage direction, 'A dead march sounded. Exeunt bearing the dead body of Martius.' Instead Aufidius, having been the first to attack Coriolanus – driven to it by Coriolanus' reaching out to stroke the livid scar on Aufidius' face that he had once given him – having kicked the dead body and stood on it until a Volscian senator stopped him, now found that 'My rage is gone' (147), without a trace of the irony the line can bear. Trying to lift the corpse under the armpits, he called 'Assist' (154) but the others scurried off the stage and he toppled back with the dead body on top of him. His final gestures, like a beetle turned onto its back, were both an embrace and an attempt to extricate himself from under the oppressive weight of the corpse, an ambiguous moment of love and submission perfectly in keeping with the production.

Like his mother, Toby Stephens's Coriolanus looked the part. Like her, he suffered from a narrow range of voice, the nasal aristocratic whine of contempt occasionally slipping but in any case constricting the possibilities in the lines. This young buck, full of himself, captain of the first XV and first XI at school, leader of the Officer Training Corps, had barely scraped a couple of A levels after much private tutoring. A man for whom the taunt of 'boy' from Aufidius was a real threat for someone still unsure of his adulthood, comfortable only in his arrogant posing but reluctant to reveal a body that was not only scarred but also showed a physical vulnerability that this striking clothes-horse would rather have kept under wraps. At Aufidius' house, dirty, bare-foot and barechested, his hair now combed back rather than forwards in the high Roman fashion, Stephens's Coriolanus was unrecognizable – I, like Aufidius, needed him to name himself. Stephens had found the comedy of the role, bellowing 'Well, mildly be it, then' (3.2.146) for instance, but he had also found the garrulity of a man who cannot control his speech and finds himself whipped along by his own unmediated attitude towards language. If the whining tone became tedious it was because Coriolanus himself is tedious. Not a great performance, it sat comfortably in a production of clarity and imagination. *Coriolanus* is a frighteningly difficult balance to achieve; Thacker very nearly managed it.

HISTORICAL MEASURES

That the same play can define different relationships to history is obvious but *Measure for Measure* has come to occupy an especial position in its negotiations with contemporary society. The two major productions of the play last year, by Declan Donellan for Cheek by Jowl and by Stephen Pimlott for the RSC, plotted the play's frightening modernity in contrasting ways: Donellan in making the play immediate and contemporary, Pimlott in gesturing at the development of British society across history from the nineteenth century to the present. Where for Donellan *Measure* was a definition of the moral relativism of the modern state, Pimlott found in it a recapitulation of the male ethos that defines the history of the Establishment, that amorphous entity to which we tend to ascribe the problems of society. Both productions followed the logic of their position with rigour and power.

Cheek by Jowl played on a minimalist set by Nick Ormerod: a black desk and some stacking chairs with a single strip of red material, suspended upstage and off-centre, offering the merest suggestion of a state banner to be echoed at the end by the red carpet unrolled for the Duke's return to the city. Objects on stage could, in this context, take on different valencies: the desk at which Angelo worked and beside which he knelt in prayer before taking on his new role at the end of 1.1, could become much more precisely the altar at which Isabella prayed by her placing a cross on it at the start of 1.4. When in 2.4 Angelo came close to raping her on the desk, the place of assault carried with it both its meanings, both an assault in his office and a blasphemous act at her shrine of veneration.

There was in all this little to distract the eye from the actors but, in his treatment of the inter-relationship of scenes, Donellan made the actors into parts of the set. Again and again the first line of a scene would be pitched loudly across the final image of a previous one before the tableau broke, the furniture was rearranged and the next scene properly began. The technique gave first lines especial portentousness but also became a part of the simultaneity Donellan was exploring. Even more striking was the sight of several characters left onstage for scenes in which they had no part, silent reminders of the play's problems: hence, for instance, Angelo wrote away at his desk through 1.3 or Claudio was seated on a chair

20 *Measure for Measure*, 3.1, Cheek by Jowl, 1994: 'She should this Angelo have married': Duke (Stephen Boxer) and Isabella
(Anastasia Hille) talk across Angelo (Adam Kotz)

upstage from the end of 1.2 until his encounter
with the Duke in 3.1. Characters could also
become figures appearing on cue in others'
narratives, or be present unseen and unseeing as
characters talked about them across them. The
continued presences counterpointed and inter-
wove with the language of the scenes, visual
reminders – but never distractions – of the
issues literally personified.

But the scenes were also imbued with nicely
observed realist details: Angelo's officer
handing Isabella a cup of tea as she waited to
talk with Angelo in 2.2 so that she then had the
problem of where to put the cup down, Escalus
giving Pompey a cigarette which he tucked
behind his ear for later, Mariana shrieking with
laughter as Isabella explained to her the 'good'
she 'comes to do' (4.1.51), or Isabella and

Mariana waiting for the Duke's return in 4.6
while checking the scripts the 'Friar' has given
them. The strength of Isabella's religious belief
made it only right that she should encourage
Claudio to kneel beside her and recite Psalm 23
after he had accepted in the single word 'Yes'
her instruction to be 'ready . . . for your death
tomorrow' (3.1.106) but his anxiety then
caused him to interject lines into the psalm
while she continued all the more strongly to
block out what he was asking of her, until he
had to put his hand over her mouth to stop the
psalm. His action here was all the more striking
given the sight of him kneeling in silent prayer
through much of the action. Claudio's faith was
apparently as fervent as his sister's, both ready
to respond to anything by trumpeting their
faith so that after her first interview with

Angelo Isabella prayed ecstatically downstage, counterpointing his soliloquy (2.2.168–92). Against this, comfortable social behaviour became a thin veneer to cover a desperate emptiness beneath for those for whom religion was not an immediate living presence, so that, for instance, Lucio's request to the Duke 'I prithee pray for me' (3.1.439) was spoken on his knees, crying and holding onto the Duke's waist, before switching back into his usual streetwise mode with its bravado now hollow.

In this context, all three principals stood out strongly. Initially the Duke, Isabella and Angelo seemed to be starting from the same moral position. But as the action developed, Isabella (Anastasia Hille) clung to her sense of virtue and ethical behaviour with a fervour that was increasingly desperate and therefore shrill, almost violent in her continued espousal of a code whose integrity was no longer in keeping with the universal corruptibility that Angelo's fall manifested. Cold and hard in her beliefs, Isabella was at the same time passionate and physical, comfortably able to place her head on Angelo's breast, stroking and touching him as she encouraged him to 'Go to your bosom' (2.2.140). But she had adopted an absolute that removed her from the world and its reality quite as much as her nun's habit so that her lesson to Angelo, 'man, proud man' (2.2.120), was both teacherly and spoken through tears, tears which would flow ceaselessly through the rest of the play as she tried to staunch them with a hankie and was left shaken and snuffling.

Terrifyingly isolated, Isabella found her code irrelevant to the world. She was rejected brutally by Claudio (Danny Sapani) at the end of the play as he embraced Juliet and kept his back firmly turned to his sister; he found it easier to hand Lucio a cross and kneel and pray for him as he was dragged off to marriage and prison than to respond to his sister's plight. Isabella finally tried to sneak away and was herself dragged back and forced, passively resisting, to hold the Duke's hand as the couples stumbled from the stage. Only with Mariana, who sang

'Take, O take these lips away' herself torchily while taking large gulps of vodka, did Isabella find a genial companion – Pimlott's Mariana, incidentally, turned not to drink but the paintbrush, working at huge abstracts in her moated grange.

If the gaps between characters were often indicated by the gulf of the stage between the two chairs on which they were seated, Angelo (Adam Kotz) and the Duke (Stephen Boxer) began the play as two connected points from which their position allowed them to diverge. Each could have done what the other did. But in their attitude to Isabella they were as one: as Michael Billington commented (*The Guardian*), 'the Duke is Angelo's double in his furtive attraction to an Isabella who represents the sexual temptation of corrective chastity'. In their exercise of rule both men explored the possibilities of power without responsibility so that their similarly logical approach to law and morality resulted only in revealing their own hypocrisy; Angelo's assault on Isabella was no different from the Duke's fixing. Isabella's reaction to the Duke's proposal of the bed-trick (3.1.245) was to leave the stage in complete shock and walk round the auditorium while he was left on stage trying to persuade her. Acquiescent rather than enthusiastic she returned to the stage, the interval coming at this point.

For the trials of Act 5, the Duke, a director in disconcerting control of his assembled cast, set up a microphone centrestage into which Isabella and Mariana, isolated on the empty spaces of the stage, had nervously to speak their accusations straight out to the audience, checking their scripts at awkward phrases like 'concupiscible intemperate lust' (98). The Stratford Isabella and Mariana were similarly isolated but not through the bare spaces around them; Pimlott had taken the extraordinary step of recruiting 'citizens of Vienna' from 'the citizens of Stratford', as the programme put it, so that each woman in turn was the sole female presence on the stage-floor while behind them were ranged dozens of middle-aged men, clad in

21 *Measure for Measure*, 5.1, RSC, 1994: Isabella (Stella Gonet) intercedes with the Duke (Michael Feast) for Angelo (Alex Jennings, left)

gowns, wigs and mortar-boards, the embodiment of the male system of the law and government, against which their pleas seemed especially vulnerable. Mariana in her red dress was discrepant enough from the black robes of the men but Isabella (Stella Gonet) now for the first time wearing a man's suit and a large crucifix seemed deliberately transgressive in her cross-dressing, an affront to the principles of religion reminiscent of the recent reactions to the prospect of female vicars. As Isabella spoke of sex with Angelo the language itself was offensively public, speaking of the most private of acts, language that should never be spoken in the presence of a woman let alone by a woman, but her simple statement 'And I did yield to

him' (101) was greeted by the violent ridicule of raucous smutty male laughter so that she yelped an interjected 'No' back at them.

The main part of Ashley Martin-Davies' huge set consisted of a curved back wall with a gallery above and, as this scene unfolded, Juliet, gagged and held back by a warder, brutalized by her experience of prison, wrestled in helpless hysteria with the appalling revelations. Her wordless witness placed the onstage action as, for instance, she pounded with her feet, desperate to stop Isabella pleading for Angelo's life. The shocks of the sequence registered with hideous emotional force so that the news of Angelo's 'private message' (457) had Isabella screaming and Mariana pounding on Angelo's weeping body. By the end, the Duke's proposal of marriage was met by Isabella's slapping his face, then kissing him and then, just as the audience was starting to feel uncomfortable with the cliché, rejecting him sharply and standing apart in tears, twitching. The final moments as the stage darkened were taken by the Duke with extreme nervousness as he looked rather shifty beside her helpless crying. It could not have been a more disconcerting ending.

Superb though Pimlott's control of the huge sweep of Act 5 was – and I could wish I had the space to describe the sequence step by step as the blocking so carefully charted the movement of the scene – it had an excellence that much of the rest of the production rather lacked. The effect was often of ideas not quite necessary, of the play burdened down by the production's materials. On either side of the forestage, for instance, a massive ducal throne confronted an electric chair which seemed a grey mirror-image of the throne of power. But the electric chair was only indicated when spotlit as the interval came and the throne used only for the Duke to sit in during the Act 5 events. The chairs offered a symbolic discourse that the production substantially refused to follow up.

Pimlott did, however, explore clashes of comedy and violence as the comic surfaces took on other hues. At his first appearance, before Escalus in 2.1, Bille Brown's Elbow was the archetypal P. C. Plod, an amiable joke; but as he hauled Pompey on in 3.1 there was a strong threat that Pompey was facing a serious beating from which only the presence of the Duke as Friar at first saved him. The picklock that defined Pompey's crime (285) was blatantly planted on him by Elbow and when Pompey in desperation bit Elbow's ear and the blood flowed the risk of police brutality was stopped now only by Lucio's entrance.

Lucio himself (Barry Lynch at his most street-wise and oleaginous) could threaten at the slightest excuse. As he munched an apple through his dialogue with the Duke in 3.1, he could drag the unwilling 'friar' into a waltz. At the end of the conversation he dropped the apple core into the friar's hood and, when the Duke plucked it out and threw it at him, turned aggressively – before pulling another apple out of his pocket and smiling with infinite malevolence. Mistress Overdone (Caroline Blakiston), confined to a wheelchair in her fur-coat and black lingerie, as a comic version of Dietrich as a brothel-keeper in 1.2, was unceremoniously dumped on the floor by the arresting officers in 3.1, accompanied by prostitutes who were bloodied and bruised from their beating.

If violence was as much a work of the state as of its subverters, then the Duke's abandonment of power was all the more culpable. Michael Feast's Duke, cultured and ironic from the start, had never had control and found in his new position of outsider the opportunity to say what he had always wanted to, seeing so graphically 'corruption boil and bubble / Till it o'errun the stew' (5.1.315–16). Nervously incompetent, he was in striking contrast with Alex Jennings's ramrod stiff Angelo, his baby-face with its smirk in contrast to the brutal authority he enjoyed wielding. Jennings's easy assumption of power meant that he could keep Isabella waiting while he finished his papers in 2.2 before slamming the book shut and striding over to shake hands. When Isabella pointed out one passage in her ever-present Bible, Jennings could instantly counter it by finding a contrary passage to show her (2.2.77–84). As his growing awareness of his own desire took over, his body sat hunched and crushed, his sense of his own worth destroyed and turned to pitiless self-loathing. The climactic scene with Isabella (Stella Gonet) moved from a hypothetical debate, a series of intellectual propositions, until he crashed to his knees at 'Plainly conceive, I love you' (141), a fall from which he quickly recovered to make 'Answer me tomorrow' (167) into a sneer that raised a laugh from the audience. Jennings's Angelo seemed limitless in his dangerousness: when he remarked to Alfred Burke's slightly tipsy Escalus that the Duke's 'actions show much like to madness' (4.4.3) he seemed to be planning to get himself off the hook by having the Duke declared insane and taking over the state himself. Crushed by the play's end he walked off to marriage so fast that Mariana was left to follow some way behind in his wake.

But neither Feast nor Jennings could compensate for the weakness of Gonet's performance as Isabella, wailing and gasping across others' lines, a performance too lush in its own emotions to raise an answering response from me. The precarious balance of the play depends on equal principals and that was unavailable. Nonetheless Pimlott had largely succeeded in anchoring his view of the play's moral politics in a construction of English society as a historically coherent object, a world whose genial acquiescence in the forms of nineteenth-century social behaviour could be threateningly exposed by the play's problems.

PROBLEMATIC HISTORIES

Directors have their own histories. Their previous work – their theatrical biographies – constitute a series of relationships within which their approach to a particular play may be defined. This is especially true when they return to a play they have previously directed. Max Reinhardt's series of productions of *A Midsummer Night's Dream* was a life-long sequence of encounters with the play, each time finding new emphases and new possibilities. But sometimes the success of one production prejudices the chances of success in a subsequent one.

Adrian Noble's 1986 production of *Macbeth* for the RSC with Jonathan Pryce in the title-role was a remarkably complete triumph, a dense and thoughtful consideration. Returning to the play in 1993 Noble seemed to have nothing left to say. There were echoes of earlier effects, like the playing of the cauldron scene at the banquet table of 3.4, but their repetition seemed now drained of interest, a gesture towards a previously strong moment of theatrical

imagination. Elsewhere Noble offered 'hardly more than a sketch' (Irving Wardle, *The Independent on Sunday*). Indeed some scenes, played in front of a downstage curtain like a Victorian front-cloth scene (for example, 1.7 and 2.4), seemed more concerned to cover elaborate scenic effects being set upstage than to be investigated for their own potential: as the Macbeths embraced at the end of 1.7, now fully resolved in their plans, the curtains parted to reveal the Scottish court at a banquet, strongly lit by candles, at the sight of which the couple started guiltily and froze before the effect dissolved too easily and the banqueting table trucked back upstage, as if the entire scene, so rich in possibility, had existed only for this one rather uninteresting surprise.

Most of the performances were similarly broad in their styles, like Denys Hawthorne's podgy Duncan, a smugly cheery man, relishing his lines but with no suggestion of a king whose murder might be troubling, or Michael Siberry's over-loud Macduff. Even Cheryl Campbell's Lady Macbeth offered only a sex-kitten given to melodramatic laughter and with swooning, whooping vowels that efficiently covered all the depths she might have wanted to plumb; no wonder that her taunting of Macbeth when his courage was slipping was met by his slapping her face (1.7.45) in response to her irritatingly childish gibes. It was only too clear from the first that the sleepwalking would be a regression to a more intense childishness.

At the production's centre lay the decision to cast Derek Jacobi as Macbeth. Jacobi is unusually capable of exploring the attractions of goodness but that is hardly a qualification for tackling Macbeth. He started as a decent and honourable soldier, apparently without any ambition, confused by the witches and ready to laugh off their prophecy until the sudden confirmation of his new title disturbed him. A sensitive man, he remained far too full of the milk of human kindness, never finding the single-mindedness of brutality – at least until he carefully hacked at Young Siward's arms and

22 *Macbeth*, 1.4, RSC at the Barbican, 1993: 'O worthiest cousin': Duncan (Denys Hawthorne) and Macbeth (Derek Jacobi)

legs before breaking his neck in an act of casual indulgence in violence. Till that point Macbeth stayed only too vulnerable and desperate in his increasing isolation. Jacobi reined in the lyricism of his voice: only in the worldweariness of the last scenes was there a glimpse of his range, eloquent in his vision of the infinite sadness of lonely old age, beautiful in his slow uncovering of the poetry here.

But it was only at this late stage that the language was allowed to take over. As John Peter commented (*The Sunday Times*), 'this most elemental of tragedies needs as little machinery as possible: hydraulics and massive, sliding furniture simply divert attention from the thunder and terror of the words'. The set was dominated by a gantry which descended

with the witches on it and left them peering down at the action; it was on this platform that Banquo was murdered, his corpse left there until it needed to reappear as ghost at the feast. But the mechanics did nothing to suggest the supernatural, inhibiting rather than helping the witches. Only in the Porter scene as the swirling dry ice took on strange shapes and the Porter was 'momentarily immobilized by some ugly intimation of hell' (Paul Taylor, *The Independent*) did the production acquire the supernatural dread and the fearsome presence of evil so greatly lacking elsewhere.

If Noble seemed hamstrung by the exhaustion of his own invention, Phyllida Lloyd was hamstrung by the inexhaustibility of her imagination in her production of *Pericles* for the

Royal National Theatre. The combination of play and theatre should have been remarkable: the limitations of the play's stage history are in themselves liberating for a director and the scenic potential of the Olivier Theatre has long been waiting for imaginative use. In a play so strongly divorced from a sense of history both in its fiction and in its after-life the director's decisions can be untrammelled by the pressures of expectation.

In the event, the production lost sight of the play. Two sets of irreconcilable oppositions remained so completely unresolved that the play was bound to disappear in the struggle. The first was between Lloyd's interest in narrative and her investigation of the play as dream, a world of infinite possibility. As Peter Reynolds sets out in his interesting account of the rehearsal process, Lloyd 'insisted on the need for everyone to keep in mind the need to "tell the story clearly"'.[8] But this laudable aim, the play as 'a literal journey', was in tension with her view of the play as 'Pericles' dream; a fantastic journey in time and space, one which breaks all the rules of logical progression' (Reynolds, *Pericles*, p. 6). Mark Thompson's set was dominated by a massive vertical disc with a huge central doorway, encrusted to suggest a moonscape and mirrored in the giant circle of the Olivier's revolve, and the powerful image offered both the world of dream and of madness, 'another form of wandering in the mind' (Reynolds, *Pericles*, p. 6). But the process of the performance denied the connections of narrative, the repetitions and mirrorings that give shape to the play, so that the production retained only the fragmentation of a dream in need of sustained analysis to find its central meanings.

The second opposition was between actors and set. As Reynolds describes, the production processes of the National mean that the set design has to be fixed long before rehearsals begin. Thompson's set, elaborate in conception and technically hugely demanding in execution, created immense difficulties with lifts repeatedly sticking, flying pieces obstinately refusing to fly and revolves demonstrating a predisposition not to revolve. After the first week of performances, some of the effects were simply abandoned and the programme carried an extra slip announcing that performances would not 'encompass all elements of the original design' but the changes, 'taken for safety reasons', had resulted in a 'slightly modified version . . . re-worked by the Director' – as frank an admission of failure as one could expect to see.

From their first encounter with the set model, 'some of the cast felt disempowered', a feeling intensified as the rehearsal process moved the focus 'from acting to staging' (Reynolds, *Pericles*, p. 4). The reunion between Pericles and Marina was initially staged with the whole disc of the revolve raised to create a sunken space, with the result that this most intimate of scenes began with Pericles completely invisible, curled up below the lip of the revolve and Marina able to be seen only from the waist up. The scene ended with the actors picking their way under the stanchions that supported the disc to find a space for Pericles to sleep. Throughout they were either invisible or dwarfed by the machinery. The restaged version, played on a flat stage-floor, allowed Douglas Hodge's Pericles and Susan Lynch's forceful Irish Marina a space in which they could act freely; if never brilliant, the second version was a tremendous improvement.

Lloyd and Thompson's free-associating dream denied the play's geography. No longer a voyager round the Mediterranean, Pericles journeyed to places of myth: a Welsh Simonides lived near the North Pole where the dance of the knights was accompanied by Pericles and Thaisa playing icicles like a xylophone; Tarsus was somewhere in Inca culture with a statue of Pericles treated as an object of cult veneration,

---

[8] Peter Reynolds, *Pericles: Text into Performance* (National Theatre Education, 1994), p. 11.

23 *Pericles*, Sc.12, RNT, 1994: Cerimon (Kathryn Hunter) revives Thaisa from her piano-shaped coffin

while Mytilene, dominated by Kathryn Hunter as a pox-ridden, rasping Bawd modelled on Barbara Windsor, was nowhere in particular. Like Viola, I kept wondering 'What country, friends, is this?'

There was a good deal of cross-gender casting to bizarre effect: Selina Cadell's Helicanus was the worst kind of girls' school-play Polonius, Tom Yang a Dionyza of screeching camp and even the virtuosic Kathryn Hunter (playing a very odd triple of Antiochus, Cerimon and Bawd) was reduced to performing strange incantatory rituals or appearing up a ladder, as Antiochus, with a long beard, sun-glasses and apparently ten-foot tall waving stick-like extensions to her arms, a position in which no performer can be expected to do much. Rather than maintaining a marginal position of controlling narration, Henry Goodman's Gower,

having first appeared from out of the lid of a piano for reasons that I could not begin to comprehend, kept popping up out of the crowd in various guises (including as Leonine), trying hard to maintain a cheeriness as all about him looked increasingly bemused. It was only too predictable that at Ephesus, as Pericles announced to Diana the story of his life, everyone else on stage was wearing headdresses like lampshades or jellyfish that covered their faces so completely that the only way one could identify Thaisa was by her bare arms (she was the only black actor in the scene) and there was no possibility of seeing her face respond to the news.

There were moments that were worth treasuring: the comic Inuit fishermen fishing at a hole in the ice, Joy Richardson's Thaisa in total terror in her piano-coffin as Cerimon revived her, Marina mourning Lychorida by draping a black veil over her discarded dress, the reformation of Lennie James's Lysimachus. But each was massively outweighed by the crassness elsewhere like the oafish Philoten (played by a man), the batiks and balloons industry Marina seemed to have set up in Mytilene or the French Diana flying in with legs posed like the Good Fairy in a pantomime.

Such a major production disaster creates its own niche in the history of Shakespearian performance but it is a history that I would rather not have to chart. The staging of some plays suggests that directors are only too willing to ignore the lessons of history while leaving behind them a trace that their successors will perhaps not heed either. Since as a reviewer I still head off to each new production with boundless optimism, I stand similarly indicted. No one could respond to the experience of such catastrophes with any belief in the inevitability of progress. Theatre historians cannot be whiggish.

PROFESSIONAL SHAKESPEARE PRODUCTIONS IN THE BRITISH ISLES, JANUARY–DECEMBER 1993

compiled by

NIKY RATHBONE

Most of the productions listed are by professional companies, but a number of productions with mixed amateur and professional casts have been included. It is interesting to note the increasing number of such productions, and the rise in the number of small professional touring companies. Information is mainly taken from newspaper reviews held in the Birmingham Shakespeare Library.

ALL'S WELL THAT ENDS WELL

Emlyn Williams Theatre, Clwyd and tour of Wales: January 1993–
Director: Helena Kaut Howson
Designer: Paul Andrew
Helena: Mari Rowland Hughes
Set in a hi-tech modern environment.

The RSC at the Theatre Royal, Newcastle: March 1993–
See *Shakespeare Survey 47*.

The Festival Players Theatre Company, tour: July 1993–
Director: Trish Knight-Webb.

ANTONY AND CLEOPATRA

The RSC at the Theatre Royal, Newcastle, and the Barbican Theatre, London: May 1993–
See *Shakespeare Survey 47*.

New Triad Theatre Company, The Village Theatre, London: October 1993–

Director: John Strehlow
Set in the 1980s.

Adaptations

Cleopatra, a ballet
Millfield Theatre, Edmonton Green: September 1993
Choreographer: Richard Slaughter
Cleopatra: Ursula Hagel
Set to music by Rachmaninov and Luigini. Based on Shakespeare, Shaw and the Elizabeth Taylor and Vivien Leigh film portrayals of Cleopatra, the ballet explored the clash of cultures. World première.

AS YOU LIKE IT

The Rose Theatre Company, Sussex, Brighton Pavilion Theatre and tour of Britain and Europe: February 1993–

D.P. Productions, tour: April 1993–
Director: Ian Dickens

The RSC at the Theatre Royal, Newcastle and the Barbican Theatre, London: April 1993–
See *Shakespeare Survey 47*.

Deal Fringe Festival: July 1993–
Director: George MacGregor
A mixed amateur and professional cast.

Illyria (London) tour of open air sites: July 1993–
Illyria is a new touring company.

THE COMEDY OF ERRORS

The Abbey Theatre, Dublin: March 1993
Director: Gerard Sternbridge
Designer: Joanna Taylor
Treated as a country and western musical.

Manchester Royal Exchange and tour: March 1993–
Director: Gregory Hersov
Designer: David Short
Fast, funny and set in a cold, north-English, modern city.

Oxford Stage Company, Oxford Playhouse, British and foreign tour: August 1993–
Director: John Retallack
Touring with *Pericles*.

CORIOLANUS

Coriolan, French text by Michael Garneau
Théâtre Repère at Nottingham Playhouse: November 1993
Designer/Director: Robert Lepage
Coriolanus: Jules Philip
First performed in Paris, 1992 and also seen in Montreal.
Projected video images and the framing of the action suggested a comparison with film newsreel.

Aquila Company, the Place Theatre, Bloomsbury, London: November 1993

CYMBELINE

Compass Theatre (Sheffield) tour: May 1993
Director: Neil Sissons
Touring with *Hedda Gabler*.

Bute Hall, University of Glasgow and international tour: August 1993
Director: François Rodinson
Students and graduates from six countries, performing in four languages. Each participating country developed certain characters, drawing on the nation's unique traditions. A narrator provided a commentary in the language of the host country.

HAMLET

The Theatre Museum, London: January 1993
Director: Miriam Segal
Hamlet: Valentine Pelka

The RSC at the Royal Shakespeare Theatre, Stratford: March 1993–
See *Shakespeare Survey 47*.

Theatre Set up, tour: June 1993–
Director: Wendy MacPhee
Hamlet: Tony Portacio

Kaos Theatre, the Niccol Theatre, Cirencester: June 1993
Director: Phil Morle
A very stylized production which highlighted imagery. Apparently Claudius addressed Rosencrantz and Guildenstern while standing on his head.

The Abbey Theatre, Dublin, Galway Arts Festival and tour of Ireland: July 1993–
Director: Fiona Shaw
Hamlet: John Lynch
Part of the Hamlet Project run by the Globe Theatre Trust, and intended to introduce sixteen to eighteen year-olds to the plays.

The English Theatre, the Lyceum, Crewe and tour: September 1993–
Director: Stephen Unwin
Designer: Bunny Christie
Hamlet: Alan Cumming
Gertrude: Eleanor Bron
Excellent reviews. Opening in Renaissance costume, the players gradually assumed modern dress. The company is the new formed touring wing of Century Theatre.

The Crucible, Sheffield: October 1993
Director: Michael Rudman
Designer: Sue Plummer
Hamlet: Robert Glenister
Excellent reviews. The Court was represented

as a world of formal etiquette and black and white geometry, contrasted with the rich and colourful world of the travelling players.

Adaptations

Antic, a ballet performed by Arc Dance Company, Sadler's Wells Theatre: April 1993–
Choreographer: Kim Brandstrup
Designer: Craig Givens
Music: Ian Dearden

Hamlet Nightmare

Dublin Project Theatre, tour: July 1993–
Director: Michael Sheridan
Hamlet: Olwen Fouere
Ophelia: David Heap
Part of the Hamlet Project. Hamlet was played by a woman and Ophelia by a man, representing a chess player who, in Hamlet's subconscious, symbolized Death.

Hamlet (Pow, Pow, Pow)

Divaldo K re-interpret *Hamlet*
Edinburgh Fringe and Lilian Baylis Theatre, Sadler's Wells, London: August 1993
Darkly comic. Hamlet escapes the play, to be dragged back and forced to perform his role by Ophelia, Gertrude and the two producers.

Hamlet, adapted by Metin Marlow

An hour-long piece for four actors, meditating on the relationship between Hamlet, Ophelia and Gertrude.
Maison Bertaux, London Fringe Theatre, November 1993

HENRY V

The Tabard, London: March 1993
Henry V: Chris Eley
A modern-dress production.

Adaptation

Odd Socks Clown Theatre: April 1993–
A new production touring English Heritage sites. The company of fifteen has lost twelve of its members and the horse, and are reduced to a company of three, playing the 'best bits'.

JULIUS CAESAR

Salzburg Festival production at the Edinburgh Festival: August 1993
Director: Peter Stein
Antony: Gert Voss
Brutus: Thomas Holtzmann
Caesar: Martin Benrath
A celebrated production, with magnificent crowd scenes, using 200 extras, but hampered by the transition to the Royal Exhibition Hall and the language barrier.

The RSC at The Other Place, Stratford and tour: July 1993–
Director: David Thacker
Designer: Fran Thompson
Music: Mark Vibrans
See *Shakespeare Survey 47*.

The English Shakespeare Company, Swansea Grand and tour: September 1993–
Director: Tim Carroll
Designer: Rae Smith
Music: Corin Buckeridge
Touring with *Romeo and Juliet*.

Adaptation

Julius Caesar, adapted by Ron Phillips
Barons Court Theatre, London: March 1993–
Caesar: Carole Street
The adaptation, with a woman playing Caesar, drew parallels with the political assassination of Mrs Thatcher.

KING JOHN

Gaslight Theatre at the Mermaid Studio, London: July 1993.

KING LEAR

The Royal Court Theatre, London: January
1993–
Director: Max Stafford-Clark
Designer: Peter Hartwell
Lear: Tom Wilkinson
Refugees crossed the stage with possessions in
supermarket trolleys, in a production which
related the abdication of responsibility to the
breakdown of order in Europe.

The RSC at the Royal Shakespeare Theatre,
Stratford: May 1993–
Director: Adrian Noble
Designer: Anthony Ward
Music: Shaun Davey
Lear: Robert Stephens
See *Shakespeare Survey 47*.

LOVE'S LABOUR'S LOST

The Wolsey Theatre, Ipswich: March 1993–
Director: Antony Tuckey
Young European actors were engaged to give
the production a Continental flavour.

The RSC at the Royal Shakespeare Theatre,
Stratford: October 1993–
Director: Ian Judge
Designer: Jean Gunter
Music: Nigel Hess
See *Shakespeare Survey 47*.

MACBETH

Leicester Haymarket: February 1993–
Director: Julia Bardsley
Macbeth: Rory Edwards
Lady Macbeth: Kathryn Hunter
A modern production using laser effects. Only
one witch appeared, miming to voice-overs.

Durham Theatre Company, Durham Cathe-
dral and tour: March 1993–
Director: Cliff Burnett
Music: Rhythm Street
Six actors in dungarees performed, relating the

play to mental illness. The throne was represented by a wheelchair. The witches' curse was
omitted from the Cathedral performances.

The Royal National Theatre, The Olivier,
London: April 1993–
Director: Richard Eyre
Designer: Bob Crowley
Music: Dominic Muldowney
Macbeth: Alan Howard.
See *Shakespeare Survey 47*.

Barons Court Theatre, London: April 1993
Director: Anthony Fletcher
Played in modern dress, with minimal props.

Dundee Rep and The Tron, Glasgow: May 1993–
Directors: Michael Boyd and Hamish Glen
Designer: Tom Piper
Macbeth: Iain Glen
Excellent reviews. The witches were played as
children, doubling as Lady Macduff's, and
the ghosts of the dead joined the march on
Dunsinane.

The Midsommer Actors Company, Saltburn
Valley Gardens and tour of open air sites in the
northwest: July 1993–
Director: Simon Corble
A promenade production using local volunteers
as extras.

Wales Actors Company: tour of Welsh castle
sites: July 1993–
Director: Ruth Garnault
Macbeth: Paul Garnault

Committed Artists, Bridge Lane Theatre,
Battersea, London: September 1993–
Director: Stephen Rayne
Macbeth: Hakeem Kae-Kazeem
A cast of black actors experienced in the classics.
The play was set in contemporary Africa. First
performed at the 1991 New York International
Festival, USA tour 1992.

The Underground Stages Company, Kents
Cavern, Torquay: October 1993–
Producer: Tony Benet
Macbeth: Shane Morgan

The company was formed to perform the play as a promenade in the linked cave system.

The RSC at the Barbican Theatre, London: December 1993–
Director: Adrian Noble
Designer: Ian MacNeil
Macbeth: Derek Jacobi

Adaptations

Macbeth

Red Shift Theatre Company: British and world tour: March 1993–
Director: Jonathan Holloway
Macbeth: Alistair Cording
The production focused on the childless Macbeths, using images of dead children, in a political allegory about dictatorship and moral responsibility. The witches were omitted. Cut to 93 minutes.

The Merry Regiment of Women by Rae Shirley

SLTC at the NATHDA Festival, Croydon: July 1993
Director: Keefe Browning
Lady Macbeth calls a meeting of Shakespeare's women characters, to protest against discrimination in Shakespeare's works.

Akogun by Rufus Orisayomi

Shaw Theatre, London: July 1993
A Nigerian adaptation in pidgin English; a multi-cultural dance-drama.
First performed in London 1991.

Hecate's Macbeth

The Little Garden at the Mermaid Theatre: October 1993
Director: Bettina Jonic
An all-women cast of singers from Portugal, France and Britain performed this adaptation of Verdi and Shakespeare.

MEASURE FOR MEASURE

Gallowglass Theatre Company: Tour of Ireland; Spring 1993

Director: Conall Morrison
Played by seven actors, using grotesque masks for the comic characters.

What You Will Theatre Company, tour of small London venues: March 1993–
Playing the First Folio text, unrehearsed, to simulate supposed Elizabethan staging conditions.

Simply Shakespeare Company at the New Market Hall, Camden Lock, London: December 1993
Director: Forbes Collins

Adaptation

Groping for trouts in a peculiar river by Stephen Jameson

Sturdy Beggars Theatre Company at the BAC, Battersea, London: June 1993–
Working in the tradition of Brecht and Marowitz, the two-year-old company re-evaluated the monarchy, British politics and the work of Shakespeare.

THE MERCHANT OF VENICE

Very Fine Productions at the New End Theatre, Hampstead, London: March 1993–
Director: Jon Harris
Designer: Rosalind Henderson
Shylock: Andrew McDonald
A production of the First Quarto text, set on the Riviera.

Bradford Playhouse: March 1993
Director: Brian Otto
Designer: Richard Grey
Shylock: David Gilman
Set in the Victorian period.

The RSC at the Royal Shakespeare Theatre, Stratford: May 1993–
Director: David Thacker
Designer: Shelagh Keegan
Shylock: David Calder
Antonio: Clifford Rose

Portia: Penny Downie.
See *Shakespeare Survey 47*.

THE MERRY WIVES OF WINDSOR

Bremen Shakespeare Company at the Globe
Theatre, London: April 1993
Director: Pit Holzworth
Played in German by an all-male cast of five,
using vaudeville and slapstick techniques, and
depicting the female characters as projections of
male fantasy.

Northern Broadsides, Salts Mills, Saltaire and
tour of the UK and India: June 1993–
Director: Barrie Rutter
Falstaff: Barrie Rutter
Black box set, mainly modern dress costuming.
Played in northern accents.

Outside Seating Theatre Company (Suffolk)
Ely Cathedral and tour: July 1993

A MIDSUMMER NIGHT'S DREAM

Bristol Old Vic: February 1993–
Director: Ian Hastings
Designer: Louise Belson
Music: John O'Hara

Century Theatre, The Grand, Blackpool and
tour: March 1993–
Director: Stephen Unwin.

Partisan Theatre Company, tour of schools in
Hull: April 1993–
Director: Phil Joseph

The Gate Theatre, Dublin: July 1993–
Director: Joe Dowling
Designer: Hayden Griffin
Music: Keith Thomas
The doubling of Theseus/Oberon, Hippolyta/
Titania and Puck/The Master of the Revels
was integral to this production in which the
Palace was transformed into an earthy, sexually
menacing fairyland.

Stafford Shakespeare Festival, The Gatehouse:
July 1993–

Director: Rob Swinton
A mixed amateur and professional cast, with
stars drawn from popular television shows.

Georgian Film Actors' Studio: Edinburgh
Festival Fringe: August 1993
Director: Michail Tumanishvili
Performed in Georgian.

Theatre Royal, York: September 1993
Director: John Doyle
Designer: James Merifield
A company of eight actors, all in white, leading
to intentional confusion through the doubling
of parts.

Eye Theatre, Eye, Suffolk: September 1993
Director: Tom Scott
Set in the hippy Sixties. A cast of eight in a very
athletic, funny production.

Pukka Theatre Company, tour, with *Romeo
and Juliet*: September 1993–
A new, mainly professional company, working
with young people.

Harrogate Theatre: October 1993–
Director: Andrew Manley
A surreal production set in a bay-windowed
living room, apparently half submerged in
water.

The Royal Lyceum Theatre, Edinburgh:
October 1993–
Director: Kenny Ireland
Set in the 1950s. The mechanicals were
portrayed as Scottish tradesmen and amateur
actors.

The Village Theatre, London: November 1993
Director: Dee Wells
Puck: John Hug
Set in India, with a multi-racial cast, the lovers
rebelling against arranged marriage, and Puck
played as a middle-aged white colonial.

The Library Theatre Company, Manchester:
November 1993
Director: Chris Honer
Designer: Michael Pavelka

Set in the 1950s with the fairies in leather and biker boots inhabiting an urban wasteland.

Adaptations

A Midsummer Night's Dream, ballet
Caracalla Dance Theatre at the Royalty Theatre, London: March 1993–
Director: Ivan Caracalla
Choreography: Abdul Halim Caracalla

A Midsummer Night's Dream, ballet
Scottish ballet; tour: March 1993–
Choreographer: Robert Cohan
Designer: Norberto Chiesa
Music: Mendelssohn and Barrington Pheloung
Cohan's choreography attempts to mix the structured approach of classical ballet with the fluidity of Martha Graham, to embody the two worlds of *A Midsummer Night's Dream*.

A Midsummer Night's Dream
Maenad, tour of central Scotland: June 1993–
Director: Eve Keepax
Three actresses worked on this version as a community play with regional groups.

MUCH ADO ABOUT NOTHING

Head to Toe Theatre Company, tour, with *Twelfth Night*: May 1993–
A new company, based in Swindon.

The Everyman Theatre, Cardiff, at Dyffryn House: July 1993

Open-Hand Productions in New College Gardens, Oxford: July 1993–
Billed as a professional group, performing in Oxford college gardens.

The Queen's Theatre, London and tour: July 1993–
Director: Matthew Warchus
Designer: Neil Warmington
Benedick: Mark Rylance
Beatrice: Janet McTeer
Produced by Thelma Holt and set in the 1930s.

Well reviewed.
See *Shakespeare Survey 47*.

Devon Shakespeare Project at the Rotunda, Oldway: September 1993–
Director: Jonathan Hales, of the Royal Court
Professionally directed community theatre.

Film version

Renaissance with Samuel Goldwyn. August 1993–
Director: Ken Branagh
Benedick: Ken Branagh
Beatrice: Emma Thompson
With Michael Keaton, Denzel Washington, Richard Briers, Brian Blessed, Keanu Reeves.

OTHELLO

Birmingham Repertory Theatre: March 1993–
Director: Bill Alexander
Designer: Kit Surrey
Othello: Jeffery Kissoon

Live Arts Theatre Company; Heartbreak Productions (Leamington) touring historic sites: June 1993–
Director: Sian Edwards
Othello: Richard Ashcroft
Iago: Peter Mimmack
The company was formed in 1991.

Ludlow Festival: June 1993–
Director: Alan Cohen
Othello: Colin McFarlane
Iago: Greg Hicks

Acting Initiative, Edinburgh Fringe Festival and tour: September 1993–
Othello: Faith Edwards
Desdemona: Thomas Mooney
Cross-sex casting was used to challenge sexual stereotypes.

Second Age at the Tivoli Theatre, Dublin, and tour of schools: October 1993–
Artistic Director: Alan Stanford

Othello: Jonny Lee Davenport
Set in the 1890s.

Adaptations

Othello or, Chaos is coming
Custard Factory (Birmingham) tour: September 1993–

Othello
Black Shakes Theatre Company, tour: November 1993–
Set during the 1981 Brixton riots, with Othello, Iago and many of the cast played as police officers.

PERICLES

Oxford Stage Company, tour: with *The Comedy of Errors*: July 1993–
Director: John Retallack
Music: Karl James
Pericles: Philip Bowen
The company also toured Japan and Poland.

Adaptation

The Seven Voyages of Pericles
The Common Players, touring open air sites in Devon: July 1993–

RICHARD II

Manchester Royal Exchange: September 1993
Director: James Macdonald
Designer: Kandis Cook
Richard: Linus Roache
Richard was played as sardonic, taunting and without self-pity, viciously arrogant, but humorous.

RICHARD III

The RSC tour continues: see *Shakespeare Survey 47* for details. The production also toured to Japan.

ROMEO AND JULIET

The ESC, Blackpool Grand and tour of the UK and abroad: January 1993–
Director: Michael Bogdanov
Designer: Chris Dyer
Romeo: Joe Dixon
Juliet: Joanna Roth
Played on a bare stage. The production attempted to reflect modern ethnic conflict.

ACT Theatre Company: The Drum Theatre, Plymouth: April 1993
Set in modern Italy with the Montagues performing rap and reggae and Mafioso Capulets.

Footsbarn Theatre Company, the Brighton Festival: May 1993
World tour. The production opened to show corpses, masked and spattered in blood, who subsequently sat and watched the action of the play.

Eye Theatre, Eye, Suffolk: June 1993–
Romeo: Benjamin Perkins
Juliet: Samantha Lewis
The principal parts were played by actors from the popular TV series *Grange Hill* and *The Bill*.

Spin-off Theatre Company, schools tour and performances in Hull and Hendon prisons: June 1993
The company has been touring schools for four years, and is now experimenting with prison performances.

The Open Air Theatre, Regent's Park: June 1993–
Director: Judi Dench
Romeo: Zubin Varla
Juliet: Rebecca Callard

The Island Theatre Company, Belltable Arts Centre, Limerick: July 1993–
Director: Terry Devlin
Designer: Fiona Cunningham
Romeo: Paul Meade
Juliet: Cathy Belton

London Bubble, touring London parks with their tent theatre: August 1993–
Romeo: Charlie Folorunsho
Juliet: Sally Mais
Performed by cast of seven.

Lincoln Shakespeare Company at the Bishop's Old Palace: August 1993
Director: Simon Hollingworth
A group of amateur and professional actors, formed in 1992.

Birmingham Repertory Theatre: September 1993–
Director: Glenda Hughes
Designer: Robert Jones
Romeo: Damian Lewis
Juliet: Josette Bushell-Mingo

Pukka Theatre Company, tour with *A Midsummer Night's Dream*: September 1993–
A professional group, with some amateur members, formed in 1992 to work with young people.

New Stage Theatre (Scotland) at the Traverse, Edinburgh and tour: September 1993–
Director: Leslie Findlay
Romeo: Paul Caputa
Juliet: Louise Montgomery
A fast, modern production, set on a darkened stage and using very creative lighting.

Mercury Theatre, Colchester: October 1993–
Director: Graham Watts
Set in the Middle East, in the present.

Orchard Theatre, Barnstaple, tour of south west England: October 1993–
Director: Bill Buffery
Designer: Meg Surrey
Skeletons hung at the corners of a bare platform stage, and attendants wore skull masks in a production which related the play to contemporary events.

Oldham Coliseum: October 1993
Director: Warren Hooper
Designer: Jacqueline Trousdale

Romeo: Nicholas Murchie
Juliet: Caroline Milmoe
Set in the 1930s Verona. Caroline Milmoe is from the cast of the television series *Coronation Street*.

The Citizens Theatre, Glasgow: October 1993–
Director: Giles Havergal
Designer: Kenny Miller
Romeo: Robert Beck
Juliet: Shirley Henderson
Conceived as a Victorian melodrama. Capulet, a Victorian industrialist, intends marrying his daughter into the aristocracy.

The Everyman, Cheltenham: October 1993–
Director: Sheila Mander
Romeo: Gerard Crossan
Juliet: Maeve Connelly
Set in modern Belfast. The school uniforms of the principal characters emphasized their youthfulness.

Chester Gateway: November 1993
Director: Chris White
Designer: Juliette Watkinson
Romeo: Raymond Coulthard
Juliet: Emily Raymond

THE TAMING OF THE SHREW

West Yorkshire Playhouse: April 1993–
Director: Jude Kelly
Designer: Paul Andrews
Katherine: Nichola McAuliffe
Petruchio: Brian Protheroe
Katherine was portrayed as physically crippled by a club foot.

The Nuffield Theatre, Southampton: April 1993–
Director: Patrick Sandford
Katherine: Louisa Gold
Petruchio: Jason Connery
Unmistakably British, set in 1930s Padua-on-Avon. The production also toured to Rouen.

The Bridge Theatre, Hebden Bridge, tour: May 1993

Director: Freda Kelsall
Katherine: Janet George
Petruchio: John Spooner

The New Shakespeare Company at the Open Air Theatre, Regent's Park: June 1993–
Director: Toby Robinson
Designer: Paul Edwards
Katherine: Cathy Tyson
Petruchio: Geordie Johnson
Set in a circus ring, and costumed as Commedia dell'arte.

Contraband at the Hen and Chicken, Highbury, London: June 1993–
Director: Rachel Lasserson
Music: Andrea Mocca
A feminist production set in contemporary Italy. The taming of Kate took place in a blood-spattered prison.

The RSC at the Theatre Royal, Newcastle and the Barbican Theatre, London: July 1993–
See *Shakespeare Survey 46*

Oddsocks Theatre Company; tour of English Heritage sites: August 1993–
Oddsocks appeared as Will Shakespeare and the Pembroke Players.

The Northcott Theatre, Exeter: November 1993–
Director: John Durnin
Designer: Kit Surrey
Katherine: Jacqueline Dutoit
Petruchio: Alan Cody
Set in an Italian film studio.

THE TEMPEST

The ESC, touring: see *Shakespeare Survey 47*.

The Lyric Players, Theatre, Belfast: February 1993–
Director: Charles Nowosielski
Music: Richard Charn
Prospero: Robert O'Mahoney
Caliban: Sheelagh O'Kane
The production showed both Prospero and Caliban, played by a woman, as full of human inadequacies.

The RSC at the Royal Shakespeare Theatre, Stratford: August 1993–
Director: Sam Mendes
Designer: Anthony Ward
Music: Shaun Davey
Prospero: Alec McCowen
See *Shakespeare Survey 47*.

South Park, Darlington: August 1993–
A co-production by Durham Theatre Company and Darlington Arts Centre, using a large cast of children.

Salisbury Playhouse: September 1993–
Director: Deborah Paige
Designer: Isabella Bywater
Prospero: Christopher Ravenscroft

The Island Theatre Company, Dublin Theatre Festival: October 1993–
Director: Terry Devlin
Also played in Kilmainham Jail.

TITUS ANDRONICUS

The Octagon Theatre, Bolton: March 1993–
Director: Lawrence Till
Designer: Carole Tweedy
Titus: Peter Harding
A mixed cast of hearing and deaf actors using a special sign language translation and cut text.

The Big Space Theatre Company, Hornsey Road Swimming Baths: August 1993
Director: John Longenbaugh
Designer: Helen Baines
Titus: John Whitelaw
A new company, performing in an unusual space. The production was noted for its violence.

TROILUS AND CRESSIDA

Tara Arts in association with Contact Theatre, Manchester; UK and international tour: September 1993–
Director: Jatinder Verma
Troilus: Andrew Mallet

Cressida: Yogesh Bhatt
Thersites: Shelley King

Opens with Queen Elizabeth I issuing 1601 proclamation expelling negroes from her dominions. A black male actor played Cressida, a white actor Troilus, a female actress Thersites, in a production which developed the themes of discrimination and division.

TWELFTH NIGHT

What You Will Theatre Company; touring London fringe venues: January 1993–
Director: Patrick Tucker
Six actors, playing the First Folio text in an attempt to reconstruct Elizabethan acting conditions.

Tilt Theatre Company, tour of south-west England: March 1993–

Head to Toe Theatre Company, Swindon, tour with *Twelfth Night*: May 1993
A new touring company.

Cannizaro Park, Wimbledon: July 1993–
Directors: Michael Lyas and Leo Dolan

Show of Hands, London; tour: September 1993–
Director: Michael Dray
A mixed company of deaf and hearing actors, present popular classics in an imaginative and innovative style.

THE TWO GENTLEMEN OF VERONA

The RSC tour: see *Shakespeare Survey 47*.
Valentine: Dominic Arnold
Proteus: Ben Miles
Julia: Alison Reid
Silvia: Sarah Jane Holm
This successful production was partly re-cast for the tour.

THE WINTER'S TALE

The Duke's Theatre, Lancaster: open-air promenade production in Lancaster Park: June 1993–

Director: Jon Pope
Designer: Liz Ascroft.

The RSC, at the Theatre Royal, Newcastle, Barbican Theatre, London and tour: See *Shakespeare Survey 47*.

THE SONNETS AND POEMS

Sweet Sessions, devised by Paul Godfrey and Nancy Meckler
Shared Experience, tour: March 1993–
Director: Nancy Meckler
Designer: Tim Hatley
Music: Peter Salem
A twentieth-century critic, trying to solve the mystery of the Sonnets, acts out the feelings that apparently inspired them.

VENUS AND ADONIS

Orchard Theatre Company, tour of south-west England: February 1993–
Director: Bill Buffery
Music: Tom Nordon
Adaptor: Cathy Turner

MISCELLANEOUS

Kicking Bardom: This professional group toured from Croydon with extracts from *Julius Caesar*, *Romeo and Juliet* and *A Midsummer Night's Dream* to complement Keystage 3 school work. March 1993–

A Tudor Maggot by Carol Carver
Stage Two Theatre Company, the Wolsey Theatre, Ipswich: April 1993
Shakespeare's company, forced by the plague to leave London, arrive in Ipswich, with a play based on the life of Cardinal Wolsey.

Shakespeare on the Streets: Deal Theatre Project: July 1993–
Director: Liz Turner
A mixed amateur and professional cast playing scenes from *Pericles*, *Macbeth*, *A Midsummer Night's Dream* in and around Deal town

centre. The project has run annually from 1987, and will now become Kent Shakespeare Project, taking the plays into schools and colleges.

Dark Ladies
Maenad, touring central Scotland: October 1993–
Director: Eve Keepax
A workshop project relating Shakespeare's female characters to women today. Maenad are a group of three actresses.

Shakespeare's Country, by Peter Whelan
The second BT Biennial play, simultaneously performed by members of amateur Little Theatre Guild theatre groups in the UK in October 1993.
A comedy set in Shakespeare's Stratford, containing elements of *A Midsummer Night's Dream*.

THE YEAR'S CONTRIBUTIONS TO
SHAKESPEARE STUDIES

I.   CRITICAL STUDIES
reviewed by DAVID LINDLEY

GENERAL STUDIES AND COLLECTIONS

The core of Graham Bradshaw's *Misrepresentations: Shakespeare and the Materialists* (Ithaca and London: Cornell University Press, 1993) is a lengthy and detailed reading of two plays, *Henry V* and *Othello*, which continues the emphasis of his earlier book, *Shakespeare's Scepticism* (1987) on the multiple perspectives and 'challenging intricacy and complexity' of the plays' dramatic thinking. Bradshaw writes illuminatingly on both plays, but it is the book's other concern – to challenge both American new historicism and British cultural materialism and to expose what he sees as their deficiencies – which will no doubt command more attention. In a sometimes witty, sometimes acerbic, and occasionally downright ungracious fashion Bradshaw berates both schools for delimiting the richness and diversity of the plays' effects through their importation of a prior agenda to their discussion. Both schools, he contends, posit a 'Them and Us' – new historicism by its emphasis upon the estrangement of the texts of the past from our present, cultural materialism by its creation of a fake 'liberal humanist' Them as against politically conscious (or 'compassionate Sussex Marxist') Us. There is justice in some of the attacks he makes upon inattentive and partial readings, though there is, too, a good deal of caricature,

particularly of cultural materialist positions. But the book as a whole sidesteps the urgency with which both schools of criticism wish to deal directly with the implication of the readers' own cultural or political position for their readings of texts. Which is not to say that Bradshaw's claims for attentive reading, founded in a view of 'Shakespeare as the directing intelligence at work within the work' do not have their own political agenda. His celebration of a sceptical, interrogative Shakespeare is, as he would acknowledge, itself inevitably historically and culturally determined. But so too, one might think, is the nature of his polemic, so much more intemperate at the expense of British critics, near neighbours in academia, than it is of the Americans.

One of Bradshaw's principal targets is the Jonathan Dollimore and Alan Sinfield collection, *Political Shakespeare*, now reissued in a second edition (Manchester: Manchester University Press, 1994) containing two new chapters by the editors. Both emphasize their felt need to 'contest' the appropriation of Shakespeare by high culture and the political Right. Dollimore projects 'an imagined production of *Antony and Cleopatra*, in the service of queer politics and creative vandalism' at the end of his chapter, while Sinfield analyses recent educational policy in Britain and the Conservative government's market philosophy for the arts. I entirely share Sinfield's hostility to the way in which Shakespeare teaching has been regulated and closed down by recent changes in the structure of school examinations, and would agree with his political analysis of what is at stake. But his privileging of the 'popular' seems to me both intellectually facile and ultimately damaging to his more serious arguments.

The debate over new historicism figures elsewhere in this year's criticism. The genealogy of the movement is investigated by Richard Halpern in 'Shakespeare in the Tropics: From High Modernism to New Historicism' (*Representations*, 45, 1994: 1–25). He argues that New Criticism and New Historicism can be seen as replicating Modernism's preoccupation with anthropology, oscillating in approach between Frazer's anhistorical correlation of myths and rituals and Malinowski's insistence upon precise cultural placement of them. He suggests that the current obsession with colonialism is itself embedded within this history, with Renaissance literature figured as the potentially unknowable, and Shakespeare as 'both guide and quarry, leading us through a cultural landscape which, as in a dream, seems both alien and our own'. Jonathan Hart takes a rather unfocussed look at what might come after new historicism in 'New Historical Shakespeare: Reading as Political Ventriloquy' (*English*, 42, 1993: 193–219).

If Bradshaw attacks from the liberal corner, Francis Barker's assault on new historicism (and post-modernism) in *The Culture of Violence* (Manchester: Manchester University Press, 1993) comes from the materialist wing. Shakespearian texts, particularly the tragedies, and especially *Titus Andronicus*, are, in his view, documents which in various ways 'occlude the violence which is culture'. Or, at least, that, I think, is what he is saying, for the book is written in such a barbarous tongue that I am frequently uncertain that I have taken the point. His case seems to rest on the fact that the 'real' poor are not present in *Lear*, and that the

wholesale judicial slaughter by hanging in Renaissance England is absent from the violence of *Titus Andronicus*. New historicism, in this account, stands guilty of conspiracy with the Shakespearian text to cancel the 'real' violence of Elizabethan culture, a violence Barker wants to expose. The book is not so much a work of literary as of cultural criticism. One chapter title of Bradshaw's book, 'Is Shakespeare Evil?' would clearly be answered unrepentantly in the affirmative by Barker.

So would it, I think, by Derek Cohen, whose own socialist beliefs and antipathy to 'liberalism' are explicit in *The Politics of Shakespeare* (New York: St Martin's Press, 1993). He discusses Othello, Shylock and Caliban as examples of society's 'unassimilable individuals'; deals with 'Shakespeare's construction of a society under siege by its own oppressed classes'; and analyses 'the use of women as essential counters in the structures of wealth and power which sustain the political culture of class'. One must respond to the energy of his writing and its use and acknowledgement of his own position – for example in his discussion of *The Merchant of Venice*, which begins with an account of his first encounter with the play as a Jewish schoolboy in South Africa. Striking, too, is his reading of Malvolio, 'stigmatized as one who was mad enough to think he could break the barriers of class'. Cohen's is emphatically an 'oppositional reading' of the kind that would make Vickers and Bradshaw foam at the mouth. It is symptomatic of the book that its concluding chapter powerfully analyses the jealousy of Othello and Leontes, but does not even mention the unlearning of that jealousy which the second half of *The Winter's Tale* enacts. But then, presumably, to want his readings to take a more inclusive view of what goes on in the plays would simply be to make evident my own 'jejune liberalism'.

Further contestation is to be found in *Shakespeare's Books: Contemporary Cultural Politics and the Persistence of Empire*, ed. Philip Mead and Marion Campbell (Melbourne: University of

Melbourne, 1993), a collection of conference proceedings dedicated to the challenging of Shakespeare's place in the culture of Australia and India. The essays are brief, but some are suggestive – those by Michael Bristol on 'Shakespeare and the *Longue Durée* of Culture', and Leela Ghandi on 'The Uses of English in Colonial and Postcolonial India' in particular.

That new historicism is still capable of stimulating good work is demonstrated by John Gillies's fascinating and appropriately wide-ranging *Shakespeare and the Geography of Difference* (Cambridge: Cambridge University Press, 1994). He locates Shakespeare in a period when an old cosmography and the culture which informed its map-making, itself of mixed classical and biblical ancestry, was giving way to a new 'scientific' geography. But, he argues, though this new geography was 'confident of its superiority to the ancient geography, energetically generating a new poetry to make sense of its radically incongruous world-image', yet it was 'still enthralled to the imagery of the past'. In the central chapters of the book *Titus*, *Othello*, *Antony and Cleopatra* and *Tempest* are analysed – and on each of them Gillies has suggestive and subtle things to offer. I find particularly useful his discussion of the ambiguous place of Venice in the geographical imagination of the period, and his demonstration of the ways in which the representation of the 'voyager' is problematically caught between a classical moral horror and a new scientific admiration. It is a thoughtful and thought-provoking book.

Miscegenation is one of Gillies's topics, and is explored also in Richard McCabe's *Incest, Drama and Nature's Law, 1500–1700* (Cambridge: Cambridge University Press, 1993). His basic proposition is that incest 'was seen to challenge some of the most basic definitions upon which society was commonly presumed to rest'. He offers a wide-ranging study of social, legal and moral arguments about incest, and of the reworking of literary motifs from Classical drama to Dryden. His Shakespearian

chapter considers primarily *Hamlet*, *Lear* and the Romances, arguing that 'the distinctive quality of Shakespeare's use of the incest motif is its restraint and subtlety, its perception of private sexual undertones in the public rhetoric of family and state, its detection of the inevitable compromises exogamy makes with incest and, on a wider scale, "natural" order with all sorts of forbidden desire'. This book offers profitable ways of 'placing' the representation of incestuous desire culturally and historically.

The central project of *Shakespeare Reread: The Texts in New Contexts*, edited by Russ Macdonald (Ithaca and London: Cornell University Press, 1994) is to investigate ways of close reading which can yet fruitfully make use of recent developments in criticism. By no means all the essays do make that engagement, and Linda Boose's piece on *The Taming of the Shrew* isn't really 'close reading' as I understand it – but does have interesting observations to make on the intersection of languages of class and gender in the play. Barbara Hodgdon takes us on a whirl round 'The Critic, the Poor Player, Prince Hamlet, and the Lady in the Dark' to examine 'how close reading constructs and accommodates the performing and performed body'. Many other essays have useful things in them, but the one that will really stick in my mind is Helen Vendler's account of how she has come towards her promised book on *The Sonnets*. She opens: 'A theory of reading might begin: Know your texts for forty years. Recite many of them to yourself so often that they seem your own speech. Type them out, teach them, annotate them'. And she ends: 'good reading never lacks a long and taxing history'. In these days of institutionalized overproduction such a principle would not come amiss for all who write on Shakespeare.

Two very different books offer particular philosophical perspectives on the plays. 'I take the historic and economic idea of the market, the historic and literary phenomenon of drama, and the theoretical vocabulary of contemporary pragmatism and mobilize them in a series of readings of plays and poems by Shakespeare.' Thus Lars Engle announces his programme in *Shakespearian Pragmatism: Market of his Time* (Chicago and London: University of Chicago Press, 1993). Drawing on Rorty, Wittgenstein and Barbara Smith among others, he posits a Shakespeare whose texts 'explore the consequences of an outlook that does without absolutes'. His model is applied to a range of texts, from the *Sonnets* to *Antony and Cleopatra*. I am not well enough versed in pragmatics to be able to judge the book as a contribution to philosophical theory, but the test is the readings of individual plays that result from it, and on this count the book works extremely well. It is not perhaps surprising that the competing economies of *The Merchant of Venice* (over which Portia is seen to exercise final control) and *Troilus and Cressida*, represented as 'a bottomless flux of evaluations', should respond well to Engle's programme. But his reading of Coriolanus as one 'who thought he lived in a state, and found, to his cost, that he inhabited an economy', offers a perspective from which the mingled responses to this problematic hero can be understood; so too, in his readings of *The Sonnets*, the Henriad and of *Antony and Cleopatra* there are many moments of illumination. It is a complex book, impossible to summarize in brief space – but one very well worth attention.

A study explicitly informed by the writer's beliefs is James Howe's *A Buddhist's Shakespeare: Affirming Self-Deconstructions* (London and Toronto: Associated University Presses, 1994). There are some intriguing overlaps offered between a Derridean and Buddhist perspective, as plays are interrogated for the ways in which they embody or stage dilemmas that are central to Buddhist teaching. In Howe's view, if Shakespeare never attains the full embracing of '*shunyata*, the absence of relative concepts, emptiness', the self-deconstructive elements in his drama are continually 'reminding us that if we will have significance, we must pretend it'.

Every teacher of Shakespeare gestures towards the importance of considering the plays as theatre; a number of studies this year valuably develop this perspective. The most substantial is Meredith Anne Skura's *Shakespeare the Actor and the Purposes of Playing* (Chicago and London: University of Chicago Press, 1993), which takes the situation and psychology of the actor as its starting point, using the testimony of modern actors to describe their sense both of power and vulnerability, of narcissism and self-abasement, and their 'childish' dependence. Though hedged with caveats, she suggests that these same ambivalences were present for Renaissance actors, and figured significantly in Shakespeare's plays. She pursues the idea of the anxiety of the actorly 'proud beggar' as it figures in the respresentation of Clowns, in plays-within-plays in the earlier drama, and in the figure of Falstaff in the Henriad and *Merry Wives*. She discusses the potential mutual hostility between actor and audience – especially in relation to *Hamlet* and goes on, in what is for me the most persuasive section of the book, to look at the ways in which a variety of plays concerned with flattery exhibit central characters who 'each experience an actor's agonies of presentation before a crowd as fickle as any theater audience'. The more problematic side of the book, deriving from Skura's psychoanalytic interests, attempts to provide 'not only a reading of the plays, but also a reading of the man who wrote them', in which *Richard III* is 'Shakespeare's Glass', and (less contentiously) the *Sonnets* figure the actor's ambivalence about his relationship with an audience, and with the craft that he practises. This seems to me altogether less compelling than the readings of the texts.

Studies in the Literary Imagination (26, 1993) contains a number of essays under the title 'English Renaissance Drama and Audience Response'. It is a particularly strong collection, with a provocative piece from Phyllis Rackin, 'Engendering the Tragic Audience: The Case of *Richard III*' (46–66), arguing that where the history plays imagine a male audience, tragedy, in its provocation of tears, implies a female auditory, and suggesting that both Richard and Richmond evidence a 'performative self-construction as the object of a feminized audience's desire'. Joel B. Altman, in '"Prophetic Fury": *Othello* and the Economy of Shakespearian Reception' (85–113), claims that Shakespeare 'exploited the psychagogic force of the enacted word – its power of marshaling the intellectual and emotional energies that produce belief – but he also deconstructed both world and belief and thematized that deconstruction'. Drawing upon a wide range of material to investigate the ways in which the play offers signs for interpretation that test the 'desire for coherence' in both character and audience, Altman puts together a suggestive and powerful account of the play. The other essays in this volume all have points of interest. Andrew Gurr's 'The General and the Caviar: Learned Audiences in the Early Theatre' (7–20), Juliet Dusinberre's '*The Taming of the Shrew*: Women, Acting and Power' (67–84) on the relationship between the apprentice boy actor playing Kate and the female audience, and Harriett Hawkins's 'Disrupting Tribal Difference: Critical and Artistic Response to Shakespeare's Radical Romanticism' (115–26) which attacks moralizing critics who have attempted to degrade Shakespeare's celebration of romantic love, all repay attention.

E. Pearlman writes a short but suggestive piece, 'Shakespeare's Projected Persons' (*Style*, 28, 1994: 31–40), in which he draws attention to the ability of a character to 'people' his speech with invented characters whose invocation produces the impression of 'depth' in the characterization of the speaker. His suggestion that Shakespeare's subtlety in using this device increased as his craftsmanship matured is convincing. Names and naming are also the subject of Marvin Spevack's packed essay 'Beyond Individualism: Names and Namelessness in Shakespeare' (*Huntington Library Quarterly*, 56, 1993: 383–98), detailing the fascination with names and naming in the plays, but suggesting that the desire for the freedom of namelessness 'is an alternative to the individualism normally associated with the Renaissance'. Joseph Lenz writes on 'Base Trade: Theater as Prostitution' (*ELH*, 60, 1993: 833–55), commenting upon the ways the theatre operated both literally and figuratively as if engaged in prostitution, and develops the continuities in a brief exploration of *Troilus and Cressida*.

Penny Gay provides a history of the performance, at Stratford since 1947, of female roles in five of the comedies. The title of her study: *As She Likes It: Shakespeare's Unruly Women* (London: Routledge, 1994) makes it pretty obvious where her sympathies lie – and, indeed, throughout the commentary there are predictable brickbats for 'conservative' productions, and enthusiasm for actresses who make their roles 'truly transgressive'. The very explicitness of Gay's approach makes her book easy and enjoyable to use – you know where you are. At the same time, however, the relentless privileging of 'newness', contempt for the conservative tastes of 'Midlands coach-parties' (it was on such trips that I first encountered Shakespeare, after all), and assorted snide but unsubstantiated remarks about the internal politics of the RSC can become tiresome.

A related, but much more incisive, discussion of the gender politics of theatrical representation is contained in Carol Rutter's 'Shakespeare, his Designers, and the Politics of Costume: Handing Over Cressida's Glove' (*Essays in Theatre*, 12, 1994: 107–28), which analyses recent performances of *Troilus and Cressida*, focussing on their 'eclectic' costuming, to suggest ways in which directors and performers respond to what she sees as the challenge of Shakespeare's Cressida, who 'if her glove is read rightly – is a gauntlet thrown down, a theatrical intervention in the cultural construction of women'.

Leah Scragg recognizes the problem of student or general reader in negotiating between what seems to be the disjunction between the outpourings of the Shakespeare industry and the relative simplicity of the enjoyment of his plays in the theatre. Her *Discovering Shakespeare's Meaning* (London: Longman, 1994) is one of a number of books designed to bridge that gap. It serves its intended readership soundly, with, for example, proper warnings about character-centred readings, an encouragement of sensitivity to verbal and theatrical artifice and sensible commentary on plays-within-plays, parallel plots and the like. But whether it really gets the first-year undergraduate up to a starting-line where he or she might be able to respond actively to the kinds of debate that currently circulate about Shakespeare is open to question. There is very little about historical contextualization, or about the politics of the plays, or about issues of gender for example, and Terence Hawkes is the only 'theorist' offered in the suggested further reading.

Two books aimed at the same audience try to give a more theoretically informed picture of the plays. Susan Bassnett's *Shakespeare: The Elizabethan Plays* (London: Macmillan, 1993), though containing useful material, is a curious product in many ways. In her effort to deal with all the Elizabethan plays there are strange emphases – the *Henry VI* plays are considered only for what they say about women, for example, and there are some groupings which seem designed to make life difficult for the author (of *Titus Andronicus* and *Love's Labour's Lost* as plays that deal with 'potential social disintegration', for example). More positively, the Elizabethan political background is (albeit somewhat crudely) invoked, and students are reminded of the theatricality of the plays – both in their own time, and by the inclusion of reference to modern performances and performers. Philip C. McGuire's companion volume, *Shakespeare: The Jacobean Plays* (London: Macmillan, 1994) is longer, yet considers only seven of the available twelve plays. This enables an analytic density in the consideration of each text – and all his readings usefully

focus on the perception of audiences in the theatre (he is especially good on the problematic of silent characters at the ending of *Measure for Measure* and *The Tempest*, for example) and he insists always on the interpretative freedom the texts enable. Sounder, perhaps, and less quirky than Bassnett, he is, however, less engaged with current critical debates.

The introduction that most overtly claims to introduce students to the reading of criticism as well as the plays is Howard Mills's *Working With Shakespeare* (Hemel Hempstead: Harvester Wheatsheaf; Lanham: Barnes and Noble, 1993). Considering a fairly limited range of plays (mainly tragedies and histories) it moves from discussion of 'voices' through 'words', 'speeches' and 'scenes' to a final chapter entitled 'gender, genre, grabbing', in what claims to be 'an accessible nuts-and-bolts approach'. Throughout Mills focuses on detail and close reading – commendable enough as a starting-point for student work – but rarely takes up larger issues of what one might do with a play as a whole. Though the book's blurb claims that it will 'help students form an independent relation to existing commentary', they are in fact guided ruthlessly in their response – nastily so by his hostility to feminist criticism. The tone of his writing is not infrequently somewhat patronizing, both towards the critics he wishes to rubbish and, indeed, towards the students who are his assumed (and sometimes directly addressed) audience. Each of these student guides has some virtues, though none perhaps quite lives up to its billing.

Stanley Wells's *Shakespeare: A Dramatic Life* (London: Sinclair-Stevenson, 1994) is both less and more ambitious than these guides. Aiming at general readers and theatre-goers, he acknowledges the debates of the academic industry, but is concerned primarily with offering an introductory guide to the whole corpus of Shakespeare's writing, including the poems and the last collaborations. Attentive throughout to the theatrical dimension, informed by his labours on the text, and urbanely sensible in necessarily brief commentary on each play, Wells has admirably met his brief.

COMEDIES

Michael Cordner, Peter Holland and John Kerrigan, editors of *English Comedy* (Cambridge: Cambridge University Press, 1994), a collection produced as a tribute to Anne Barton, observe that: 'Writing about comedy continues to seem less prestigious and culturally significant than writing about tragedy' in what is a leitmotif of virtually all the books reviewed in this section. Though one or two papers seem rather thin, there are a number of strong contributions to the volume. I especially enjoyed Richard Beadle's essay, 'Crab's Pedigree', which places Lance's dog in *The Two Gentlemen of Verona* in its historical and narrative traditions, suggesting that his appearance in the play may owe something directly to Tarleton's comic routines, but also arguing that the dog may function as something darker in its link to 'an ancient line in sexual conquest through farcical deception, the excremental emblem of lust and defilement'. For Barbara Everett, in a warmly humane account of '*Much Ado About Nothing*, The Social Comedy', the seriousness of the play depends upon the way its realistically maintained portrait of a social world in Messina comes under the cure of the 'truth of feeling' manifested by Beatrice and Benedick from their independent, individual and marginal position in that world.

Peter Wolfensperger, in *Shakespeare: Impartial and Partial, Strategies of Persuasion in the Comedies* (Tübingen: Francke, 1994) brings reception theory to bear on *Comedy of Errors* and *Much Ado About Nothing* to test the possibility of discerning Shakespeare's own commitment to particular positions within the plays. He concludes that *Errors* is a play in which 'the playwright refuses to leave his hiding place and to commit himself', whereas in *Much Ado*, analysis of the macro and microstructure of the play leads him to the conclusion that the audience are led inevitably to privilege Benedick as the moral centre of the play, and therefore to view him as, to some extent, Shakespeare's mouthpiece. It is a very detailed account of each of the plays, and usefully represents a critical school that is perhaps not enough known in Anglo-American criticism. But the underlying schematism of the approach may not necessarily be to every reader's taste.

G. Beiner, in *Shakespeare's Agonistic Comedy: Poetics, Analysis, Criticism* (London and Toronto: Associated University Presses, 1993) essays a more comprehensive analysis of the genre, distinguishing the 'agonistic', which aims at punishment and expulsion of threat, from the 'comedy of love', which ends in inclusion and reparation. Three plays, *Merry Wives*, *Merchant* and *Twelfth Night*, are singled out as those which contain a fully agonistic element. The effect of Beiner's taxonomic method is to produce very severe, delimited judgements. Shylock, for example, is the antagonist who simply must be expelled; 'the play is not a liberal text', and however qualified the opposition between Christian and Jew in the play, 'they may be imperfect, he is atrocious'. The book usefully draws attention to the way various comic strategies are interrelated in the plays, but the method ultimately seems to me rather inflexible.

Acting Funny: Comic Theory and Practice in Shakespeare's Plays, ed. Frances Teague (London and Toronto: Associated University Presses, 1994) collects together a number of serviceable essays both on comedies, and on comic elements in tragedy and history, with Christy Desmet's 'Shakespearian Comic Character: Ethos and Epideictic in *Cymbeline*', arguing for the importance of ethical characterization through rhetorical strategies, seeming to me the most interesting.

Before turning to individual plays it is worth noting a suggestive, if slightly wispy, article by Peter Erickson, 'Representations of Blacks and Blackness in the Renaissance' (*Criticism*, 35,

1994: 499–527) which considers the represen-tation of blacks in European art, focussing on the picturing of paired white and black female figures, and then links this tradition with the pairing of 'light' and 'darker' women in some of the comedies.

I come to David Wiles's *Shakespeare's Alma-nac: A Midsummer Night's Dream, Marriage and the Elizabethan Calendar* (Cambridge: D. S. Brewer, 1993) with some sympathy. Like him, I do not believe that locating a text in a specific occasion is necessarily a cause of a simplification and reduction of its potential to 'mean' in other contexts or for other readers. Wiles's book is devoted to strengthening the claim of the Carey-Berkeley wedding as the play's occasion. But it seems to me that the book is at its strongest in its more general exploration of festive rites (particularly of St Valentine's Day) that the play echoes and in its demonstration of the significance of astrology to Elizabethan habits of mind. Precisely because this is a play with masque-like elements, to identify the par-ticular occasion has much less total effect on interpretation than is the case with an analysis of full-blown masques: it's in the effort to get towards the identification of the occasion, and in the study of Elizabethan marriage habits and custom en route that the book succeeds best.

There is a certain kind of criticism which rejoices, it would seem, in its own extravagant absurdity. Bruce Thomas Boehrer begins con-fidently 'Although no one has paid much sus-tained attention to the fact, *A Midsummer Night's Dream* is patently about bestiality' ('Bestial Buggery in *A Midsummer Night's Dream*', in *The Production of English Renaissance Culture* (Ithaca and London, Cornell University Press, 1994, 123–50)). By a twisted wit, the play becomes 'a bit like a Protestant marriage-manual constructed out of animal pornogra-phy'. As an example of a criticism which takes vehicle for tenor in its exploration of metaphor this essay cannot be beaten.

A scattering of individual articles explore various aspects of the comedies with varying success. In a piece which relates to Engle's study noticed above, Mark Thornton Burnett argues that gift-giving and exchange form the matrix of *Love's Labour's Lost*. His 'Giving and Receiv-ing: *Love's Labour's Lost* and the Politics of Exchange' (*English Literary Renaissance*, 23, 1993: 287–313), pointing out that a dispute over tribute payments is a central plot-motor of the play, discusses the unstable relationship of gift-giving and monetary transaction in the text, suggesting that it reflects the transitional nature of late sixteenth-century society in general, and more particularly, that it encodes the problem-atic of court patronage in the last years of Elizabeth's reign.

Paul Gaudet offers an interesting reading of the exchange between Jessica and Lorenzo which begins the fifth Act of *The Merchant of Venice*. He sees the dialogue, with its references to Troilus, Thisby, Medea and the rest as playing out a power-game in which Jessica resists Lorenzo's male 'signifying practices', and by her self-association with Medea in particular suggests a sense of disappointment and betrayal which complicates the romantic closure of the play. ('"A Little Night Music": Intertextuality and Status in the Nocturnal Exchange of Jessica and Lorenzo', *Essays in Theatre*, 13, 1994, 3–14).

Twelfth Night is placed in a theological framework by Maurice Hunt, who sees it as endorsing a Hookerian, liberal protestant Providence (where virtuous conduct contri-butes to salvation) in Viola, while satirizing Malvolio's Puritan orthodoxy that admitted no human agency. ('Malvolio, Viola, and the Question of Instrumentality: Defining Provi-dence in Twelfth Night', *Studies in Philology*, 90, 1993: 277–97).

According to Karen Bamford, *Cymbeline*, though related to *Lucrece*, 'offers a far more disturbing vision of gender politics. Imogen's heroism is central to the play, but it is the heroism of the beaten wife.' She is 'a tragi-comic Lucrece whose "wounded chastity" redeems both family and country'. (*Essays in Theatre*, 12, 1993: 51–61).

Barbara A. Mowat valuably considers the figure of Autolycus as constructed out of colliding 'infracontexts', associating him with 'a century-long struggle among and within texts as to how individuals and state should respond to those in distress', a struggle between charity on the one side and wariness of being taken in by the undeserving poor on the other; between harsh treatment of the 'rogue' and recognition of the ways in which the actions of the rich drove others to poverty. ('Rogues, Shepherd, and the Counterfeit Distressed: Texts and Infracontexts of *The Winter's Tale* 4.3', *Shakespeare Studies*, 22, 1994: 58–76). C. B. Hardman suggests, in 'Shakespeare's *Winter's Tale* and the Stuart Golden Age' (*Review of English Studies*, 44, 1994: 221–9) that, though less overtly than in other Jacobean plays, Shakespeare deploys imagery and ideas derived from classical representation of the Golden Age to surround the figures of Hermione and Perdita and thereby unsettle Jacobean political rhetoric.

But two comedies dominate the journal output this year, *Measure for Measure* and *The Tempest*. Julia Briggs, noting that Shakespeare may have been the first dramatist to bring the familiar narrative motif of the bed-trick to the stage, develops some of the implications of this 'unsavoury' device in her 'Shakespeare's Bed-Tricks' (*Essays in Criticism*, 44, 1994: 293–314). In a series of useful contrasts with its function in Italian novelle, and, particularly, in Sidney's *Arcadia* (which she suggests may have influenced the legal surroundings to the device in *Measure for Measure*), she defines Shakespeare's more problematic stance, where the bed-trick brings the 'sexual dissidents', Bertram and Angelo, 'back into the community' but yet leaves a 'disturbing suspicion at the end that their marriages are founded on mistakings, on a transient desire for an unattainable woman'.

It is on Isabella's position at the end of the play that a number of articles concentrate – and I'll deal with them in descending order of optimism. Mark Taylor's Horneyan psychoanalytic approach allows him to believe that at the end of *Measure for Measure* the Duke's proposal is accepted, and that for both of them this represents a curative coming to terms with their 'personality type'. His 'Farther Privileges: Conflict and Change in *Measure for Measure*' (*Philological Quarterly*, 73, 1994: 169–94) relies upon the reader's acceptance of the proposition that 'so precisely and completely do the three main characters of *Measure for Measure* correspond to the basic types of [Horney's] paradigm that it is as if she formulated it with them in mind'. Less certain is Karl F. Zender's 'Isabella's Choice' (*Philological Quarterly*, 73, 1994: 77–93), which represents the play as attempting to find a way out of the absolute binary opposition in which it begins, where the worlds of 'vice' and 'virtue' can have no middle term, and suggests that through Mariana's flexibility Isabella gains 'insight into the nature of love and shame, and into the power of one to make bearable the other'. But at the end he ducks (as a critic can, but as I would suspect an actress cannot) the question of her response to the Duke, suggesting instead that the wholesale resistance of all characters to romantic closure, since none of the couples speak to one another, means that we have to 'decline to choose between the options'. Carolyn E. Brown begins as if she is going to end up on the optimistic side, suggesting that the Duke and Isabella engage in a covert wooing, where the bed-trick is a vehicle for the expression of repressed fantasies for both of them. But she then turns to the claim that the Duke's trickery at the end forces her (but not himself) to stage 'the latent sexual import of her actions', and that her silence may signify her 'psychic breakdown'. ('The Wooing of Duke Vincentio and Isabella', *Shakespeare Studies*, 22, 1994: 189–219.) Laura Lunger Knoppers also believes that the Duke's conduct towards Isabella at the end of the play is repellent. Her '(En)gendering Shame: *Measure for Measure* and the Spectacles of Power' (*English Literary Renaissance*, 23, 1993: 450–71), however, is not based on psychoanalytic reading, but (rightly, I think) places the play in the contexts of the shaming rituals enjoined by the Ecclesiastical Courts. She suggests that though the play seems 'to move shame from women to men, from sexual to political offenses', the enactment of an apparent shaming of Isabella in her confession links her to the shaming of the Whore. The Duke restore her 'honour', yet in the process reveals the foundation of female honour in patriarchal mastery. Though I would want to contest this reading, it seems to me much the most challenging of the articles on the play's ending, taking its place with a number of recent articles that have addressed the play's links to the practices of the 'bawdy courts'.

A different perspective is provided by A. D. Harvey, who suggests, in 'Virginity and Honour in *Measure for Measure* and Davenant's *The Law Against Lovers*' (*English Studies*, 75, 1994: 123–32), that the nature of Davenant's revisions indicates that 'the whole issue had ceased to have any living, dynamic interest. Isabella's honour has simply become a convenient piece of dramatic machinery.'

A number of articles on *The Tempest* seek to negotiate with the colonialist reading of the play. Richard Halpern produces a newly inflected version in his '"The Picture of Nobody": White Cannibalism in *The Tempest*', in David Lee Miller, Sharon O'Dair and Harold Weber, eds., *The Production of English Renaissance Culture* (Ithaca and London: Cornell University Press, 1994, 262–92). Gonzalo's Utopian speech, borrowing from the culture of the Amerindians, but erasing their presence from his ideal commonwealth, typifies the way in which Western culture is always already the product of mixture (or 'mestizoisation') which it attempts to deny. Interestingly Gonzalo's fantasy is juxtaposed with Caliban's desire to found an imagined commonwealth through his rape of Miranda, demonstrating the way that the play sides with neither colonizer nor colonized. Other writers finesse the colonialist reading in different ways. William M. Hamlin suggests that Renaissance ethnography is much more ambivalent about native cultures than is

often argued, and that it moves, as *The Tempest* does, 'toward human exclusiveness' ('Men of Inde: Renaissance Ethnography and *The Tempest*', *Shakespeare Studies*, 22, 1994: 15–37). Arthur Kirsch, in his essay 'Montaigne and *The Tempest*', from a collection which has a wider value than can here be illustrated, *Cultural Exchange between European Nations during the Renaissance*, ed. Gunnar Sorelius and Michael Srigley (Uppsala, 1994, 111–22), argues that Montaigne's pervasive influence on the play has been understated in the past, and that full recognition, especially of the importance of the essay 'Of Cruelty', redirects attention to what he sees as the play's preoccupation with compassion. Prospero's learning of forgiveness, and the 'imaginative sympathy which animates our individual responses to the play', resurrect the claim to the play's essential humanity. For John S. Hunt, '*The Tempest* ... supports [Prospero's] socially ordained political authority, but rebukes his ambition to reach beyond ordinary human limitations' ('Prospero's Empty Grasp', *Shakespeare Studies*, 22, 1994: 277–313). Perhaps the most interesting reconsideration of Prospero is offered by Jonathan Bate in 'The Humanist *Tempest*', in *Shakespeare, La Tempête: Etudes Critiques*, ed. Claude Peltrault (Besançon: Université de Franche-Comté, 1994, 5–20). He locates the play within the humanist theory of education, suggesting the limitations and inadequacies of Prospero's own performance as Erasmian teacher and the ways in which this makes of the play 'a humanist critique of humanism'. The battiest argument is David Porter's suggestion that it is the fear of sexual inadequacy which motivates Prospero's attempts to bring all other characters to a childlike acquiescence. ('His Master's Voice: The Politics of Narragenitive Desire in *The Tempest*', *Comitatus*, 24, 1993: 33–44.)

The music of *The Tempest* generates two articles this year, both tending to recuperate a positive view of the play. Howell Chickering considers in detail the two surviving Robert Johnson settings, arguing that the kinds of uncertainty of effect that critics have ascribed them may or may not be true of the play's theatrical actions, but are not true of the music itself, which has a 'stability of effect that does not vary when interpretations vary'. ('Hearing Ariel's songs', *The Journal of Medieval and Renaissance Studies*, 24, 1994: 131–72). Robin Headlam Wells, in 'Prospero and the Myth of the Musician King', wants to restore the play to the 'general discursive field of Neoplatonism', giving us a Prospero who 'employs the arts of poetry, music and spectacle to civilize his subjects and restore harmony to his kingdom'. The book from which this piece comes – *Elizabethan Mythologies: Studies in Poetry, Drama and Music* (Cambridge: Cambridge University Press, 1994, 63–80) – also contains essays on the musical iconography of *Henry IV* ('Falstaff, Prince Hal and the New Song', 44–62), and on *Twelfth Night*, arguing that the music there 'reflects the idea not of social harmony and discord, but of mutability' ('"Ydle shallowe things": love and song in *Twelfth Night*', 208–24).

Finally, Brian Gibbons focuses on the dramatic procedures of the play, particularly on the way in which all its narrative movements are interrupted and redirected, involving the audience in revising their generic assumptions as the play proceeds. It is a device which 'brings out the quintessence of drama, its commitment to the live moment of performance, of existential risk'. ('*The Tempest* and Interruptions', *Cahiers Elisabéthains*, 45, 1994: 47–58.)

HISTORIES

In the articles I have encountered this year almost all attention has been focused on *Henry V* – a play which has become (as in Bradshaw's book) a test-case for critical affiliation. Three historicist essays offer ingenious, but not equally compelling readings. '*Henry V*'s association between theatrical enterprise and the enterprises of a dauntingly masculine monarch grants theater not the power of subversion, but rather the power of patriarchy, which is asserted over and against the waning and increasingly disparaged power of female rule'. Thus begins Katherine Eggert's 'Nostalgia and the not Yet Late Queen: Refusing Female Rule in *Henry V*' (*ELH* 61, 1994: 523–50). In the argument that follows she points to a variety of ways in which the play seems determined to marginalize the female – Henry's ancestry is traced no further back than Edward III; Katherine's place as ancestor of Elizabeth through her subsequent marriage to Owen Tudor is nowhere mentioned; the French are consistently feminized. But in the end, she argues, the play replicates its political moment both in its urgent desire for male rule, and its anxieties about the nature of the project. A perhaps more surprising reading is offered by Jeffrey Knapp, who argues that for Shakespeare 'the new public theaters seem to have represented a marvelous device not to "fight against God's word", as some preachers claimed, but to save it from the preachers'. 'Preachers and Players in Shakespeare's England' (*Representations*, 44, 1993: 29–59) is ingenious in suggesting that anticlericalism and the demystification of Harry's holy war, mediated by the Chorus's emphasis upon spectatorly participation, demonstrates that 'Shakespeare believed his audience could achieve some form of communion through the spiritual sacrifices inspired by his theatre.' The most suggestive reading is offered by Claire McEachern, in '*Henry V* and the Paradox of the Body Politic' (*Shakespeare Quarterly*, 45, 1994: 33–56), even if, as a whole, the essay is not entirely clear in its direction. At the centre of her argument is the recognition that 'changes in critical fashion notwithstanding, discussion of *Henry V*'s ambivalence frequently takes place in terms of Henry's character', and most often operate by setting up 'an antipathy between hegemonic power and fellow feeling, a binary in which Henry's humanity exists in an inverse proportion of "his" accommodation of state interests'. She argues that in Elizabethan political language the image of the body was multivalent, applying both to the body of the state and of the monarch, and that it contained within it the potential to symbolize the disorderlinesses either of 'levelling' or of 'tyranny'. She demonstrates that 'the play's representation of the paradox of monarchical personhood shares in the labile terms of Tudor–Stuart ideology generally'.

Seeking a way beyond 'the old dichotomy between ironic and heroic interpretations' of *Henry V*, P. K. Ayers focuses on Henry's problematic use of language, its failures and successes, concluding that 'it is Henry's fate to remain, simultaneously and paradoxically, both master and prisoner of the languages he has mastered and the time he has redeemed'. ('"Fellows of Infinite Tongue": *Henry V* and the King's English', *SERL*, 34, 1194: 253–77.) Michael Neill takes a much broader view of questions of language in his 'Broken English and Broken Irish: Nation, Language, and the Optic of Power in Shakespeare's Histories' (*Shakespeare Quarterly*, 45: 1–32). Full of material, some familiar, some less so, about the English colonial project in Ireland, the underlying argument seems to be that the English ambition to 'incorporate' the Irish is what, itself, produced the idea of Irish nationhood amongst the warring septs of the land.

Firmly of the view that the play demystifies war and exposes the play of class interests, Robert Lane produces a detailed and fierce indictment of Branagh's film of the play, concluding: 'Abandoning Shakespeare's probing examination of the problematic origin and product of male comradeship in war, Branagh instead reinforces the cinematic spectacle's rehearsal of the timeworn notion that warfare provides the optimal occasion for men to achieve their highest fulfilment.' ('"When Blood is their Argument: Class, Character and Historiography in Shakespeare and Branagh's *Henry V*', *ELH*, 61, 1994: 27–52.)

A more traditional and straightforward suggestion of the importance to the play of Plutarch's *Life of Alexander* is offered by Judith Mossman ('*Henry V* and Plutarch's *Alexander*', *Shakespeare Quarterly*, 45, 1994: 57–73), where she argues that Henry is presented more favourably than his classical model, but that the structure and the shaping of the play owe much to Plutarch, whom Shakespeare found useful 'not only for filling out the subtle texture of the Alexander comparisons but also for suggesting ways in which a portrait of a national hero could be made more memorable, more moving, more universal'.

TRAGEDIES

Titus Andronicus seems to be coming in from the critical wilderness, for in addition to Barker's book noticed above, it is the focus of at least three articles this year. Naomi Conn Liebler suggests, in 'Getting it All Right: *Titus Andronicus* and Roman History' (*Shakespeare Quarterly*, 45, 1994: 263–78) that Smyth's 1550 translation, *The History of Herodian*, provides a context for the play in its view of Rome 'dominated by female influence that subverted everything understood by the ideology of *romanitas* and governed by a miscegenized culture'. In the same journal Katherine A. Rowe's 'Dismembering and Forgetting in *Titus Andronicus*', (297–303) descants upon the significance of hands in the play, using both Renaissance emblems, and Freud's essay 'Fetishism' to argue 'that Titus's severed hand should be understood as part of a fetishizing tradition that makes the capacity for effective action contingent on disability'. The argument is not always clear, and some of the readings of emblems seem to me questionable; nonetheless the paradox that 'if dismemberment symbolizes loss of effective action in the world, it is clearly the condition of political agency in the play' is worth pursuing. In 'Textual Politics in *Titus Andronicus*: "Record", Maxim and an Icon of Justice' (*AUMLA* (*Journal of the Australasian Universities Language and Literature Association*), 91, 1994: 1–19) Heather Kerr considers two examples of legal texts within the play,

Saturninus' 'Record' and the maxim of 1.i, setting them in the context of legal theory to indicate ways in which the play dramatizes competing views of law and authority.

Joan Ozark Holmer mounts a persuasive and useful case for the influence of *Vincentio Saviolo His Practice*, a 1595 translation of the Paduan master's treatise on fencing, on *Romeo and Juliet*. She suggests many ways in which the precise language of this treatise finds echo in the play, but also draws attention to the way its concern with the ethics of duelling offers a complex moral surround for the 'aggressive, masculinist ethos' that the characters within the play manifest. ('"Draw, if you be men": Saviolo's Significance for *Romeo and Juliet*', *Shakespeare Quarterly*, 45, 1994: 163–89.)

As usual, *Hamlet* attracts a good deal of attention, of very varied quality. By far the most suggestive and powerful article is that by Steven Mullaney, 'Mourning and Misogyny: *Hamlet*, *Revenger's Tragedy* and the Final Progress of Elizabeth, 1600–1607' (*Shakespeare Quarterly*, 45, 1994: 138–62). He situates the play in the uncertainty of the last years of Elizabeth's reign and in the context of the increasing misogyny of the period, which he allies to mourning – a proleptic mourning for the dying Queen in the case of *Hamlet*, retrospective in *The Revenger's Tragedy*. The thesis enables a persuasive and rich reading of the encounter with Yorick's skull, seen as decisive in enabling movement from melancholy to mourning. In a psychoanalytic turn he links the fact that the skull provokes 'a triumphant reading and declaration of female mortality' with the observation that Yorick's death must have taken place when Hamlet was seven years old – the age of 'breeching', or when boys passed from the hands of women to the hands of men. Stuart M. Kurland also concentrates on the late-Elizabethan date of the play in his '*Hamlet* and the Scottish succession' (*SEL*, 34, 1994: 279–300). He picks up an old suggestion that the play builds into itself the anxiety about the succession of James to the throne of England,

and to the circumstances of the Essex rebellion. After a detailed demonstration of English anxieties at the end of the century he briefly surveys the political uncertainties of the play. The trouble is that one scarcely needs the 'evidence' of the first part of the essay to arrive at the very general conclusion of the last. I have some sympathy with 'topical' reading – but it needs to be prosecuted with more determination than it is in this essay.

A number of less ambitious pieces may be briefly noted. Melancholy and nostalgia inform Naomi Conn Liebler's reading of Hamlet's lament for the hobby-horse, taken to stand for the play's intent to 'reclaim tradition and all that it implies for legitimacy' ('Hamlet's Hobby-Horse', *Cahiers Elisabéthains*, 45, 1994: 33–45). William Collins Watterson's 'Hamlet's Lost Father' (*Hamlet Studies*, 16, 1994: 1–23) sees Yorick as 'a merry father standing in dialectical opposition to the play's numerous patriarchs'. In the same journal the fact that Hamlet addresses Horatio first as 'you', only modulating to 'thou' halfway through the play, is taken by John Halverson to suggest that Hamlet and Horatio did not know one another well before the play's beginning, and therefore what is represented is a growth of mutual understanding and respect as the play progresses. ('The Importance of Horatio', 57–70.) Hamlet's paralyzing desire for perfect knowing is interestingly explained by R. Chris Hassel, Jr in his 'Hamlet's "Too, Too Solid Flesh"' (*Sixteenth Century Journal*, 25, 1994: 608–22) as a symptom of the spiritual illness which Luther called the 'prudence or wisdom of the flesh'. Feminist concerns are addressed by Martha C. Ronk, who suggests: 'If Hamlet threatens to become all language and eventually all story, Ophelia as his counterpart becomes all picture.' She analyses the troubling significance of Gertrude's ekphrastic description of the dying woman as an act of allegoresis which points 'insistently beyond itself', moving Ophelia beyond the play 'to stand in a realm apart', so that, like the ghost, she both causes and stands for the fear of the uncanny. ('Representations of Ophelia', *Criticism*, 36.1., 1994: 21–44.)

In a typically witty, yet careful and densely argued piece (also printed in *Shakespeare Reread*, noticed above), Patricia Parker discovers in the phrase 'close dilations' terms which can be made to mean in a number of ways simultaneously. She links the political suggestion of 'spying' and 'secret accusation' with anatomical languages of 'uncovering, dilating and opening the "privy" place of women', and suggests that these implications play across one another in both *Othello* and *Hamlet*. Her style of 'close reading', which attempts to 'attend to the characteristic terms not only of the plays but of the culture contemporary with them,' thus, as it were, historicizing a formalist criticism, is exciting, returning one to the text with enthusiasm. ('*Othello* and *Hamlet*: Dilation, Spying and the "Secret Place" of Woman', *Representations*, 44, 1993: 60–95.) A rather more straightforward feminist perspective is offered in Ruth Vanita's '"Proper" Men and "Fallen" Women: the Unprotectedness of Wives in *Othello*' (*SEL*, 34, 1994: 341–56). She takes as her starting point the proposition that: 'The peculiar painfulness of *Othello* . . . springs from its dramatization of the ordinary, the normal, and its revelation of that normality as inherently brutal and horrifying.' Using the failure of Lodovico to intervene when Othello strikes Desdemona, compared with the readiness of onlookers to assume that the striking of Montano by Cassio is a public act which needs to be punished, she argues that the murders of Desdemona and Emilia are represented primarily as the tragedies of women in whose deaths the audience is complicit with the perspective of 'those men of Cyprus and Venice who silently witnessed the abuse of Desdemona and failed to intervene'. To the heaps of speculation as to Iago's motivation Karl F. Zender brings the suggestion that his 'worsting' by Desdemona in 2.1, where she exposes 'the inability of his manipulative rhetoric fully to masquerade as a language of affection', is a significant episode.

The play, then, registers at one level the ultimate failure of Iago's attempt 'to gain mastery over language and over the love it has the power to communicate'. ('The Humiliation of Iago', *SEL*, 34, 1994: 323–39.)

Regarding *King Lear* through the glass of Freud and Lacan (with Derrida urging on), Philip Armstrong's 'Uncanny Spectacles: Psychoanalysis and the Texts of *King Lear*' (*Textual Practice*, 8, 1994: 414–34) considers the doubling of texts, of kingdoms, of characters and of critical responses to be seamlessly symptomatic of the play's preoccupations with blindness and sight, mirroring and doubling, leading to a final identification of 'the most uncanny element of all, the gaze, as that radical alterity inhabiting the scopic field'. Perhaps for those with more sympathy towards psychoanalytic approaches than I have this makes sense.

In 'The Historiographical Evolution of the Macbeth Narrative' (*Scottish Literary Journal*, 21, 1994: 5–23) Kenneth D. Farrow provides a fascinating account of the earlier Scottish sources of the life of the King. Only tangential to Shakespeare's play, in that most of these sources were unlikely to be consulted by the playwright, the ways in which the morality of the story is continuously tidied up, and the emergence of the three witches as malign figures is yet interestingly traced.

'Shakespeare's Romans, it seems, think by the eye and watch one another habitually.' From this proposition, and considering various ways in which *Julius Caesar* employs theatrical spectacle and illusion, Fumio Toshioka develops his argument that Brutus, in *Julius Caesar*, is fatally misled into a 'grand illusion' which closes 'without even a touch of disillusionment on the part of the hero'. ('Theatre, Identity, and Brutus' Grand Illusion', *Studies in English Literature* (The English Literary Society of Japan, Tokyo) 70, 1994: 129–47.)

Theatricality is also seen as the central preoccupation of *Antony and Cleopatra* in G. A. Wilkes's amiable but unsurprising 'Excellent Dissembling: A View of *Antony and Cleopatra*',

(*Sidney Studies in English*, 19, 1993–4: 31–9). A more thoroughgoing approach to the play is essayed by Peggy Muñoz Simonds, using emblem literature to argue that the love of Antony for Cleopatra is represented as an addiction to chance, or to Fortuna, rather than to Sapientia. ('"To the Very Heart of Loss": Renaissance Iconography in Shakespeare's *Antony and Cleopatra*', *Shakespeare Studies*, 22, 1994: 220–76). For all her learning, it seems to me that the play will not be flattened into the moralizing emblematic frame that Simonds makes its master-text.

A notable feature of this year's criticism is the way in which *Coriolanus* seems to be gradually moving into a more prominent place. Its ambiguous (but politically very incorrect) hero could perhaps take over from Henry V as a focus for differently politicized readings. To Lars Engle's study (above) can be added Tetsuya Motohashi's 'Body Politic and Political Body in *Coriolanus*' (*Forum for Modern Language Studies*, 30, 1994: 97–112), which identifies two sets of conflicting conceptions of Rome. The first is a dialectic between a multiple state which embraces compromise and a military state which generates authoritarianism; the second a clash between images of 'Father Rome and Mother Rome' (both represented in Volumnia). The climax of the play, Coriolanus' submission to his mother, is 'so painfully moving because Coriolanus, for the first time in his life, realises his fate, which is, in fact, the expression of a Roman contradiction'. This is a useful recognition of the way in which Rome itself produces the fate of the hero – of a play in which the 'Hydra-like Body Politic finally devours the body of this political viper'. A more comprehensive revaluation is offered by T. McAlindon in '*Coriolanus*: An Essentialist Tragedy' (*Review of English Studies*, 44, 1993, 502–20), an article which applies the theory of tragedy developed in his *Shakespeare's Tragic Cosmos* (1991). The contrarieties of fire and ice, Mars and Venus, masculine and feminine are elaborated in the text; the moment of Corio-

lanus' retreat from Rome signals his achievement of an 'heroic integrity . . . his tragedy being that he reaches such a consummation only through death'. The whole careful analysis (particularly useful in its emphasis upon the symbolic function of Virgilia) is framed by and as an attack upon the 'anti-essentialism' of materialist reading, in the belief that 'each tragic world is culturally distinctive but at the same time it is grounded on a construction of reality which Shakespeare's contemporaries considered to have a timeless validity'. If these essays in different ways seem to recoup Coriolanus himself, the potentially explosive political effect of the play is noted by Pascal Ory in a brief account of its reception in France on the eve of the death of the Third Republic ('L'Affaire Coriolan: Shakespeare contre la République', *L'Histoire*, 180, 1994: 74–5). No compromises here, for he regards the play as 'l'une des plus violentes diatribes antidémocratiques qui aient franchi les siècles'.

Shakespeare's perhaps least studied tragedy, *Timon of Athens*, is claimed by Jonathan Baldo as the play in which Shakespeare comes closest 'to entertaining the fantasy of a levelled humanity before reinstating difference'. His 'The Shadow of Levelling in *Timon of Athens*' (*Criticism*, 35, 1993: 559–87) see the play's 'generality and abstractness' as helping to make it 'one of Shakespearian tragedy's most vigorous acts of self-examination'.

POEMS

The poems seem to have returned to favour as objects of critical attention this year (even if the quality of discussion is not always of the highest). I have to confess that my linguistic incompetence makes me unable to comment securely on the most substantial collection of all, *Shakespeares Sonette in europäischen Perspectiven*, ed. Dieter Mehl and Wolfgang Weiss (Studien zur englischen Literatur, 5, Münster, 1993). Michael Spiller's *The Development of the Sonnet, An Introduction* (London: Routledge, 1992) covers the period from the thirteenth century to Milton, and in its focus on form and the uses of language is an extremely useful primer for students. The chapter on Shakespeare focuses on the poet's 'characteristic and unique' concern with 'the insecurity of his own selfhood'. The nature of the self presented in the sonnets is, indeed, the focus of a number of essays. Comparing Donne's *Holy Sonnets* with two of Shakespeare's Martin Coyle in 'The Subject and the Sonnet' (*English*, 43, 1994: 139–50), suggests that in each something of a modern subjective consciousness is to be discerned. Jane Hedley's 'Since First Your Eye I Eyed: Shakespeare's *Sonnets* and the Poetics of Narcissism' (*Style*, 28, 1994: 1–30) argues that the 'psychic profile of Narcissism' which critics such as Pequigney have seen as informing the first 126 sonnets can be extended to assist in understanding the macrostructure of the sequence, and the 'microstructure' of individual sonnets. She sees in the sonnets to the young man 'an oscillating rhythm of identification and estrangement, fullness and emptiness that is continually being recircumstanced', and explains the conjunctions and disjunctions between them as an embodiment of the problematic of Narcissism. Raymond B. Waddington considers Sonnet 20 in his 'The Poetics of Eroticism: Shakespeare's "Master Mistress"' (Claude J. Summers and Ted-Larry Pebworth, eds., *Renaissance Discourses of Desire*, Columbia and London: University of Missouri Press, 1993, 13–28), setting it in the context of Classical and Renaissance representations of androgyny and of the myth of Priapus to clarify its 'profoundly ambivalent eroticism'. In another essay in the volume, which alludes to *Troilus and Cressida*, but might have equal consequence for the reading of the *Sonnets*, Joseph Cady continues his dispute with the argument of Alan Bray and others that 'homosexuality . . . was not a sexuality in its own right' in the early modern period. ('Renaissance Awareness and Language for Heterosexuality: "Love" and "Feminine Love"', 143–58). M. L. Stapelton varies the focus by considering the Dark Lady sonnets, suggesting, not entirely convincingly, that they are not simply anti-feminine, since 'the lie to be unraveled is that the dark lady is evil and that Will is a reliable narrator; we might conclude from these sonnets that neither premise is true, and that Will knows it'. (' "My False Eyes": The Dark Lady and Self-Knowledge', *Studies in Philology*, 90, 1993: 213–30.) In a rather elusive piece: 'Shakespeare's Sweet Leaves: Mourning, Pleasure and the Triumph of Thought in the Renaissance Love Lyric' (*ELH*, 61, 1994: 1–26) Elizabeth Harris Sagaser tries to distinguish three of the *Sonnets* (29, 30, and 122) as 'poems in which thought of the beloved is represented as vital and good in and of itself'. But for me at least, the grounds of distinction appear less than clear, and the argument that follows less than compelling. David Thatcher, in 'What a Lark: The Undoing of Sonnet 29' (*Durham University Journal*, 86, 1994: 59–66), simply throws up his hands, concluding that the poem 'cannot be undone, because, patently overdetermined as it is, it eludes our most determined grasp'. Finally, Gunnar Sorelius posits a suggestive analogue for the *Sonnets* (and early comedies) in 'The *Hypnerotamachia* and Spenser's and Shakespeare's Ruins' (in *Cultural Exchange*, noticed above, 133–42). Colonna's text, he tentatively suggests, meditates in an interestingly parallel fashion on the collocation of architectural ruins and love.

Venus and Adonis, says Katherine Duncan-Jones, 'has still failed to find a modern popular market'. In her delightful ' "Much ado with Red and White": the Earliest Readers of Shakespeare's *Venus and Adonis*' (*Review of English Studies*, 44, 1993: 479–501) she charts the immediate reaction to the poem, from its appropriation by the demented William Reynolds, to whom Venus stands for the Queen, Adonis for himself, through echoes and rewritings by Drayton, Heywood and many others to suggest that the narrative was 'above all a poem which exemplified the rhetoric of courtship. It was entrancing, sexually exciting, and open to numberless fresh applications.' This, in pointed contrast to the reaction of readers from Coleridge to contemporary (male) critics who have felt 'threatened by the overwhelming physicality of Shakespeare's Venus'.

In *The Rape of Lucrece* Philomela is twice invoked as a parallel, but, in Jane O. Newman's account, 'Philomela, Female Violence, and Shakespeare's *Lucrece*' (*Shakespeare Quarterly*, 1994: 404–26), the failure of the poem to mention her revenge upon Tereus is a mark of the way Shakespeare's text sets particular limits to Lucrece's potential for action. Endlessly reduplicated in the scholarship which has maintained the invisibility of the 'Philomela' possibility, Newman argues, Shakespeare's elision has compelled readers into 'a position of critical identification with and reproduction of the Roman matron's suicidal politics', a collusion she wishes to overthrow. It is a clear and cogently assembled argument, but it does, I think, simplify the responses to Lucrece's suicide that the poem permits. In a rather similar, but less focussed fashion, Joyce Green Macdonald argues that 'renouncing speech and history, Lucrece is nonetheless appropriated for the purposes of both. The conclusion of the poem speaks the contradictions and perils inherent in the Renaissance productions of doctrines of female sovereignty' ('Speech, Silence and History in *The Rape of Lucrece*', *Shakespeare Studies*, 22, 1994: 77–103.) John Roe comes at the poem from a very different angle in his 'Pleasing the Wiser Sort: Ethics and Genre in *Lucrece* and *Hamlet*' (*Cambridge Quarterly*, 23, 1994: 99–119). He begins with the moral question posed by Lucrece's suicide to the Church Fathers, including St Augustine, who argued: 'If her homicide is extenuated, her adultery is established; if she is cleared of adultery, the murder is abundantly proved.' Roe is not particularly concerned with the issues of gender and power that this represen-tation of the dilemma of Lucrece might raise; instead he focuses on the ways in which the poem develops and exposes contradictions in attitudes to chastity that suffuse the Petrarchan tradition, finally to 'exonerate Lucrece and pin the blame where it has always belonged'.

REISSUES

Robert Ornstein's *Shakespeare's Comedies* (1986) is reissued in paperback by Associated University Presses, as is Vivian Thomas's study of *Julius Caesar* in the Harvester New Critical Introductions series. E. A. J. Honigmann has edited the *British Academy Shakespeare Lectures, 1980–89* (Oxford: Oxford University Press for The British Academy, 1993), including essays by a number of distinguished Shakespearians. Three essays by Albert S. Gerard, on *Twelfth Night*, *Troilus* and *Othello* are to be found in *Baroque Tragedies: Comparative Essays on Seventeenth-Century Drama* (Liège, 1993). John Wain has edited two revised Casebooks, on *Othello* and *Macbeth*, each of which includes some recent criticism, and an editorial health warning about critical theory in the introduction.

The most welcome of all the reissues is Anne Barton's *Essays Mainly Shakespearian* (Cambridge: Cambridge University Press, 1994). In addition to previously published work ranging from her first essay on *Love's Labour's Lost* to the 1992 'Parks and Ardens' the volume includes a characteristically urbane lecture on 'Comic London', and her very persuasive '"Wrying but a little": Marriage, Law and Sexuality in the Plays of Shakespeare', which surveys customary and legal practices surrounding marriage contracts as a prelude to a discussion of Imogen and Posthumus' relationship in *Cymbeline*. It is marked, as are all her essays, by an easy authority in dealing with a wide range of material, careful particularity in reading her chosen texts, and a blessed clarity of exposition.

2. SHAKESPEARE'S LIFE, TIMES, AND STAGE
reviewed by MARK THORNTON BURNETT

A quick inspection of current titles in Shake-spearian criticism suggests that theory has now come of age. The new historicism, gender-related approaches and contextual studies dominate, and equal attention is given to restoring the profile of Shakespeare's neglected contemporaries. It would appear as if the margins of the text have finally subsumed the dramatist. A closer investigation, however, highlights the continuing vitality of author-centred readings and the ways in which Shake-speare serves as a prompt for wider-ranging cultural interpretations. Critical efforts are focusing increasingly upon appropriations of Shakespeare, shifting interest away from the Renaissance itself and towards its importance for a later generation of writers and producers.

I

In recent years the new historicism, cultural materialism and varieties of materialist feminism have altered the complexion of Renaissance scholarship, and, taking their cue from previous publications, these newer assessments see Shakespeare as one discursive strand in a larger, contradictory cultural matrix. Prominent among the latest group of studies indebted to the new historicism must stand Jean E. Howard's *The Stage and Social Struggle in Early Modern England* (Routledge, 1994), an exciting account of the controversial place of the theatre, puritan polemic against plays, and the ideo-logical and political uses of spectacle. Exploring such dramas as the histories, *Much Ado About Nothing* and Thomas Dekker's *The Whore of Babylon*, Howard unpicks the dangerous meanings embodied in cross-dressing while also arguing for the empowerment of women attending contemporary playhouses. Very occasionally questions about different kinds of playgoer and playhouse rest unresolved, but this does not diminish the book's key contri-

bution: Howard's commendable achievement is to discuss the social impact of a number of lesser known plays and to establish negotiation as a critical term that goes well beyond the subversion/containment binarisms that be-devilled much previous new historicist work.

Howard carries her theory confidently, always combining sophistication with accessi-bility; in contrast, Linda Charnes, in *Notorious Identity: Materializing the Subject in Shakespeare* (Harvard University Press, 1993), is slightly less manageable in terms of her ideological em-phases. The basic thesis that Shakespeare's choice of a number of 'historical' characters, such as Richard III, Cressida and Antony and Cleopatra, involved reflections upon the com-modification of identity, conceptions of the past and the process of representation is attrac-tive. These 'characters' are read as meditations upon legend, as struggles for subjectivity and as functions of theatrical effect, and the argument entails some brilliant local insights. Although Charnes has anticipated many of the questions to which her perspective gives rise, some nig-gling difficulties remain. Are there degrees of reinscription among the many 'texts' she covers, and how defensible is her decision to favour a stance of theoretical pluralism? In addition, the constant tendency of her writing to qualify can blur the point being made; this produces an impression of a debate that staggers even as it shapes the study's dexterous move-ments around a densely articulated central theme.

The impact of the new historicism on the humanities is reflected in anthologies as well as in individually authored monographs. Three collaborations carry through the implications of a materialist critique with varying successes. Margo Hendricks and Patricia Parker have edited an excellent volume, *Women, 'Race', and Writing in the Early Modern Period* (Routledge, 1994), which is to be applauded in that it combines post-colonial theory and European-inflected dialogue in a series of essays concentrating on women writers and gendered representations. As Hendricks and Parker point out in their introduction, 'race' has been generally overlooked by new historicists, and the collection succeeds admirably in building upon and changing the concerns of an older critical outlook. Personally anecdotal and intertextual, pedagogically self-aware, and historically precise and interrogative, the contributors go a long way towards undoing categories of difference, complicating models of colonial exchange and domination and resistance, and recovering an indigenous experience. Perhaps the most impressive essay is Patricia Parker's, a penetrating appreciation of *Othello* that sets the play in relation to discourses of discovery and secrecy with considerable finesse. A more uneven collection centring upon issues of nationality is represented by *Shakespeare's Italy: Functions of Italian Locations in Renaissance Drama* (Manchester University Press, 1993), edited by Michele Marrapodi, A. J. Hoenselaars, Marcello Cappuzzo and L. Falzon Santucci. Italy emerges from the book as a site within which questions about alien cultures and ethnocentric mentalities can be confronted, and several contributors bring useful Italian sources to bear upon their materials. But a smaller number of essays fails to develop observations about metatheatre (Agostino Lombardo) and the dubious opposition between 'appearance and reality' (Mariangela Tempera), and, taken as a whole, *Shakespeare's Italy* seems more of a prolegomenon to a longer and more systematic project than a finished statement.

It is an index of the extent to which new historicism has filtered through to the arts in general that established historians are responding to the insights gained from theoretical enquiry. Kevin Sharpe and Peter Lake's *Culture and Politics in Early Stuart England* (Macmillan, 1994) is an attempt by historians to introduce some of these developments to students, and to this end the editors assemble revisionist work

from across the disciplines. Some pieces (for example, those by Martin Butler and David Norbrook on courtly and republican literary cultures respectively) are subtle and felicitous persuasions, and it is a pity that their standard is not imitated throughout. Writing on royal authors, Kevin Sharpe is surely to be queried in his compartmentalization of gender and politics; similarly, Peter Lake might be challenged in that his discussion of murder pamphlets fails to take account of reception and audience. More seriously, despite its claims, the volume avoids direct collisions with theory, underestimates the role of popular rituals, contains little on class or on gay and lesbian sexualities, and is sometimes critically out-of-date. The only genuinely new historicist essay (by Leah S. Marcus on pastoral) is reprinted.

Many of the new historicist titles are the work of American scholars, and the British equivalents, such as Kevin Sharpe and Peter Lake's anthology, tend to be more guarded in their theoretical orientations. This can function positively, as other British contributions to the reconfiguration of the period serve to demonstrate. Andrew Hadfield undertakes a complete revaluation of the sixteenth century in his vigorously argued *Literature, Politics and National Identity: Reformation to Renaissance* (Cambridge University Press, 1994). Indebted to but never wholly dependent on recent discussions of nation, Hadfield writes against conceptions which divide the Renaissance into neatly demarcated literary units. Instead, by exploring the contrasting vernacular and poetic idioms enlisted by such authors as John Bale, William Baldwin, George Ferrers, George Puttenham, Philip Sidney, John Skelton, Edmund Spenser and Thomas Wilson, he charts attempts to forge a national history and moves well beyond pre-existing definitions. He is at his most eloquent when detailing areas of overlap between nationalism and ideas about speech, when contextualizing the generic diffuseness of his chosen texts, and when speculating about the effects of the Reformation on a reading audience.

While her *Dekker and Heywood: Professional Dramatists* (Macmillan, 1994) is intended as a less specialized work, Kathleen E. McLuskie makes equally valuable points about the relationship between audience taste (in the popular theatres) and literary production. Her book has the merit of recognizing the social complexity of neglected dramatists as well as defining the serious intellectual claims made by the popular playhouses. The Earl of Essex's rebellion, the political role of apprentices in the 1590s, and the accession of James I all feature as telling pressures on the growth of a consumer-oriented professional theatrical repertoire. As concerned to scrutinize the politics of dramatic form as to pinpoint ambivalent images of the metropolis, McLuskie shows herself no less adept in appreciating representations of women, in ways which reveal changing social relations and the influence of popular cultural traditions. A robust reappraisal of the chrono-logical and thematic development of each dramatist, *Dekker and Heywood* operates at the same time an incisive commentary upon the interplay between theatrical experiment and gendered modes of conduct.

The new historicism has thus stamped its imprint across a broad expanse of scholarly endeavour, and generally the effect has been to advance knowledge in uncharted areas, ampli-fying constructions of marginalized voices or rescuing familiar names from critical obscurity. The historicist enterprise has had the notable advantage of tilting enquiry back towards women as writers and as representations, and, indeed, gender questions loom large in the present crop of titles. Unfortunately the results have been mixed in the extreme. A disappoint-ing example is Annette Drew-Bear's *Painted Faces on the Renaissance Stage: The Moral Sig-nificance of Face-Painting Conventions* (Bucknell University Press, 1994), the moralistic slant of which is clear from the outset. Drew-Bear has read widely in the drama of the period and is in good command of the literary background to the convention, but her dogged pursuit of

'moral implications' and 'dramatic purposes' limits her survey's ideological potential. It is not clear why cosmetics became so urgent a pre-occupation in the Renaissance, nor are the racial and political dimensions to her subject fully aired. One has little sense of the plays them-selves as organic entities, and the decision to focus on selected scenes allows few opportuni-ties to explore original performance circum-stances. Only flat conclusions are finally advanced: 'face-painting offered [for Jonson] a . . . fruitful image of pretense' (p. 92) and 'The verbal and visual images of painting [in Shake-speare] underscore [a] central concern with false appearances' (p. 99). A harder criticism must be reserved for Carol Hansen's *Woman as Indi-vidual in English Renaissance Drama: A Defiance of the Masculine Code* (Peter Lang, 1994). In this extraordinary book, whose bibliography con-tains only three items of criticism published since the early 1970s, Hansen turns to Hey-wood, Middleton, Shakespeare and Webster to claim that the 'masculine code' (which is never adequately explained) led to 'disintegration, defiance, and death for women, and to madness for men'; from this astounding declaration, she moves on to suggest that Cleopatra alone emerges as an 'individual' as she has the 'cult of Isis' to lend her support (Preface). A host of problems accompanies this critical procedure. 'Individual' is rarely problematized; the 'mascu-line code' is presented as seamlessly negative; the dramatic sample is woefully impoverished; and the prose displays an essentialist bias against which the occasional theoretical remark is oddly pitted. Women are divided up into binary categories; 'masculine' and 'feminine' are accepted unreservedly as active concepts; and 'contradiction' barely enters the discussion. It is difficult to be more sympathetic towards a work labouring under the illusion that early modern printed books in the Bodleian Library are manuscripts (pp. 157–60, 205–6).

Two related studies which address gender issues from a theatrical angle with far greater sophistication come as a welcome relief.

Women's roles form only part of Lloyd Davis' book, *Guise and Disguise: Rhetoric and Characterization in the English Renaissance* (University of Toronto Press, 1993), an accomplished analysis of the ways in which the use of disguise 'foregrounds the equivocal aspects of rhetorical and dramatistic identity' (p. 12). The social and political aspects of disguise are suitably rehearsed in a series of carefully packed chapters on Ben Jonson's *Bartholomew Fair*, James I's *Basilicon Doron*, John Lyly's *Campaspe*, John Marston's *The Malcontent* and Elizabethan prose fiction. One chapter, however, deals with disguise and androgyny, and dramas such as Francis Beaumont and John Fletcher's *A King and No King* and *Philaster* are cited as challenges to the sexual motives that underlie images of the essentialist self, an argument that leads to intriguing parallels being drawn between Renaissance culture and postmodern views about subjectivity and language. A sharper reading might have speculated about the particular theatres where disguise dramas were staged, and it would be satisfying to know why 'a certain predictability is found in the motif' (p. 129) by 1609, but these omissions do not interfere with the book's overall treatment of an abundantly interesting cultural phenomenon.

The Usurer's Daughter: Male Friendship and Fictions of Women in Sixteenth-Century England (Routledge, 1994) by Lorna Hutson is more striking still, possibly because of the high level of critical engagement it demands. Hutson's concern is to establish points of correspondence between new humanist ideas about male friendship and representations of articulate women, and in her ensuing discussion of conduct books, prose fiction, and Terentian and Shakespearian drama, she suggests that there is an economic dimension to fictions about women's infidelity, that 'masculinity' is articulated as a form of husbandry, and that trust between men depended on notions of 'credit' and exchange. Arguably this approach takes important attention away from questions about women's

agency and empowerment; in addition, it might be felt that some of Hutson's historical claims and definitions are open to debate. However, the writing is never anything less than stimulating, and, if the elaboration of the argument is difficult, the book in its entirety offers an innovative and rewarding reading experience.

One final effect of the new historicism, in addition to orienting the axis towards the place of women in literary discourse, has been to revive interest in the work of Shakespeare's contemporaries. Accompanying the decentring of Shakespeare has been an attempt to bring his contemporary dramatists and writers into the mainstream of critical debate. Thomas Healy's *Christopher Marlowe* (Northcote House, 1994) employs recent thinking about the historical embeddedness of literary texts in a refreshing critique of the playwright's resistance to established norms and embracing of new social possibilities. The 'Writers and their Work' format of the series does not leave Healy free to expand upon all of his opening proposals, although he is able to consider the plays' treatment of social fluidity, their moments of self-parody, and their Protestant militarism. This is a short but worthwhile study, which is only marginally spoiled by the unjustified observation that the *Tamburlaine* plays may have been performed together (p. 55) and by incongruous references to modern soap operas (p. 65). Shakespeare's plays, and the relationship between their aesthetic self-consciousness and representations of social distinctions, occupy one chapter of Peter Holbrook's *Literature and Degree in Renaissance England: Nashe, Bourgeois Tragedy, Shakespeare* (University of Delaware Press, 1994), a work which is, however, more directly concerned with pursuing these arguments in a wider literary context. For Holbrook, popular prose and plays such as *Arden of Faversham*, *A Woman Killed with Kindness* and *A Yorkshire Tragedy* are primary instances of literary forms as social modes: Nashe's work shows his complex role as an insider and outsider; domestic drama uses an aristocratic genre (tragedy) to negotiate the status of mainly middling classes. The book constitutes a useful corrective to constructions of 'society', despite its reluctance to theorize its texts more forcefully and to provide a material reading of the period's social instabilities.

Perhaps the best of the mainly non-Shakespearian titles is Gordon McMullan's *The Politics of Unease in the Plays of John Fletcher* (University of Massachusetts Press, 1994). McMullan regards Fletcher as keenly responsive to social and political tensions, and, in the plays, conflicts between London and the country, England and the colonies, and women and men are key manifestations of the forces within and against which the dramatist worked. The study has much to recommend it, and a mark of its originality is McMullan's meticulous discussion of Fletcher's plays in the light of the interests of his patrons, the Hastings family, Protestant aristocrats who were disaffected from court and favoured a theatrical aesthetic. Accordingly, McMullan brings a shrewdly political reading to Fletcher's deployment of pastoral themes, to his representations of aristocratic responsibilities, and to his experiments in masque entertainments. Any future study of Beaumont and Fletcher will surely be indebted to McMullan's fine work, which broadens the application of new historicism and provides fresh ways of conceptualizing the processes of collaborative writing practice.

II

From the previous sections, it might be assumed that new historicism and its offshoots are now the dominant forces in the academy. Even in books which have apparently little connection to the imperatives of the new historicist project, the traces of a materialist critique can usually be found. This is not to suggest that more 'traditional' kinds of historical scholarship have completely disappeared. Several examples of work which does not strongly identify itself with a particular theoretical position are evident in the current selection of titles. These might loosely be described as belonging to the more established genre of 'source study', although a number of the volumes under consideration do not yield easily to such a strict labelling of their scope and purposes.

On the one hand, research into the 'literary and philosophical background' to Shakespeare's work continues unabated. Anna Baldwin and Sarah Hutton have edited *Platonism and the English Imagination* (Cambridge University Press, 1994), the first compendium which aims to assess the influence of Plato on English literature, showing in discrete chronological stages how writers used Platonic and neo-Platonic ideas in their work. There is no single theme which ties the collection together; rather, its strength resides in the distinction of the individual essays, such as those by John Roe on the adventurous, mocking treatment of Italian neo-Platonism in English Renaissance poetry, and by Stephen Medcalf on the Platonic contexts of *The Phoenix and the Turtle* and *Troilus and Cressida*. Their methodological approach is broadly similar to that of Theodor Meron in *Henry's Wars and Shakespeare's Laws: Perspectives on the Law of War in the Later Middle Ages* (Clarendon Press, 1993). In this book, Meron traces the medieval regulations of conduct in battle which lie behind accounts of the historical Henry V and Shakespeare's realization of the monarch; after rehearsing general ideas, he proceeds to map specific instances in an argument that eventually illuminates the drama as well as changes in modern legal procedures. The book tends to leap bewilderingly between medieval and modern concepts of warfare, and Meron never quite decides if Shakespeare's Henry V might be described as conventional; nevertheless, his study is brightly clear-sighted, and he brings to it all the expertise of a professor working in a law department.

On the other hand, traditional forms of historical research are now being married to more recent work on power and patronage, a development which is apparent in several books about the relationship between drama, the arts and popular and élite cultures in general. David Wiles' *Shakespeare's Almanac: 'A Midsummer Night's Dream', Marriage and the Elizabethan Calendar* (D. S. Brewer, 1993) contends that the play was commissioned for the wedding of Elizabeth Carey, the grand-daughter of the Lord Chamberlain, and it is by taking this occasion into account that we can understand the drama's astrological allusions and formal parallels with masques and pageants, and speculate about its early performances. Wiles' method is to pursue such allusions relentlessly, and while the breadth of evidence is impressive, eventually it is not clear how his study differs from an older historicism and how many of his connections are coincidental. There are some discordant notes in Robin Headlam Wells' *Elizabethan Mythologies: Studies in Poetry, Drama and Music* (Cambridge University Press, 1994), too, such as the author's need to point out passages of 'extreme lyrical beauty' (p. 3) whenever they present themselves. But this is to do the book a disservice. *Elizabethan Mythologies* is a wonderful disquisition on art both as a source of aesthetic pleasure and as a means of social control. It contains a wealth of scholarly information and invention, which are skilfully applied to chapters on the Elizabethan lute song, the symbolic geometry of the Renaissance rose, architecture and the court lyric. In this ballet around a series of related musical and artistic productions, Wells is unfailingly subtle and insightful. A firm believer in the author's intentions and the inherent meanings residing in the text, Wells is rather more essentialist in his treatment of Shakespeare, although he is not averse to favouring some new historicist accounts and argues for the importance of art as a philosophical system and a material fact with a winning conviction and confidence.

The tradition of hunting down Shakespeare's 'source' material, if the activity can be so described, would appear to be alive and well. And work by such critics as Wells is advancing knowledge in significant directions. Looking at current academic practice more leisurely, however, reveals that it is not so much Shakespeare's use of history as history's use of Shakespeare to which the critical profession is veering. The idea of Shakespeare himself as a 'source' seems to be attracting the greatest volume of interest. One such example of the present tendency is Anthony J. Berret, S. J.'s *Mark Twain and Shakespeare: A Cultural Legacy* (University Press of America, 1993). Shakespeare is the key to Twain's self-understanding and artistic development, Berret believes, a claim which involves several problems. Despite some caveats, Berret employs Shakespeare as a universal yardstick, thereby demonstrating an inadequate grasp of the recent dismantlement of the dramatist's cultural status. As a result, the book never progresses very far beyond suggesting that Shakespeare represented for Twain the 'robust life-style of the English Renaissance' (p. 13), an 'antique flavor' (p. 112), a 'profundity' (p. 148) and perennial 'human' themes.

The same cannot be said for Marianne Novy's *Engaging with Shakespeare: Responses of George Eliot and Other Women Novelists* (University of Georgia Press, 1994), a cogent reconsideration of the preoccupations of several literary periods and a polished intellectual exercise. Novy discusses those women novelists who responded to Shakespeare's presence, and, while sidestepping the issue of patriarchal constructions of the 'anxiety of influence', she still manages to throw light on creations of Shakespeare which helped some women to reflect upon specific needs and concerns. Focusing on Jane Austen, Charlotte Brontë and George Eliot, and later on Virginia Woolf, Margaret Drabble, Angela Carter and others, Novy illustrates the contention that Shakespeare appealed as an outsider, an artist of wide-ranging identification and a performer: in short, as a charged system of cultural meanings and references. In textual appropriations of his plays, Novy writes, there can be seen a will to expand upon genres or to play them off against each other, and a broader development whereby class positions in Shakespeare are translated into questions about changing gender hierarchies. A narrower criticism might want to fault Novy for an overly sensitive ear to echoes and allusions, and for sometimes hesitating to entertain a more radical feminist ideology. An open evaluation would prefer to praise the uniqueness of her exploration of a vital fictional tradition, and her interpretation of increasingly competing rewritings of Shakespeare's mythical abilities.

What distinguishes these studies is the way in which Shakespeare functions as a repository of values and mentalities that later generations are drawn to change and contest. His work is represented as the impetus for a range of literary and cultural experiments, some of which bear a very tangential relation to their bardic originator. A number of the appropriations involve a performative dimension, particularly as far as regards adaptations of Shakespeare for film, television or the theatre. Manfred Draudt has edited Richard Peake and Charles Mathews' *Othello, the Moor of Fleet Street* (Francke Verlag, 1993), an 1833 burlesque. He has done a competent job on the copy-text, which he recovers from a manuscript copy in the British Library. Shakespeare's *Othello* is only dimly glimpsed in Peake and Mathews' version in which the African general is reduced to a London street-sweeper, and it is this process of textual transformation that one would expect the edition to explicate. Unfortunately, Draudt offers no such reading, choosing instead to unfold questions relating to the play's authorship and provenance. Limited in their theoretical overview, his introduction, notes and appendixes lack the necessary cultural elements that might have added some zest to a rather uninspired editorial undertaking.

A more substantial body of criticism goes further towards exploring connections between wider cultural changes and 'Shakespearian' rewritings, specifically theatrical and cinematic productions. The Shakespearean play becomes the raw material out of which is fashioned a looser text, which operates as a sensitive register of peculiarly modern imperatives. *Foreign Shakespeare: Contemporary Performance* (Cambridge University Press, 1993), edited by Dennis Kennedy, gathers linked essays dealing with the importance of Shakespeare's drama for non-English theatres. Text and translation theory, the place of the visual, divergent acting and directing strategies, the role of the audience, and political appropriations and conflicts are all considered in the volume. While it fulfils the essential task of querying Anglo-centric Shakespearian conceptions, the book's actual content is less arresting. The contributions generally eschew close analysis, spend an inordinate amount of time expounding the genesis of their selected productions (in China, Czechoslovakia, France, Germany, Italy, Japan and Russia) and leave too many questions unresolved, although there are a couple of notable exceptions: Avraham Oz's account of the necessarily sympathetic portrayals of Shylock in Israel elucidates the shaping of the country's theatrical realizations by a nationalist agenda. The 'Afterword: Shakespearean Orientalism' shows the editor bravely trying to turn the collection from what could strike some readers as a set of extended play reviews into a meatier collaborative endeavour, and he is certainly provocative in his observations. Fascinating reflections on the theoretical bases of transculturalism are forwarded, and there is a considered effort to speculate about why a 'foreign' Shakespeare continues to be performed: it is only to be regretted that Kennedy's curiosity and enthusiasm do not percolate through to the anthology as a whole.

In the two publications which address Shakespearian appropriations from cinematic and televisual perspectives, grander claims and conclusions are again fitfully sustained. *Screen Shakespeare*, a special 1994 issue of *The Dolphin* – a journal published by Aarhus University Press and edited by Michael Skovmand – addresses the filmic tradition of *A Midsummer Night's Dream*, Polanski and Welles' versions of

Macbeth, Brook's *King Lear* and Kurosawa's *Ran*, and the recent directorial work of Branagh, Greenaway and Zeffirelli from an array of critical positions. The quality of the collection varies: some contributors are inward-looking to the point of obscurity, as Bernice W. Kliman's scrupulous but unanalytical survey of cuts to Welles' *Macbeth* proves, while others, such as Susanne Fabricius in her essay on the 'universal human' (p. 98) appeal of Branagh's *Henry V*, couch their points in a far-fetched essentialist language. These essays are offset, however, by Ib Johansen's fine Bakhtinian reading of the folkloric elements in Kurosawa's *Ran*, and by Claus Schatz-Jacobsen's nuanced unravelling of the dialogic relationship shared by literary texts and cinematic images in Greenaway's *Prospero's Books*. *Screen Shakespeare* contains highlights and frustrations in equal measure.

In *Watching Shakespeare on Television* (Fairleigh Dickinson University Press, 1993), H. R. Coursen devotes a whole book to the Shakespearian screen. He looks with gusto at Shakespeare as a cultural phenomenon and at the videocassette as text, describing productions ranging from Olivier's *Hamlet* and Welles' *King Lear* to Zeffirelli's *Hamlet* and Branagh's *Henry V*. The prose is enlivened by moments of acute commentary, and the idea that the Shakespearian script represents both a locus for prevailing cultural anxieties and 'a set of signals to be decoded . . . in radically different ways' (p. 69) is helpfully developed. Notwithstanding these positive features, Coursen is hampered by his argumentative framework. He admits that many of the films on television with which he is concerned originated in a widescreen format (p. 32), and yet the book does not do enough to acknowledge such discrepancies in the sample of evidence selected. Two chapters (on the endings of different versions of *Hamlet* and a psychological approach to *Othello*) do not seem to fit with the rest of the volume, and the poorly printed stills make an unfavourable impression. *Watching Shakespeare on Television*

is a book to enjoy for its sprightly isolated details and to question for its collapsing of representational distinctions.

III

Critical readings of Shakespearian rewritings often shade into discussions of the more conventionally performative dimensions of the dramatic experience. In debating appropriations of Shakespeare's work, these interpretations touch upon seminal questions about the nature of the theatre, the plays' contemporary impact and their subsequent revivals. It is the project of some recent titles to address precisely these issues, and to give an account of sixteenth- and seventeenth-century playhouses as well as the status of modern theatrical institutions and performances. Editorial research on play-texts is showing itself to be as important in deepening an understanding of the theatre's changing role and determining influence.

The historical aspects of the development of early modern theatrical institutions furnish the keystones for two studies, which offer synthetic and archeologically intricate approaches to their subjects. The first book fares less well than the second. In *Art Imitates Business: Commercial and Political Influences in Elizabethan Theatre* (Bowling Green State University Popular Press, 1993), James H. Forse attempts to explain the 'difficulties' of English Renaissance drama by considering the playhouse as an essentially financially motivated project. The book that emerges fails to escape the constraints of its assumptions and never manages to expand into a coherent argument, to the extent that it is difficult to tell for whom its bland remarks are intended. Useful lists of theatrical wage-earners are provided, but Forse is not always scrupulous in revealing sources for his tables and calculations. The dating of plays is questionable; the writing rehearses views familiar from older accounts; and the tone is alternately chatty and anti-theoretical. And either the author or the type-setter must stand accused of atrocious transcriptions: 'Marlow' (p. 206) is credited with a new drama entitled '*Dido, Queen of Corinth*' (p. 182); Marston apparently wrote '*Historio-mastix*' (p. 281); Robert Devereux becomes Robert 'Devereaux' (p. 289); and other names in the bibliography are misspelt. It is an altogether regrettable and careless production. Graham C. Adams avoids such pitfalls in his precisely elaborated *The Ottoneum Theater: An English Survivor from Seventeenth-Century Germany* (AMS Press, 1993). This study of the Ottoneum theatre in Germany, erected in 1604 to 1606 for the staging of English plays, explores with exemplary rigour acting troupes, the building's measurements and dimensions, and correspondence relating to its early history. More effort might have been made to identify particular dramas in the repertoire, and comparisons with the Globe and the Rose remain frustratingly brief. Yet Adams has produced a useful, specialized and reflective work of reconstruction, whose value is only slightly marred by the unevenly reproduced illustrations.

The shifting fortunes of companies and playhouses in earlier periods are generating an obvious interest, and, in a parallel fashion, attention is coming to focus on the institutional pressures placed upon modern theatrical enterprises. One disadvantage with this critical tendency is that genuine enquiry can be swamped by the minutiae of myopic obscurity; one advantage is that the ideological underpinnings of current performative practices can be more openly debated. In *Shakespeare and the Birmingham Repertory Theatre 1913–1929* (The Society for Theatre Research, 1993), Claire Cochrane promises a number of exciting revaluations. In addition to launching the careers of Olivier and Richardson, the theatre (the first of its kind in the country) was characterized by innovative production methods, which (under the direction of the founder, Sir Barry Jackson) formed part of a more general movement in performance aesthetics, away from period detail and towards streamlined efficiency. However ground-breaking this central thesis sounds, the

book as a whole does not live up to its packaging claims. The chapters mainly consist of reviews of the theatre's productions, and they are crammed with bewildering and inelegantly punctuated citations and lists of dates and names. One wonders if the material is sufficiently important to justify a book-length project: it is certainly wearing to be forced to wait for a contextual criticism that does not adequately materialize. Cochrane's talents do not stretch to broaching the wider implications that this kind of research deserves, and her evident enthusiasm – 'I was hooked on Shakespeare for life' (p. 148), she gushes – cannot rescue the study from its more glaring omissions.

In a superior league is Russell Jackson and Robert Smallwood's edited *Players of Shakespeare 3: Further Essays in Shakespearian Performance by Players with the Royal Shakespeare Company* (Cambridge University Press, 1993), a collection which investigates with a more pronounced sensitivity the work of a modern theatrical organization. Thirteen actors and actresses assess the roles they played with the RSC between 1987 and 1991, and the plays include *As You Like It, Cymbeline, Hamlet, Henry VI, King John, Measure for Measure, The Merchant of Venice, Much Ado About Nothing, Richard III* and *Titus Andronicus*. The essays constitute a unique opportunity to enjoy access to the player's creative process, to the kinds of mental preparation undergone before a production is staged; and the pieces which work best (by Deborah Findlay on Portia, and Nicholas Woodeson on King John) introduce challenging complications, centring upon how to adapt to changes during a performance run and how to flesh out a character who appears to be emotionally inarticulate. The prefatory materials are shrewdly and self-consciously formulated, despite minor inconsistencies. Why the RSC is chosen for discussion is not explained convincingly, and there are good reasons for casting the net wider in future volumes. Once or twice the effect of the perspective is to normalize Stratford-upon-Avon as the prime location of the Shakespeare industry, and to marginalize the distinct contribution of other provincial theatrical activity. These, however, remain minor objections to what is otherwise a distinguished collective venture.

It is with surveys of productions of single dramas that discussions of modern theatrical conditions can be seen in their best light. The larger developments that affect directors and producers, and the changing status of particular play-texts, are finely described in a (still small) sample of recent critical work. Hugh M. Richmond has written the *King Henry VIII* (Manchester University Press, 1994) volume for the 'Shakespeare in Performance' series. Six major twentieth-century productions are described (by Kevin Billington, Howard Davies, Tyrone Guthrie, Trevor Nunn, Paul Shepard and Herbert Beerbohm Tree), and the directors' growing reliance on naturalistic stage business and an elaborate reconstruction of Tudor settings is established. Apart from arguing forcefully for the critical importance of *Henry VIII*, Richmond also elucidates the reasons for the play's perennial appeal: 'In the case of the role of the King,' he writes, 'it anticipates our modern concern that art represent the uncertainties and ambiguities of contemporary reality' (p. 24). This refreshing approach permits Richmond to account for the individual successes of various productions, and to weigh up the challenge posed by Trevor Nunn's *Henry VIII*, which invited the audience's participation in political history, reflecting 'the increasing politicisation of public life in the 1960s and 1970s' (pp. 93–4). Throughout, Richmond's own experience in the theatre (he produced the play at Berkeley in 1990) is used profitably to mediate historical providentialism, to address notions of representationalism and referentiality, and to adjudicate between a range of directorial decisions and emphases.

Attending to the fortunes of Renaissance drama in the modern playhouse has encouraged a corresponding interest in the plays' textual status and availability. Not only have critics scrutinized the relationship between a dramatist's activity and company practice; they are simultaneously producing working editions of neglected theatrical experiments, which deserve to be realized in commercial performance. A notable example is Barry Weller and Margaret W. Ferguson's edition of Elizabeth Cary, Lady Falkland's *The Tragedy of Mariam, The Fair Queen of Jewry*, to which is appended *The Lady Falkland: Her Life* by one of her daughters (University of California Press, 1994). Elizabeth Cary, Lady Falkland (1585/6–1639) converted to Catholicism in 1626, and her sufferings for her faith belonged to an ongoing spiritual struggle, as the biography testifies. *The Tragedy of Mariam, The Fair Queen of Jewry* is a Senecan work, composed in about 1603 but only published ten years afterwards. This is the first attempt to combine the text and the life, and it is a splendid accomplishment. The discussion of the play raises such matters as Herodian antecedents, the influence of neoclassical dramaturgy, the 'closet' tradition, links with other contemporary productions, and Shakespearian affinities, and it gains immeasurably from acknowledging recently discovered manuscripts and questioning earlier attributions. These high scholarly standards continue into the section on the life, written in 1643–50 by one of Cary's daughters who was a nun in the Benedictine Convent at Cambray. Wary to tie the text to a particular daughter, and scrupulous in their assessment of dedications, Weller and Ferguson print a very readable version of the narrative, without yielding to the temptation to weigh down their notes with digressive commentary. Their modernized edition is a comprehensive and significant addition to a growing body of historically and theatrically informed studies.

The Tragedy of Mariam, The Fair Queen of Jewry is an occasional publication, and it would be welcome to see more such editions with a similar format. It is reassuring, therefore, that the established editorial series are maintaining their programmes and making available the work of lesser known as well as more canonical writers. Volume fifteen of *Collections*, published for the Malone Society by Oxford University Press (1993), contains four pieces: Ralph Crane's transcript of *A Game at Chess* (Bodleian manuscript Malone 25), the part of 'Poore' (from an anonymous late morality), musical and dramatic records from the Middle Temple, and a set of letters relating to fireworks staged for an Elizabethan royal occasion. In this gathering of disparate materials there is little to criticize and much to praise. David Carnegie might have written rather more on the provenance of the play from which 'Poore''s part is taken, as in his previous articles, although the description is probably as full as the Malone Society design allows. The transcript of *A Game at Chess* will be of interest as the Bodleian version exhibits the 'massed entries' device also found in three first folio comedies, *The Merry Wives of Windsor*, *The Two Gentlemen of Verona* and *The Winter's Tale*. The fireworks correspondence (from Sir Henry Killigrew to the Earl of Leicester) is very plausibly redated to the 1560s, when Leicester was eager to entertain the queen at his newly acquired Kenilworth estate. Although the Malone Society is faced with a diminishing sample of important documents, as increasing numbers of manuscripts make their way into print, it has still produced an unexpected and variegated collection, which illuminates dark corners of the period's dramatic and cultural history. Peter Happé's edition of Ben Jonson's *The Devil is an Ass* (Manchester University Press, 1994), however, is less successful in illuminating the mysteries that this rumbustious Jacobean comedy presents. The theatrical qualities of the play are particularized; some of its social contexts are enumerated (including the implications of witchcraft); Jonson's debt to Dekker and medieval moralities is evaluated; and recent adaptations are surveyed. What is missing is a more penetrating account of the royal objection to the play's printing, of the precise ways in which it offended the court. Questions of this nature have implications for

censorship and prompt speculation about the delay between composition and publication: Happé is an acute theatrical commentator but makes a poorer political explicator.

IV

The volume of studies devoted to reproductions of Shakespeare would seem to indicate that bardolatry can no longer haunt the corridors of English departments. Shakespeare has been removed from his pedestal, his place taken by interdisciplinary negotiations and intertextual conflicts. In another sense, Shakespeare still functions as a charged source of fascination, and the will to reveal the 'man' behind the 'work' has not been entirely extinguished. Pursuing this well-trodden critical path leads to some obvious irrelevances as much as it introduces a number of surprising discoveries.

D. Allen Carroll has edited *Greene's Groatsworth of Wit, Bought with a Million of Repentance* (1592), attributed to Robert Greene and Henry Chettle, for Medieval and Renaissance Texts and Studies (1994). He explains several authorial problems and identifies William Cecil, Marlowe and Nashe as the targets of some of the pamphlet's allusions. Would this edition ever have been conceived, however, were it not for the hypothesis that Shakespeare is the intended victim of the dismissive reference to the 'upstart Crow'? In a helpful appendix, Carroll summarizes the main lines of the debate, suggesting that a charge of impudence is being levelled. But the final argument could have been offered in an article rather than an edition, and a reader might find the rest of the pamphlet lacking in sustaining interest. When the Shakespearian sections are finally delivered, moreover, it is a feeling of disappointment that dominates; as Carroll observes: 'Something ambiguous hovers at the center of [the] expression just at the point where we might hope . . . for a clue to [Shakespeare's] early practice as a dramatist' (p. 132).

The predilection for explaining Shakespeare

in terms of a biographical narrative is clearly visible in two books in which the dramatist is discussed according to diametrically opposed approaches. Neither study advances knowledge of the drama, but both show in different ways the attractions that bardolatry exercises. *Shakespeare in the Stratford Records* by Robert Bearman (Alan Sutton, 1994) assembles all the Stratford documents relating to Shakespeare and sets them in their contexts. No critical unease undermines Bearman's strict reliance upon documents as facts: his is a historian's perspective, which places the utmost trust in archival sources. Despite the inflexibility of the methodology, Bearman writes well about two recent items – concerning land Shakespeare purchased in 1602 and the lease of his birthplace – and, to his credit, he is not opposed to being speculative, as when he suggests that Anthony Nash was Shakespeare's business representative. By contrast, speculation is the watchword (and the downfall) of the far inferior *The Startup Papers: On Shakespeare's Friend* by R. A. Hunt (Images Publishing, 1993). Two main ideas inform the book's discussion: George Chapman was the 'rival poet' of the sonnets, and 'W. H.' was William Hole, the engraver. Once Hunt has delivered these (dubious and irrelevant) hypotheses, he proceeds to illustrate biographical fallacies in abundance. The point is, surely, do the ascriptions really matter? The 'author' is no longer the point of origin, and, as Hunt develops his theme, musing about the 'School of Night', continually misspelling the name of the Huntington ('Huntingdon') Library and rhapsodizing about 'just how beautiful language can be' (p. 84), one tends to lose patience. 'I can only hope', writes Hunt, 'that readers will excuse my imaginings' (p. 147). This reader does not.

One cannot accuse Marvin Spevack of bardolatry, although his *A Shakespeare Thesaurus* (Olms, 1993) might be seen as a by-product of an industry obsessed with detailing every facet of Shakespeare's dramatic output. Indeed, such a volume would probably not exist were it not

for the Shakespearian connection. Nevertheless, Spevack states his case carefully rather than with awe-struck infatuation, and his thesaurus is a work to admire. It constitutes an attempt to organize and classify Shakespeare's entire vocabulary: thirty-seven main groups have been formed (including eight hundred and ninety-seven sub-groups), and the concepts range from the physical world to sense perception, law, religion, time and space. Interests such as motion and communication are represented; objects and things are detailed; and other classes concerning oaths and foreign words are available. Inevitably these are somewhat eclectic and personal choices. There will be some classifications that do not appear. As Spevack himself acknowledges: the 'open and fair' (p. ix) decisions are based on a classified inventory that is essentially 'handmade' (p. xiv). These subjective elements do not take away from the value of the thesaurus; they do, however, make one aware of the limitations of such enlightening projects.

It is difficult to know where to place William Empson's *Essays on Renaissance Literature* (Cambridge University Press, 1994), the second volume of which, edited by John Haffenden, is devoted to the drama. Empson's criticism fits into no clearly recognizable category. Insofar as he privileges the Shakespearian text, he might stand trial for bardolatry, even though he is demonstrably concerned with uncovering less canonical literary forms. He was probably a New Historicist when Stephen Greenblatt was a mere freshman, and yet his writing carries no obvious theoretical appurtenances. Textual matters occupy him sometimes fully, sometimes not at all. Empson answers to no conventional idea of the critic and is the master of traditional analysis at one and the same time. How, then, can his essays be characterized? On the positive side, they touch upon key political preoccupations (namely, marriage and inheritance) in such plays as *The Spanish Tragedy*; establish the importance of laughter as opposed to censure in Jacobean comedy; rescue the

Duchess of Malfi from critical obloquy; and suggest that Hermetical and magical lore, inherited from the ancients, were telling influences on late Elizabethan dramatists. Less favourably, Empson's prose can be unpredictable, eccentric, reactionary and arcane. While John Haffenden has edited the pieces with the loving touch of a

disciple, some are too short and others overly repetitious. If he is contrary, however, Empson never fails to be invigorating, and his essays offer a salutary reminder of some of the skills that modern scholarship might do well to imitate: with one foot in the past, his work still has an important bearing on the present.

3. EDITIONS AND TEXTUAL STUDIES
reviewed by H. R. WOUDHUYSEN

When considering some of the editions and textual studies published in the last year or so, it is hard not to be reminded of the Chinese curse, 'May you live in interesting times.' On the one hand, the theories and certainties of the New Bibliography seem to be coming under more and more pressure with the beginnings of a movement proclaiming the death of the editor and the arrival of the New Textualism. On the other hand, the well-disciplined advance of the Oxford and Cambridge series continues, producing high-quality scholarly editions which stand firm against some of the most pressing current doubts and questionings. Editors and anti-editors lob brickbats over the parapet at their enemies (or simply ignore one another), and what Shakespeare did or did not write continues to receive detailed attention. All categories are questioned – but not at the same time, for that way, and this is what makes the times so worrying, madness lies.

I

It was Christmas Eve in *The Times Literary Supplement* and under the heading '*Hamlet* by Dogberry' Brian Vickers effectively laid into Graham Holderness's and Bryan Loughrey's edition of *Hamlet* Q1 in the Harvester 'Shakespearean Originals: First Editions' series.[1] Vickers attacked their grasp of textual history and scholarship, dismissing their 'fiction that the pirated Quarto makes sense on its own' and

concluded that the 'Harvester editors have presented the texts in an ideologically predetermined frame, denying editorial responsibilities while performing some of them sloppily.' Vickers's powerful polemic was perhaps aimed not just at Holderness's and Loughrey's slim volume, but at the growing trend which in addition to questioning what 'bad quartos' are, also believes (to put it crudely) that the editor's task is to make the textual materials available in an unmediated form so that the reader is allowed to construct whatever sort of edition he or she wants or needs. Not surprisingly Vickers's review drew responses both from the '"bad quartos" are first versions' school, but also from the 'editors are the agents of textual oppression' faction. Evert Sprinchorn appeared for the first group, arguing against a theory of memorial reconstruction and concluding that 'The only tenable conclusion is that Q1 is mainly Shakespeare's and that it shows the effects not of piracy but of playhouse tampering.'[2] Vickers was not impressed by Sprinchorn's arguments and dismissed them as 'a hopeless mixture of irrelevant anecdote, fallacious argument and inaccurate scholarship' and certainly, despite his protests, it was hard to see that Sprinchorn had made a particularly con-

---

[1] *TLS*, 24 December 1993, pp. 5–6. The Harvester series was briefly mentioned in *Shakespeare Survey 46* (1994), p. 254.

[2] *TLS*, Letters, 21 January 1994, p. 15.

vincing case.[3] Meanwhile on the same page where he was dealing with Sprinchorn, Vickers himself was coming under attack from Holderness and Loughrey, who concluded their letter by saying: 'To the extent that we have been introducing readers to the furtive and perverse pleasures of engagement with corrupt and diseased texts . . . the role of bawd [i.e. Pompey] perhaps suits us better than the persona of "simple constable" [i.e. Dogberry].' The dispute – as such disputes do – then descended into personal details (it turned out that none of the main participants was able to go to the 1994 Stratford conference's seminar on editing), pointing out mistakes in publishing history, and to arguments about who had said what and whether it was justified or not.[4]

The argument managed to be diverting and mildly tiresome at the same time. The defenders of the 'bad quartos' made indefensible claims about them, while proudly picking at the scab of ideology. Vickers and Jenkins held the line and yet, because of the nature and the location of the row, failed to dispose of doubts and anxieties which some textual scholars have about the subject. The problem of 'Shakespearean Originals: First Editions' was dealt with more satisfactorily (and without reference to the *TLS* correspondence) in an admirable article by Janette Dillon.[5] Dillon set out to question what she called 'a new orthodoxy, an orthodoxy of performance', including 'the degree to which the printed text is capable of being used as evidence about the material practice of performance' (p. 74). First, she attacked the binary opposition of author and stage which condemns the first while exalting the second, before moving on to criticize the Holderness and Loughrey view that *Hamlet* Q1 'comes closer than the other texts to actual Jacobean stage practice' (p. 77: their words) – her target here was the 'unitary notion of Jacobean stage practice'. She then considered four aspects of Q1 which Holderness and Loughrey had discussed as showing its superiority. Q1's length led her to conclude that 'We

cannot refer to "the playhouse" as a singular concept . . . different texts may be appropriate to different performances' (p. 78). The evidence of Q1's title-page 'cannot be used as testimony for the faithfulness of its text to any single performance' (p. 79). When she turned to '*Memorial reconstruction/Pirating*' Dillon drew on unpublished work by Peter Blayney, who has pointed out that Humphrey Moseley's much-quoted account in the Beaumont and Fletcher folio of private transcription by actors should be taken to refer to memorial reconstruction. 'It seems unlikely', Dillon concluded, 'that any of the publishers [of the "bad quartos"] considered their ventures fraudulent' (p. 80). Her point is that while denying the memorial-reconstruction theory, Holderness and Loughrey 'assume the link between playhouse and text which is primarily supported by this theory' (p. 81). Furthermore, there is no reason to believe that the quarto may tell us more about the playhouse than it does about memory itself or about the printing shop. Equally, there is no evidence that 'Q1 as it stands was ever performed' (p. 82) and, although it may be put on the stage nowadays, that reveals more about the current state of the theatre than it does about 'the nature of historical performances or printed texts'. Like Vickers, Dillon pointed out that Holderness's and Loughrey's text of the play has been edited and adapted, just as it must be if it is to be performed. If performance it is to be 'the holy grail of Shakespeare studies' (p. 85), the large variety of possible contemporary performances has to be acknowledged and 'the specific practices of performers in particular locations' need to be discussed (p. 86). Editors driven by perform-

---

[3] *TLS*, Letters, 4 February 1994, p. 15; see also Sprinchorn's letter in 1 April 1994, p. 15, and Harold Jenkins's judicious response 15 April 1994, p. 17.

[4] *TLS*, 4 March 1994, p. 15, 8 April 1994, p. 19, 29 April 1994, p. 19.

[5] 'Is There a Performance in this Text?', *Shakespeare Quarterly*, 45 (1994): 74–86.

ance merely replace the quest for authorial authenticity with another 'equally mystified and immaterial' grail (p. 85). Dillon's final points are provocative and important:

we still lack any very firm evidence about the transmission of Elizabethan dramatic texts generally and are therefore not in a position to make judgments about the consistency of *any* surviving printed texts with what was performed on the Elizabethan stage . . . We know that printed texts are the product of printing houses; we do not know how directly or indirectly they may relate to what was performed.

(pp. 84, 86)

Although her argument was focused on the specific claims made by Holderness and Loughrey, Dillon's discussion of the current editorial belief in the inherent superiority of performance-related texts is a challenging one.

Dillon's sharp piece was commendably short, but was preceded in the same journal by a much longer and more discursive article about 'The Materiality of the Shakespearean Text' by Margreta de Grazia and Peter Stallybrass.[6] If Dillon's argument is finally rather pessimistic about our ignorance, de Grazia's and Stallybrass's article, which evokes the 'New Textualism', goes beyond a simple anti-editorial position to argue that any sort of text or edition will do: 'There is no intrinsic reason *not* to have a modernized, translated, rewritten "Shakespeare." In an important sense, that is all we *can* have' (p. 282). The inverted commas around Shakespeare's name give something of their programme away. While they begin by examining the falsifications which the editing of the plays and poems have produced since the eighteenth century, their larger aim is to question the ideology which allows that there is or was an 'authentic Shakespeare . . . some ideal "original" behind the text' (p. 256). Like Dillon they organize their account under four headings. First, they argue that what is generally taken to be a single work may possess 'multiple names as well as multiple texts' (p. 258) and, quite reasonably, that authorship cannot be determined on the basis of title-pages or of

collections for which theatrical companies or stationers may have been responsible. In their next section, 'Word', they have some good discussions of the editorial treatment of individual words, such as the 'weyward' or 'weyard' sisters in the Folio text of *Macbeth*, and conclude it is regrettable that in editing and modernizing words, editors tie down and limit their meaning, or as they put it, 'the mutable Renaissance signifier disappears' (p. 266).

When they turn to 'Character' they observe, interestingly, that following Rowe's 1709 edition, Pope was 'the first editor to read Shakespeare with a list of dramatis personae preceding every play' (p. 267). But their point is that early texts are often irregular in their speech prefixes and that 'When dramatic nomenclature is made uniform, the variability of Elizabethan and Jacobean theatrical books and manuscripts is phased out' (p. 269). They continue by asserting that just as there is no 'fixity of character' in the early texts, 'neither is there fixity of gender', seeking to prove their claim by looking at the textual history of the Sonnets and at 'recent work on the construction of gender' (p. 272). Finally, they consider the 'Author' who, they determine, is partially a construct of compositors, stationers and editors (p. 273). They begin this section by looking at the spelling of Shakespeare's name which is 'itself a variable material sign inscribed in books, not a fixed essence that lies imperceptibly behind the text' (p. 275). By challenging 'the category of solitary and unitary authorship', their doubts concerning his 'unity and integrity' eventually lead them to question 'the category of author' (p. 276). Rather surprisingly, their grounds for this are that it is impossible to justify the arguments, based on palaeographical evidence, that the hand which wrote the six extant signatures can be identified with Hand D in the manuscript of *Sir Thomas More*: 'The construction of a single autograph

---

[6] *Shakespeare Quarterly*, 44 (1993): 255–83.

from six disparate signatures is not unlike the construction of a single play from multiple texts' (p. 278) – the double negative, 'not unlike', is telling. Therefore, all early texts can be 'recognized as autonomous and deserving of textual and critical attention . . . all intertextual and intratextual variants are claimed in the name of a revising Shakespeare' – a Shakespeare (or 'Shakespeare') who anyway must also be appropriated within 'our new knowledge of collaborative writing, collaborative printing, and the historical contingencies of textual production' (pp. 278–9). Since, as they argue, 'there is no "original"', modern editions of whatever kind cannot be accused of deviating from or betraying it (p. 282). Presumably there are therefore no readings or editions which are better or worse than others, only ones which are different. The 'solitary genius . . . is, after all, an impoverished, ghostly thing compared to the complex social practices that shaped, and still shape, the absorbent surface of the Shakespearean text' (p. 283). In this despairing vision, the two editions which de Grazia and Stallybrass seem to approve are Michael Warren's *The Complete King Lear* and, more surprisingly, Stephen Booth's Sonnets.

II

So, editorial and textual times have changed to such an extent that the Emperor's new clothes are genuinely greeted by a large and cheering crowd as the height of fashion and good taste: walking naked is all the rage – 'Off, off, you lendings!' But scepticism and doubt need not necessarily lead to a sort of editorial despair or madness. Dillon's article is a sobering reminder of how limited is our knowledge of certain aspects of the theatre and of publishing history. When editors refer to the superiority of performance texts to non-performance texts – and she must have been thinking of the Oxford and Cambridge series here – what exactly do they mean by 'performance'? It is a good question, one that deserves to be pursued. But the

question 'What are "bad quartos"?' remains. Memorial reconstruction may explain how they were put together, but why and under what circumstances this was done and what their status was in print are uncertain. What did the buyer of *Hamlet* Q1 think he was getting and did he feel cheated by his purchase? '*Enter two Centinels*' Q1 begins, and the owner of the British Library copy noted that they were 'now call'd Bernardo & Francisco'; '*Corambis*' in 2.1, he reported, is 'Now call'd Polonius' and the *Mousetrap* is set 'In later Editions' in '*Vienna Gonzago* the Duke's Name his Wife's *Baptista*'. He corrected several of Q1's more eccentric readings but there is no sense that he felt he had bought the wrong edition of the play, merely that there were later editions of it and that 'now' some features of it were different.

If memorial reconstruction seems the most likely explanation for the texts 'bad quartos' contain, it is not the only possible one. As Vickers pointed out in his initial review of Holderness's and Loughrey's edition, Duthie and Hart disposed of shorthand as the means by which the texts were assembled. But they did so, inevitably, on the basis of their knowledge of 'the available systems' – available that is to modern scholars. But there were, or at the very least may have been, systems available to Shakespeare's contemporaries about which we know almost nothing and which may have been sufficiently flexible for a variety of legal, political, religious, personal or even theatrical uses. This is not to argue that 'bad quartos' were compiled from shorthand reports – that would not explain all their features – but to point out that the categories and established facts on which the New Bibliography (or even the 'New Textualism') was built can only be provisional and contingent. The last decade or so has seen just such a questioning of the bases for the modern understanding of the foundations of Shakespeare's texts – for example, by William B. Long of 'promptbooks', by Paul Werstine of 'foul papers' and of 'bad quartos', by David Bradley of stage plots and by a variety of scholars about authorship matters.[7] It is not hard to imagine that at some point there will be a serious assault on the traditional bases for compositor identification and their results. Equally, while Trevor Howard-Hill's labours on the work of Ralph Crane have been intensive and widespread, they are limited to his dramatic manuscripts which form only a part of his overall scribal activities. Crane is generally agreed to have supplied copy for five or six plays in the First Folio, but the possibility that in fact another scribe was (or other scribes were) copying his work might be worth considering. At a more fundamental level, as scholarly understanding of the economics and mechanics of the London booktrade develops, the familiar accounts of how and why Shakespeare's plays were published in quartos are beginning to look rather threadbare. The fact is that there are serious limits to our knowledge of the basic materials, as well as problems with their interpretation, which editors and textual scholars tend to take for granted. It is a sobering thought that while twentieth-century bibliographical research has been much concerned with trying to discover the nature of the copy which was sent to the printer, no certain example of printer's copy for a dramatic work survives: we simply do not know what such copy might have looked like.

Some fundamental questions of this kind are addressed in Gary Taylor's and John Jowett's book *Shakespeare Reshaped 1606–1623*, a late contribution to the 'Oxford Shakespeare Studies' series.[8] This contains three principal pieces: the first concerns 'Act-Intervals in the London Theatres, 1576–1642'; the second reviews the problem of 'Theatrical, Editorial, and Literary Expurgation' in the light of the 1606 Act to Restrain Abuses of Players; and finally there is a long account of 'Theatrical Interpolation in *Measure for Measure*'. There are also six appendices, of which four are devoted to *Measure* and the two others to the printer's copy for *2 Henry IV* and to 'O' and 'Oh' in Renaissance plays. *Shakespeare Reshaped* at last

supplies the research on which some of the textual decisions in the Oxford edition were based: in fact it was completed in 1985, before the publication of the *Textual Companion* in 1987, and then returned to in 1989. There are, however, few references to books or articles published after 1989, giving rise to a curious situation in which, for example, Taylor and Jowett do not allude to Gibbons's or Bawcutt's 1991 editions of *Measure*. This is unfortunate and contributes to the impression that *Shakespeare Reshaped* has rather been left behind. It is a collection of pieces written with characteristic drive and determination: the outlines of the essays are usually clear, but there is a huge amount of detail whose purpose and direction are often a little hard to grasp. Taylor's and Jowett's arguments are dense and their range of evidence wide, veering towards the comprehensive. But in a book in which detail counts for so much, it is surprising that there are many errors, misquotations and inconsistencies. Most of the mistakes are admittedly minor ones of no great immediate significance, but they do tend to make the reader anxious about the formidable quantities of supporting

---

[7] William B. Long, '"A bed / for woodstock": A Warning for the Unwary', *Medieval and Renaissance Drama in England*, 2 (1985): 91–118, 'Stage-Directions: A Misinterpreted Factor in Determining Textual Provenance', *TEXT*, 2 (1985): 121–37, and '*John a Kent and John a Cumber*: An Elizabethan Playbook and Its Implications', in ed. W. R. Elton and William B. Long, *Shakespeare and Dramatic Tradition: Essays in Honor of S. F. Johnson* (Newark, London, and Toronto, 1989), pp. 125–43; Paul Werstine, '"Foul Papers" and "Prompt-Books": Printer's Copy for Shakespeare's *Comedy of Errors*', *Studies in Bibliography*, 41 (1988): 232–46, and 'Narratives About Printed Shakespeare Texts: "Foul Papers" and "Bad" Quartos', *Shakespeare Quarterly*, 41 (1990): 65–86; David Bradley, *From Text to Performance in the Elizabethan Theatre: Preparing the Play for the Stage* (Cambridge, 1991).

[8] Gary Taylor and John Jowett, *Shakespeare Reshaped 1606–1623* (Oxford: Oxford University Press, 1993) in the Oxford Shakespeare Studies series.

evidence which appear to be handled with such ease.[9]

The three essays are concerned with 'kinds of interference' which 'must have reshaped Shakespeare's plays much more drastically than the occasional errors of compositors or sophistications of scribes' (p. 1). It is hard to feel that they really amount to a coherent account of the forces at work on the texts of Shakespeare's plays between 1606 (presumably chosen because of the Act against stage profanity) and 1622 (presumably selected on the basis of its being the year in which work on the First Folio began). And although there is some cross referencing and a few overlaps between the essays, the book gives the impression that it is made up of off-cuts from *The Textual Companion*.

The first example of interference, analysed by Taylor, takes the form of a change in theatrical conventions which led to the introduction of intervals between acts. Taylor surveys the practice of dividing plays into acts in the public and private theatres, at Court, in the children's companies and in academic performances. He rejects the two-part dramatic structure espoused by Emrys Jones (among others) as an anomaly (p. 11), arguing that plays were either performed continuously or with act intervals. Different practices obtained in different circumstances, but his most striking piece of evidence is that all of the 245 extant plays written for London Companies between 1616 and 1642 are divided into five acts (p. 4). Before then intervals were used in private theatres, but they did not occur in public ones until about 1610 (p. 22). 'Plays written after 1615, and plays written for the children's companies, were printed with act-divisions; excepting those by Jonson, plays written for the public stage between 1592 and 1606 (inclusive) were not' (p. 25). The change came after 1606 (p. 12), '*c.* 1607–10' (p. 25) or 'after 1608' (p. 238), taking 'a decade or more to become universal' (p. 26); it coincided with the King's Men's acquisition of the Blackfriars playhouse in 1608 and performances there from 1609 or 1610

(p. 30). They adopted the conventions of the children's companies in their theatre. Other companies followed the example of the King's Men (pp. 32, 36–7), and quite rapidly plays began to be written to reflect the new interval forms (pp. 37–40): this can be detected in *Coriolanus*, *The Winter's Tale*, *Cymbeline*, *The Tempest* and *The Two Noble Kinsmen* (pp. 40–2). Plays 'published after *c.* 1610 may have had act-divisions imposed on' them, especially if they were 'revived in or after 1609' (pp. 42–3). Printers were not responsible for introducing these divisions: 106 out of 108 quarto reprints of plays between 1610 and 1660 'leave the plays undivided' (p. 18). All the Folio's Comedies have act-divisions, but three plays, set from 'non-theatrical early texts', have divisions which 'seem clearly mistaken, and presumably editorial' and so inauthentic: these are *The Comedy of Errors*, *The Taming of the Shrew* and *All's Well that Ends Well*. The first of these, however, was designed for Gray's Inn where act-intervals would have been expected (pp. 44–5). The next play set in the folio was *Henry V* whose 'act-divisions are grotesquely inappropriate' (p. 46), but after that the editors seem to have given up trying to impose such

---

[9] Among errors which might affect the book's arguments are the following: p. 99 'the iambic pentameter norm would be achieved if we added "God's" [to *Measure* TLN 996] Grace goe with you, *Benedicte*.' which should read '*Benedicite*'; p. 113 in the discussion of '*within*' stage directions the reference to *Richard II* TLN 2587 should presumably be to 2573, but the same page has another of this kind at TLN 2535, hence such directions do not 'occur only three times' outside *Measure* in the canon, but four times; p. 118 here there are said to be 'fifty-eight "oh"s to only seven "o"s in Folio *Measure*', but in Table II. 2 on p. 250 the figures are given as fifty-six to seven; p. 125 n. 52 (on p. 126) the note about *The Witch*'s 'imprisond-Obscuritie' is not in Middleton's but in Crane's hand; p. 290 Jump did not assert that 'a text printed from a prompt-book "would normally be less distinctly removed from the author's manuscript than would one printed from a more 'literary type'"', but that it would be less 'distantly removed' than 'one printed from a manuscript of a more "literary type"'.

divisions. Taylor then goes on to discuss plays which may have been revised to take the new performing conditions into account, concentrating on *King Lear* (pp. 48–50) whose revision must therefore be dated to after *c.* 1608.

The evidence deployed here strongly supports Taylor's argument. In the new private theatres a simple pause, some dramatic action or music filled the intervals (pp. 6–8); immediate re-entrances between acts start to occur (pp. 21–2); choruses or presenters appear in plays until 1609, but after 1612 they do not; instead they are replaced by '"classical" lyric choruses' (pp. 24, 37). Intervals would allow candles to be trimmed (but they could have been trimmed during performances); the theatres' better facilities for music led to its greater use (p. 31). Intervals probably helped increase sales of food and drink. And yet, while thinking about 'kinds of interference' – the authorial, theatrical or editorial imposition of act-divisions – there is still the question of length of performance to consider. To take one example, Folio *Lear* is long enough without act-divisions: add four intervals, even of the shortest duration, and it is hard not to believe that some part of the text would have to be cut. The implications of Taylor's arguments in this first essay are potentially disturbing, not least to ideas about performance texts.

The introduction of act-intervals around 1607 came a year after the passing of the 'Act to Restrain Abuses of Players' in 1606 which sought to purge the stage – but not the page – of profanity. Taylor's second essay, ''Swounds Revisited', seeks to explain the 'apparently random expurgation of Folio texts' (p. 51). The expurgation 'may result from interference in the theatre after May 1606, interference in the printing-house in 1622–3, or interference by particular scribes at any time up to 1622–3' (p. 52). He begins by arguing that the treatment of the deeply offensive 'zounds' was a special case, the result of editorial interference (pp. 54–5). Apart from this anomaly, 'the printers or publishers of the Folio did little to expurgate their copy; instead, they reproduced profanity as they happened to find it in the materials available to them' (p. 58). The removal of profanity in *King John* shows that the copy for the Folio was prepared by two different scribes, working in or after 1606: they were preparing a new prompt-book for a possible revival (pp. 58–64). The absence of profanity in Folio *Othello* and in *Hamlet*, whose texts do not derive from prompt-books, suggests they were subject to 'deliberate "literary" bowdlerizing' (pp. 65–6). Taylor's lengthy discussion of Folio *2 Henry IV* leads him to maintain that its expurgation may have been authorial, the result of revisionary work after 1606 (pp. 66–70): the Folio was set from manuscript, rather than from printed copy (pp. 245–7). Similar arguments lead him to detect revisionary work on *Othello* and *Lear*, but not on *Hamlet* whose oaths were cut in or for the printing-house (pp. 71–6).

Expurgated texts therefore 'reflect late theatrical practice' (p. 76) and plays like *Hamlet* and *1 Henry IV* which retain their profanities must derive from private transcripts (p. 78). The evidence suggests Crane did not censor the texts he copied, but it is possible that scribes restored profanities when copying manuscripts from censored theatrical texts: expurgation indicates theatrical origins, but 'the presence of profanity in a printed text is certainly *not* good evidence of the ancestry of the manuscript the printer used' (p. 85). The cases of *Macbeth* and *All is True* show that 'some transcripts reinstated profanity' (pp. 85–7). Taylor turns finally to four Folio plays written before 1606 which have been purged – *The Merry Wives of Windsor*, *The Two Gentlemen of Verona*, *King John* and *Measure for Measure* – and examines readings in them where he believes profanities might or should be restored (pp. 90–105). He concludes that editors should look at 'the problems of profanity globa[l]ly' and 'do something to solve' those problems by emending the text (pp. 105–6).

The third essay in *Shakespeare Reshaped* was

jointly written by Jowett and Taylor and fills some 130 pages. The argument is long and involved, but its main outlines are clear. Two passages in *Measure for Measure*, they argue, 'were added after Shakespeare's death, on the occasion of a late theatrical revival' (p. 108). Ralph Crane prepared the Folio copy for the printers from an expurgated theatrical manuscript, a prompt-book revised after 1606 (pp. 109–19). The first passage Jowett and Taylor look at is the 'notorious crux' in 4.1, the relationship between the Duke's Place and Greatness lines in that scene and his couplets on the same subject in the preceding one, 'No might, nor greatnesse in mortality', (3.2 or 3.1): they reject the traditional explanation that the lines in 4.1 were moved from 3.1 to fill a gap (pp. 119–23). Instead, they begin their enquiry by questioning the authenticity of the song 'Take, oh take those lips away' which begins 4.1. They believe Fletcher originally wrote it for *Rollo, Duke of Normandy* (which has a second verse for it), and that *Rollo* can be dated to the summer of 1617 or a little later. In other words, the song and the material at the beginning of 4.1 constitute a late and not very appropriate theatrical interpolation which is unlike Shakespeare's writing or his dramaturgy elsewhere. The lines following the song (TLN 1776–96) 'are, at best, undistinguished' (p. 137) and the whole beginning of 4.1 'points to its being a late theatrical interpolation' (p. 140).

If the suspected interpolation is removed, the powerful outlines of a 600-line long continuous scene can be discerned, whose closing moments introduce Mariana. Jowett and Taylor propose that it is not the relationship between 'Oh Place, and greatnes' and 'No might, nor greatnesse in mortality' which needs disentangling, but that 'Oh Place, and greatnes' and his concluding couplets in 3.2, 'He who the sword of Heauen will beare', have been transposed (p. 143). If the speeches are transferred and the interpolated matter removed, the reconstructed scene makes better sense dramatically (pp. 140–51). The key figure in this recasting is

Lucio who exits just before the Duke's 'No might, nor greatnesse in mortality' speech. Earlier in the play, there is evident duplication of material in 1.2 which begins with Lucio's entry. The shorter of the duplicating passages (TLN 176–82) can be readily assigned to Shakespeare: crowding on the page in F suggests these seven lines should have been omitted. If the longer passage (TLN 153–71) is removed, then much more material has to be cut with it, from as far back as Lucio's initial entrance (TLN 96). All of this material looks like a later interpolation, padding out the beginning of the play 'with extra comic material . . . suitably bulky and suitabl[y] bawdy' (p. 155) and expands Lucio's part. Again, his part in 1.2 is unlike Shakespeare's usual dramatic practice (pp. 156–9), suggesting that the beginning of the scene 'is an unShakespearian interpolation'. Its duplication, language, style and dramatic structure, support this contention (pp. 159–65). And, if TLN 96–171 are an interpolation, local difficulties also suggest that Mistress Overdone's words before Pompey enters (TLN 172–4) and the transition involved in the Folio's creation of a new scene, 1.3, especially relating to Juliet's awkward entry (suspiciously duplicated in 5.1), are also later work (pp. 165–71).

A fresh examination of the topical allusion in 1.1 concerning James's dislike of crowds (TLN 76–81) shows that the play was originally written between September 1603 and March 1604 (pp. 171–7). The interpolations, however, post-date *Rollo*'s composition probably in mid-1617; Overdone's topical allusions in TLN 172–4 refer to 1619–22 and the reference to the King of Hungary (TLN 97–101) fits 1620–2: the new material (including a reference to a pirate (TLN 103)) was therefore probably added in 1621 (pp. 177–86). A lengthy consideration of who may have written the interpolations follows, in which evidence of several kinds, especially of parallels, is surveyed: at its end, Middleton emerges as the most likely author for the material in 1.2 (pp. 186–226) and Webster as a possible candidate for 4.1 (pp. 226–31).

Additions were commissioned because *Measure* seemed rather short and because (like *Macbeth* in which Middleton is also thought to have had a hand) it lacked a song (p. 232). Without the interpolated passage in 1.2 'the play gets off to a rather lighter, more clearly comic start' (p. 233): in relation to the rest of the play, the Lucio-expanding passage 'testifies to the brilliance of [Middleton's] writing and the craft of his remodelling – and to the intensity of his own commitment to the issues the play raises' (p. 235). On the other hand, Jowett and Taylor conclude by saying that the 'interpolations weaken' the play, 'confuse its structure, and contribute in some small measure to the dissatisfaction many critics have felt with its mixture of genres' (p. 236).

There are, inevitably, problems with this bravura argument concerning *Measure*. Although their examination of the interpolated passages is exhaustive, Jowett's and Taylor's explanation of why new material was added to the play is distinctly thin. Equally, they say little about what the larger implications of their discoveries, in terms of rewriting and adaptation elsewhere, might be. As so often in textual and editorial studies, by not looking fully at alternative explanations for real or perceived difficulties and characteristics, the evidence – however scrupulously presented – is inevitably tilted in one direction. Brian Vickers's recent suggestion that material in the play may have been inserted by Shakespeare after 1607 puts one large cat among a flock of pigeons.[10] *Shakespeare Reshaped* contributes a mass of new material for editors to think about, and although it is professedly not a comprehensive study of the subject (p. 2), some readers may feel it adds up to little more than a series of closely argued possibilities, which seek to justify editorial interference. 'In some sense', Jowett and Taylor write, 'our entire investigation amounts to no more than an attempt to demonstrate that editors should indeed do what many of them have always wanted to' and emend the problematic passages in the play (p. 232).[11]

Part of the trouble lies in the continuing acceptance of orthodoxies (both new and old). In a 'Post-Script' Taylor takes it as axiomatic that 'Shakespeare's plays *were* written for performance' (p. 237) but, as Dillon's article suggests, this view is not as simple as it at first appears. For some plays, *As You Like It* and *Antony and Cleopatra* for example, in the absence of early records of performance some editors have even suggested that they were not written for the stage. For others, such as *Hamlet* or *King Lear*, Shakespeare may well have known that they could never be realized in the form which the extant texts represent – whether with or without act-intervals. To operate as editors by recognizing 'Shakespeare's commitment to collaborative performance' (p. 237) and to believe that the script of the first performance represents 'the first complete text of the play' (p. 238) begs rather a large number of questions. Taylor goes on to discuss the way in which the presence of scene-divisions in a Folio text is more likely to indicate copy set from a scribal transcript than from authorial papers or a prompt-book (pp. 239–41). The Folio, he argues, was prepared from 'literary transcripts' as opposed to 'holograph pre-scripts by a margin of (at least) nineteen to nine, or (at most) twenty-two to seven' plays (p. 242). The result of this is that 'the bulk of Shakespeare's œuvre comes down to us in editions which reflect non-authorial literary transcripts' (p. 243). In acknowledging this position, Taylor points out that this was the conclusion Sir Sidney Lee had put forward before the New Bibliography began 'its search for the uncontaminated authorial pre-script'. It may be evident to some that the Oxford Shakespeare project is

---

[10] Brian Vickers, 'Shakespearian Consolations', *Proceedings of the British Academy*, 82 (1993): 268–9.

[11] The recent reception of Robert F. Fleissner, *Shakespeare and the Matter of the Crux: Textual, Topical, Onomastic, Authorial, and Other Puzzlements* (Lewiston, Queenston, Lampeter, 1991), shows that the rage for emendation could not be said to have cooled.

not the herald of a magnificent new age of investigating Renaissance dramatic texts, but is instead the swansong of the old age. Sometimes, it feels that it is not the spirit of Greg, McKerrow or Pollard (or Lee for that matter) which hovers over modern textual work, but of John Dover Wilson.

The questions of attribution which Jowett and Taylor pursue are also at the centre of Jonathan Hope's stimulating book on *The Authorship of Shakespeare's Plays*.[12] Although it has a large number of fearsome-looking graphs and tables, Hope writes clearly and concisely: his methodology and findings are quite comprehensible and he largely eschews statistics. In fact he is fully aware of the limits of stylometry (pp. 8–9, 17), but also sees that his own approach to the subject 'illustrates the necessity for authorship studies to be cumulative, for cases to be built on a variety of independent tests, rather than just one type of evidence' (pp. 108–9). On its own his method 'will never be able to give a categorically positive attribution for an anonymous play – it can, though, confirm that a named author for whom a comparison sample exists could have written a play' (p. 149) or a particular part of it. After explaining what socio-linguistics are, he moves on to consider three separate determinants which were all changing in early Modern English: the auxiliary 'do', relative markers and 'thou' and 'you' – the last of these is the most limited as a discriminator and is used only in relation to *All is True* (p. 67). In addition to Shakespeare, the dramatists whose work he has analysed are Fletcher, Marlowe, Dekker, Middleton and Massinger. The second part of Hope's book applies these determinants to the Shakespeare–Fletcher and the Shakespeare–Middleton collaborations, to the attributed plays in the second issue of the third folio, 1664, and to other apocryphal plays. For each work there is a brief history of previous attribution studies, then the evidence of auxiliary 'do' and of relative markers is presented and analysed, and a summary supplied. The book's last chapter usefully summarizes again all Hope's authorship findings for each play (pp. 150–5).

His results are, briefly, as follows. In the Fletcher collaborations, Hoy over-estimated Shakespeare's hand in *All is True*, but was right about their respective shares in *The Two Noble Kinsmen*. Theobald's *Double Falsehood* (*Cardenio*) is not a forgery, but shows evidence of two hands at work which conform to Shakespeare's and Fletcher's in some of their usages of auxiliary 'do': 'the scenes up to and including 2.02 appear to be more "Shakespearean", while the later ones are more "Fletcherian"' (p. 151). Hope finds a second hand involved in *Timon of Athens*, but is not certain it is Middleton's, perhaps because 'subsequent Shakespearean revision has blurred the evidence' (p. 151). There is not enough material in attributed passages in *Macbeth* to allow them to be analysed. The traditional division of *Pericles* stands, with the possibility that it is 'a final draft by Wilkins of a collaboration between him and Shakespeare in which Wilkins contributed more to acts 1 and 2 than in the remainder of the play' (p. 152). *The London Prodigal* is a collaboration in which Fletcher may have been involved. *Thomas, Lord Cromwell* is not collaborative nor by any of the major writers of the period. As Henslowe's diary records, *Sir John Oldcastle* is collaborative. The evidence for Middleton's involvement in *The Puritan* and *A Yorkshire Tragedy* is not clear-cut. There may be links between Marlowe and *Locrine* and *Arden of Faversham*, but the evidence is by no means conclusive. *The Birth of Merlin* may be a collaboration. Shakespeare could have written *Edward III* which remains 'the best candidate from the apocryphal plays for inclusion in the canon' (p. 154). Auxiliary 'do' evidence suggests that Shakespeare could have written *Edmund Ironside*, but the play's low frequency of relativization makes

---

[12] Jonathan Hope, *The Authorship of Shakespeare's Plays: A Socio-Linguistic Study* (Cambridge: Cambridge University Press, 1994); an earlier article by Hope was mentioned in *Shakespeare Survey* 45 (1993), p. 202.

this unlikely: it 'stands as a strong candidate for further detailed examination of possible Shakespearean authorship' (p. 154). Hand D's contribution to *Sir Thomas More* is insufficient for analysis, but at least two authors contributed the play's original scenes.

Hope is all too aware of the limitations of socio-linguistic studies of attribution. The sample size has to be sufficiently large at both a local and an overall level: he found that five plays 'give a more than adequate sample' (p. 9). But writers also may choose to write in uncharacteristic styles, deliberately archaizing their plays (p. 14), or indulging in quite different sorts of dialogue (pp. 45–6). Their writing may also be affected by generic factors (pp. 47–8), by 'style, genre, character, and transient emotion in literary texts' (p. 64). Textual interference can also play a part (p. 48) – only in *Richard III* were relative markers changed between quarto and Folio (p. 33) – but generally the discriminants were not 'regarded as interchangeable by scribes and compositors' (p. 5). Despite this, one weakness of Hope's book lies not in the fact that he assembled his material by hand, but in his vagueness about what texts he used to gather it. He says that he used 'modern facsimiles of the earliest available authoritative texts', microfilms and 'modern diplomatic editions' (p. 15). Most of his quotations come from the Folio and since *Lear*, *Othello* and *Troilus* are among his Shakespeare sample texts, his casual account of the texts from which he gathered his raw data is surprising. It is a pity that he did not take *Measure for Measure* into account in his study and it would certainly be interesting to know what would happen if his methods were applied to the *Henry VI* plays.

Hope's book is a useful addition not just to questions surrounding what Shakespeare did or did not write, but to discussions of attribution theory. His scepticism and willingness to see socio-linguistic analysis as only one among a variety of tools are refreshing. The linguistic evidence he has gathered is certainly powerful and rigorous: it is the 'socio' part of the theory, relying variously on the author's date and place of birth, class, urban or rural background, education and so on which appears to be rather flabby (pp. 8, 11–12, 19–20, 59–60). If more were known, for example, about George Wilkins there might be some explanation as to why, despite being born a decade or so later than Shakespeare, his use of auxiliary 'do' is so similar to his collaborator's (p. 108).

III

If Taylor is right, and as few as seven Folio plays were set from holograph manuscripts, there is still a startling discrepancy between the quality of their texts (and the texts of other quartos allegedly set from holograph copy) and that of the first quarto of *King Lear*. The New Cambridge Shakespeare has launched its 'The Early Quartos' series with Jay L. Halio's edition of Q1, a sequel to his Folio-based text published in 1992.[13] He says the edition 'is essentially a unique one, founded upon a fresh examination of the early texts' (p. ix). The new edition has no commentary and no glossary. Q was printed 'from Shakespeare's foul papers, or rough draft' (p. 1), but how Nathaniel Butter and John Busby got hold of the manuscript they gave to Okes 'remains a mystery' (p. 2). The copy 'was often illegible or nearly so', because Shakespeare's hand was hard to read and because the manuscript was heavily revised (p. 4). Halio admits that not all the evidence points in this direction and pays some attention to 'actors' "gags" or interpolations' which could derive from performances, but which might equally reflect Shakespeare 'in the heat of rapid composition' (pp. 4–5). Other evidence for authorial copy can be deduced from stage directions, speech headings, mislineation, spellings and punctuation (pp. 4–7). Halio then goes on

---

[13] *The First Quarto of King Lear*, ed. Jay L. Halio (Cambridge: Cambridge University Press, 1994), in The New Cambridge Shakespeare: The Early Quartos series.

to discuss the printing of Q, analysing the stints of compositors B and C, with a particularly detailed discussion of the quarto's distinctive spellings and punctuation (pp. 10–12). The evidence is not unambiguous, but Halio argues that a great deal of it points to autograph copy. His discussion of the proof-correction of Q is good, emphasizing that the readings of corrected formes are not necessarily the 'true' ones – he takes 2.4.79 ('The fierie Duke, tell the hot Duke that *Lear*,') as his leading example (pp. 17–18). And he rightly cautions that 'those attempting to edit Q *Lear* must use F with caution' (p. 20).

When he moves on to discuss Q2, he stresses that it derives entirely from Q, with no 'resort to any other copy' (p. 22). And while he believes that Q2 was used in the preparation of F, he maintains his belief that Jaggard's compositors did not use an annotated copy of Q2, but a manuscript from which to set the play. In a final short section he discusses the significance of the differences between Q and F. He believes that the later text 'was revised, possibly by Shakespeare himself, for performance, possibly at the Blackfriars Theatre sometime after 1609' (p. 24). There are, he argues, 'two defensible texts' of the play, 'one more "literary", the other more "theatrical"' (p. 26). Even so, he is forced to admit that whoever was responsible for cutting the trial scene, 3.6, in F 'and it could have been Shakespeare – doubtless underestimated the powerful impact the scene can have upon an audience' (p. 25). The invocation of the theatre here deserves further attention in the light of Dillon's article and of Taylor's arguments about act-intervals and their possible effect on playing-times. Halio is deliberately tentative in some of his claims about Q, but there are also moments when he seems over confident. For example, when thinking about the messy manuscript from which he believes Q was set, he first suggests reasonably that if it was a reported text the publisher would have demanded 'cleaner copy'. But with a modern editor's point of view, he then goes on to imply

that the publisher would not have demanded better copy if what he had was 'the author's original manuscript' (p. 5). Equally, he has nothing new to say about the date of the supposed Folio revision.

Halio's text is almost entirely accurate.[14] On the other hand, his textual commentary which has clearly cost him a great deal of effort is unfortunately full of errors. Most of these are minor ones affecting spelling, punctuation or typography, but there is a sufficient number of serious mistakes to alarm the user.[15] On three occasions Halio has changed his mind about emendations to Q readings he printed in the appendix to his 1992 edition: he returns to Q for 3.1.10 'Strives in his little world of man to outscorn', where earlier he had adopted Muir's 'outstorm'; at 3.6.16 he rejects Theobald's 'justicer' for Q's 'justice', and later in the scene at line 44 he sticks to Q's 'join-stool' instead of Pope's 'joint-stool'. Turning to individual readings in his textual notes, Halio attributes a very large number of Q's errors to simple misreading on the compositors' part, with some omissions, some misprints, some mispunctuation, a sprinkling of eye-skip, substitutions and simple guesswork. Consequently, he feels that Q is in need of much more radical emendation than Weis did in his 1993 parallel-

---

14 One error occurs at 3.2.1 *for* 'Blow, winds, and crack your cheeks!' *read* 'Blow, wind, and crack your cheeks!'; and he has some difficulty with stage directions at 1.2.107 *for* '[*Enter*] EDGAR' *read* 'Enter EDGAR' and at 4.2.95 where *for* 'Exeunt' *read* 'Ex[eunt]'.

15 Among these are: 1.2.92 'Treasons' for F's 'Treason'; 1.4.250 'thourt disuentur'd' for Q's 'thourt disuetur'd'; 2.2.79 Q2 does not read 'Then' with F, but 'Than'; 2.4.74 'Fiery? fierie quality' for F's 'Fiery? What quality'; 3.2.75 'good' for Q's 'my good'; 3.4.103 'tode pole' for Q *uncorr.*'s 'tode pold'; 3.4.107 'stockt, punish'd' for F's 'stockt, punish'd; 3.5.17 *read* perseuer] F; perseuere Q; 3.7.57 *add* bare F; 4.2.0 *add* F includes Oswald in the entry; 4.6.78 'would be' for Q2's 'would he'; 5.3.114 SD2 *delete* 'with a trumpet F'.

There are also a few misleadingly inaccurate references: 1.1.121 for 1.1.120; 2.2.37 for 2.2.39; 3.7.99 for 3.7.98; 4.1.43 for 4.1.41.

text edition. There are some hundred or so passages in which the two editors differ in their approach to Q's text, and in the majority of these cases Weis sticks to Q while Halio either emends from F or offers a new reading of his own. Sometimes his motive for doing this is evidently linked with a desire for metrical regularity and correctness.[16] But at others it reflects a simple feeling that Q does not really make sufficient sense. The introduction and the Textual Notes section allow him to discuss briefly a large number of problematic readings. However, there are still some occasions where one would like to ask both editors to explain why their editions differ. For example, at 1.4.214 Halio adopts F's 'then' for Gonorill's 'Be then desired . . . A little to disquantity your train', while Weis is content to retain Q's 'Be thou desired . . .', making the daughter change pronouns in the course of the sentence. Again, at 2.4.202 Halio adopts F's 'I looked not for you yet', where Weis sticks to Q's 'I look not for you yet'. Edmund's closing line in 3.3 is emended from F to read 'The younger rises when the old do fall' by Halio, but Weis retains Q's 'Then younger . . .' Edgar tells his father that he climbs the cliff 'up it now' in Halio's F reading (4.6.2), but 'it up now' in Weis's Q version. Neither editor comments on the Q/F variants.

But the balance does not go all one way. Halio adopts Q in some instances where Weis has had to use F. Where Weis printed 'Woe that too late repents' (1.4.245), Halio ingeniously sees a way of retaining Q's 'We' by reading 'We that too late repent's!' (1.4.225). At 2.1.118 he follows Stone's lead and makes Regan complete Cornwall's 'You know not why we came to visit you?' by asking 'This out-of-season, threat'ning, dark-eyed night?', where Weis (2.1.119) felt forced to adopt F's 'Thus out-of-season thredding dark-eyed night'. Halio follows Blayney at 3.6.60 'brach or him' where Weis adopts F's 'lym'. Most surprisingly, drawing on Thomas Clayton's arguments, Halio finds 'several kinds of sense' (p. 134) in uncorrected Q's notorious 'My foot usurps my

body' (4.2.27) to retain it against the corrected 'A fool usurps my bed.' Elsewhere he shows a fairly considerable debt to the Oxford edition,[17] but he also has some attractive new readings, for example restoring what is probably a missing 'there' to Edgar's 'and there, and there, and there again!' at 3.4.48–9. At line 89 in the same scene his emendation has been anticipated by Weis (3.4.100). Halio has Dover cliff at 4.1.70 look 'sternly in the confinèd deep' where Q and F have 'firmely' and 'fearfully' respectively. 'The clearest gods' at 4.6.73 'make their honours', fusing Q's 'made their' with F's 'make them'. Partly adopting Blayney's emendation in Oxford, Gloucester is made to say at 4.6.211 'The bounty and the benison of heaven / Send thee boot, to boot.' Finally, Halio tries to sort out Q's version of Edgar's line in 5.3.120 by printing 'Yet am I noble. Where is the adversary': Weis seeks to solve the problem by modernizing Q's 'are I mou't' to 'ere I move't'.[18]

Halio's edition is predicated on the view that the Folio text of *Lear* represents a revision by Shakespeare of the quarto version. While it is undoubtedly useful to have Halio's new edition,

---

[16] Halio makes the following emendations to Q to regularize the metre: 1.1.60, 1.4.6, 1.4.228, 2.2.144, 2.4.112, 3.4.4, 3.4.132(?), 3.7.71, 3.7.102, 4.1.34, 4.1.36, 4.6.65, 4.6.180, 5.3.24, 5.3.280, 5.3.293, 5.3.315. Most of these changes are the result of omissions in Q.

[17] For example, at 2.4.68 Halio adopts Oxford's 'Mere insolence' for Q's 'Mere Iustice' or F's 'Mere fetches'; not very happily at 3.4.112 he retains Oxford's 'Smolking' for F's 'Smulkin' and Harsnett's 'Smolkin'; at 3.6.5 Halio prints 'The gods discern your kindness!' where Weis defends a transitive use of Q's 'deserve' to mean requite; or again, at 3.7.15 Halio follows Oxford's 'questants' where Weis adopts 'questrists' from Q by way of F. Halio follows the Stone–Oxford reading at 4.2.10 'What he should most defy seems pleasant to him' where Weis adopts F's 'dislike' in his Q text. See also 4.2.55 'flaxen biggin threats', 4.6.226 'baton' and 5.3.141 'My right of knighthood' for Q/F 'By right of knighthood'.

[18] There is a nice modernization problem with Edgar's song 'Come oe'r the bourn, Bessy, to me' (3.6.20), which Weis renders as 'burn' meaning 'brook'.

the reader must be constantly aware of exactly what claims are being made for the status of the text which is being presented. In the end there is something of a division in the book itself, for while on its title-page it announces itself as *The First Quarto of King Lear*, the running-title for the play is printed as *The History of King Lear*: there is a difference. It would be wrong to criticize Halio for trying to have his cake and to eat it, to walk naked under a heavy overcoat, but it is disingenuous to present 'accessible' editions of quartos (of whatever kind, but especially those not usually selected as copy-texts) and at the same time set them in a pre-determined scholarly context.

Jowett and Taylor report that Peter Blayney does not believe the Folio revisions are by Shakespeare. In a brief article Ann R. Meyer puts forward some evidence against the whole revisionary idea arguing in effect for a conflated text of the play.[19] She argues first that Qa's 'crulentious' at the beginning of 3.4 represents a simple misreading of F's 'contentious' and Qb's a compositorial sophistication. Later in the same scene, Qb's correction of Qa's 'come on bee true' to 'come on' represents a failure to carry out the correction of a misread 'come vnbutton heere' fully. Meyer then turns to the mock trial in 3.6 which she argues was so inexpertly cut from the Folio that its 'omission was not authorial' (p. 140). Finally, she looks at the play's closing moments and examines the printing of its last sheet. It was set seriatim, and the outer forme was ready before the inner was complete – the compositors reckoned that the play's last page could be left blank. Yet while the outer forme was being printed off, the compositor realized that there was not enough space in the final pages of the inner forme for what he still had to set. He crowded, cut, and adapted the material to make it fit the available space and at the same time managed to perpetrate mistaken speech assignments (there are nine in the sheet). While her first two examples of Q's misreadings are suggestive but not conclusive, Meyer adds another voice to the chorus of those who find

the omission of the mock trial in F unfortunate. But her account of the relationship between the printing of the play's final sheet and its text in Q is definitely striking. On the other hand, while L4r of Q1 has a rather crowded look, it also has a fine 'FINIS' taking up three or four lines, one or two of which could have been used by the compositor to set his text. Meyer's argument is a provocative one (not so far removed from Weis's), which is well worth coming back to.

IV

'There is no avoiding edited Shakespeare', Brian Gibbons writes in the General Editor's preface to The New Cambridge Shakespeare: The Early Quartos, 'the question is only what kind of editing'. *King Lear* has emerged as the prime contender for editorial arguments and different practices, with *Hamlet* ('fat and scant of breath') puffing at its heels: *Dr Faustus* has also joined the race again with an important reconsideration by David Bevington and Eric Rasmussen of the two texts of the play and the problems of its authorship and of its revision.[20] Modern editorial work seems to encourage a sort of purist textual integrity ('We have decided nevertheless against facing-page texts', Bevington and Rasmussen explain (p. x), 'since each play needs to be read in and for itself') and, sometimes – even at the same time – a heavyish-handed degree of interference. Of course Shakespeare has to be edited (even the barest photo-facsimile involves complicated editorial decisions), but editing is part of a

[19] *Shakespeare Reshaped*, p. 193 n. 185; Ann R. Meyer, 'Shakespeare's Art and the Texts of *King Lear*', *Studies in Bibliography*, 47 (1994): 128–46.

[20] Christopher Marlowe and his Collaborator and Revisers, *Doctor Faustus: A- and B-texts (1604, 1616)*, ed. David Bevington and Eric Rasmussen (Manchester: Manchester University Press, 1993) in The Revels Plays series and Eric Rasmussen, *A Textual Companion to 'Doctor Faustus'* (Manchester: Manchester University Press, 1993) in The Revels Plays Companion Library series.

process which involves publishers and readers as well: contemporary editing may be dependent on practical and commercial decisions which go beyond the apparent disinterestedness of bibliographical and textual theory.

Something of this can be seen in the two most recent additions to the Oxford Shakespeare, Michael Neill's *Anthony and Cleopatra* – already the audience is shifting in their seats – and R. B. Parker's *Coriolanus*: at least he does not try to argue that the play should be renamed *Cor-eye-olanus* as Peter Hall mistakenly did; indeed (see 5.6.92) he argues strongly against this.[21] Both editions of what T. S. Eliot called 'Shakespeare's most assured artistic success[es]' are full and long, both occupying exactly 388 pages, with introductions of well over a hundred pages. Hanging over Neill's *Anthony* is David Bevington's edition which is a hard act to follow – not that Neill is under his shadow. He takes his own line with the play to produce a useful and often stimulating volume which scholars and critics will wish to consult. His introduction is long and pays particular attention to the history of the play in performance and there are many good moments in his commentary. And yet, his edition as a whole does not quite capture the 'happy valiancy' which Coleridge found in the play. Neill begins his introduction by saying acutely that the play 'is recognizably the work of a dramatist at the confident height of his powers – an artist who feels he can do *anything*' (p. 1). But the edition itself sometimes gives the impression that Neill feels constrained by his task, not quite able – for whatever reason – to say or to do what he really wants. 'If ever a Shakespearean play called for music, processions and Tadema-like excesses in bathroom marble,' he quote James Agate as saying, '*Antony and Cleopatra* is that play' (p. 35). But his own critical introduction or '*Interpretation*' tends more to Peter Brook's 'minimalist version' (p. 37) than to Beerbohm Tree's (or Trevor Nunn's, for that matter) Orientalism.

He argues persuasively that 'Shakespeare

seems more than usually willing to break or challenge the rules of dramatic construction' in the play (p. 2) so that its 'most extraordinary effect lies in Shakespeare's capacity to draw a superb theatrical climax out of seeming anticlimax' (p. 99). Despite this, Neill is finally sceptical about the play as a whole, concluding that it 'does not, of course, end on a note of unambiguous triumph' (p. 129). He refers early on to its 'unstable brilliance' (p. 68) and he seems much happier with its instability than with its brilliance. 'For what the play does', he says in a telling passage, 'is to pit a classical "Roman" notion of fixed and stable identity, embodied in the heroic image of Anthony, against the incarnation of its Montaignean opposite in Cleopatra, and to expose the classical ideal as chimerical and ultimately self-destructive' (p. 85). The French philosopher makes another appearance when Neill argues that the play is 'an attempt to explore Montaignean subjectivity from within' (p. 82 and see also 4.15.2–14): it 'renders the constitution of the "self" so intensely problematic' (p. 131 and see 1.1.44–5, 2.2.4, 4.16.48, 54). The difficulty with this approach is that it plays down so much that is attractive and exciting about *Antony and Cleopatra* – the very Coleridgean '*feliciter audax*', the 'happy valiancy', with which Neill begins his introduction. Neill's reading brings out powerfully the play's 'paradoxical tendency to hollow out and undermine its own most cherished values' (p. 74), but might be thought to understate its equally important engagement with the world of the imagination.

He floats the idea 'that the play was never actually performed in Shakespeare's lifetime' (p. 23), but is interested in problems of its staging, particularly in Cleopatra's death which he insists takes place on a day-bed rather than a

---

[21] *The Tragedy of Anthony and Cleopatra*, ed. Michael Neill (Oxford: Oxford University Press, 1994) in The Oxford Shakespeare series and *The Tragedy of Coriolanus* ed. R. B. Parker (Oxford: Oxford University Press, 1994) in The Oxford Shakespeare series.

throne (p. 47). On several occasions in the commentary he describes how lines have been spoken or scenes performed (see 2.2.197, 2.6, 4.9.24, 4.13.43, 4.16.13–33, 5.2.76–92). But he is also willing to suggest how lines might be spoken (see 1.2.175, 1.3.35–7, 3.13.88). Like Bevington and like other editors in the Oxford series he is particularly aware of the problems of the play's lineation, to which he devotes a separate appendix.[22] One of his initial points is certainly worth pondering in a wider context, that 'a dramatist accustomed to writing in blank verse may reproduce its cadences in his prose from time to time' (p. 371). But he believes that lineation has a dramatic part to play in interpretation. For although he allows that 'amphibious' lines can reflect the play's indeterminacy, he also argues that the lineation can convey something of the tone or formality of the speeches (pp. 371–2). Some of his commentary reflects this view and he relines quite freely.[23] On the other hand, he admits that rearranging the sentries' speeches in 4.3 may efface an attempt to 'represent nervous, halting exchanges, full of tense pauses and hesitations' (p. 374).

Neill devotes another appendix to pronoun usage, in which he convincingly discusses Shakespeare's careful modulation of pronouns in the play, concluding that 'readers (and actors) need to be constantly alert to the social and emotional shadings involved' (p. 369).[24] There are a number of good notes, for example on Cleopatra's 'my becomings' as opposed to 'being' (1.3.97, see also 4.15.2–14 and 20), or on 'the significance of the verb *do* in a play which repeatedly opposes heroic *deeds* to erotic *doing*' (1.5.15–16 and see 2.7.80). He interestingly compares 'the question-and-answer game' played by the lovers in 1.1 to 'the standard repartee between Lady and Fool' in *Twelfth Night* 1.5; Octavia's first speech in 3.4 with Blanche's in *King John* 3.1.253–62; and the contrast between the night-scene with the watch, 4.10, and the 'colour of what has gone before', with the 'gloomy battlements and

brilliantly illuminated court in the opening of *Hamlet*'.

These observations reveal Neill's sharp eye for the play's dramatic structure, but his fondness for modifying some details is less attractive. His greatest weakness is for dashes – a passion he shares with Nicholas Brooke's *Macbeth* in the same series. There are just over 300 of them in a play of under 3,500 lines. The effect is sometimes a little overwhelming as in 1.3.22–34 containing seven of them or at the end of Antony's speech in 3.11.22–4:

Leave me, I pray, a little – pray you now –
Nay, do so; for indeed I have lost command –
Therefore I pray you – I'll see you by and by.

The Folio itself has five dashes in the text of the whole play. He persuasively capitalizes 'Love and her soft Hours' in 1.1.46, but does the same less convincingly for 'Idleness your subject' at 1.3. 93. The Folio's capitalization of 'Famine' in 1.4.59, he notes, 'points up the allegory', and he defends leaving Cleopatra's 'I am marble constant' (5.2.240), meaning 'constant marble', unhyphenated on the grounds that by printing 'Marble', F suggests the word is a noun. But it is the modernizing of proper names which presents him with a real opportunity to stick his neck out. He settles for 'Camidius', despite

---

22 Even so there are a few mistakes in his list of changed lineation: he omits F's division after 'him' in 1.2.86; his 1.2.89–90 should refer to 1.2.88–90; an 'F' has dropped out of 2.1.16–17; 2.2.34–5 should report F as printing 'I . . .I' as one line; 195–6 in the same scene appear as prose in F; and 4.15.9–10 are set as prose in F.

23 See 1.2.117–19, 1.2.130–1, 1.4.85 ('the cool tone of Caesar's reassurance is emphasized . . . by the slightly enigmatic way in which it is left hanging upon a half-line'), 1.5.76–8 ('the half-lines are used to significant dramatic effect'), 2.2.28–32, 2.2.147–8 ('a significant pause is appropriate'), 2.3.11–15, 3.3.26–7 ('the natural pausing created by the end-stopped line, is enough to dictate the slight pause required'), 3.11.70–3, 4.3, 4.16.10 ('the metrical gap probably signals that ['O sun' is] to be treated as a long drawn-out cry').

24 See also 1.2.175, 1.3.70–1, 1.4.34–5, 2.6.24–9, 2.6.72–80, 2.7.55, 2.7.86, 3.4.11, 3.6.29, 3.7.27, 3.13.86, 3.13.98, 3.13.173, 4.2.7, 4.15.36, 5.1.11, 5.2.176.

finding the Oxford editors' choice of the form 'puzzling' (p. 132), and 'Dercetus' because it is 'phonetically a little closer to North' and to the Countess of Pembroke's 'Dircetus' (p. 133). More controversially, he has decided to follow the Folio's spelling of 'Anthony' because he believes 'we can be reasonably certain that . . . it represents the dramatist's own preference', and adds that 'only a misleading antiquarian habit . . . can justify the retention' of 'Antony' (pp. 134–5) – despite this he retains '*Antoniad*' (3.10.2). His decision is part of a general view that anachronisms 'ought to serve as warnings against inappropriate attempts to "Romanize" the play' (4.4.14 and see 1.3.71).

The choice of 'Anthony' is also predicated on the play's having been set from 'good copy close to the dramatist's own foul papers' (p. 133) and he detects several occasions which reveal authorial uncertainty, changes of intention or simple failure to work out stage directions fully (see 1.2.112.1, 1.5.34, 3.7.72, 4.3.0–6, 4.4.0.1–2, 4.4.24, 4.16.0.1, 5.2.317.1 where the Guard's 'rustling in' 'belongs more with the imaginative excitement of an authorial manuscript than with the practicalities of a theatrical prompt-book'). Despite (or perhaps because of) this he does his best to retain Folio readings where he can, preserving, for example 'quick winds' (1.2.110), 'an arm-gaunt steed' (1.5.48, conjecturing '*argent* = clad in silver armour'), 'Tawny-fine fishes' (2.5.12) because 'there is no reason why Cleopatra should not imagine her fish as if tricked out in cloth-of-gold finery'; he defends the 'perfectly manageable five-stress line' caused by the tautology of the 'young Roman boy' at 4.13.48 as 'an over-emphatic expression of contempt'.

When he cannot defend F, he tends to stay with traditional emendations. For example, at 2.1.21 where he feels that Steevens's 'waned lip' is clinched by the parallel 'wayned face' in Cary's *The Tragedy of Mariam*; he sticks with Hanmer's 'breathless, power breathe forth' at 2.2.239 and with Rowe's 'Is't not denounced' at 3.7.5 because it 'gives the easiest sense'; he

adopts F2's 'He lessens his requests' at 3.12.14 rather than F's 'Lessons', even though 'the distinction would be virtually impossible to convey to an audience'; he keeps to Theobald's 'The rack dislimns' (4.15.10), defending the coinage by reference to the proverbial 'to limn in water'; he includes Hanmer's 'but' in 'he but mocks / The pauses' (5.1.2–3), saying that its omission 'sharpens Caesar's ironic edge by allowing a slight mocking pause'; and finally (and least happily), he keeps Theobald's 'an autumn 'twas' (5.2.87) while accepting that F's 'An *Anthony* it was' 'is nevertheless not wholly impossible in this compressed speech'. And when the traditional readings are unacceptable, he moves to more recent ones. He adopts Dover Wilson's conjecture for Agrippa's 'There she appeared triumphantly indeed' (2.2.195) because F's line, which lacks an adverb, 'seems incomplete, or at the least inappropriately weak'; he draws on Oxford's reading at 2.5.104 'That act not what thou'rt sure of', which 'has the advantage of simplicity and clarity, as well as being graphically plausible'; he admits Johnson's conjecture which Oxford adopted for Enobarbus's 'mooted' rather than F's 'meered' question at 3.13.10; he uses Pope's 'caparisons' at 3.13.26 while pointing out that F's '"comparisons" sometimes appears as a corrupt form of "caparisons"' and accepts Collier's emendation to line 71 later in the scene; in 4.5 he reassigns Eros' and the soldier's speeches to Scarrus, since they are 'evidently addressed to the same scarred veteran whose advice Anthony ignored at Actium'. He has few new readings of his own, but conjectures that at 4.13.24–5 Shakespeare wrote 'Betrayed I am / O this false soul of Egypt' while printing F's 'Betrayed I am. / O this false soul of Egypt' because the short sentence 'seems a little weak on its own'. There are two substantive errors in the text.[25]

---

[25] At 1.2.79 a speech-prefix is wrongly assigned to Charmian, giving her two speeches in succession: it should be given to Cleopatra. At 2.7.101 *for* Caesar's 'Than drink too much in one' *read* 'Than drink so much in one.'

Other minor errors include textual commentary for

If Neill sometimes gives the impression that he was not quite doing what he wanted to do, R. B. Parker's edition of *Coriolanus* occasionally makes the reader wonder whether he really wanted just to edit the play or to write a book about it. In the end he has produced a very accurate, even exemplary, edition. He has read widely and thought deeply; at times he writes quite movingly about the play. He has done his Roman duty by *Coriolanus*, but although he recognizes it is 'brilliantly complex' (p. 1), he is not warm in its praise. Parker's introduction is very long and ranges widely, including much material on the play's contemporary background as well as psychoanalytical accounts of its interpretation and even a short section on Shakespeare's Political Development. These matters are also dealt with in the commentary, where the stage history (which is done very well in the introduction) and references to the play in performance occur again and again. All of this is very valuable, and there is a great deal of it: Parker has been given ample space to capture and to explain the play's complexity.

He begins by dating the play to late 1608, perhaps in part to early 1609 (p. 7), and by suggesting that Shakespeare's understanding of the political world had expanded by then to investigate 'a triple interaction between three forces: individual character; that individual's institutions, including the family which is the basic institution; and society as a whole, which is at the same time the product and the cause of the other two' (p. 11). Shakespeare found in Coriolanus' Rome a place where 'public ethos and private tragedy' could be 'for the first time located clearly in the middle ground of family neurosis' (p. 13). The sources for Coriolanus' make-up include Prince Hal, Hector, Othello, Hamlet, but above all King Lear – some of these characters' plays share an anticlimactic structure (pp. 13–17). Parker examines Shakespeare's changes to Plutarch's account, his reshaping of its characterization and action. Most of all he brings out the play's use of

'"overdetermined" choices: decisions, that is, for which no motives are given, not because there are none but because too many, conflicting emotional subtexts are possible' (p. 30).

When he turns to the play's contemporary background, Parker writes at length on the events which lie behind its treatment of the plebeians' revolt. These include riots in the Midlands in 1607–8 against corn prices and enclosures (pp. 34–7), the position of the gentry in the early seventeenth century (pp. 37–8), and both royal and local disputes over authority and legitimacy (pp. 38–43). The point of these is that the 'play is politically sophisticated enough to open up such issues and to expect [the] audience to appreciate them', for *Coriolanus*'s 'special brilliance . . . is its insight into the mutual influence of psychology and politics' (p. 43). Parker then goes on to survey the play's treatment of the political, the psychological and the philosophical, especially in relation to Martius himself and his mother. 'The crucial phrase', he writes, 'on which the whole play hinges, is Aufidius' taunt of "boy of tears"' (p. 48). Just as Martius is Volumnia's creation, so she is Rome's: his tragedy is to have both elements of Rome's and mother's boy in his make-up (pp. 53–4), which result in the play's recurrent concern with sex and warfare (pp. 55–6), not least in his relations with Aufidius (pp. 57–9). Drawing on a wide range of writers from Freud to R. D. Laing, Parker argues that Shakespeare comes to see 'the familial link . . . as the truly *political* core of human society set against the constant flux of history' (p. 63). Martius' struggle with the self, with his uniqueness and individuality, is both the cause and the result of his 'punitive self-fashioning'

4.16.74 and 5.2.160.2 on the wrong pages (pp. 217, 311); footnote numbers which need adjusting (pp. 22 n. 4, 79 n. 3, and commentary to 4.16.92); the reference to Sir John Davies at 2.3.36 should be to John Davies of Hereford (not the same person at all) and at 3.1.1 there is an unusual and suggestive word division 'hor- / semen'.

(p. 65), which finds its centre in the line 'O, me alone! Make you a sword of me?' (1.7.77). Parker interprets his behaviour in the light of Elias Canetti's *Crowds and Power*, finding in Martius a 'pattern of compulsive repetition' which forces him to risk his life to confirm his '"uniqueness"' (p. 68). The result is that 'His death is a last act of aggression, his final humiliation of Aufidius' (p. 69); 'stoic individualism' turns death into 'self-assertion' (p. 70). Even by this stage Parker is not yet half way through his meaty introduction.

Next, he looks at the play's style, pointing out its use of hyperbole (p. 70), semi-soliloquy (p. 71), argumentativeness (p. 72), antithesis (p. 73), overpackedness (p. 74) and energy (p. 75), before discussing its imagery. This relies on 'three main image clusters: grain/nurture/cannibalism, body/blood/sex, and language/acting' (p. 77). Finally, in this part of the introduction Parker gets on to the play's first production, suggesting it may have been written with performance at the newly acquired Blackfriars in mind (pp. 87–8). This may account for the play's elaborate stage directions (Shakespeare may have been in Stratford at the time) and for its use of debate and of legal language which would have appealed to an Inns of Court audience. Parker discusses various problems in the play's staging, including how the Romans are to be '*beat back to their trenches*' in 1.4 (p. 92), what sort of costumes are called for (pp. 96–8), the play's use of noise and of silence (pp. 100–2), of hands and of kneeling (pp. 102–5), and its treatment of Coriolanus' death (pp. 110–13). When he gets on to the play's modern stage history, Parker's material is particularly well organized under headings: '*Ideological*', '*Right-wing*', '*Anti-heroic*'[26] and '*Left-wing*' approaches or interpretations, '*Historical Relativity*'[27] and '*Post-modernist Interpretation*'.

When it comes to the text Parker is equally thorough and keeps his head well down, although it is not clear quite what he means when he says that F is 'the definitive text for the play' (p. 136). He disagrees with Taylor about its act-divisions, suggesting that they 'were probably done by someone other than Shakespeare' (p. 137).[28] F's spellings, lineation and stage directions show that it was set from a manuscript which was 'close' to Shakespeare's 'working manuscript' (p. 138), 'before a fair copy was made' (p. 141), 'a draft that still required revision', not 'a fair copy' (p. 143), 'a penultimate draft in which he was still to some extent "thinking through" the play' (p. 147). Parker argues that most of F's distinctive features can be explained by this and there is no need to resort to arguments about playhouse or editorial annotation.

As a result Parker's text is very 'clean', with careful attention paid to F's punctuation and lineation: it also has very few slips.[29] The Folio compositors A and B misread their copy on some twenty or so occasions, the worst cases being at 3.1.100 where 'Ignorance' was substituted for 'impotence', 3.3.53 where 'accents' was set as 'Actions' and 5.2.18 where 'verified' should have been 'varnished'. Most of their other graphic mistakes were probably the result of misreading only one or two letters in their

---

26 This section includes a brief account of John Osborne's adaptation *A Place calling Itself Rome* (1971) which was turned down by the RSC on the 'grounds that it was too like Shakespeare's original' (pp. 124–5).

27 Parker provides a description of a production at the Old Globe Theatre of San Diego in 1989: 'This updated the Volscian war to the United States' struggle against the Sandinistas of Nicaragua, with Coriolanus identified with Colonel Oliver North giving evidence before a Senate tribunal, Volumnia and Virgilia associated with Rose and Ethel Kennedy (the former lethal in a wheelchair), and Menenius as a southern, white-suited, "pork-barrel" senator' (p. 131).

28 Cp. *Shakespeare Reshaped*, pp. 40, 46 n. 130.

29 At 3.1.65 Menenius should say 'Not now, not now' instead of 'Now now, not now'. The stage-direction '*Enter a Gentlewoman*' at 1.3.25.1 is in F (TLN 387). Lartius' 'I'll lean upon one crutch and fight with th'other' (1.1.240) should perhaps read 't'other' with F. The scene heading on p. 195 should read 1.7 not 1.8. The sudden appearance of Petrarch in the introduction (p. 33) is presumably a learned slip for Plutarch.

copy. Parker detects one certain and one possible example of dittography (2.1.160–1 and 3.2.102) – a third (3.1.327) could just as well be 'a false start in Shakespeare's papers' – one piece of compositorial eye-skip (2.3.239) and two omissions (4.6.14 and 5.2.62–3). The manuscript copy had marginal or interlinear corrections which the compositors misplaced (1.7.82–4, 1.10.0–1, 3.1.237 etc., 5.1.67–9). They mistook the stage direction *'cum aliis'* for the name of a character *'with Cumalijs'* (3.3.136.2), were baffled by Shakespeare's neologism 'exposure' (4.1.37) which they set as 'exposture' and were misled by the presence of 'gods' to set 'pray' for 'prate' (5.3.48). Twice in 2.1 they had to stretch verse to fill the column (2.1.154–7 and 177–87) but on another occasion the compositor was simply misled by the manuscript (2.1.232–9) and elsewhere the apparently deliberate waste of space 'surely marks an emphatic pause' (3.2.63). In a characteristic way, Parker resolves the play's few cruces without much fuss. Coriolanus' cry 'O, me alone!' (1.7.77) is punctuated to suggest that it is 'ecstatic' rather than, say, a joke. He wants the parasite to be made 'an ovator for th' wars' (1.10.45–6, that is 'one who receives a public ovation') since F's 'Ouerture' was pronounced in the same way; and he wears a 'wolvish toge' (2.3.111) as a result of a simple misreading which led to F's 'tongue'. Volumnia tells her son to wave his head, 'Which offer thus', instead of the more usual 'With often, thus' (3.2.80). Parker's own new readings (3.2.18 and 21, for example) are modest and credible.

There is an extraordinary amount of material in Parker's edition, almost all of which is good and sensible. It is extremely well informed by a detailed and practical knowledge of performances, but also by a sense of the play's theatricality. His commentary pays particular attention to the themes, such as parallels to *King Lear* or contemporary allusions, which he writes about

in his persuasive introduction. If some of his reading of *Coriolanus* is in its own way overdetermined, then that – like his measured and cool response to it – is appropriate: after all, editors inhabit the world of their texts more closely than most readers. The solid virtues of his work stand far away from tendentious projects and superficial arguments.

The New Bibliography rightly concentrated much attention on the discovery of the nature of the copy underlying a printed text. Current orthodoxy detects, with more or less certainty, authorial manuscripts behind both quarto *King Lear* and Folio *Coriolanus*. Okes's compositors have been found to be inexperienced and inaccurate, while F's A and B (despite perceived differences in the quality of their work) have been deemed more competent. Yet while the quarto has been taken for a 'bad' text of some kind, a modern editor of *Coriolanus* can print his play from F with – lineation and punctuation apart – very little interference. Are these differences to be put down to printing-house practices and circumstances alone, or is there a more fundamental problem about modern conceptions of what sorts of manuscripts were set in type and how they came into the hands of printers? Familiar categories and explanations need to be questioned, but new answers need to be viewed just as sceptically. These are interesting times, in the current as well as the cursing sense, but perhaps they mark the end of an era, not yet the beginning of a new one. There is now a millennial feeling about editing and textual theory, in which Shakespeare is allowed to have written nonsense which merely represents another version or at worst another traducing of his work. In time the mood will pass, but any fresh approach to the subject might well start by looking again precisely at the fundamental materials with which Greg, Pollard, McKerrow and Chambers concerned themselves, especially the manuscripts.

BOOKS RECEIVED

This list includes all books received between September 1993 and September 1994 which are not reviewed in this volume of *Shakespeare Survey*. The appearance of a book in this list does not preclude its review in a subsequent volume.

Blits, Jan H. *The End of the Republic: Shakespeare's 'Julius Caesar'*. Maryland: Rowman and Littlefield, 1993.

Burrow, Colin. *Epic Romance: Homer to Milton*. Oxford: Clarendon Press, 1993.

Carlin, Patricia L. *Shakespeare's Mortal Men: Overcoming Death in History, Comedy and Tragedy*. New York: Peter Lang, 1993.

Curren-Aquino, Deborah T. *'King John': An Annotated Bibliography*. New York and London: Garland, 1994.

Deutsche Shakespeare-Gesellschaft/Deutsche Shakespeare-Gesellschaft West: Jahrbuch, 1994. Verlag Ferdinand Kamp, Bochum, 1994.

Korte, Barbara. *Körpersprache in Der Literatur*. Tübingen: A. Francke Verlag, 1993.

Nelson, Alan H. *Early Cambridge Theatres: College, University, and Town Stages, 1464–1720*. Cambridge: Cambridge University Press, 1994.

Shakespeare, William. *Antony and Cleopatra*. Ed. by Mary Berry and Michael Clamp, Cambridge School Shakespeare. Cambridge: Cambridge University Press, 1994.

Shakespeare, William. *Hamlet*. Ed. by Susanne L. Wofford, Case Studies in Contemporary Criticism. Boston and New York: Bedford Books of St Martin's Press, 1993.

Shakespeare, William. *'A Lover's Complaint': Deutsche Übersetzungen von 1787 bis 1894 Festgabe fur Dieter Mehl zum 60 Geburtstag*. Berlin: Erich Schmidt Verlag, 1993.

INDEX

The index includes titles of books referred to in the review articles.

INDEX

INDEX

INDEX

INDEX

INDEX

INDEX

INDEX

INDEX